AF575641

LOST AND FOUND

TIME, TIDE, AND TREASURES

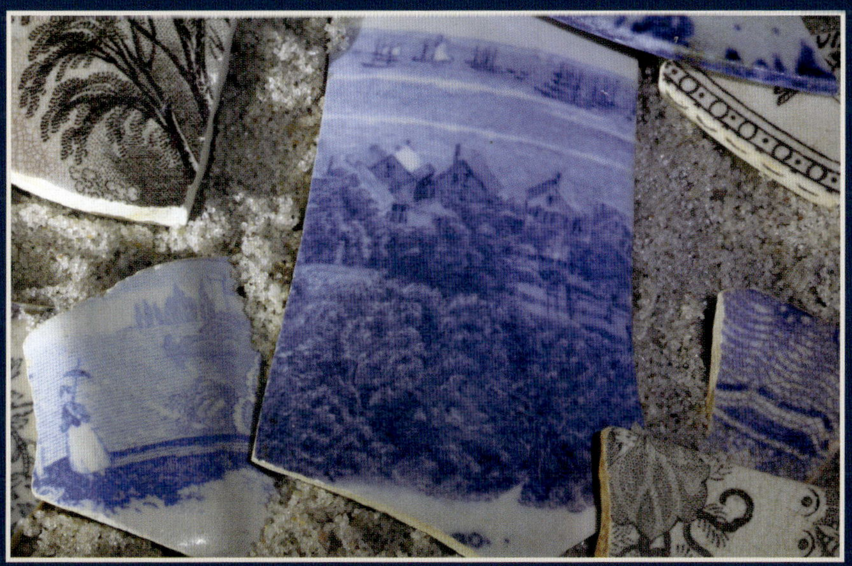

Amy Heller

Gail Browne

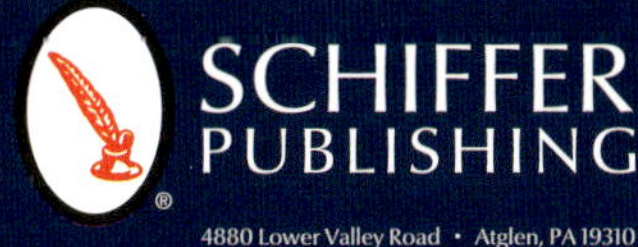

SCHIFFER PUBLISHING

4880 Lower Valley Road • Atglen, PA 19310

Other Schiffer Books on Related Subjects:

Contemporary Cape Cod Artists: Images of Land and Sea, by Deborah Forman, ISBN 978-0-7643-4451-0

Art from Cape Cod: Selections from the Cape Cod Museum of Art, by Edith A. Tonelli and Deborah Forman, ISBN 978-0-7643-5134-1

Art from Above Cape Cod, by Christopher S. Gibbs, ISBN 978-0-7643-5747-3

Library of Congress Control Number: 2019947461

Cover design by RoS

Cover photo: Paul Bowen collection: metal drawer with whale inner ear bones, clay marbles, bones, buttons, and other objects. Photo by Amy Heller

Back jacket: Amy Heller and Gail Browne at the Cultural Center of Cape Cod. Photo by Bart Weisman

Conceptual design and text: Gail Browne
Photography: Amy Heller, unless otherwise noted
Research and interviews: Amy Heller and Gail Browne

Type set in Cinzel/Staccatto222/Optima

ISBN: 978-0-7643-5942-2
Printed in China

Published by Schiffer Publishing, Ltd.
4880 Lower Valley Road
Atglen, PA 19310
Phone: (610) 593-1777; Fax: (610) 593-2002
E-mail: Info@schifferbooks.com
Web: www.schifferbooks.com

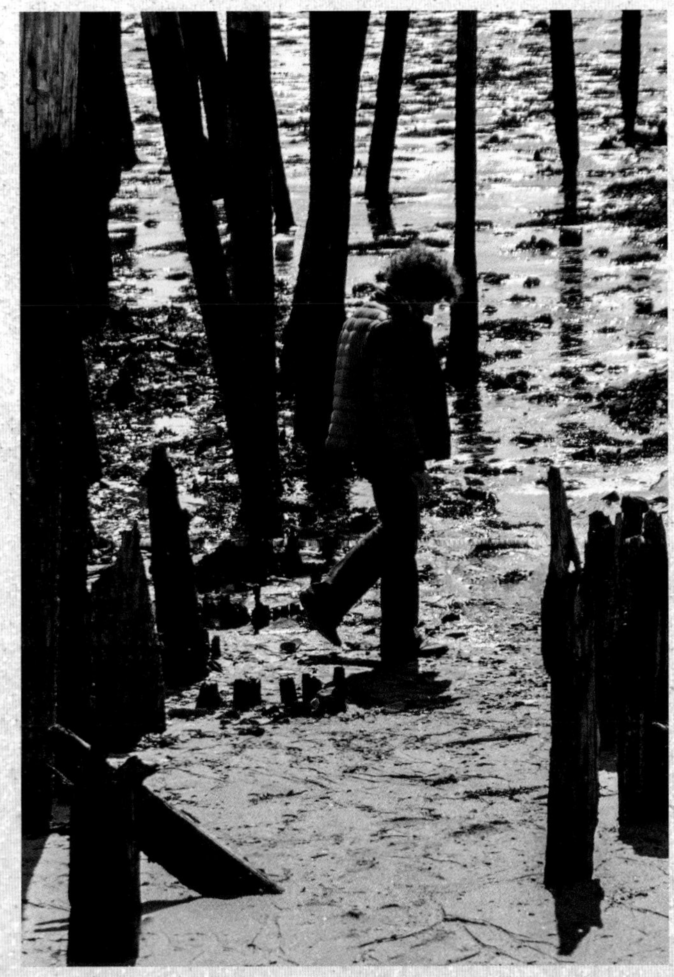

To J. C. and K. B., who inherited sand in their shoes. —With love, G. S. B.

Thank you to my coauthor, Gail Browne. A special thank-you and appreciation to my husband, Bart Weisman, for being the greatest supporter of all my endeavors, and whose love has provided a firm foundation for my life. And finally, to my late mother, Adele Heller, whose nurturing, love of Provincetown, and beachcombing led me to this unique story. She epitomized all that is beautiful about Provincetown.—A. H.

Contents

FOREWORD

Over the years, I've often been asked for my opinion of artifacts and treasures that explorers have discovered from around the world. When I was first contacted for my opinion of objects local beachcombers had picked up along our beaches, I politely attempted to explain that I was traveling, or at the dentist.

Having said that, for anyone who has ever wandered a beach and dreamt of discovering treasure, you'll find it in *Lost and Found: Time, Tide, and Treasures*. This amazing photographic chronicle takes you step by step, inch by inch, on the relentless, fifty-year-plus forage of six local beachcombers, who, while not praying for moon tides, scoured every sandbar, ancient dock piling, and crab grotto in the Provincelands in search of history.

To understand the scope and cross-cultural diversity of the relics discovered by these tireless wanderers, this book provides a tantalizing peephole into our past and those who first walked these sands.

If only pipestems could talk.

Plus ultra.

—Barry Clifford, underwater archeological explorer best known for discovering the pirate ship *Whydah*

ACKNOWLEDGMENTS

We are grateful to the artists who participated in our book, and the museums and galleries that helped provide images and information. Although each artist's work and beach collections were varied, we all shared a common bond of our connection to and love of Provincetown, a passion for beachcombing, and our lives dedicated to being artists, inspired by the tip of Cape Cod. We thank them for the hours of interviews and for sharing their collections with us.

Peter Schiffer, president of Schiffer Publishing, gave us the green light and license to express our creative ideas. Senior editors Sandra Korinchak and Cheryl Weber have been a guiding force in every part of the process. We thank them and graphic designer Jack Chappell for making this book see the light of day.

A special thank-you to Lisa Tate and her family for allowing us to premiere some of the beautiful photographs from the Cook Collection.

To Nell Husted, for permission to use her beautiful poem from her book *Provincetown Cuts*. It is the essence of what we are expressing in our book.

We would also like to thank photographers Patricia Burke, John Caplice, and Vincent Guadazno for their time and talent.

Thanks to Dave Drabkin for his knowledge of all things Provincetown.

Introduction

This spit of sand was visited by the Vikings in 1004, Bartholomew Gosnold in 1602, and, of course, the *Mayflower* and her passengers in 1620. After a difficult time of finding it generally inhospitable, the surviving passengers, Pilgrims as we know them, pulled up anchor. However, in the following one hundred years, many others found the land full of opportunities. The physical attributes of a deep harbor protected by a hooked finger of land attracted fishermen, smugglers, and other entrepreneurs, and it earned the nickname Helltown.

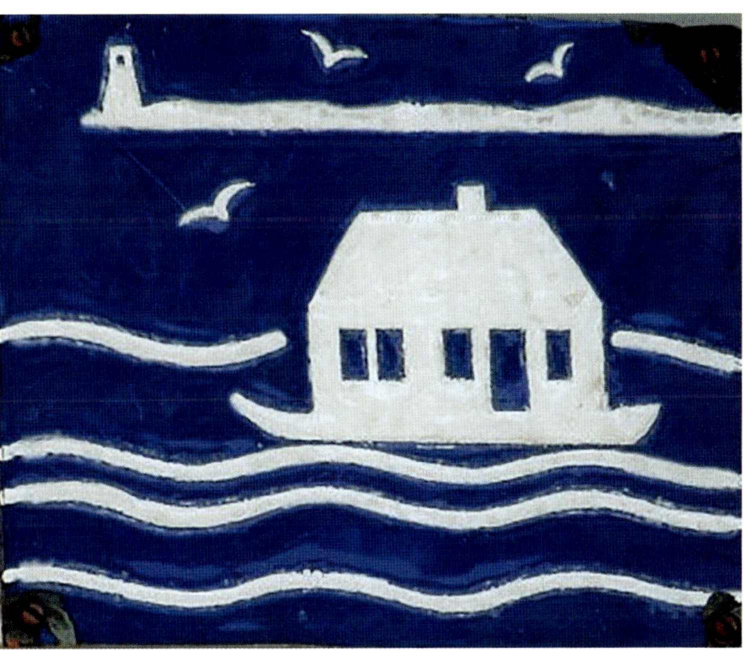

The reputed outpost spanned from Long Point to Herring Cove. As many as 120 people fished and processed incoming catches of whales and fish for food, oil, and fertilizer. Carts pulled by horses transported the commodities into town daily for trains bound for New York City.

Provincetown achieved legitimacy by incorporating in 1727. The town boasted one of the largest fishing and whaling fleets. With stability and prosperity came the development of more than fifty wharves to handle the daily waterfront business. This success attracted Portuguese people, who settled in Provincetown over a period of two centuries. It also created a bounty of ancillary businesses to support the growing population.

The settlement houses from Long Point were floated over on scows to become part of the booming village. Today, these floaters are recognizable by their blue-and-white plaques, designed and executed by Provincetown jeweler Claude Jensen.

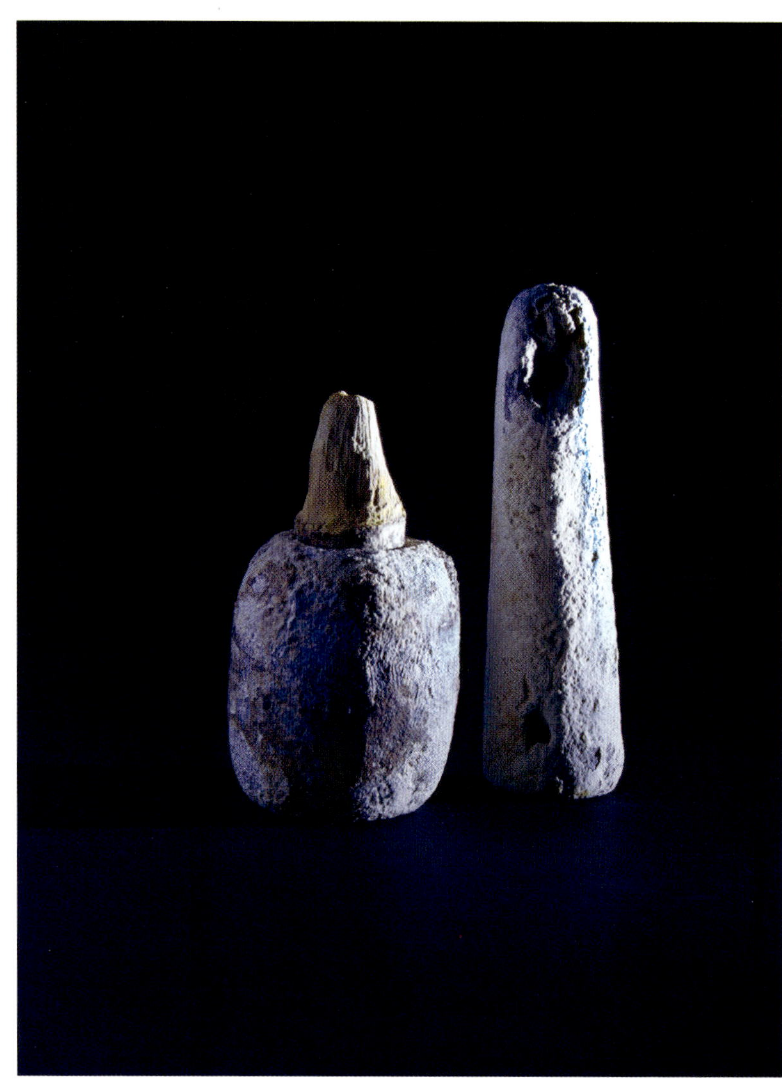

Through all these transitions, the harbor was the most obvious place to dispose of unwanted rubbish. Embodiments of the local history were either washed out to sea or sunk in the sand.

The experience of discovery transports us to a different time and place limited only by our imaginations. Every piece here contains its own narrative; collectively they portray a rich and meaningful personality and history that defines this vibrant community at the edge of the world.

Adapting to natural and domestic forces through four centuries, Provincetown has shown a tenacity to survive with grace, creativity, and generosity of its bounty. The people who have come before us leave us this legacy.

Amy Heller, an artist with deep local roots, was passing by a Provincetown gallery when something caught her eye: the artwork in the window was nestled in a deep bed of ceramic beach shards. The sight triggered a flashback to the Provincetown summers of her childhood. That moment led to a friendship with coauthor Gail Browne and was the genesis for this book, showcasing beachcombing artists whose personal collections inspired their work.

What also surfaced was a historical narrative of Provincetown as told through the objects themselves. Some of it is factual, some is distorted, and some is rhetorically accurate. However it is viewed, we hope to impart our collective perspective on this unique culture at the end of the road.

We humans feel the pull of consumption, the epitome of capitalist nirvana. And yet the rhythms of life—the moon's pull, the life force of Earth's water—continue to inhabit our unconscious selves. As we step onto the sand, we are primitive again. We walk, we pause to discover, we find tangible evidence of our connection, we are transported.

Those of us who collect from the sea find our subconscious directing our focus. The creative act is a result of a special alchemy and is a confluence of two parallel streams: one of the spirit and one of the tangible.

Independent of each other, the six artists represented here have been collecting from Provincetown beaches for decades. Some literally employ the detritus in their work. However the artists interpret their experience, the commonality is the mystery and history embedded in the objects, crossing all barriers to inspire with their beauty and wonder.

As a footnote, Provincetown's beachcombing territories, unlike the Thames in London, are unregulated. Walk lightly with respect to the archeological nature of these beaches and their artifacts. Acknowledge that you are walking through past lives. No shovels, please.

A local historian with an impeccable memory, George Bryant (1937–2015), was said to have struggled to save Provincetown one plank, one nail, one cultural artifact at a time. In that vein, this book is an attempt to legitimize and remind us of characterizations that have always made Provincetown special. It seemed most logical that in their resurrection, the sunken detritus be presented chronologically and by category, as a shared collective.

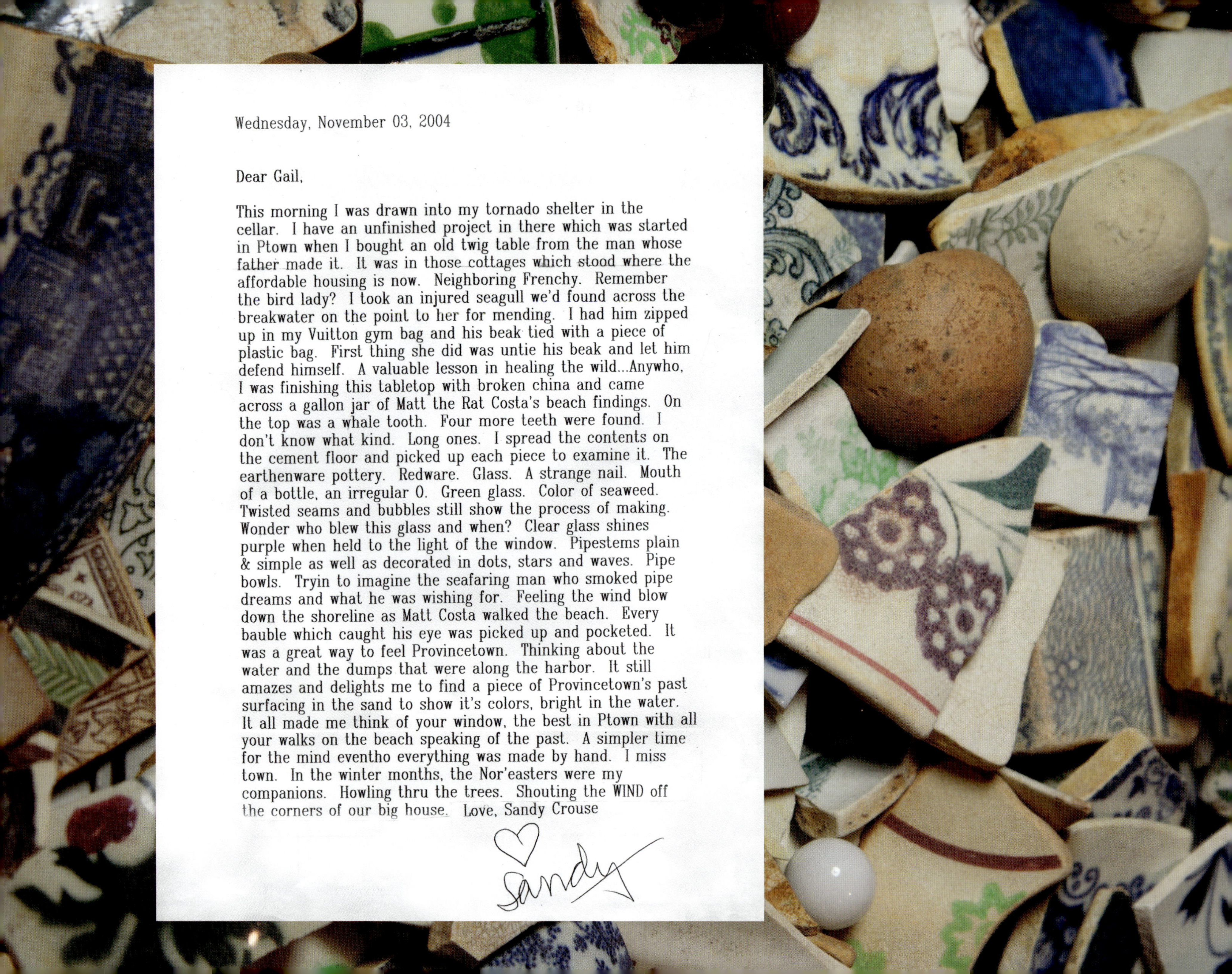

Wednesday, November 03, 2004

Dear Gail,

This morning I was drawn into my tornado shelter in the cellar. I have an unfinished project in there which was started in Ptown when I bought an old twig table from the man whose father made it. It was in those cottages which stood where the affordable housing is now. Neighboring Frenchy. Remember the bird lady? I took an injured seagull we'd found across the breakwater on the point to her for mending. I had him zipped up in my Vuitton gym bag and his beak tied with a piece of plastic bag. First thing she did was untie his beak and let him defend himself. A valuable lesson in healing the wild...Anywho, I was finishing this tabletop with broken china and came across a gallon jar of Matt the Rat Costa's beach findings. On the top was a whale tooth. Four more teeth were found. I don't know what kind. Long ones. I spread the contents on the cement floor and picked up each piece to examine it. The earthenware pottery. Redware. Glass. A strange nail. Mouth of a bottle, an irregular O. Green glass. Color of seaweed. Twisted seams and bubbles still show the process of making. Wonder who blew this glass and when? Clear glass shines purple when held to the light of the window. Pipestems plain & simple as well as decorated in dots, stars and waves. Pipe bowls. Tryin to imagine the seafaring man who smoked pipe dreams and what he was wishing for. Feeling the wind blow down the shoreline as Matt Costa walked the beach. Every bauble which caught his eye was picked up and pocketed. It was a great way to feel Provincetown. Thinking about the water and the dumps that were along the harbor. It still amazes and delights me to find a piece of Provincetown's past surfacing in the sand to show it's colors, bright in the water. It all made me think of your window, the best in Ptown with all your walks on the beach speaking of the past. A simpler time for the mind eventho everything was made by hand. I miss town. In the winter months, the Nor'easters were my companions. Howling thru the trees. Shouting the WIND off the corners of our big house. Love, Sandy Crouse

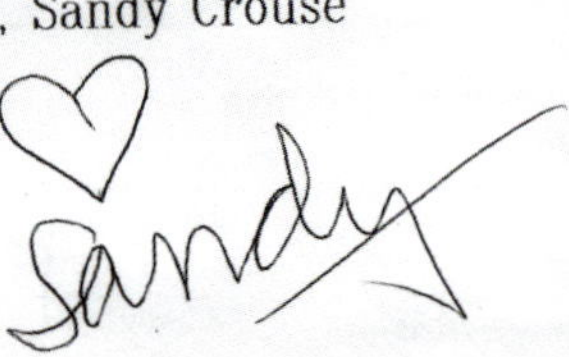

White May

by Nell Husted

White May west wind

Blowing the harbor green

Egrets asleep in the marsh

In bridal plume

Wild shad white on the dune

White beach plum

By the side of the road

All the way to Herring Cove

There in the white-capped waves

A face like a man's

Looks toward the blossoming shore

Dives and is gone.

Part 1.
The Artists/Beachcombers

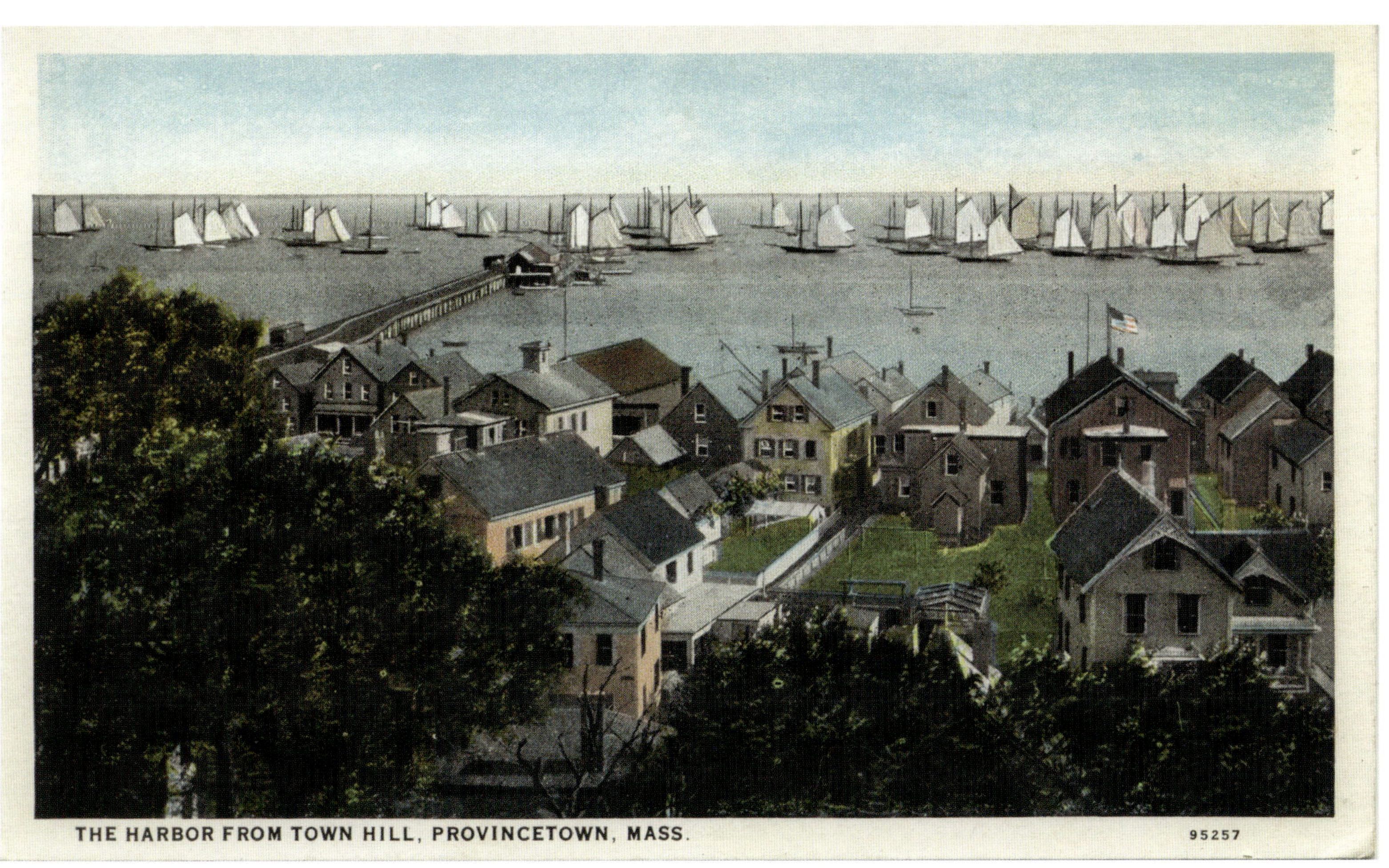

Amy Heller

My love of the sea and the beauty surrounding it started at an early age, passed on to me by my mother, Adele Heller. Spending every summer with my family in Provincetown, she and I would take beach walks at Herring Cove, known then as New Beach. We would collect glacial pebbles, shells, seaweed, and any other gifts offered. Some summers we lived on the Provincetown Harbor. When the tide was low, we would walk through warm pools of water, searching for treasures. My mother's collection included old bottles, ceramic shards, sea glass, clay pipes, ceramic doll parts, driftwood, and whalebones. She had an arsenal of techniques, the most notable being her special dance in which she would wiggle down with her big toe until she hit pay dirt. A squeal of delight and voilà, another medicine bottle for her collection! Her sense of delight was infectious.

Winters in the Washington, DC, area were made brighter by her collection on the kitchen windowsill and inspired me to imagine what surprises lay ahead. One day at the end of summer vacation, when the movers came to take our possessions back home, they could barely lift the steamer trunk. My mother had to confess that she was "smuggling" white quartz stones, which she used to create a spectacular Japanese garden next to our willow tree. Provincetown has a long history of bootlegging all sorts of things, but usually beach stones weren't among them.

Although my main interest was collecting shells (much lighter than stones), when I was eight I found a bisque doll leg (*see photo*). I was so delighted with my discovery that I decided beachcombing for man-made objects would be fun too. My pastime developed over time, but my serious collecting came later in life when I discovered that I loved motion, and collecting windup toys became my passion.

I went to Hampshire College in Amherst, Massachusetts, and received a BA in fine art. I detoured to the Smithsonian Museums and the National Gallery of Art, where I worked as an exhibit specialist. Leaving the government, I took some classes at a community college and fell in love with photography, and I earned my MFA in photography at George Washington University. My thesis was on the history of human locomotion photography, and my portfolio of photographs were black-and-white time/motion studies of the human figure à la Eadweard Muybridge. I also taught photography, drawing, and design on the college level at the community college where I had taken classes. Then I worked for *US News & World Report* as a photo researcher/editor and also curated an exhibit at the Newseum called "Unforgettable Photos." My artwork took a back seat for a while, but one day my husband (we got engaged in my darkroom at

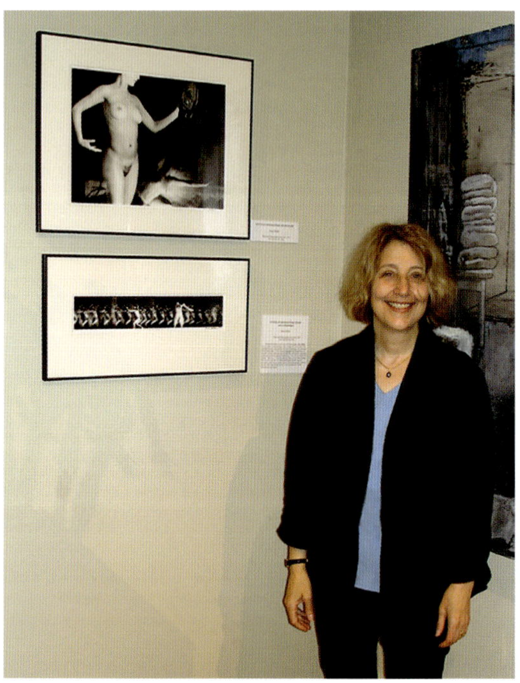

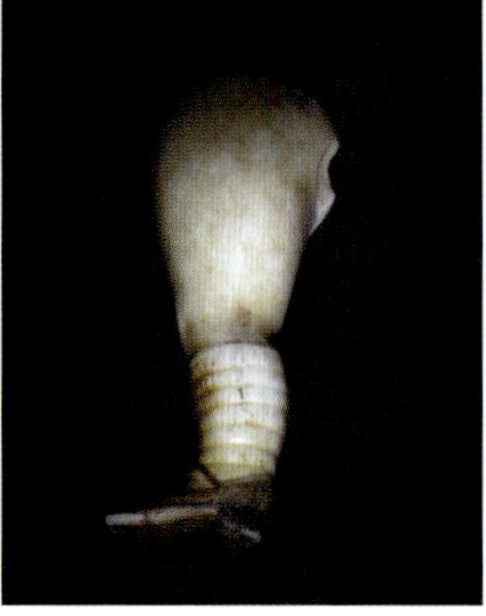

Nothing but the sea
and yet with every breeze
the smell of lilac.

—Haiku by Adele Heller (1922–1997)

GWU) said he wanted a change of scene; he had fallen in love with Cape Cod and especially Provincetown (my second ancestral home). We moved there in 2003 and never looked back. We bought an apartment on the Provincetown Harbor at the old Ice House Condominiums and enjoyed nine years there before moving to nearby Orleans.

Both my husband and I experienced a rebirth of our artistic leanings: he became a full-time musician and is something of a local celebrity on the Cape. Living in proximity to Provincetown, the oldest continuous art colony in the United States, has been inspirational. Surrounded by the sea, I started pursuing my art more steadily. Drawn to the natural world, I find beauty and grace in the simplest discoveries: intertwining seaweeds, dancing skate egg cases, lyrical forms of sand and sea. Recently I have been making cyanotype photographs on fabric, inspired by the blue sky, using figures resembling skate egg cases and, in some artworks, using the actual egg cases. In addition, I incorporate light, motion, and three-dimensional figures. My work is included in collections both here and abroad, including the Provincetown Art Association and Museum, the Cape Cod Museum of Art in Dennis, the Dimock Gallery, and many private collections.

However, the story of this book began when I decided to revisit working with clay, something I had enjoyed in high school (where I met my future husband, Bart Weisman; his band class was next to my art class). I signed up for a hand-building pottery class with artist Gail Browne. I thought it would be a good idea to meet with her first, so I walked to her gallery in the center of Provincetown and was thunderstruck. Her front window was overflowing with beautiful pottery shards that she had collected from the beach over the years. Her collection took my breath away. Seeing it reawakened fond memories of the beach walks I took with my mother, and of her collections that surrounded us back home.

Gail and I talked, and the rest is history. I signed up for her class and loved every minute of it. We became fast friends, and little by little she showed me more of her collection. She had an unbelievable volume of gorgeous finds: dolls, marbles, coins, metal, clay pipes, inner ear bones of whales, jewelry—and things you can't even imagine. One day we talked about writing a book about beach collections. We selected four other artists with beachcombing collections, connected to Provincetown and to us, and started photographing their treasures. We interviewed them years ago, and again just recently. We are excited to put into words and photographs the stories behind these found objects, and our love of Provincetown.

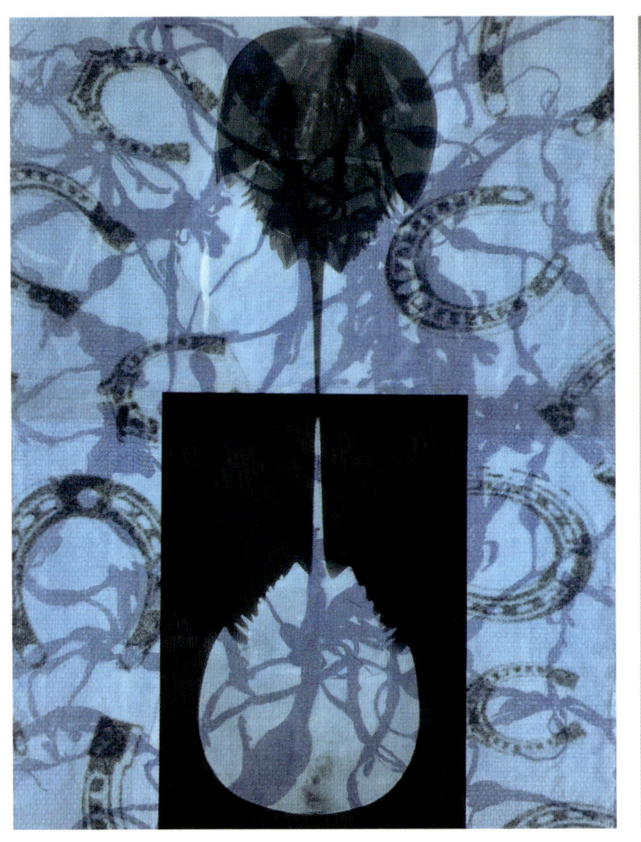

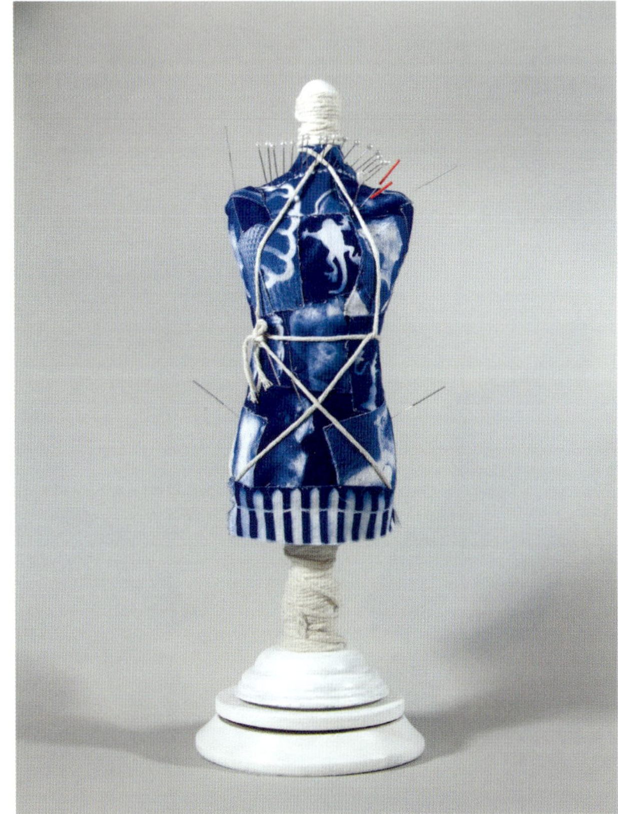

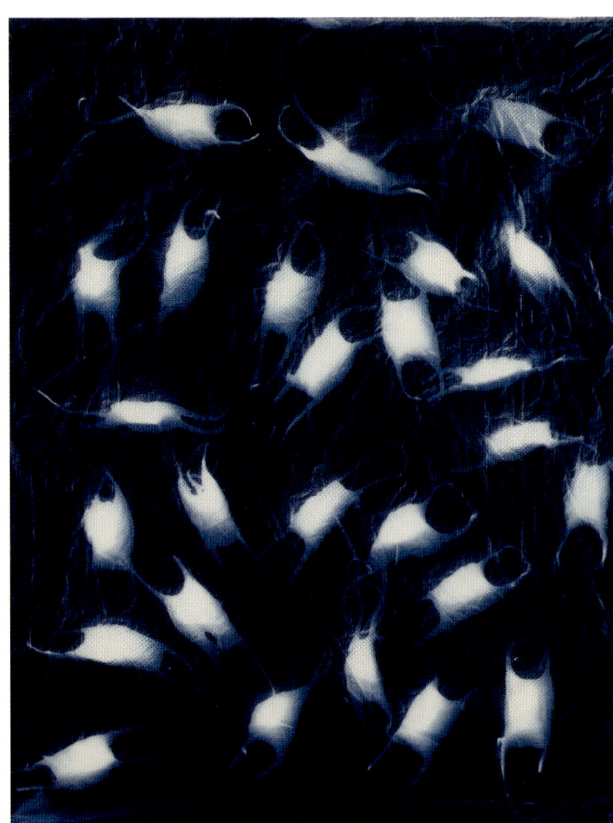

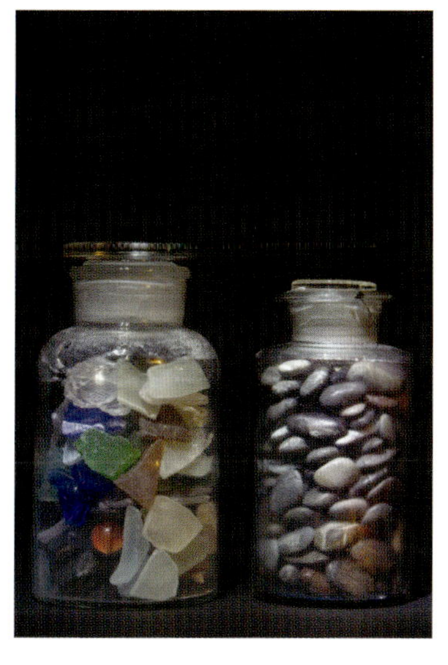

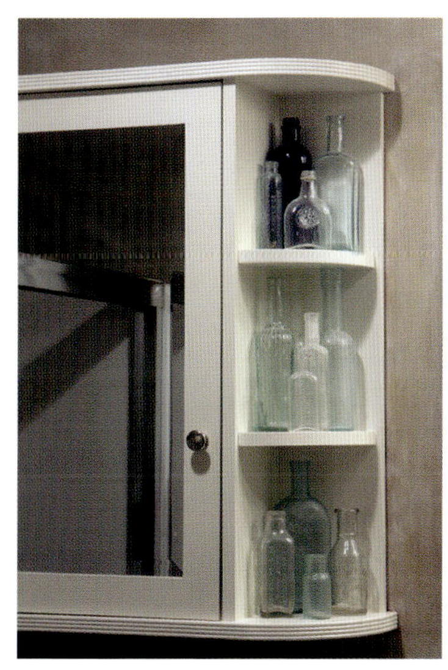

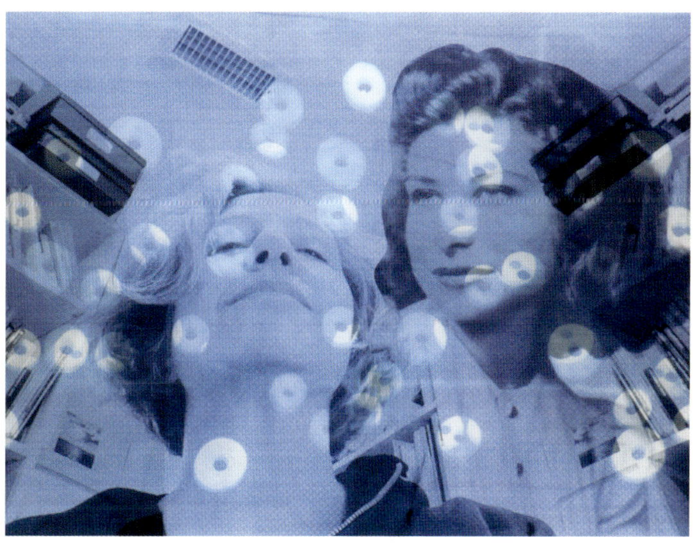

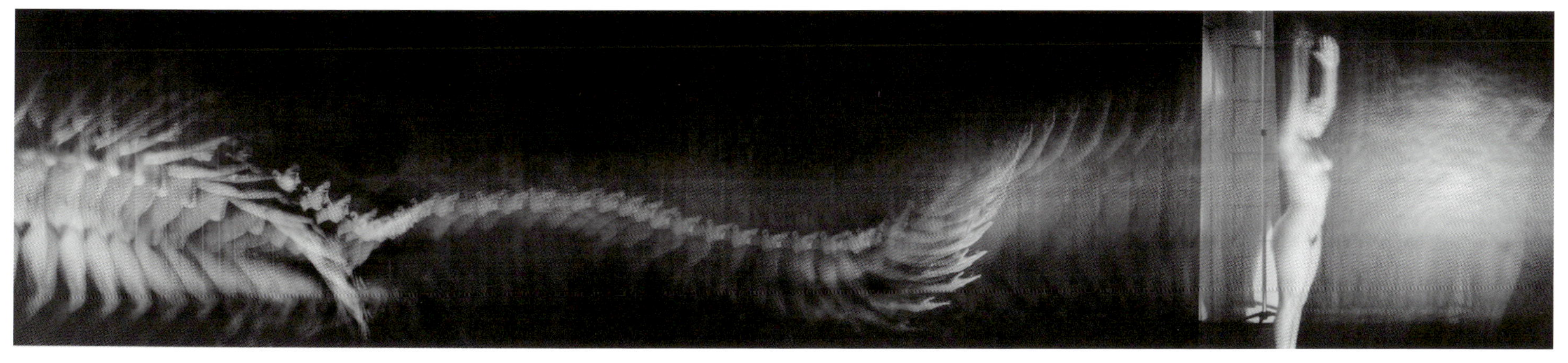

Gail Browne

Flying into Provincetown aboard a DC-10 on a sunny day in May 1966, it felt as if I'd left Cleveland, Ohio, far behind. The dunes, the forest, and the rambling roses on picket fences pushed it all back into timelessness that was more a state of mind. Once unpacked, I strolled the neighborhood and gazed out over the bay from Saint Mary's Church. The tide was high and the waves slapped hard against the concrete bulkhead. The following morning I crossed Commercial Street, anticipating the feel of sea spray on my face again. Seeing the tide so far out made me realize I had much to learn in this new place. But I also discovered that the ocean had relinquished its secrets. And a beachcomber was baptized.

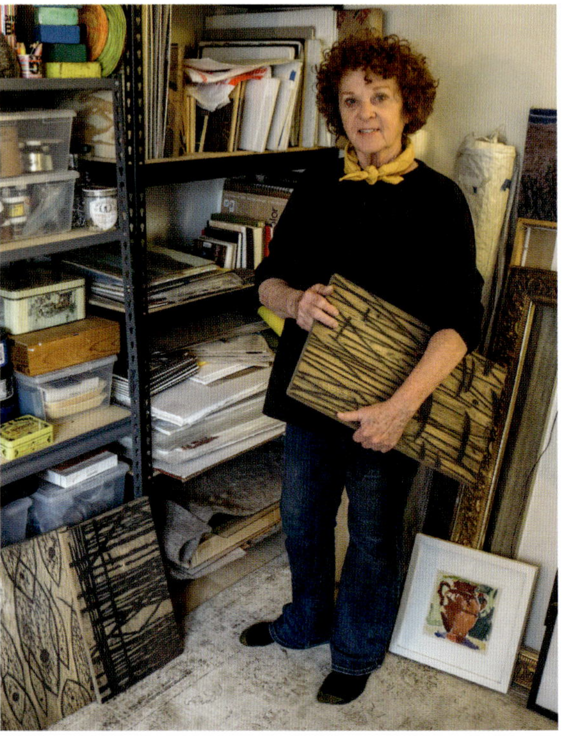

Across from the White Horse Inn were wooden poles, remnants of the former wharf of the derelict fish-packing plant called the Ice House. Scattered among the poles, seaweed, and tidal pools were bits and pieces of ceramics, glass, bricks, and other industrial refuse, evidence of a former life. The Ice House was a ghost of its former self, housing pigeons and other free-roaming animals.

After receiving a BFA degree in graphic design in 1970 from the Cleveland Institute of Art, the memory of studying painting that initial summer in Provincetown drew me back permanently. However, it wasn't until the mid-1980s that my beachcombing became a passion. My children and I spent summers at the West End beaches. To acclimate the girls to the water and teach them to dive, I tossed pieces of old shards into the sea to be retrieved from the bottom. And at low tide we went beachcombing. It became time away from the demands of the day.

I believe that my lifelong painting experience has sharpened my eye to catch the slightest differences in shape and color. From initially painting the landscape to externalizing the emotional impact of a nuance, for me the fading wharves are not unlike intimate places of worship. Today they exist as sculptural icons, bare bones of a culture that built Provincetown. At their roots lie the spoils. Meandering among them, transported across the spectrum of time, the wharves serve as inspiration and stand as cathedrals to the spirit of Provincetown.

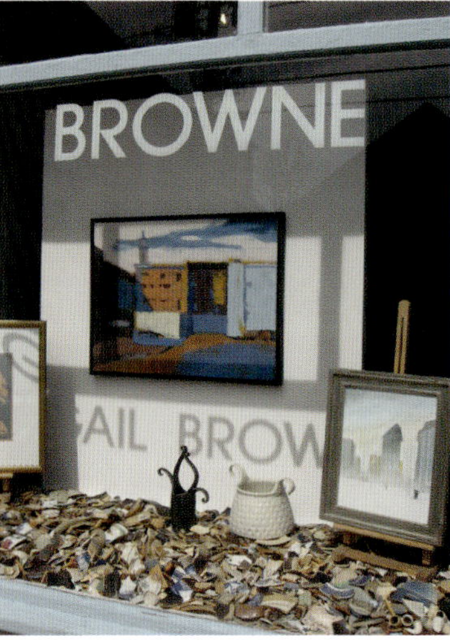

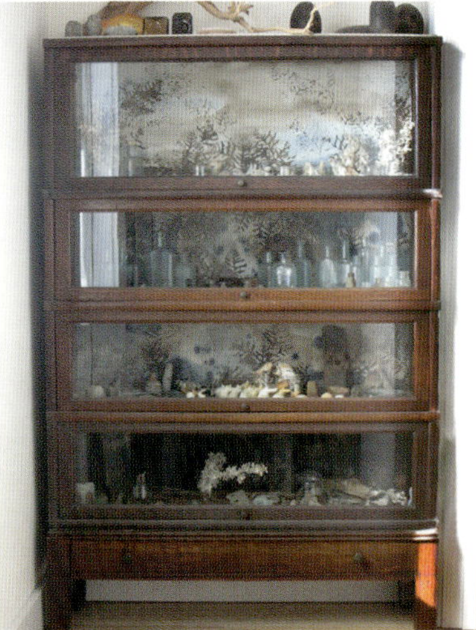

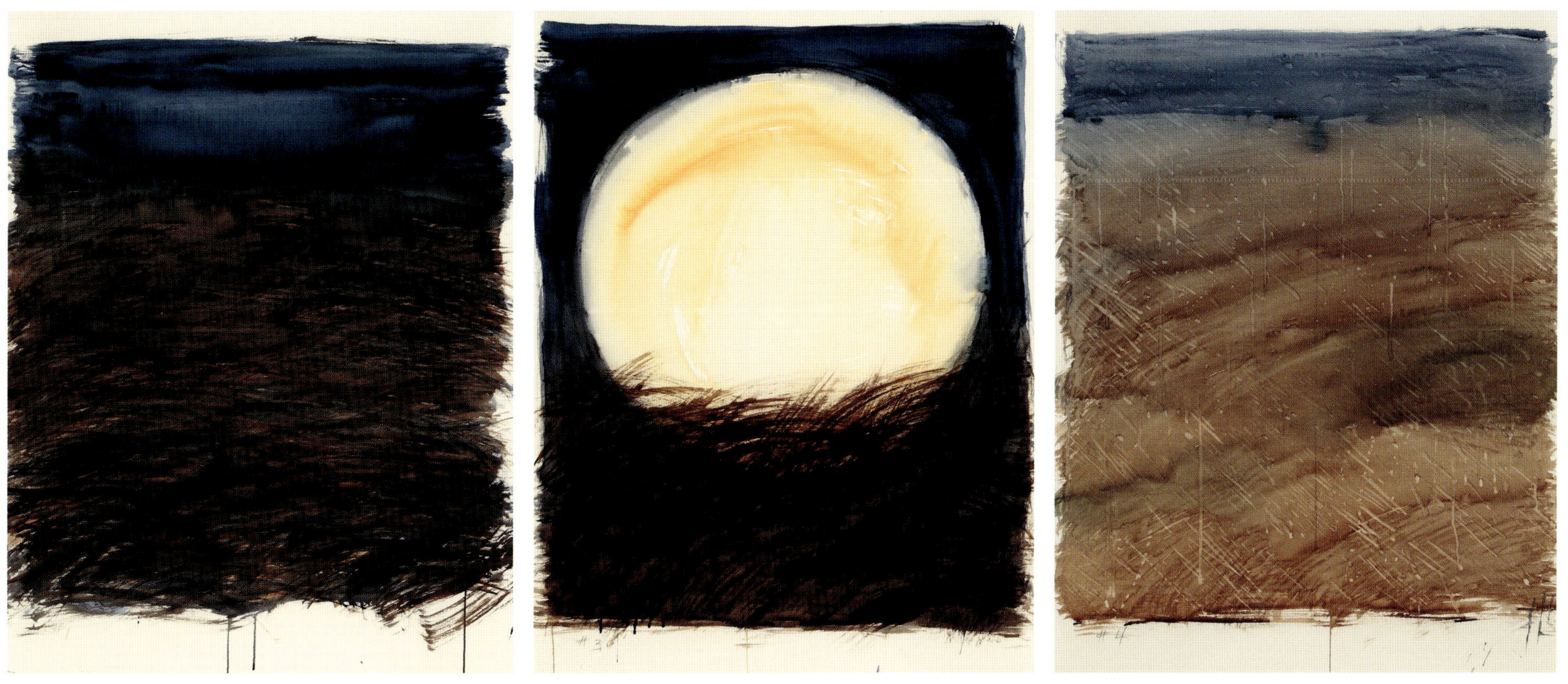

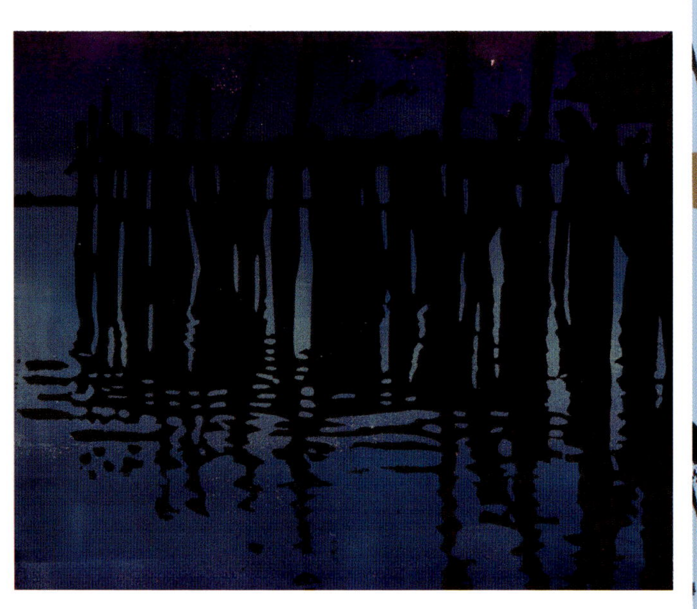

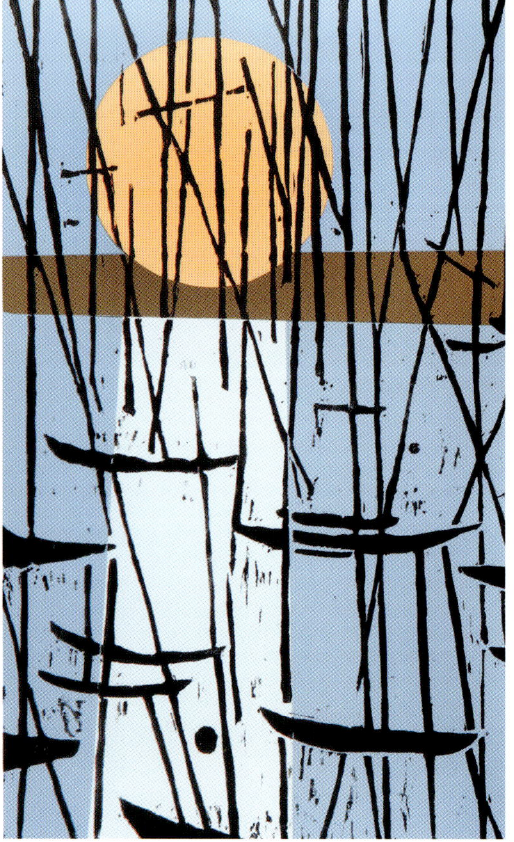

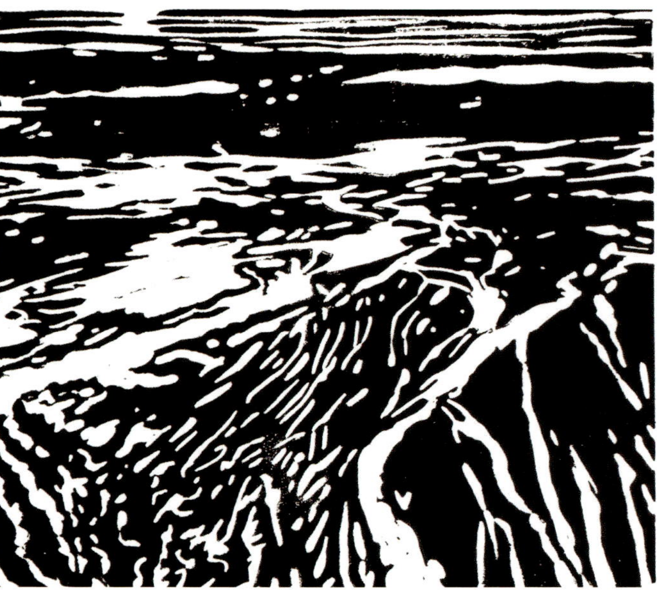

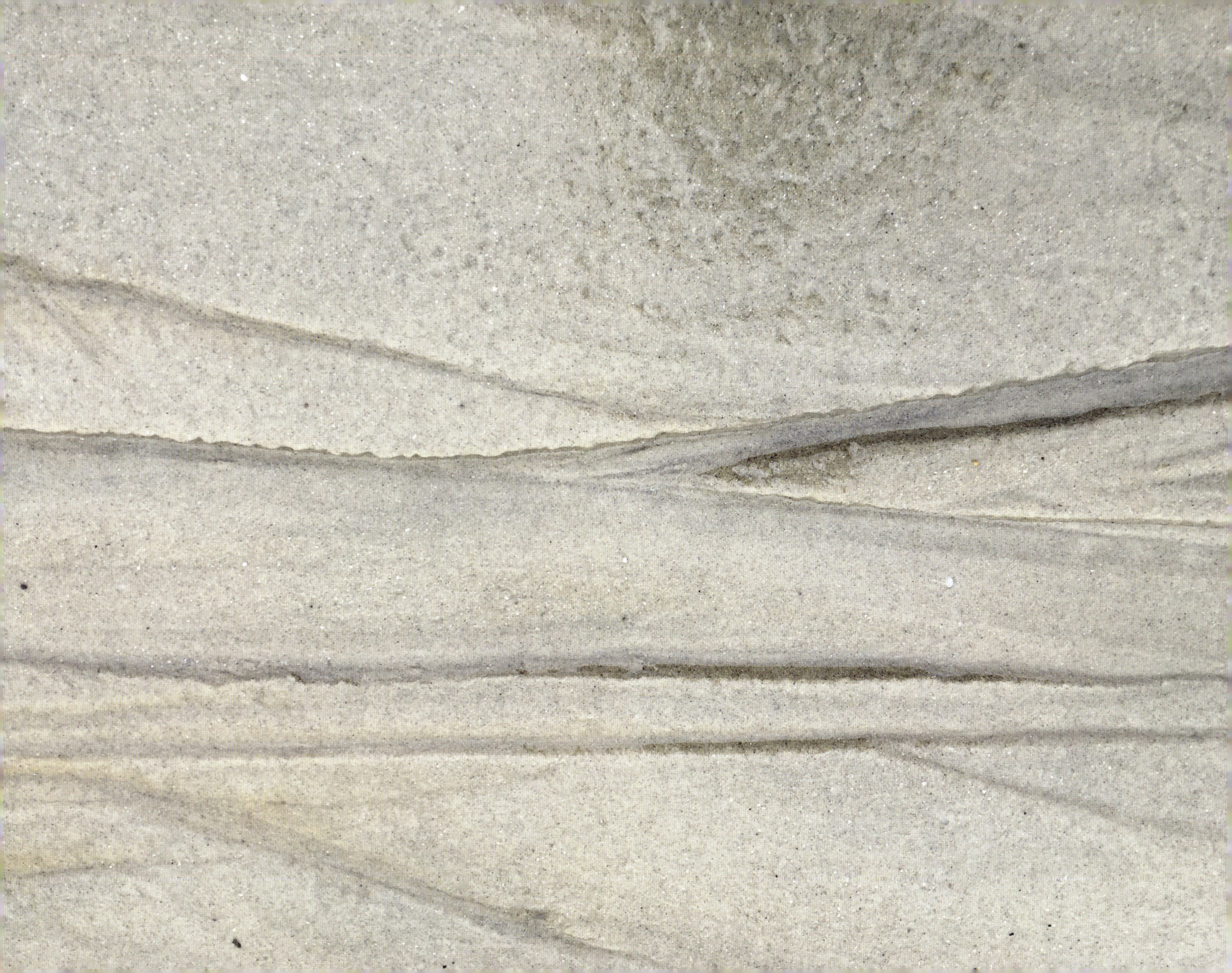

JUDY BERKOWITZ

Fertile ground for major US cultural shifts in the late 1950s to mid-'60s, Provincetown has a long-standing reputation as a place of tolerance, birthing the human genus of the Provincetown "washashore," what locals call nonnative, year-round residents. Characteristically youthful, this generation of visitors made an impact. Among them was Judy Berkowitz, a college student and free spirit who'd migrated from the East Village in New York.

In the early 1960s, Judy lived for a brief time in a shack in the woods of Tasha Hill. Waitressing at a Commercial Street establishment paid for her bohemian lifestyle until adulthood insinuated itself.

After graduating from City College of New York, Judy opened a store in the East Village called Opening Line, featuring her one-of-a-kind clothing designs. Her circle of friends in the Village included some now-famous artists and musicians. Memories of fishing nets and ropes found their way into her creations. Obligations kept her from Provincetown until 1991, when she started revisiting Provincetown as often as she could. These visits would take her to the boatyards, where she scavenged anything nautical.

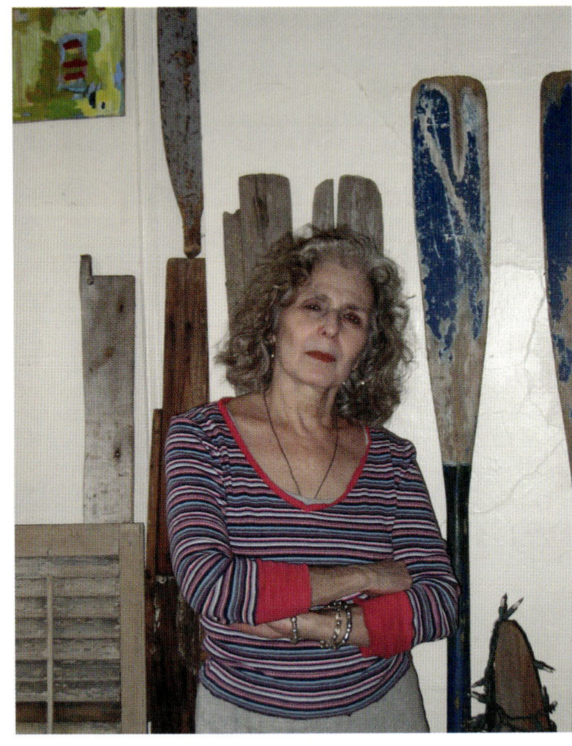

Judy has repurposed some of the objects from her collection. The most unusual piece was made from saw blades and other jetsam and resembled a pot of flowers. She entered it into a Provincetown Art Association and Museum (PAAM) show, where it made the catalog cover. Her collected objects include fishing baskets, wooden oars and oarlocks, old bones, nails, paintbrushes, metal objects, and colored rope.

Of the ropes, she says: "They're so beautiful, and they're different shapes too. There's this dark-green one that's kind of oblong. Then there's another longish one that's another shade of orange . . . it's puffy. Then there's another longish orange one, much lighter, slightly different shape, round at the bottom, opposed to one that's square on the bottom. I love these; I have them hanging where I can see them every day. They're works of art, really."

Judy recalls quite clearly how barren the boatyard beaches seemed the last time she visited Provincetown: "There were hardly any treasures there . . . I don't know if it's because the boats weren't going out that much anymore." She is looking for a future home for her legacy and has considered returning some of her pieces to the sea.

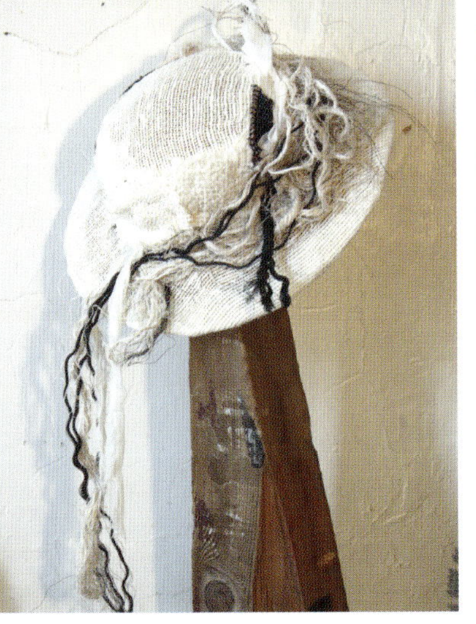

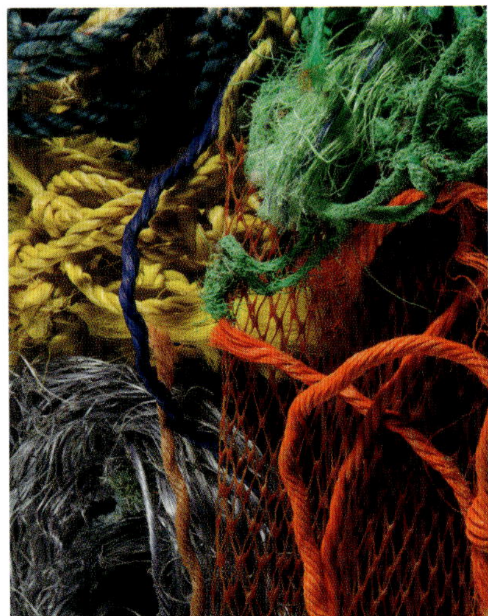

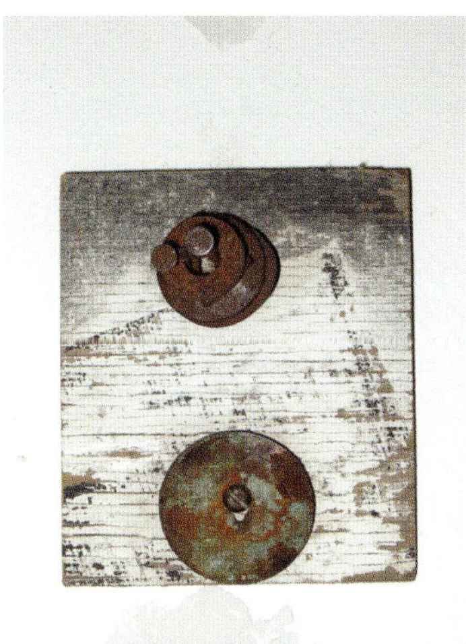
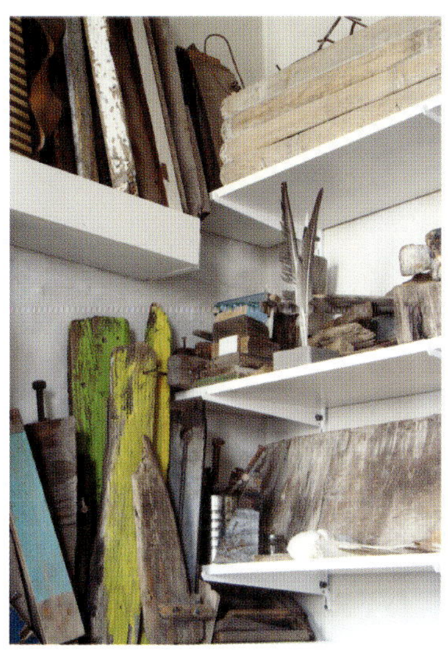
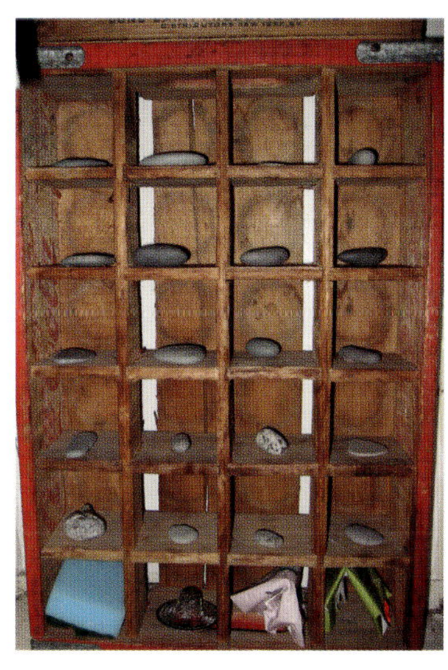
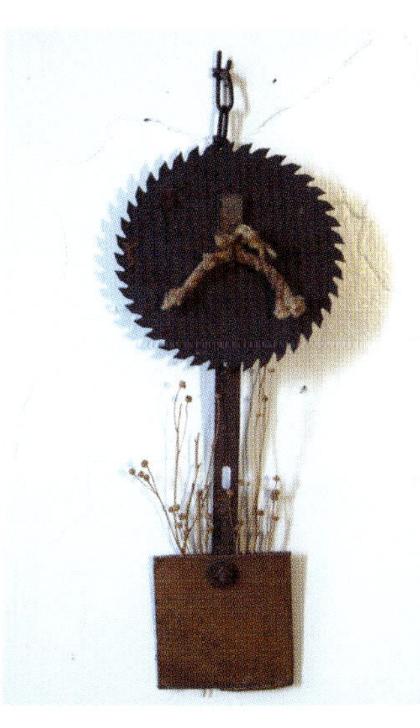
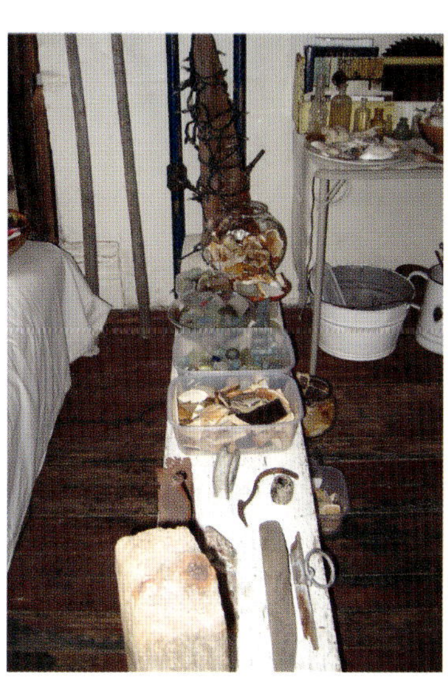

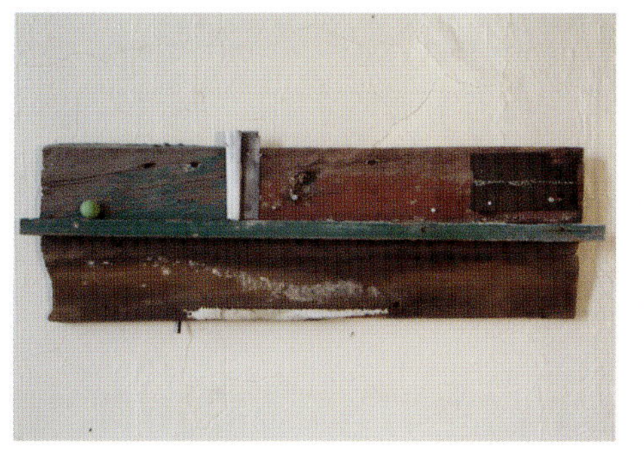
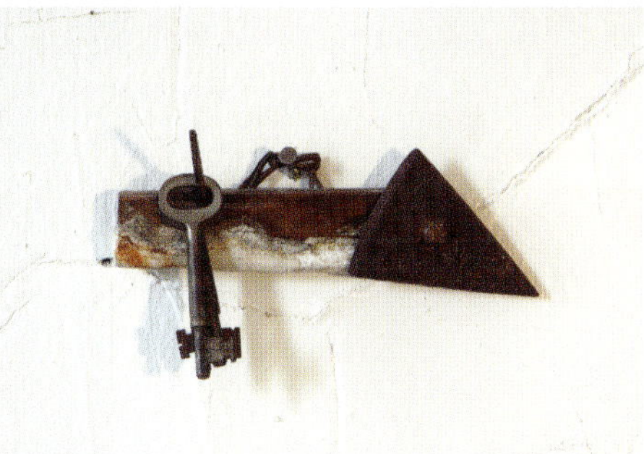
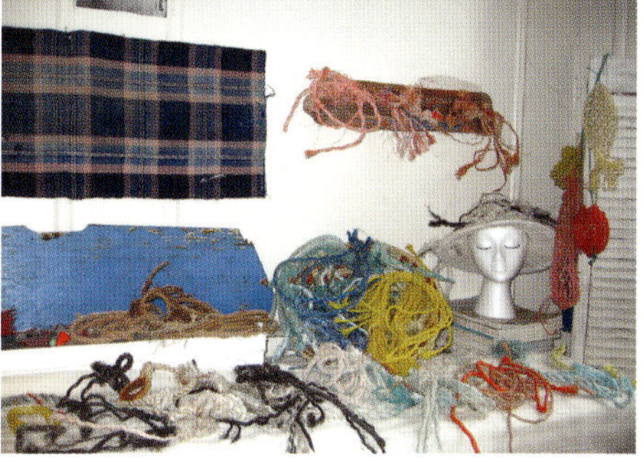
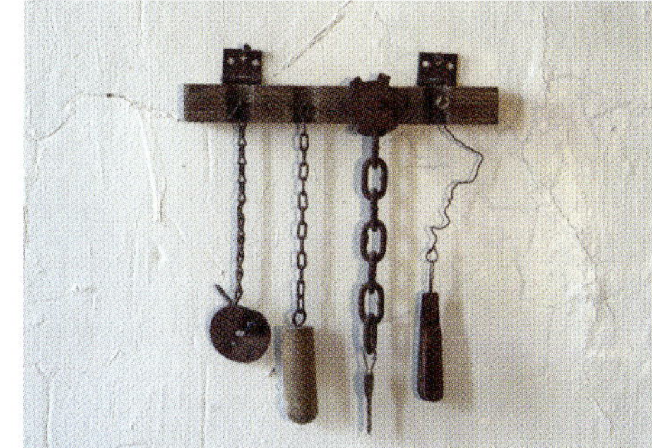

Betty Bodian

Betty Bodian is the quintessential New Yorker: self-contained, confident, no-nonsense, and resourceful. Born in Newark, New Jersey, she attended the High School of Music and Art in New York City and studied fashion and design at Cooper Union. She also possesses a sense of wonderment and creativity, and an appreciation of the ethereal. It seems impossible that anyone with her qualities wouldn't be compelled to investigate the secrets held by the powerful tides.

Betty's history with Provincetown spans over sixty years. She arrived in 1953 and met her future husband, Al. In the mid-1960s they lived in the center of town near the Old Reliable Wharf. Construction on the Lopes Square parking lot began around this time. There was a good deal of dredging, which amounted to the wholesale archeological excavation of an old garbage dump.

Over the decades, Betty and Al spent summers in Provincetown, usually on the water. On a routine beach walk, Betty experienced something extraordinary. She looked down to see bottles everywhere on the sand. "They were just lying there . . . beautiful! I didn't gather them all up because it occurred to me that they were always there, and it was like a farm that kept producing." Of course it didn't, but Betty was hooked.

"It turns out that my middens are very limited," she says, referring to the trash treasures she likes to collect. "It's very odd, it's really like *Brigadoon*: I go out in July and find something in a given spot. . . . I can never find it again until the next July. Isn't that crazy?" Traditionally, beachcombers don't discuss locations. And prevailing seasonal winds scour or build up the sand, which affects the hunt.

Asked about her most amazing find, she talks excitedly about the smallest things: clay pipe bowls, pipestems. And then, the gold button. Not just any gold button, but solid gold with her initial on it—an extra special gift from the sea. Her favorite bottle finds are "Doctor Hough's Anti-Scrofula Syrup," found near Bryant's Market, and "Water Safe Kidney and Liver Cure." Betty recalls that she went running to local historian George Bryant with the kidney cure bottle, fresh out of the water. He looked at it and said jokingly, "I'm only interested in bottles with liquor in them."

Betty painted in oil, then acrylic and watercolor, and is inspired by the sea and the transparency of the bottles she finds. She was a member of the Group Gallery in Provincetown, the Atlantic Gallery in SoHo, and more, and her work is in the permanent collection at the Cape Cod Museum of Art, the Provincetown Art Association and Museum, and private collections.

Back in New York, she displays her bottles staggered on a sunny windowsill. I see them as a diorama of the New York skyline, but Betty is transported to Brigadoon.

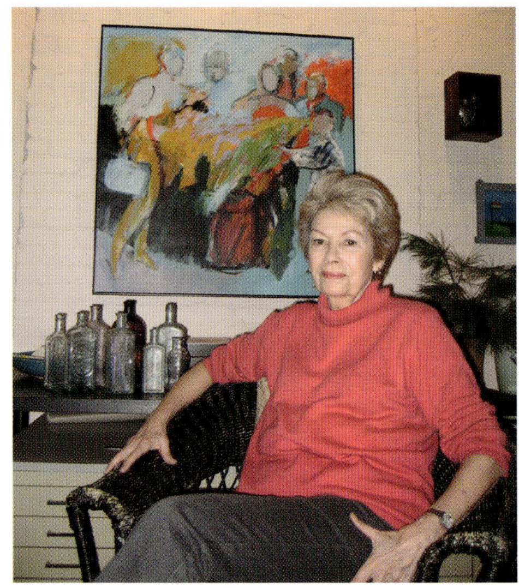

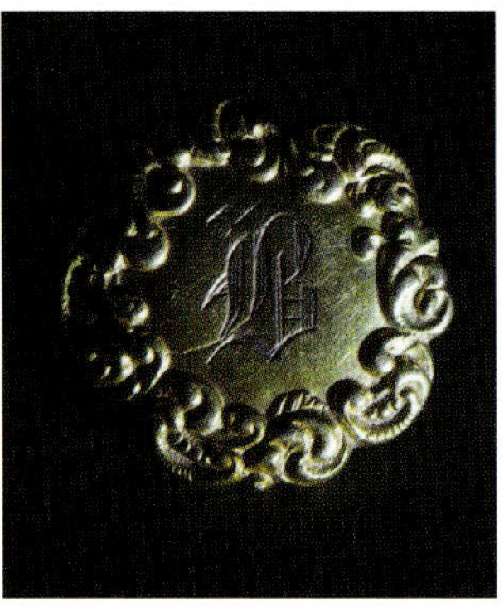

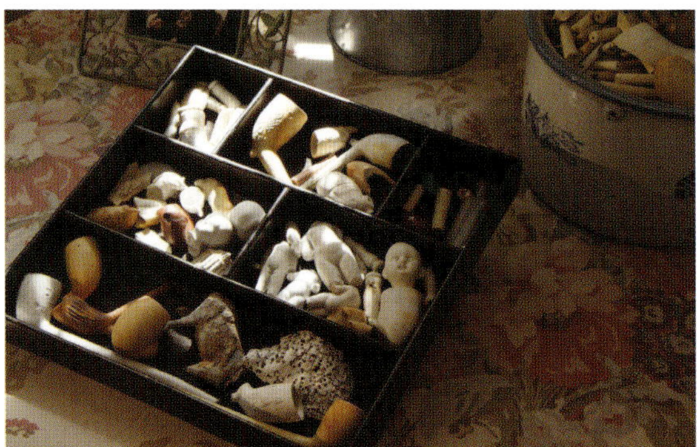

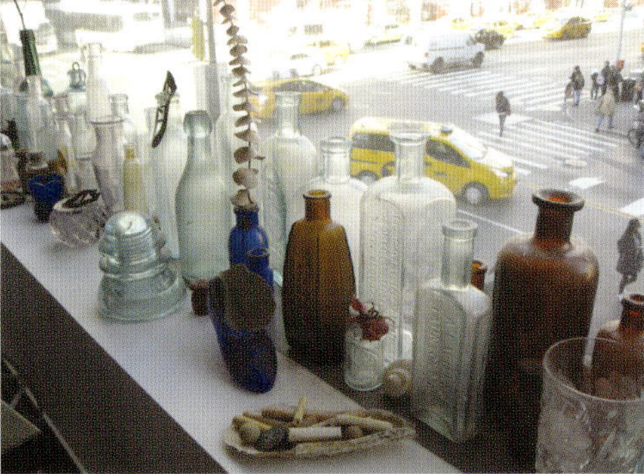

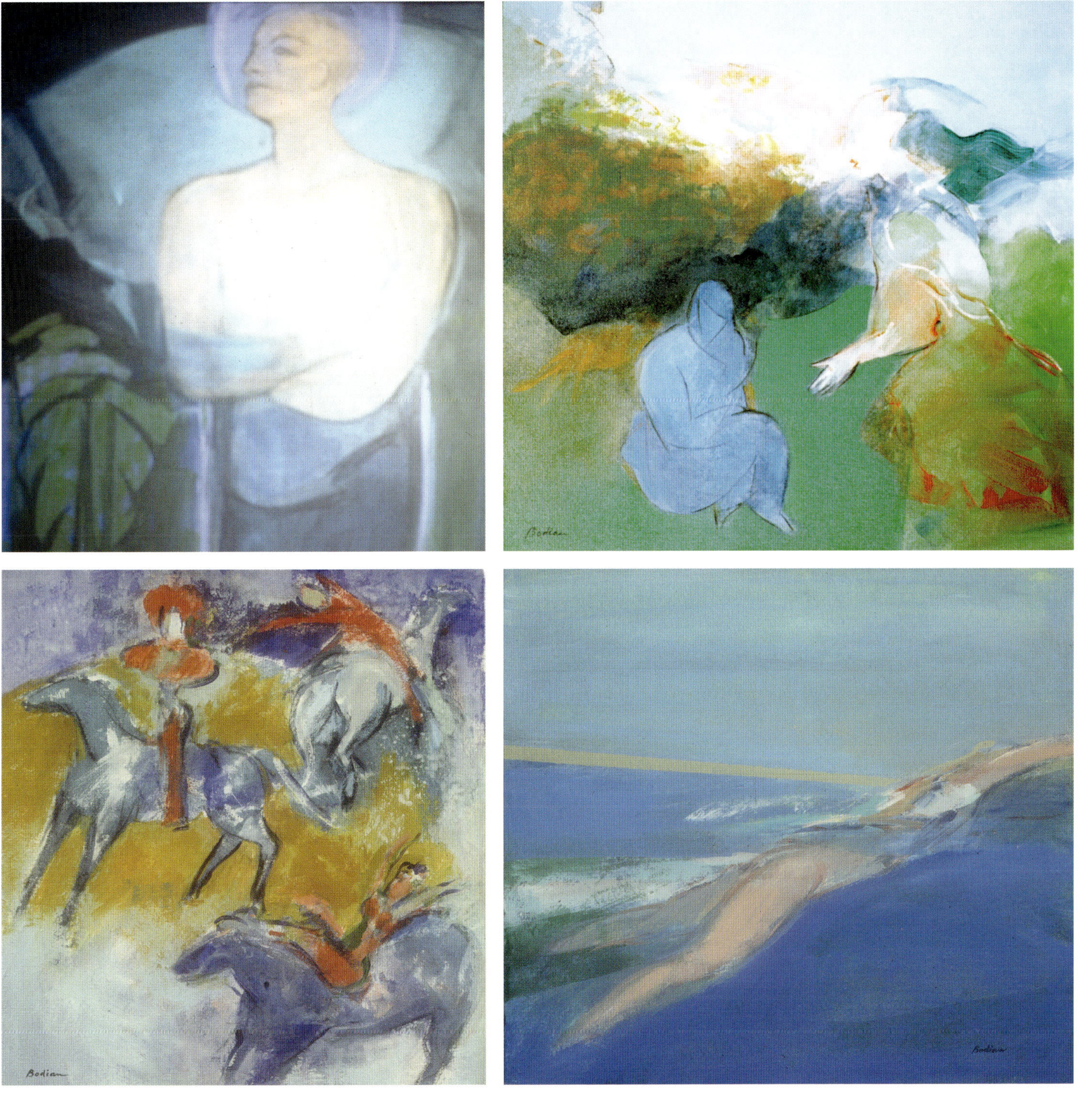

Varujan Boghosian

In the 1940s, members of the summer artists' community in Provincetown read like *Who's Who in American Art*, and crossing the town line was like entering a utopian vision not unlike Shangri-La. In fact, Varujan Boghosian stayed at a summer compound at the end of Miller Hill Road called "Shangri-La." The year was 1946, and he was one of many artists studying with Henry Hensche (1899–1992), a student of painter Charles Hawthorne who taught color theory at the Cape School of Art for more than fifty years.

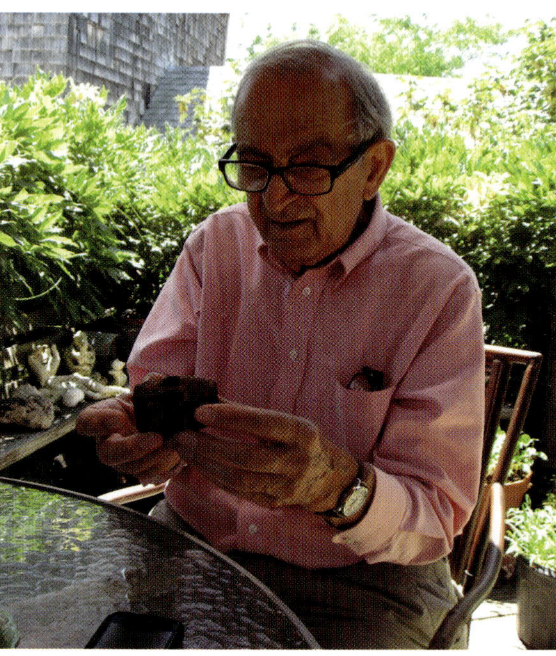

Varujan has continued his summer pilgrimages to Provincetown ever since. At one point the local newspaper, the *Provincetown Advocate*, ordained him "Greatest Beachcomber." They might have considered a second accolade as a consummate antiques collector, as his humor and intelligence are expressed through the implementation of his unique and beautiful antique finds. His daughter and Kahlil Gibran's daughter played on the sand in the West End, past Sal's Place restaurant. Farther west were a few abandoned fishing boats from which Varujan would salvage wood embellished with geometric cuts, portholes, and ships knees and ribs. Soon he was incorporating these salvaged objects into his sculptural pieces.

What locals call the "Backside" of the Atlantic Ocean was also a rich source of salvaged wood. The Peaked Hill Bars were well known as a ship graveyard. Wood from abandoned wrecks provided lumber for building beach shacks still in use today. It also provided material for Varujan, who would carry the wood into town across the great dunes. A window structure became an artful sculpture, now in the collection of the Phoenix Art Museum. The Whitney Museum in New York City has a piece made from a wooden structure he reclaimed near Highland Light.

It was fortuitous that Varujan should meet and correspond with artist Joseph Cornell (1903–1972), an American artist and pioneer of assemblage. Perhaps this association inspired Varujan to work smaller. As he matured as an artist, the frame or box became the stage for expressions of the human condition, inspired by Greek mythology. His beach finds are elevated in his artwork to reflect the human condition: love and loss, possession and liberation, pain and pathos, time and decay.

"I never found any great jewelry or any great coins, but my greatest treasure was found by a boatyard," he says. "It is a little lion, a flat lion with a little base, lead, and a big mane. The rust has congregated around his head."

Varujan attended Yale University and has been a Fulbright scholar, as well as artist-in-residence at the American Academy in Rome, and a Guggenheim Fellow. He taught art for many years, most recently at Dartmouth College, and lives in New Hampshire. Varujan exhibits his work at the Berta Walker Gallery in Provincetown and Wellfleet, and at the Kent Gallery in NYC. His work has been exhibited nationally and internationally and is in permanent collections at the Metropolitan Museum of Art, the Museum of Modern Art, the Whitney Museum of Art, the Cape Cod Museum of Art, and the Provincetown Art Association and Museum.

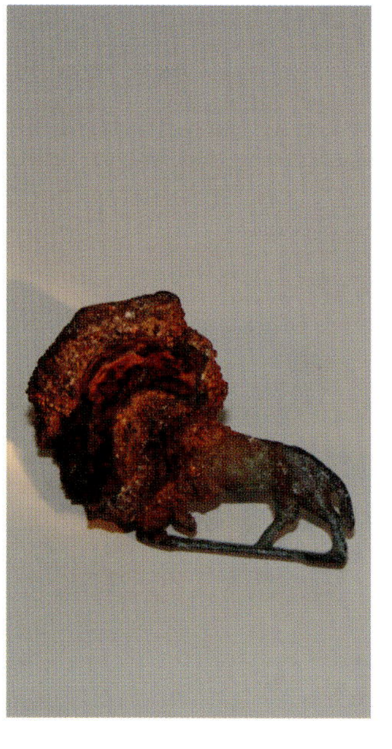

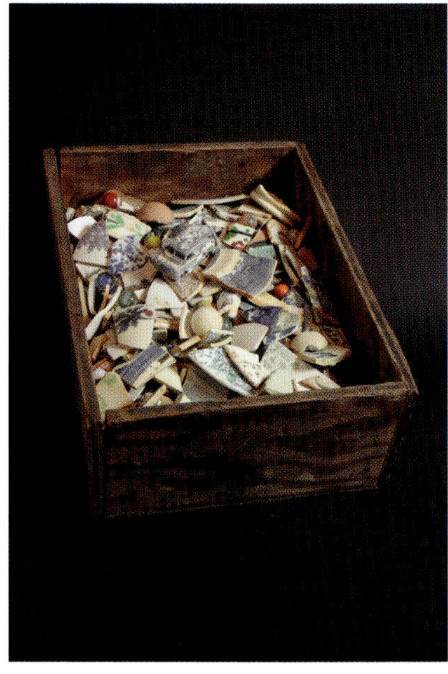

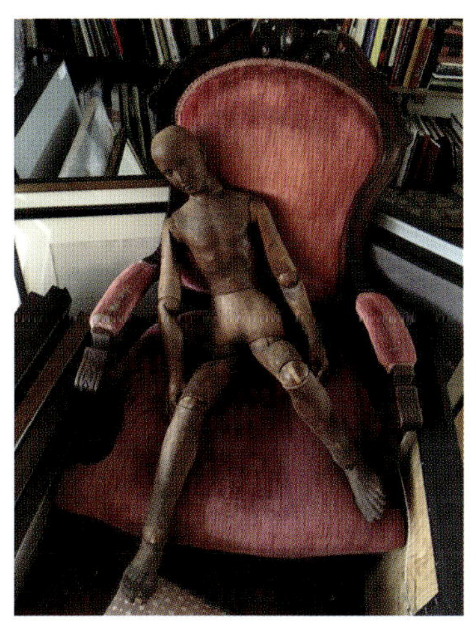

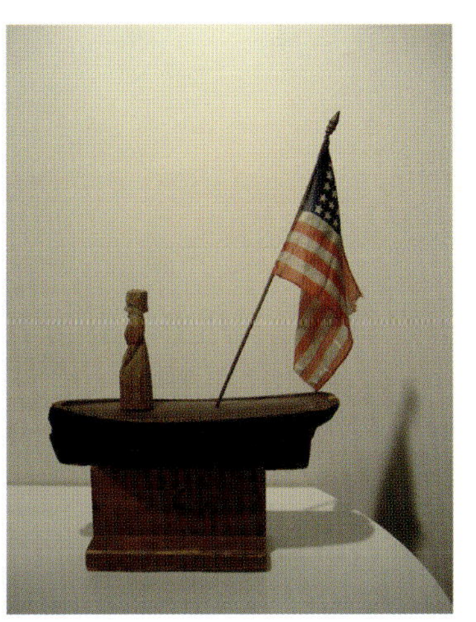

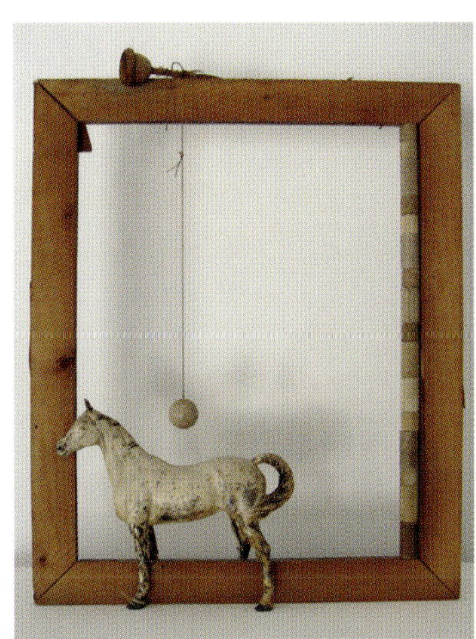

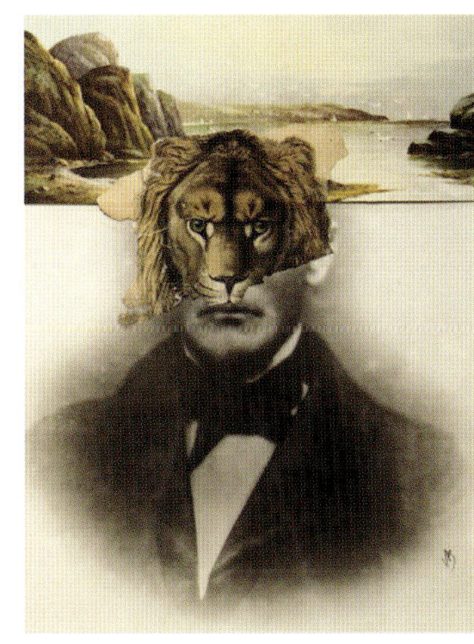

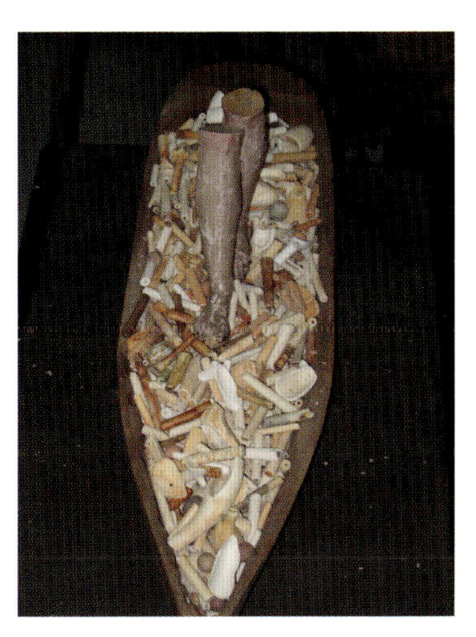

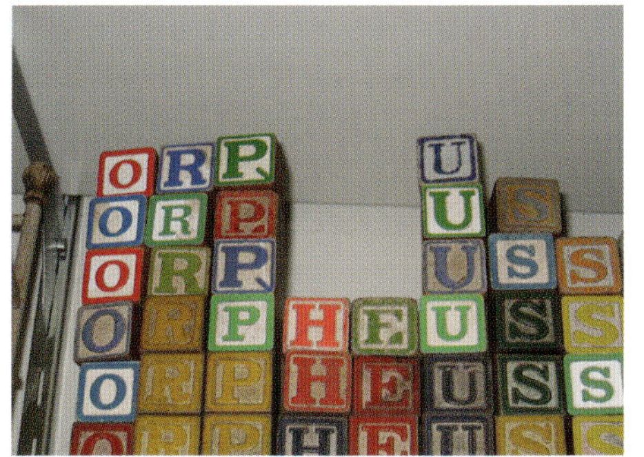

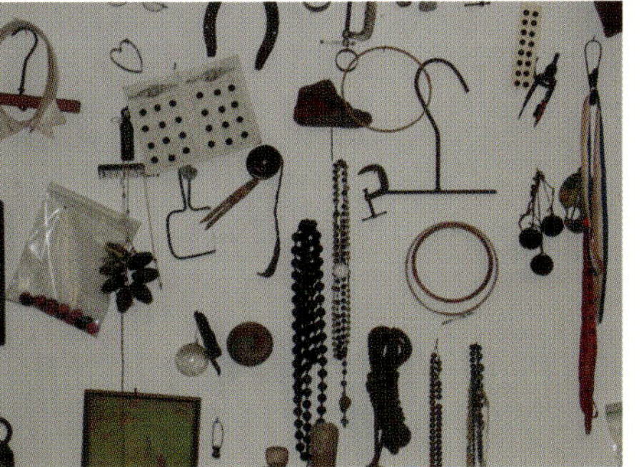

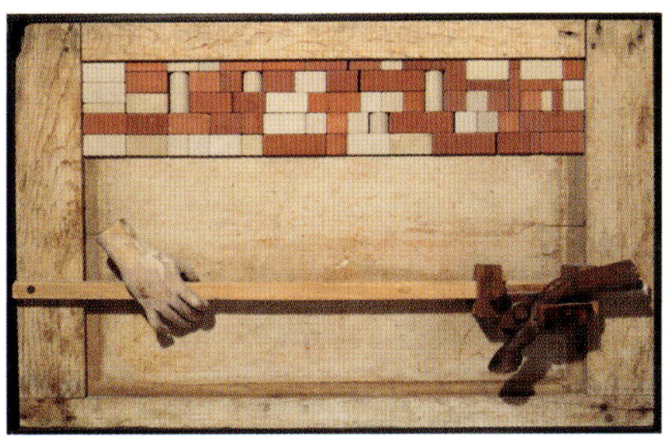

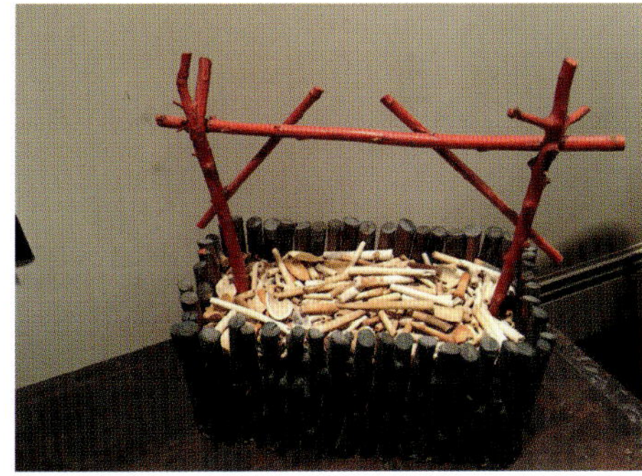

Paul Bowen

Paul Bowen is an iconic artist of modern-day Provincetown with two feet in Vermont, where he now lives with his wife, Pamela Mandell. He came to Provincetown after graduate school and became the visual arts coordinator at the Fine Arts Work Center (FAWC), a nonprofit offering residencies in the visual and written arts. His mark on the town's contemporary art legacy is indelible, as is Provincetown's history on him. He is a natural-born beachcomber and readily admits to being addicted to the search.

The shards, pipes, pipestems, bottles, and other objects of daily life do not physically appear in his work but inform his aesthetic. Wooden boatbuilding fragments define Paul's language of form and purpose by reflecting the past, and he uses the salvaged wood he collects in his sculptures.

His beachcombing treasures include a sizable number of pilot whale inner ear bones. "When a pilot whale beached itself or when a pod of pilots was spotted in the harbor, they were chased into shore and butchered for their oil," he says. "Captain Taylor Cook and others used the oil from the heads as clock and watch lubricant, because it is very fine oil." Teeth are occasionally discovered today, sawed off at the jawline.

"In front of the Coast Guard wharf is a big clump of tar that has fish netting imbedded in it," Paul says. "Fishermen had to tar the cotton nets to preserve them." Fishing and whaling built and sustained the town, and the industry's remnants still show up: ships knees, old wooden winches, wooden wagon wheels, planking, rusted chains. These items often show up in his sculpture. "It is amazing how the rust eats and stains the wood, so beautiful."

Characteristically, he isn't obsessive about pottery shards unless they are special, like the white vase with pink roses. For five or six years Paul collected the fragments of that vase and finally glued it back together. "That is how insane this business [of collecting] is," he says.

Born in Wales, Paul grew up by the sea. He studied at the Chester School of Art in Chester, England; Newport College of Art in Newport, Wales; and the the Maryland Institute College of Art in Baltimore. His work is in collections here and abroad, including the Museum of Fine Arts, Boston; the Solomon Guggenheim Museum, New York City; the Walker Art Center, Minneapolis; Provincetown Art Association and Museum; and the Cape Cod Museum of Art, Dennis. He is represented by the Albert Merola Gallery in Provincetown and the Big Town Gallery in Rochester, Vermont.

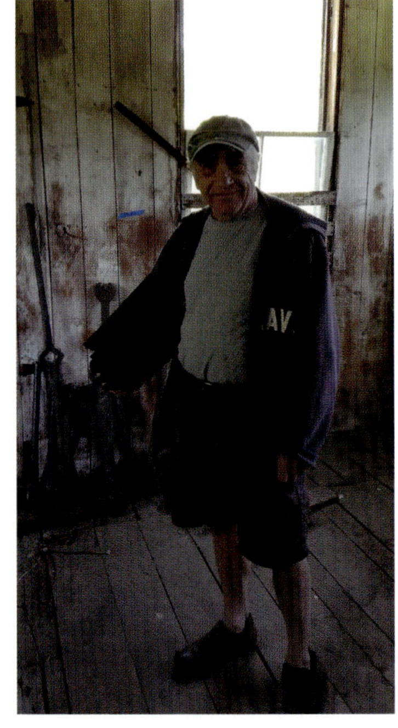

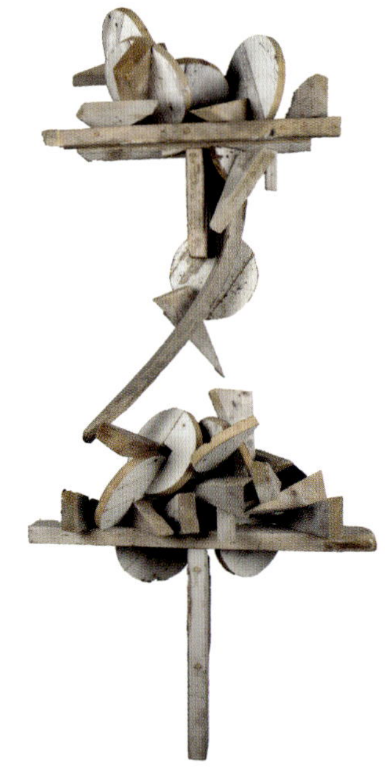

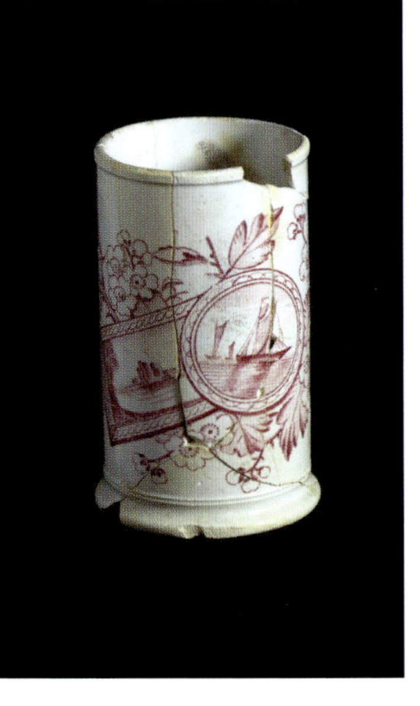

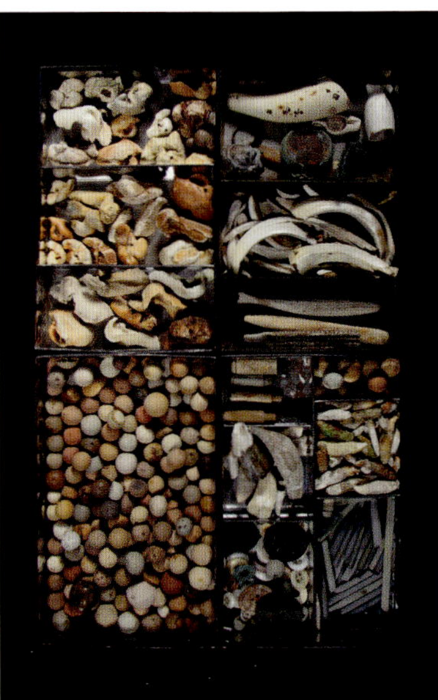

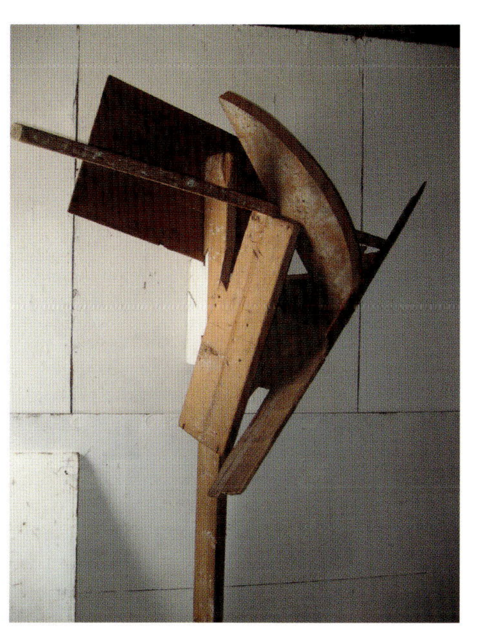

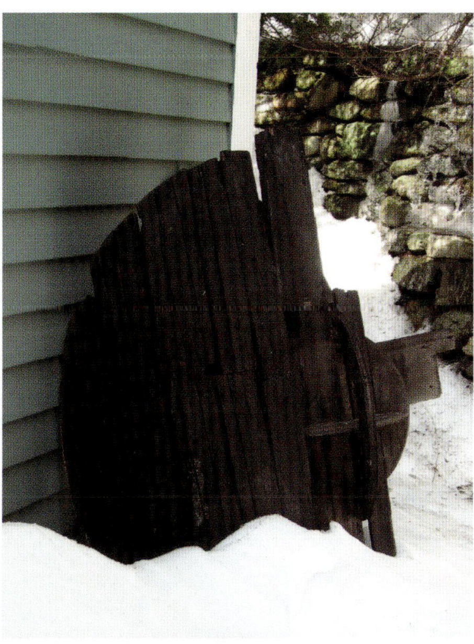

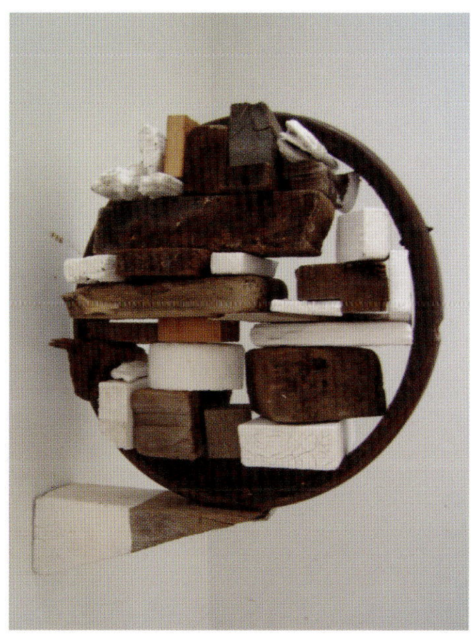

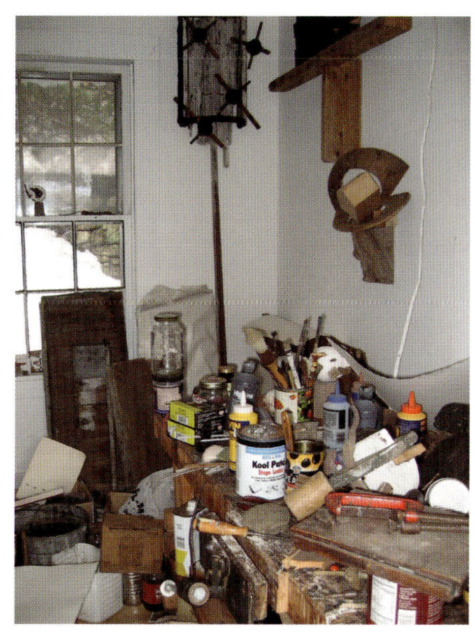

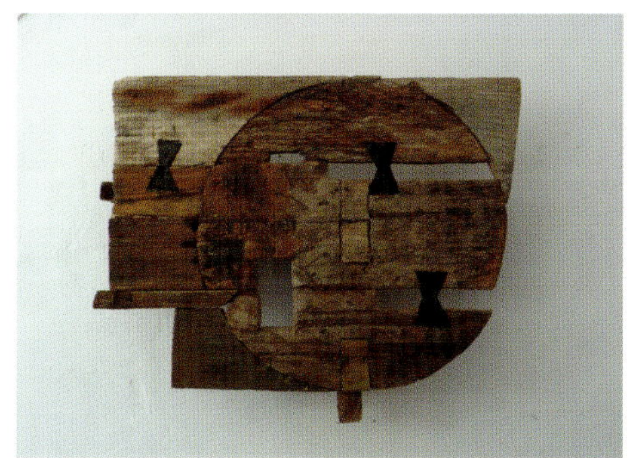

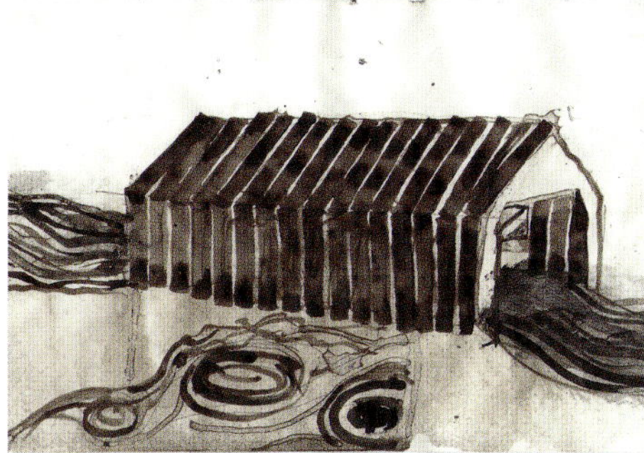

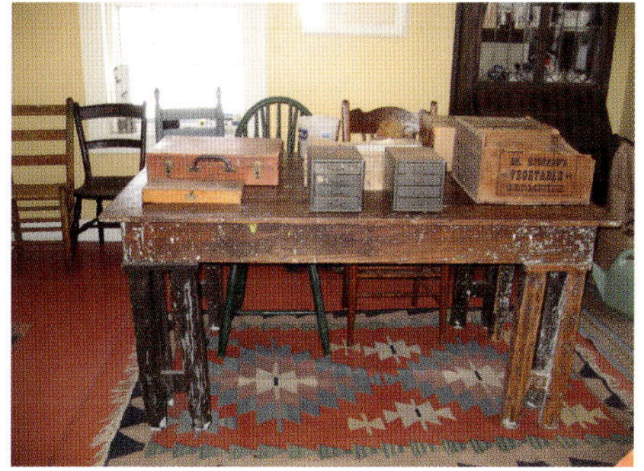

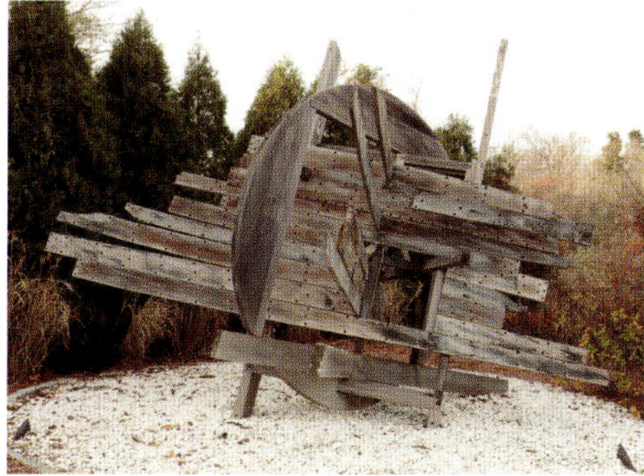

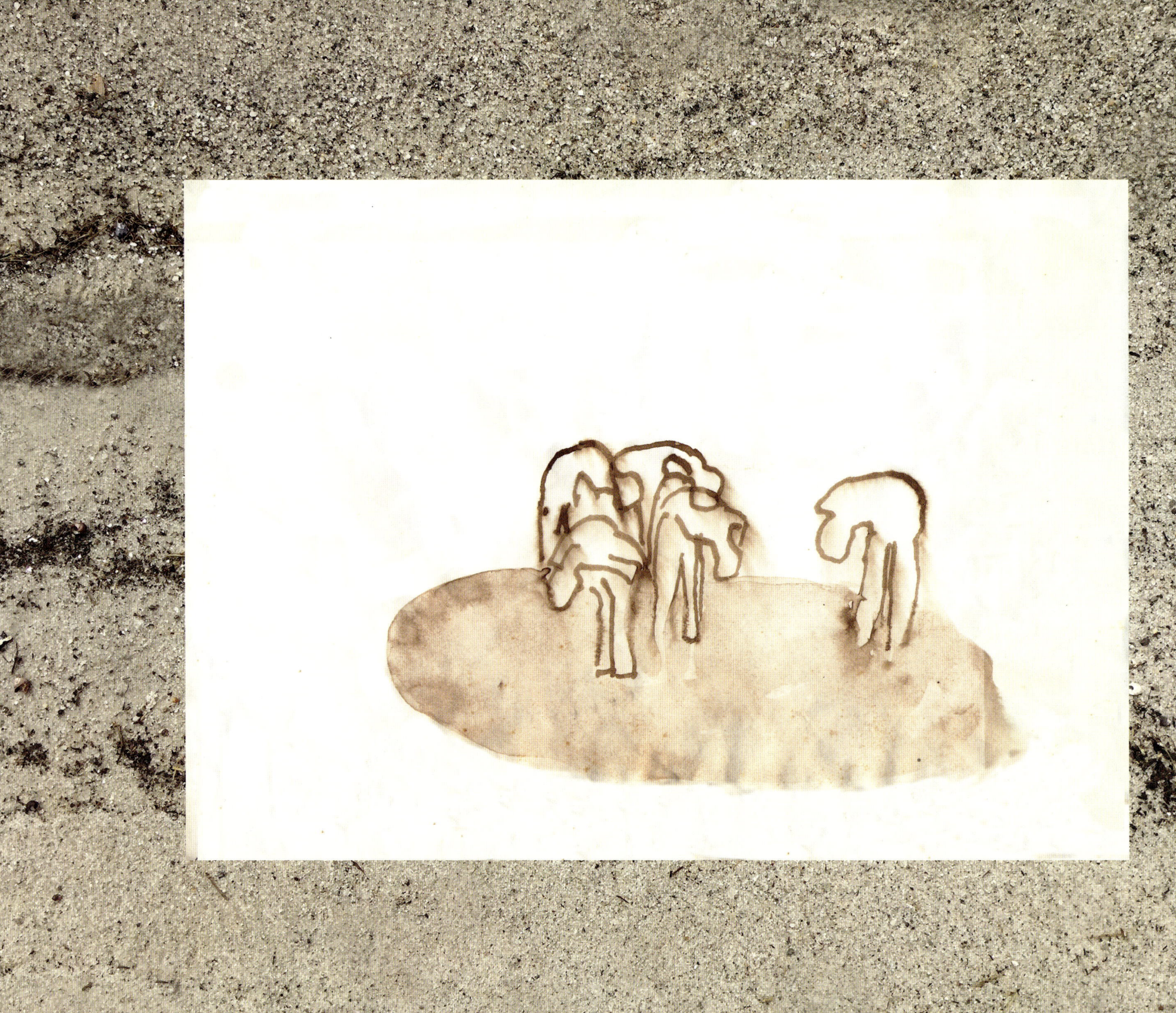

Part 2.
The Collections

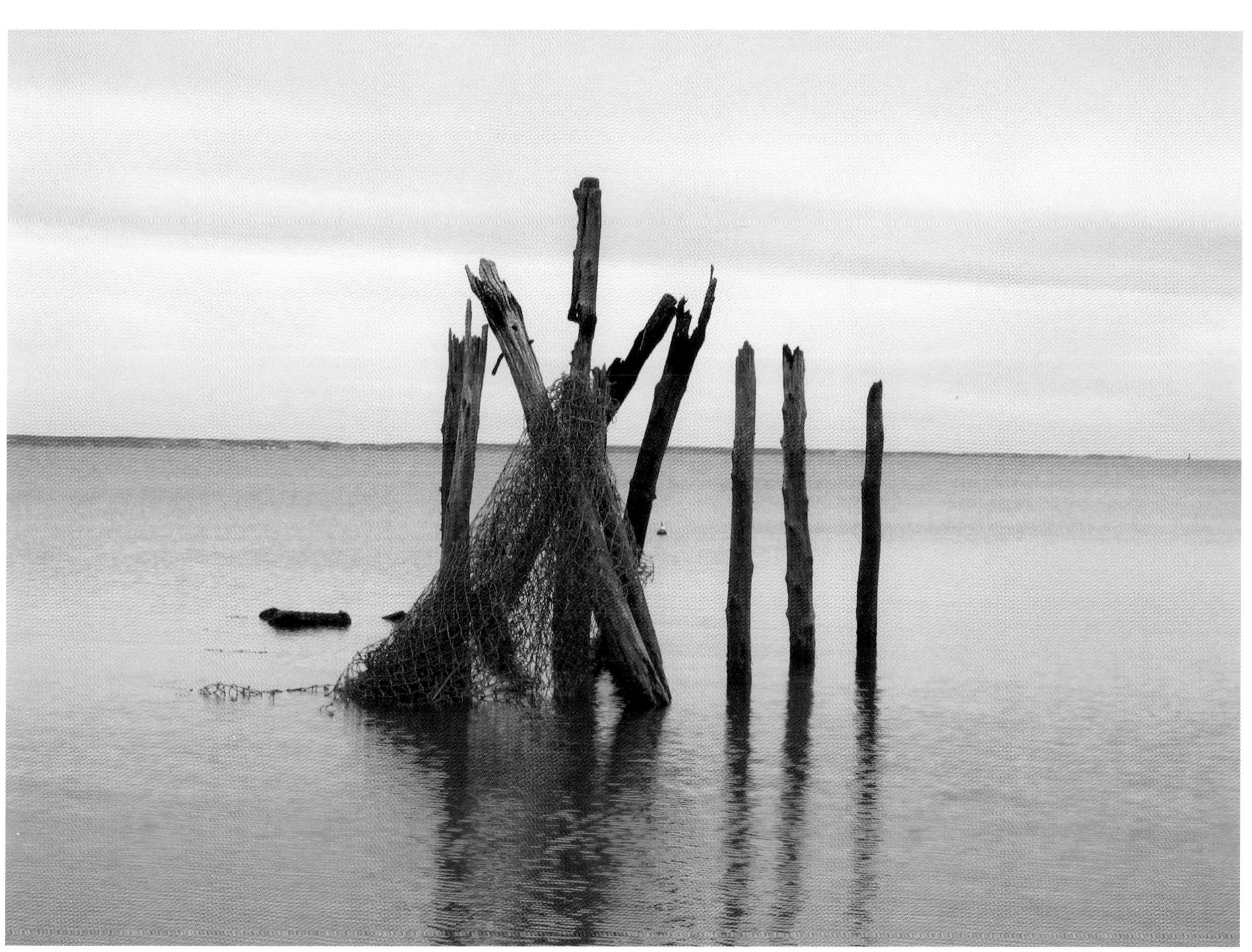

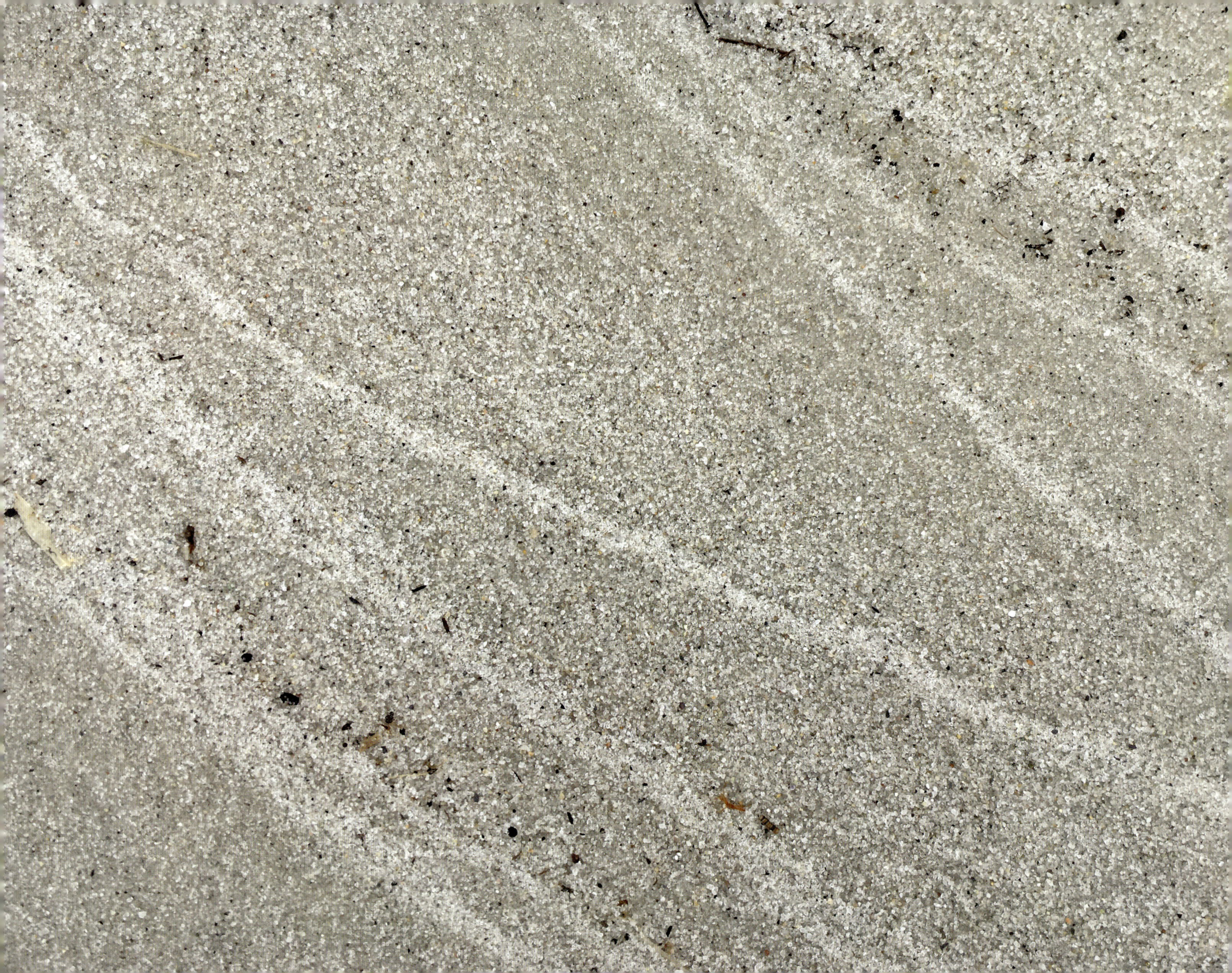

INDIGENOUS PEOPLES

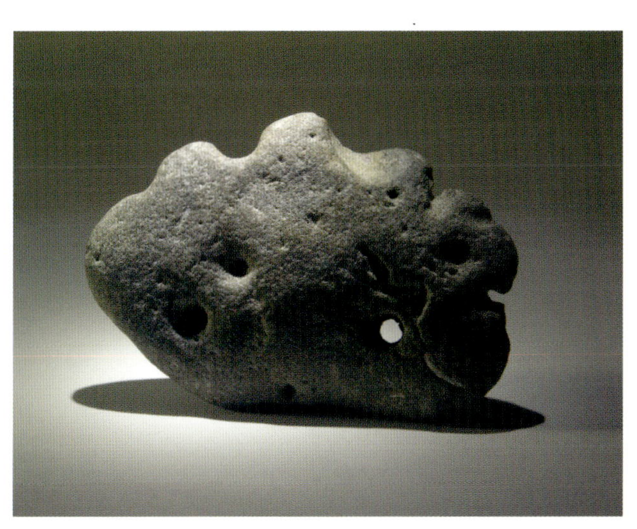
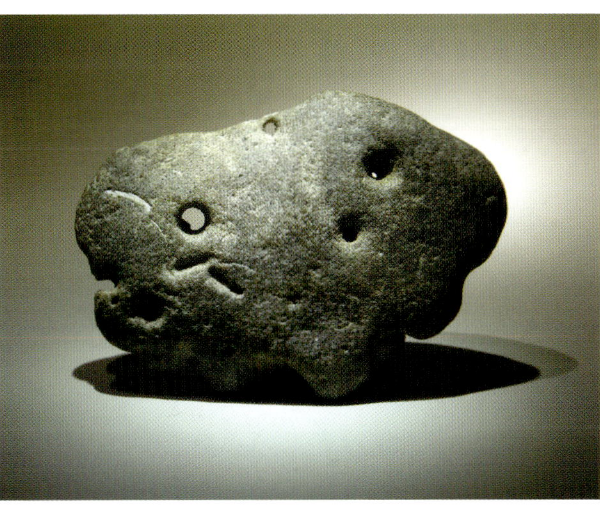
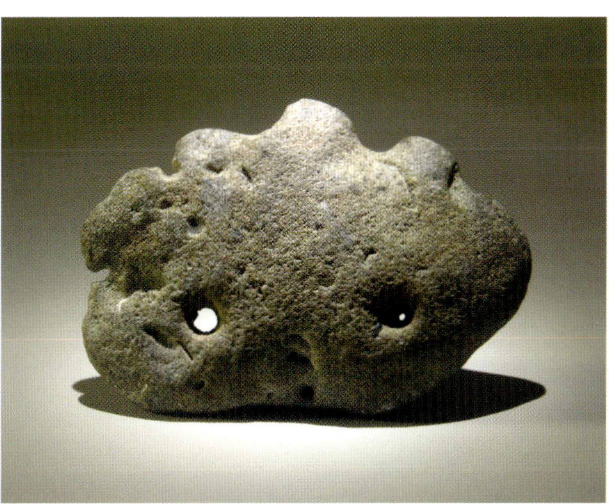

It is widely believed that the indigenous peoples migrated to this continent via the Bering Strait, reaching the eastern continental coast 8,000–10,000 years ago. Flint and granite were essential to tool-making, and the inhabitants secured their success by trading with people to the north. When the English settlers arrived, the indigenous peoples traded with them for other items such as glass beads.

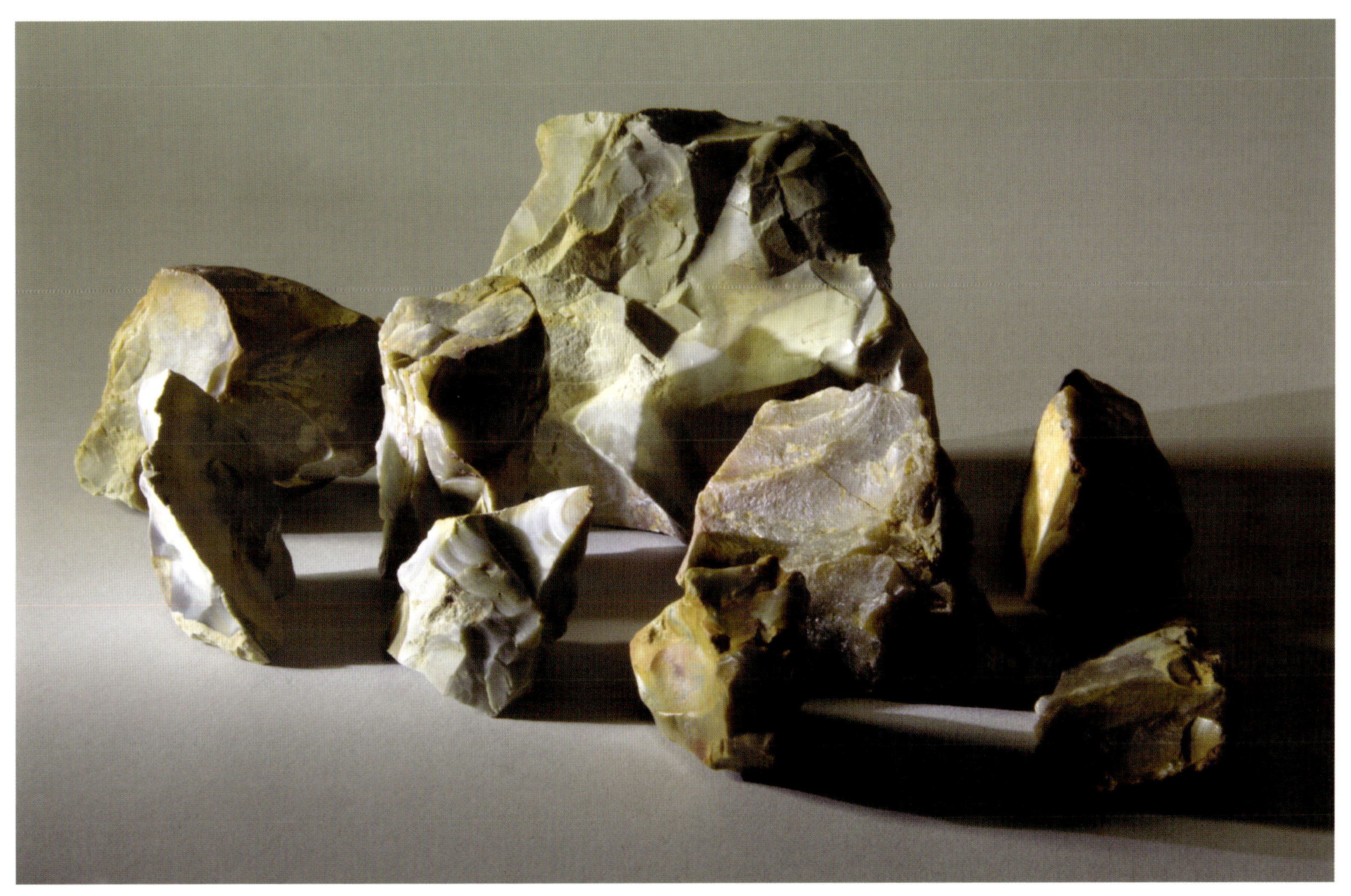

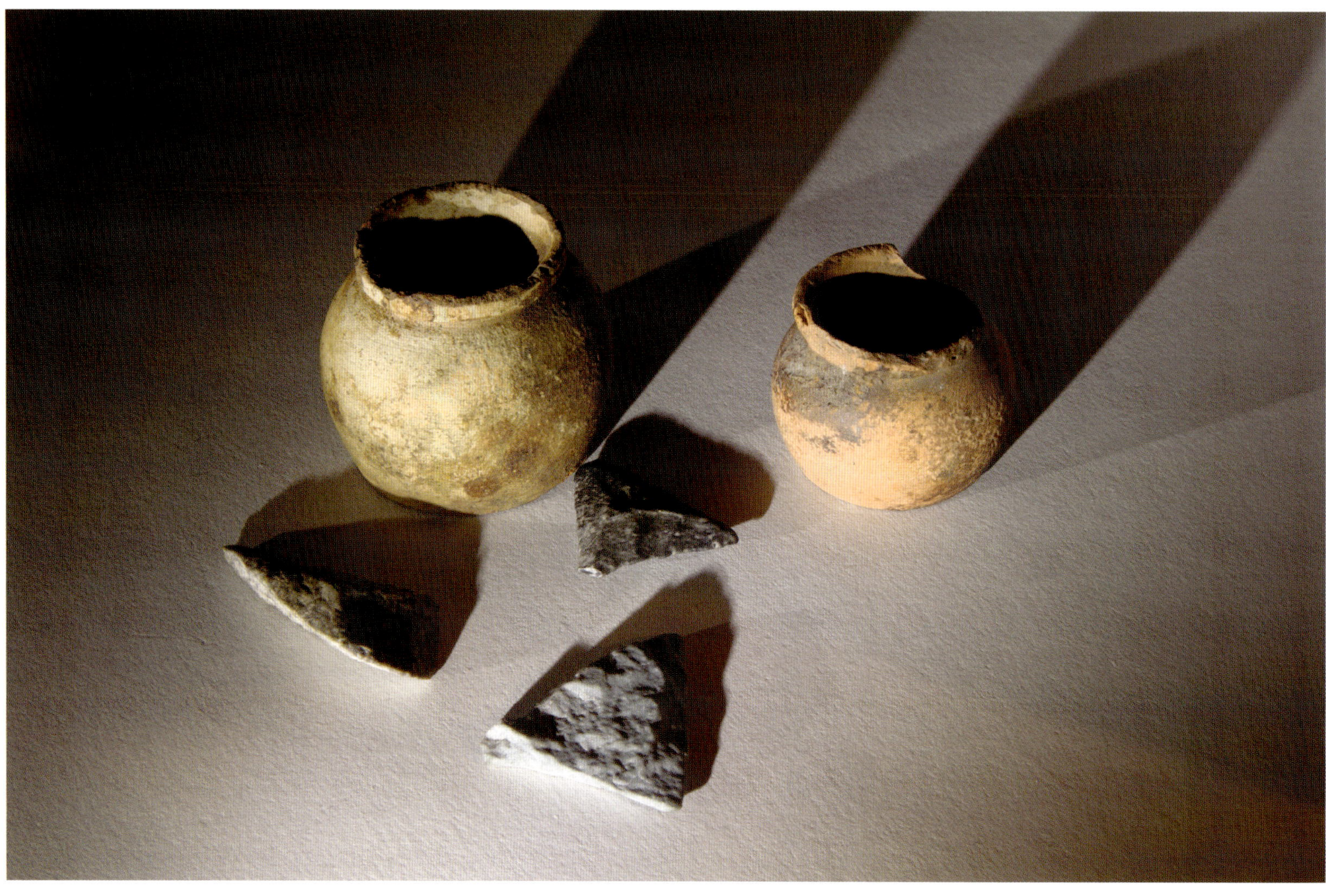

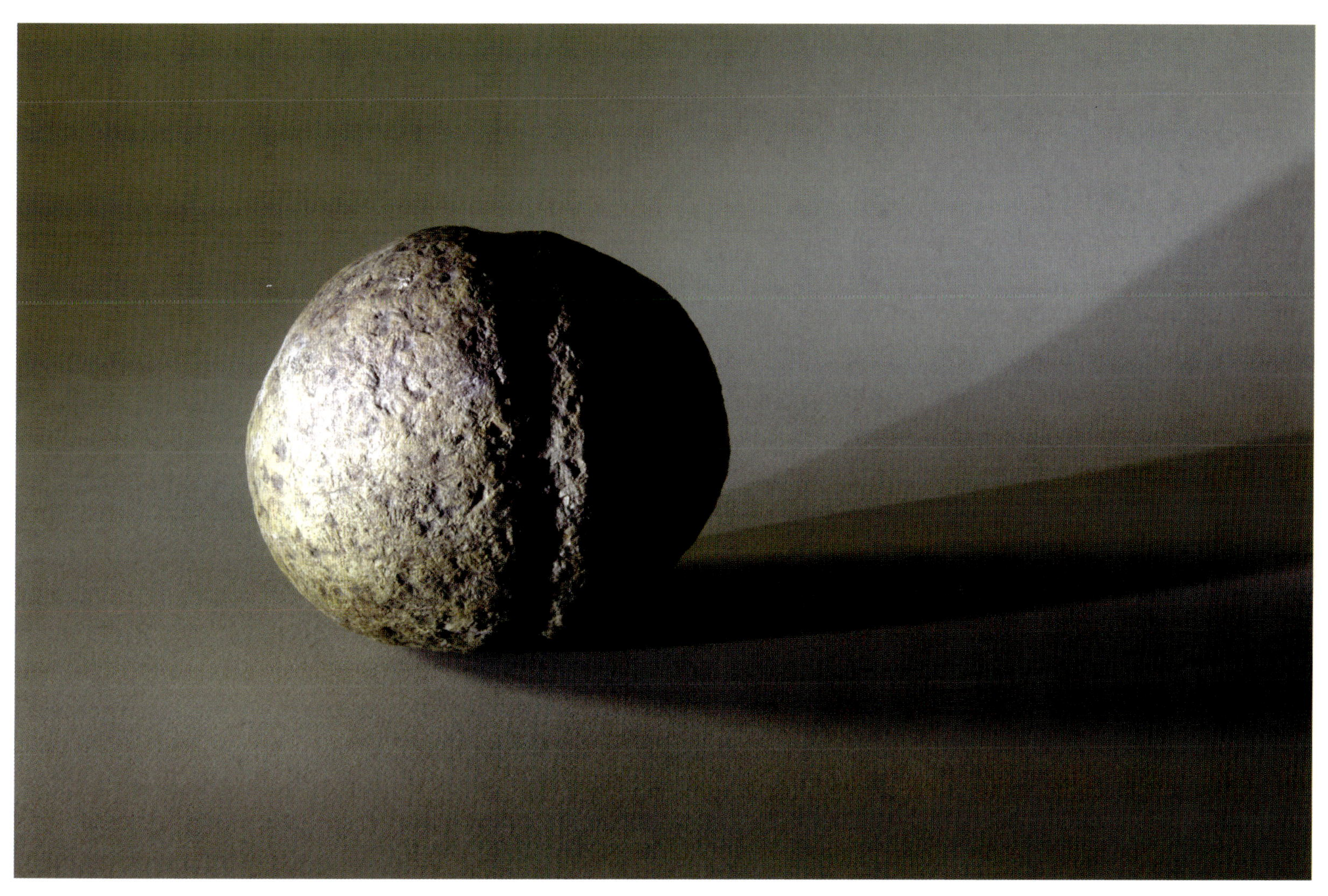

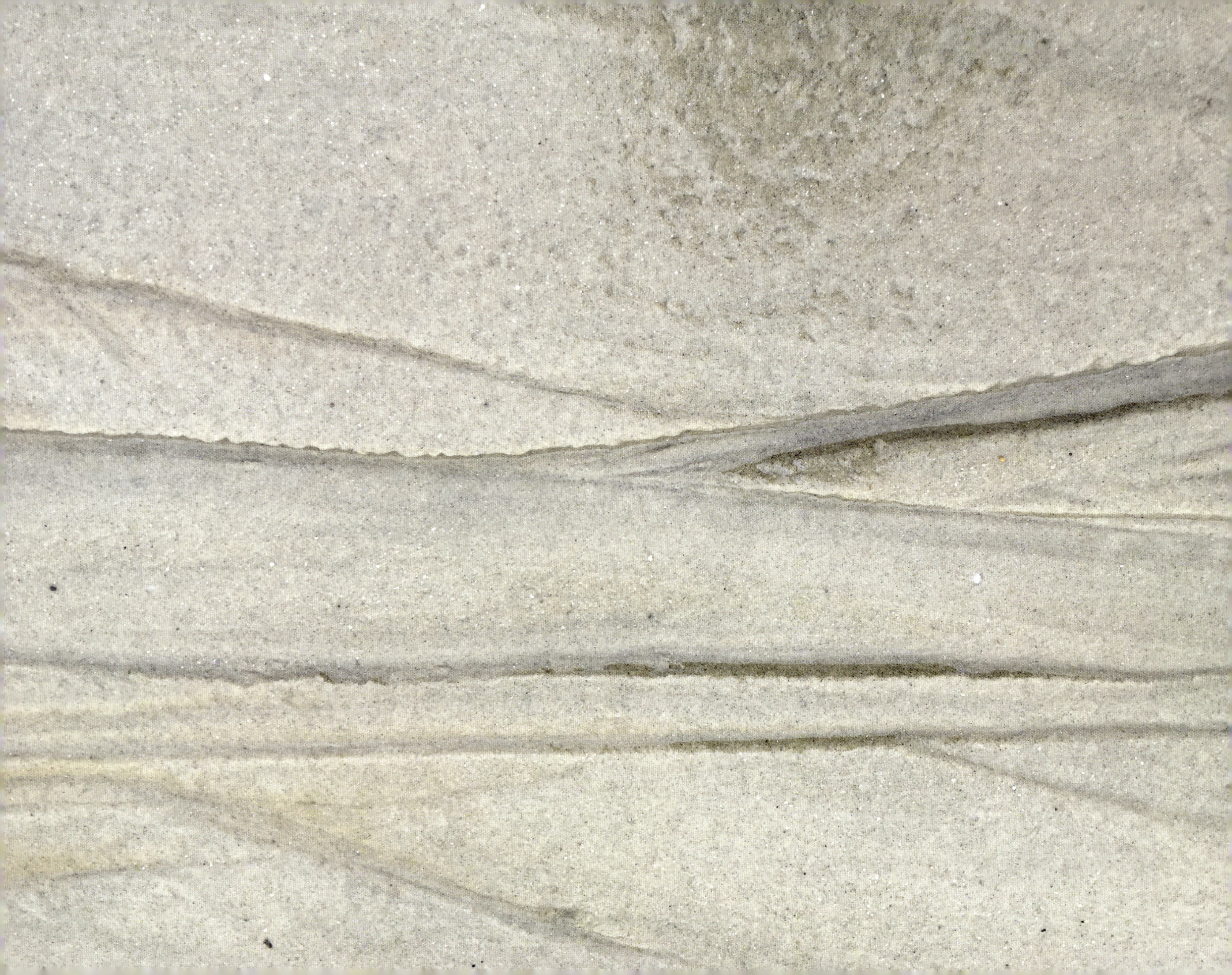

WHALING

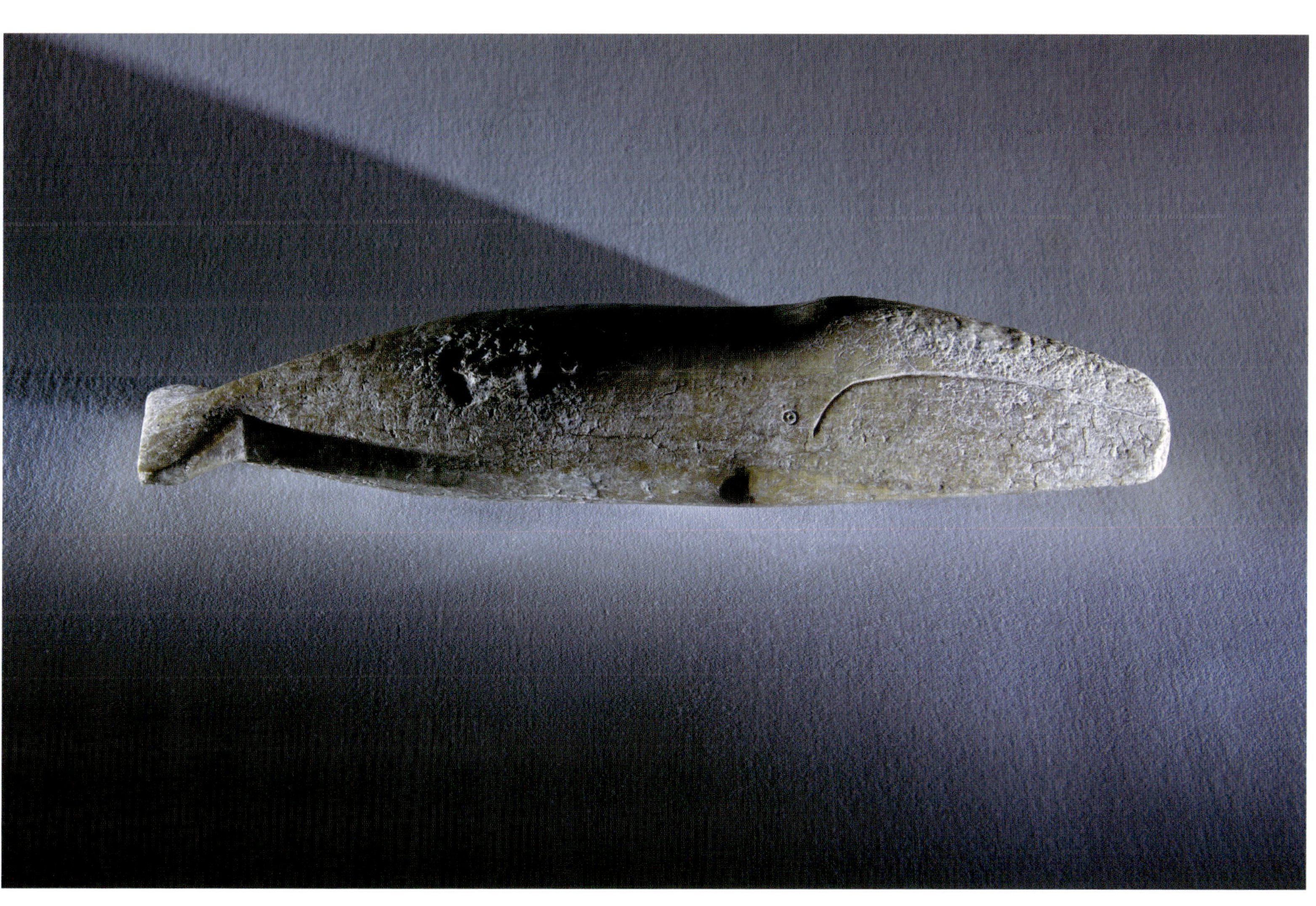

When the *Mayflower* dropped anchor in Provincetown Harbor, it was obvious that whales were plentiful. Early exploration of nearby waters revealed scores of blackfish (the colloquial name for pilot whales, also known as drift whales), which were especially abundant in Wellfleet Harbor. The Pilgrims observed indigenous peoples culling stranded or beached blackfish to use as a food source. The newcomers did the same, and a local economy developed around whale oil. In winter, Cape Cod Bay, referred to as the North Sea, was also fished for slow-moving right whales, whose thick layer of blubber made them highly buoyant and easy to see.

In less than a century, as whales in immediate waters became scarce, an offshore whaling industry developed, fueled by high demand for fine oils. Provincetown grew rich and the waterfront developed as a complex center for processing and distributing this valuable resource. It also attracted Portuguese fishermen who were skilled whalemen.

Ship logs show that Provincetown whaling ships sailed the globe: the British West Indies, Hudson Bay, the Grand Banks, Bermuda, India, Cuba, Java, and Africa. Gone for months at a time, seamen brought home riches and tokens of their travels.

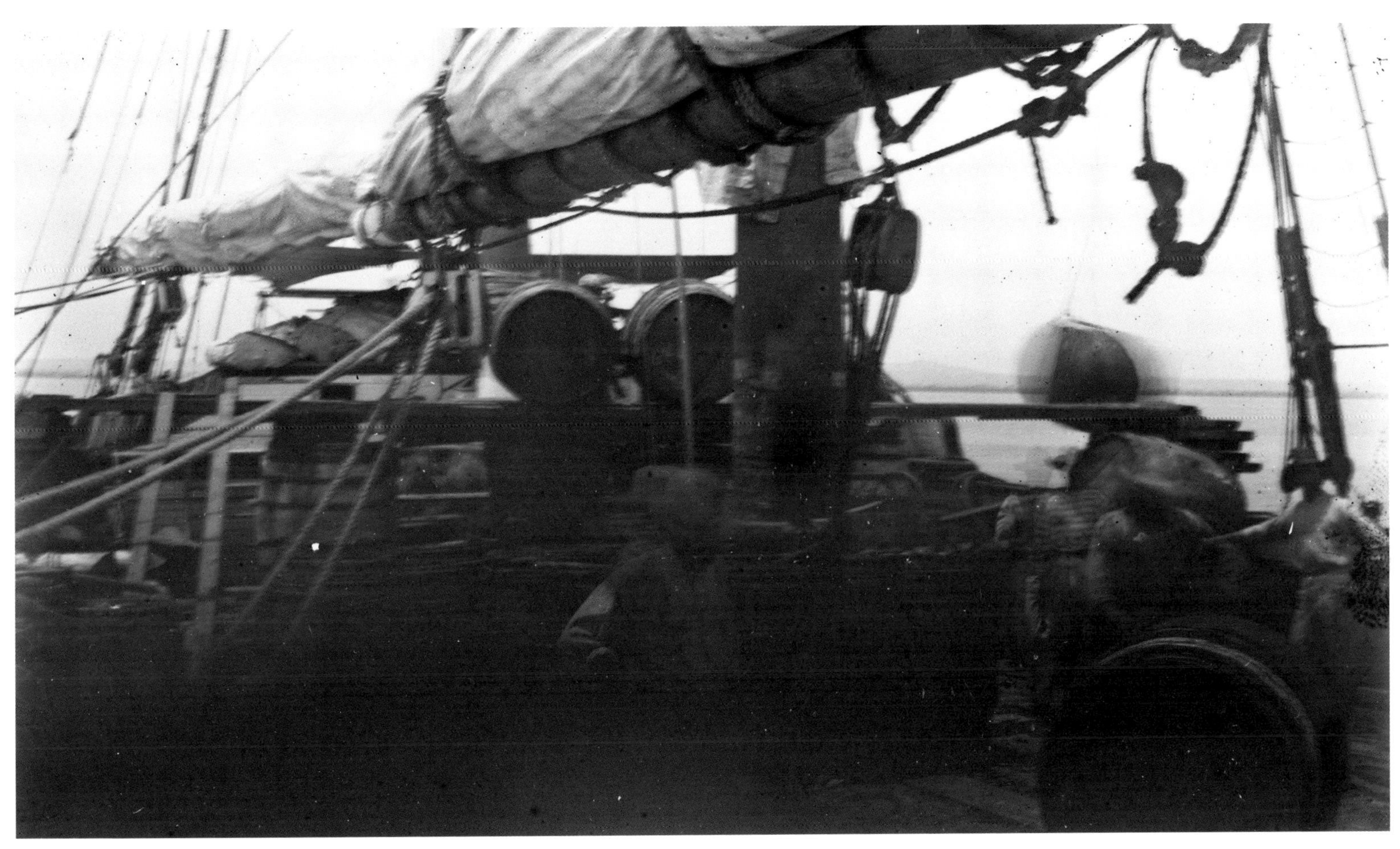

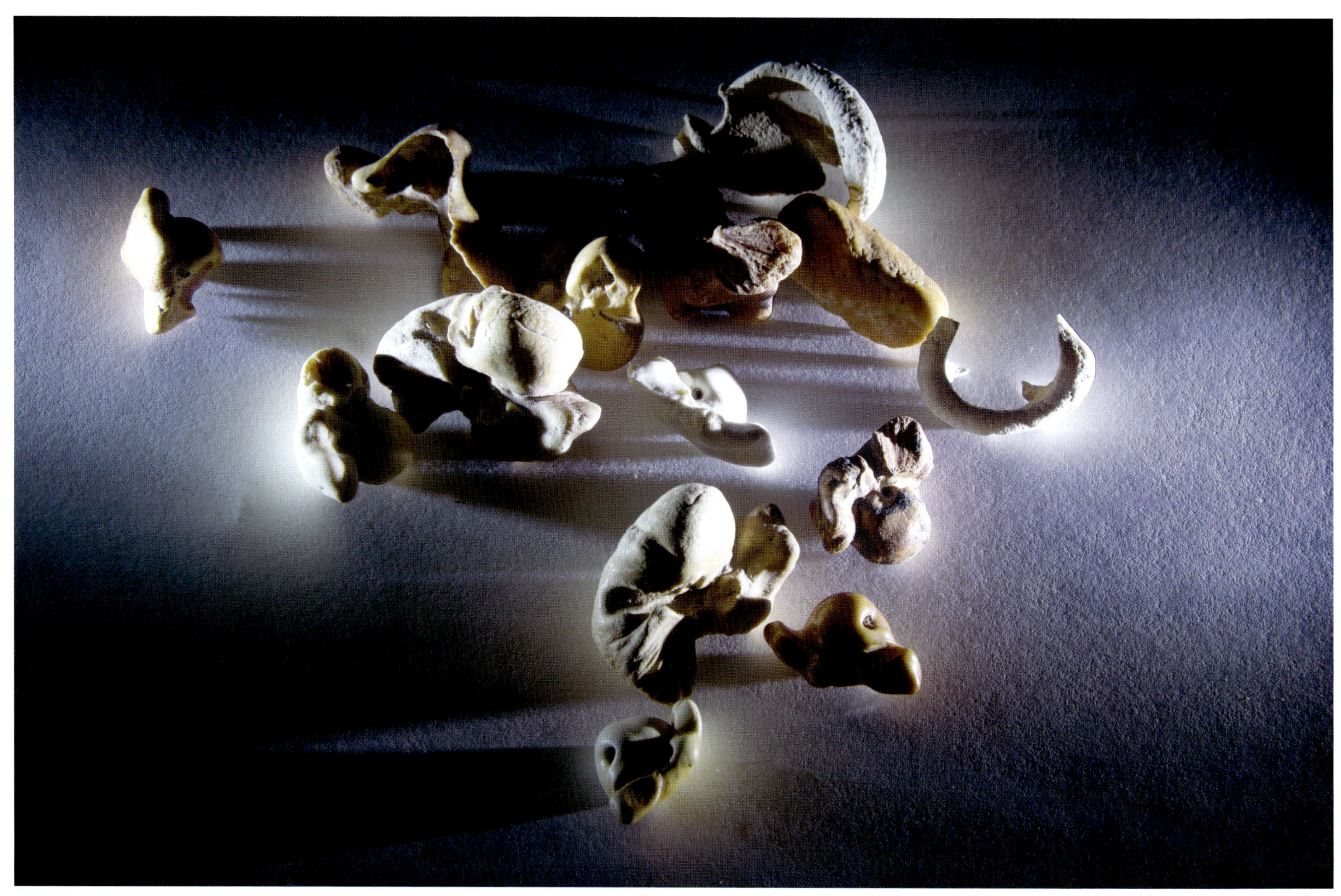

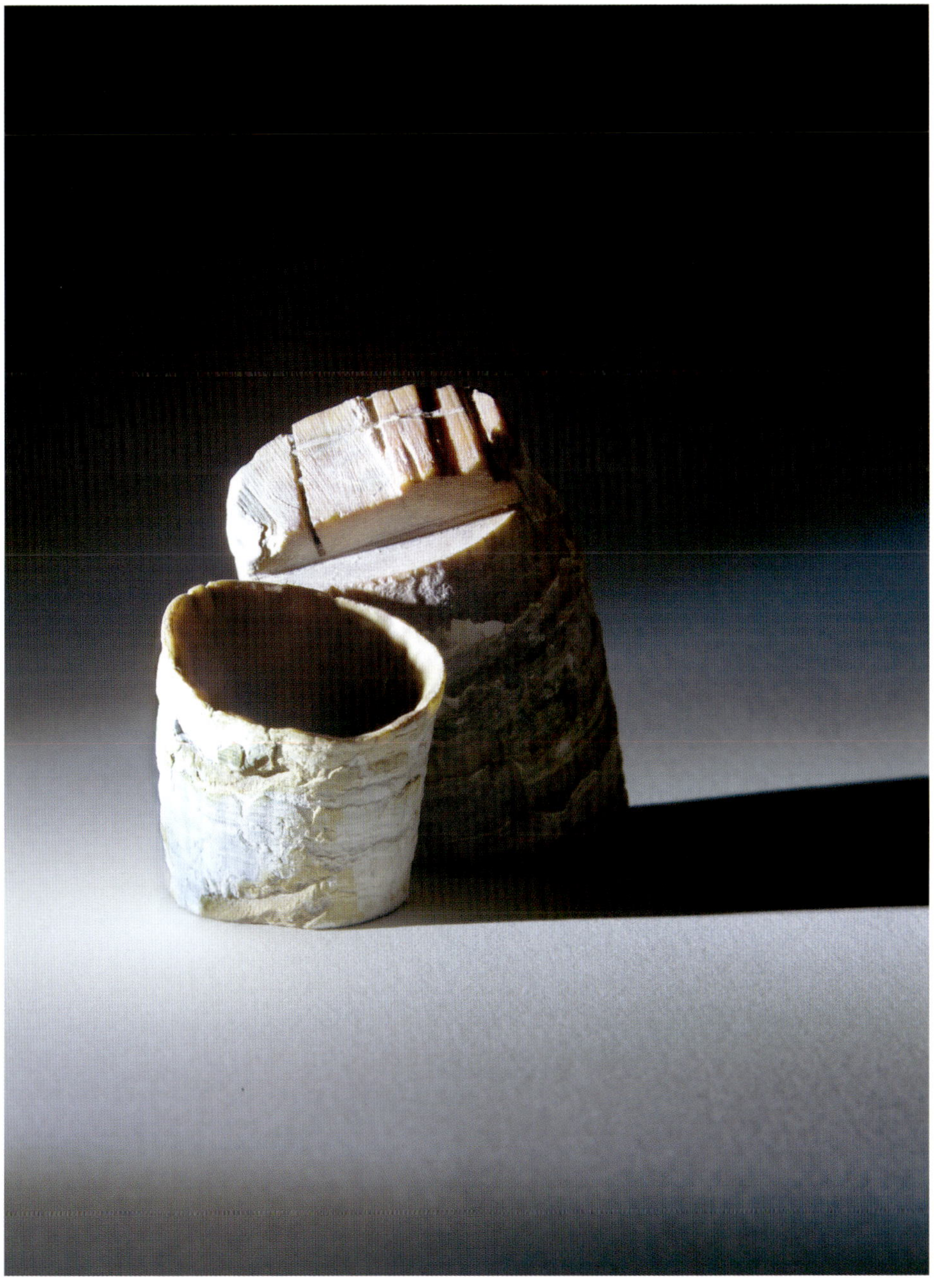

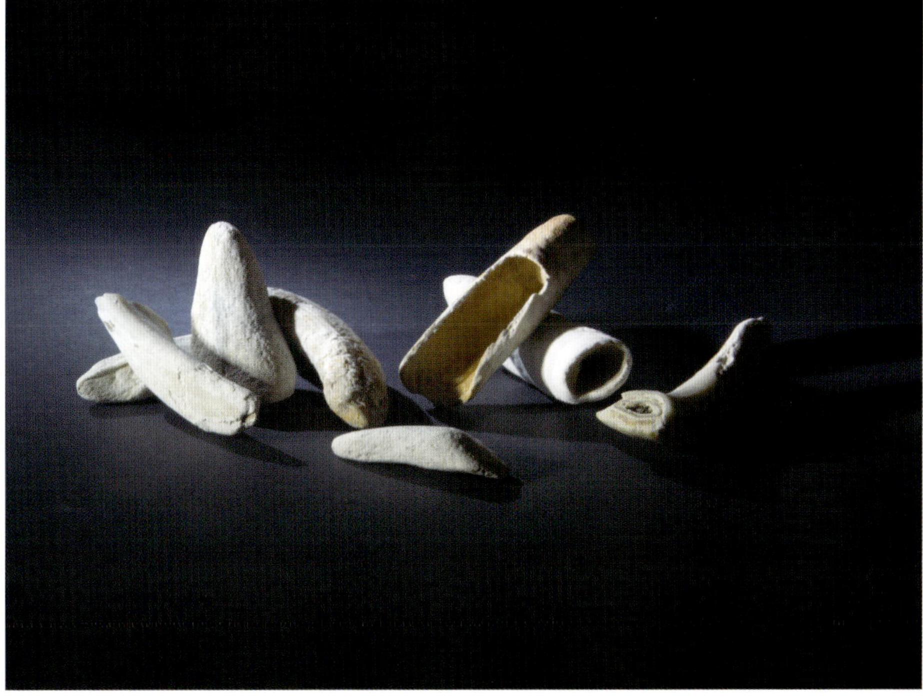

PROVINCETOWN SEA MONSTER

Boston, September 28, 1719:

"On the 17 Instant there appear's in Cape-Cod harbor a strange creature, his head like a Lyons, with very large Teeth, Ears hanging down, a large Beard, a long Beard with curling hair on his head, his Body about 16 foot long, a round buttock, with a short Tayle of a yellowish colour, the Whale boats gave him chase, he was very fierce and gnashed his teeth with great rage when they attacked him, he was shot 3 times and Wounded, when he rose our of the Water he always faced the boats in that angry manner, the Harpaniers struck at him, but in vain, for after 5 hours chase, he took him to sea again. None of the people ever saw his like before" (Miller and Smith 1996).

Written in 1719, shortly after the *Boston Gazette* was founded, this article is attributed to Benjamin Franklin, uncle to the famous inventor. Some attribute it to the patriot Benjamin Franklin himself, since his brother James was the *New-England Courant* editor.

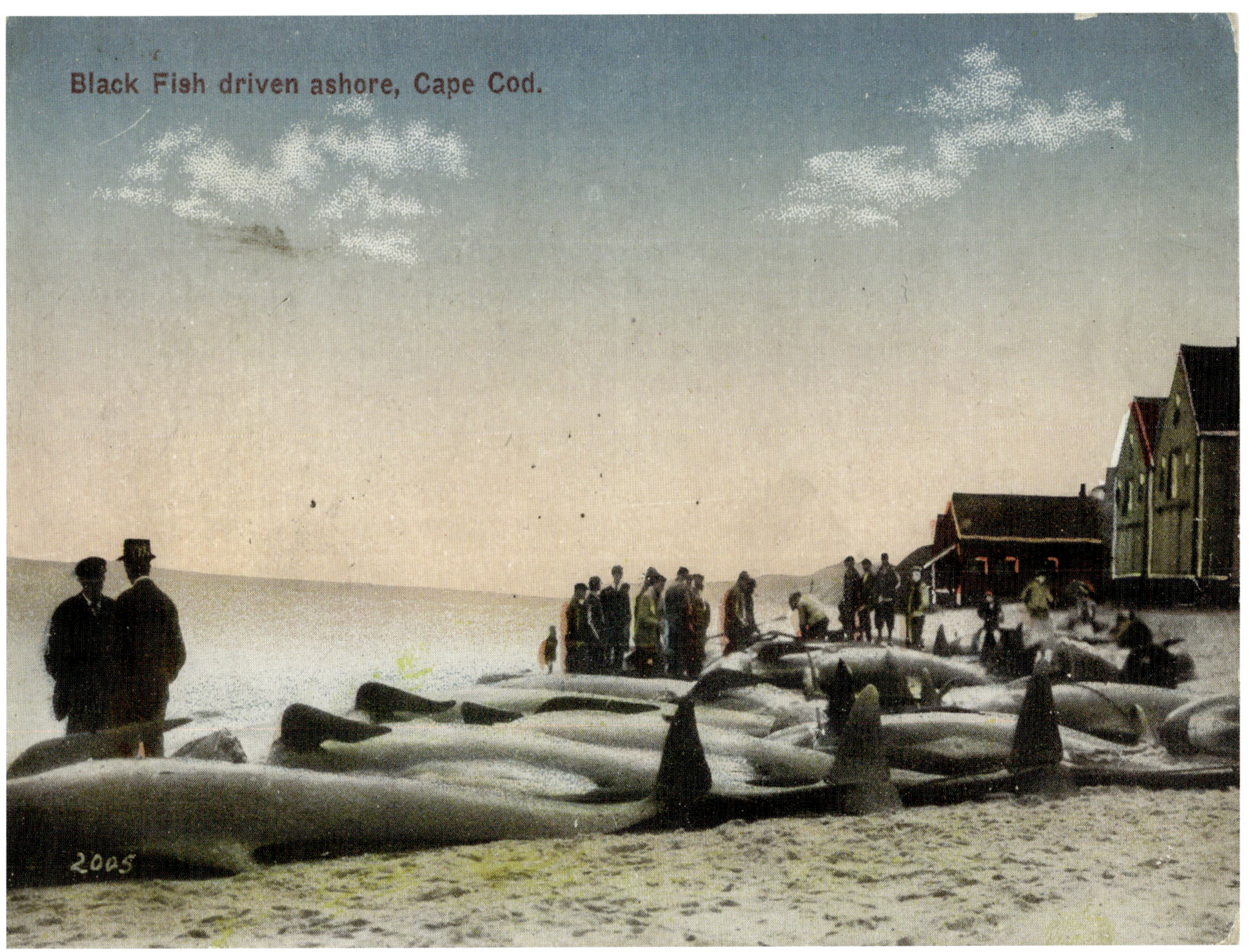

Bryant's Market displayed a photo of local resident David Conwell Stull, wearing his bowler hat, cutting off the head of a pilot whale in front of the market. He was a Provincetown businessman known as the Ambergris King. Ambergris was a secretion culled from whale intestines that was used to stabilize perfume, a rare and valuable resource.

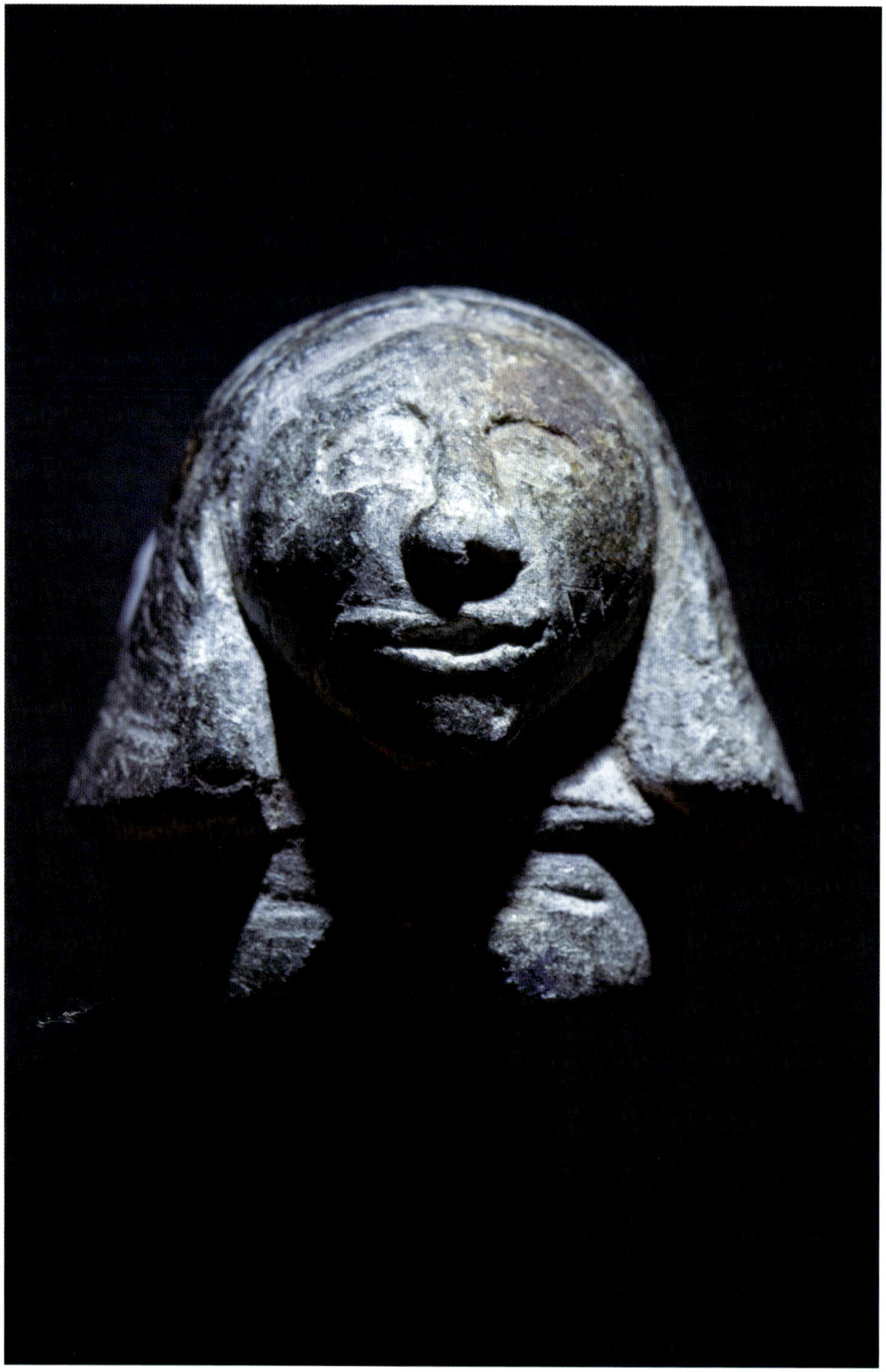

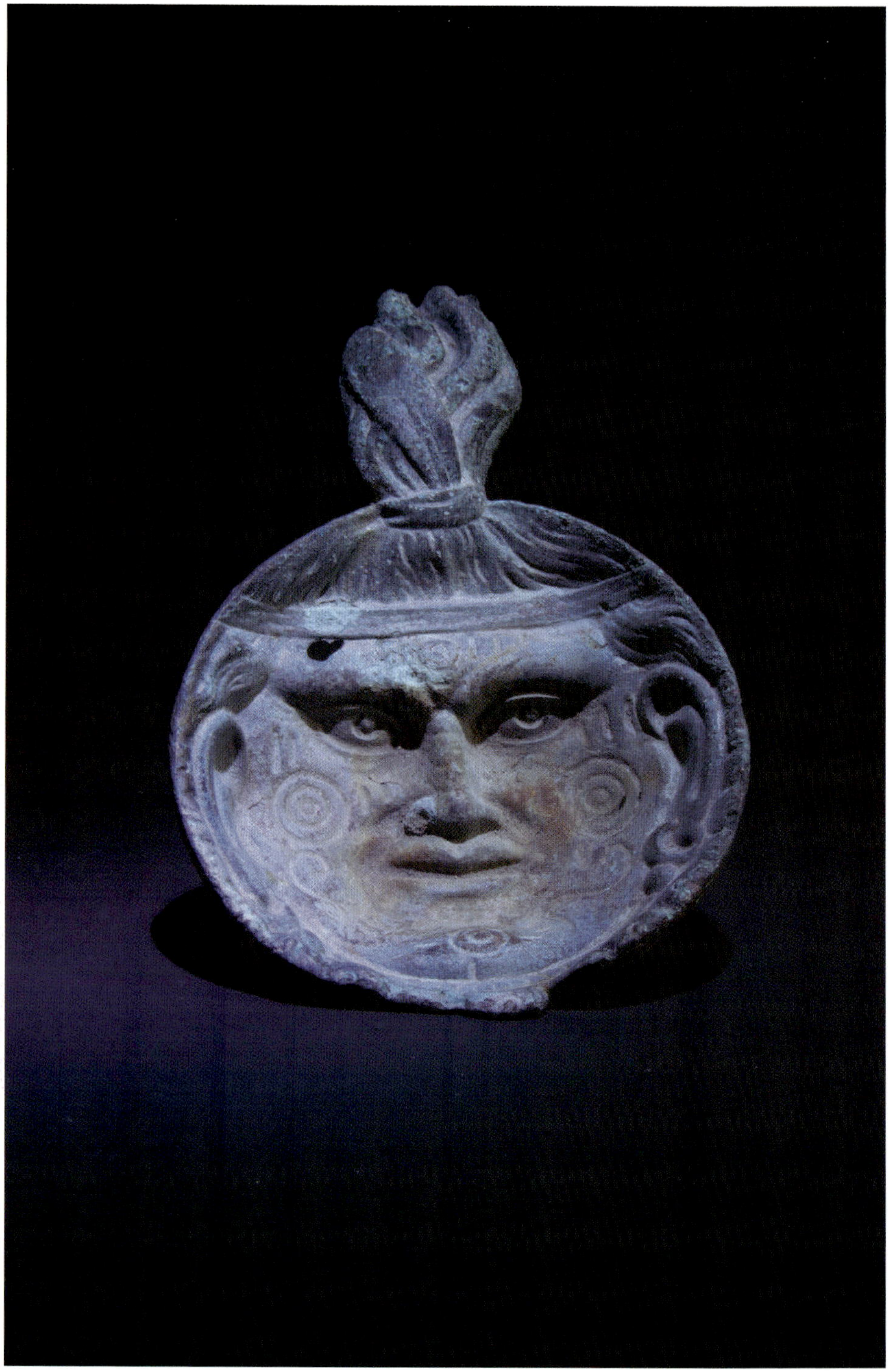

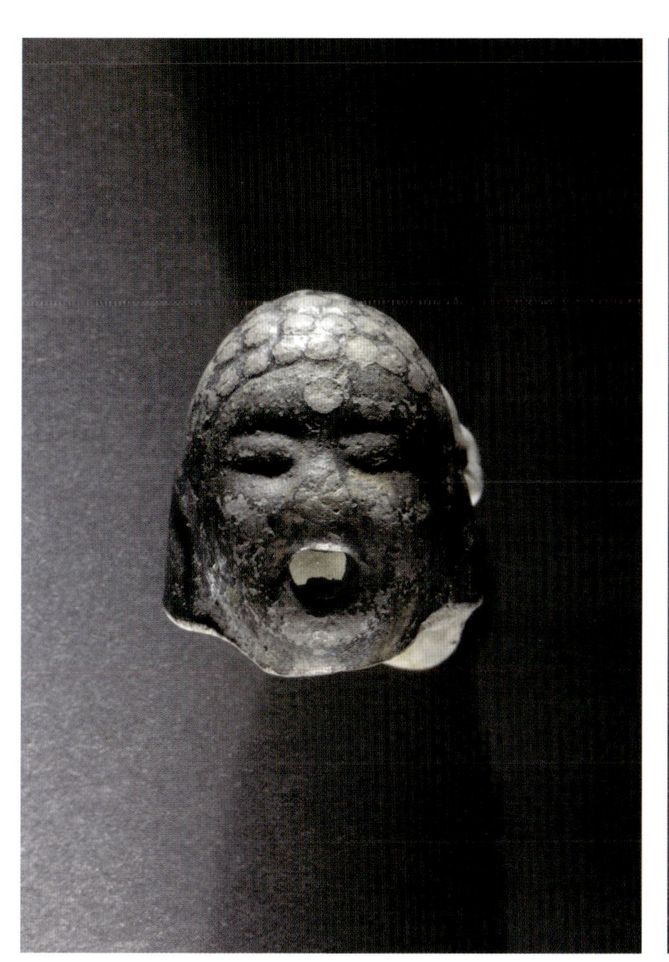
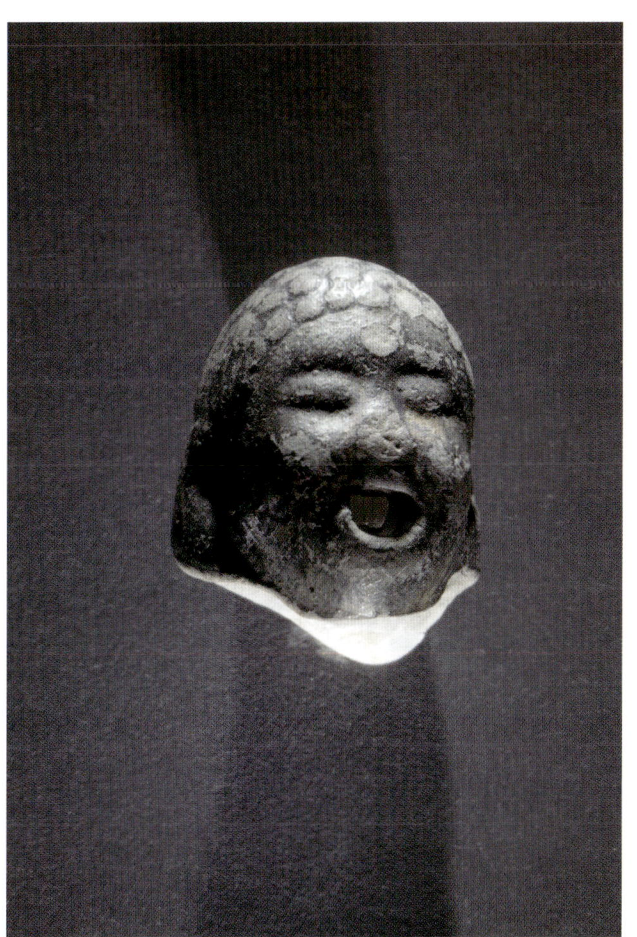
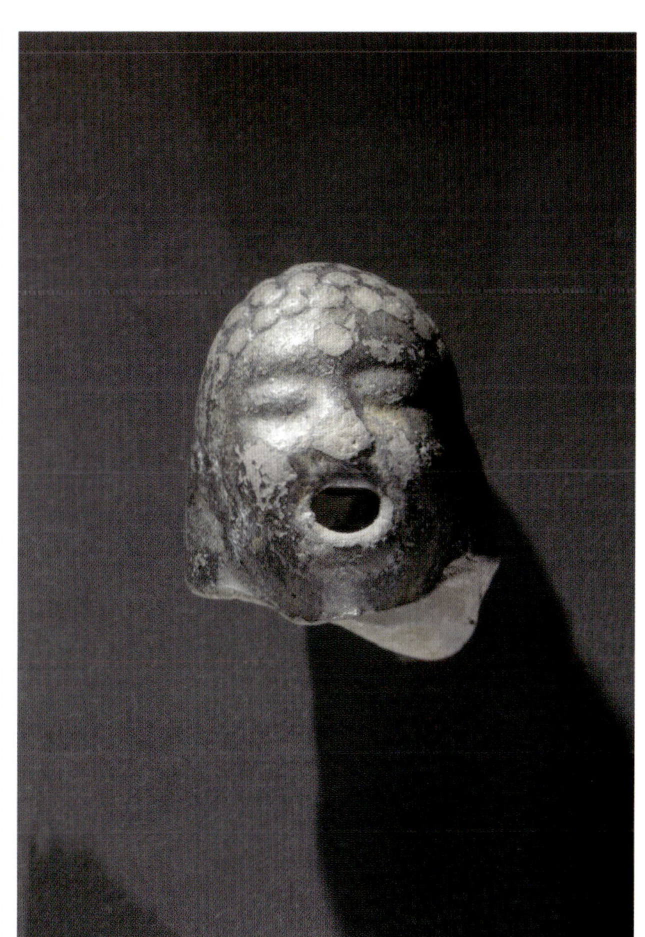

FISHING

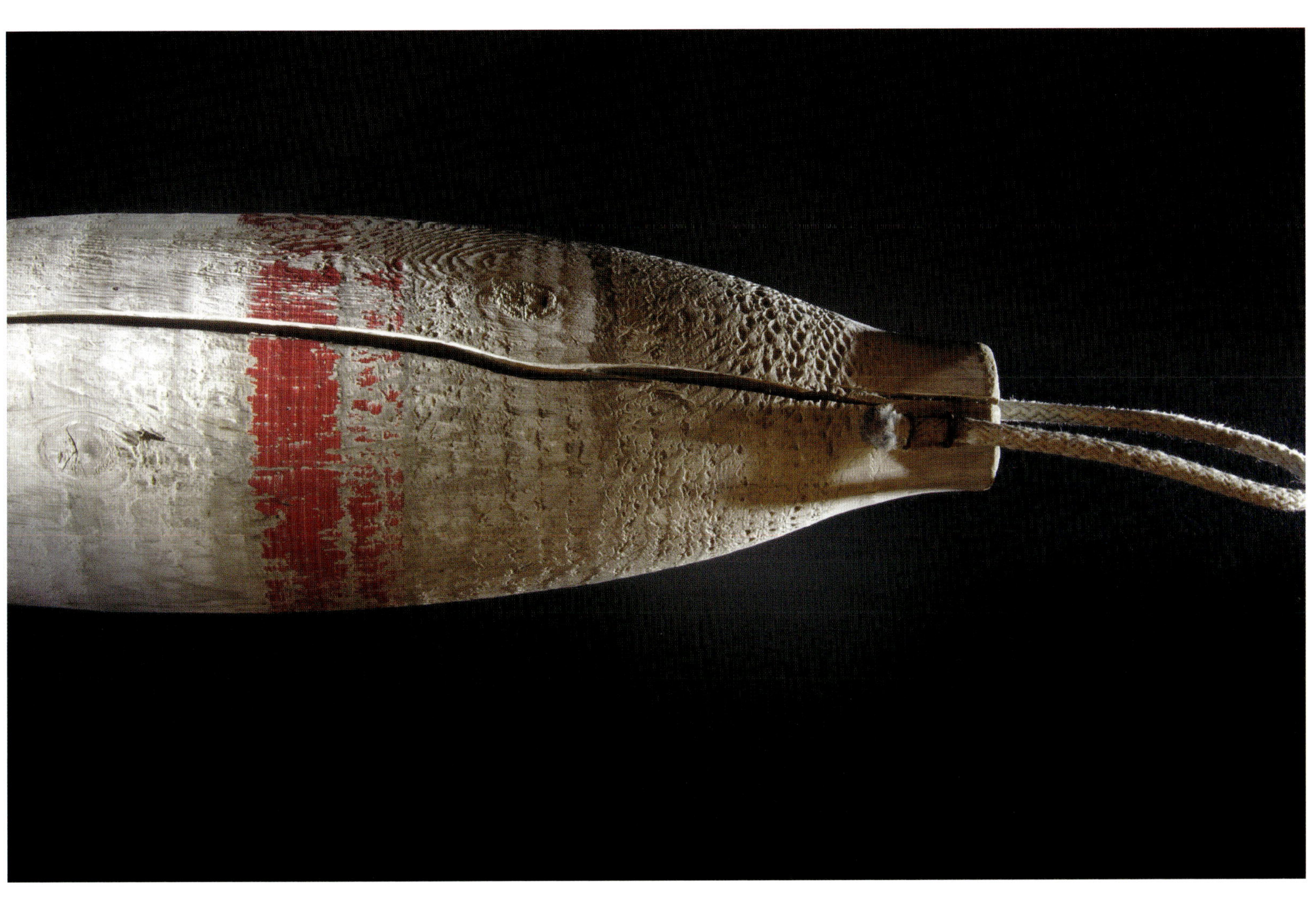

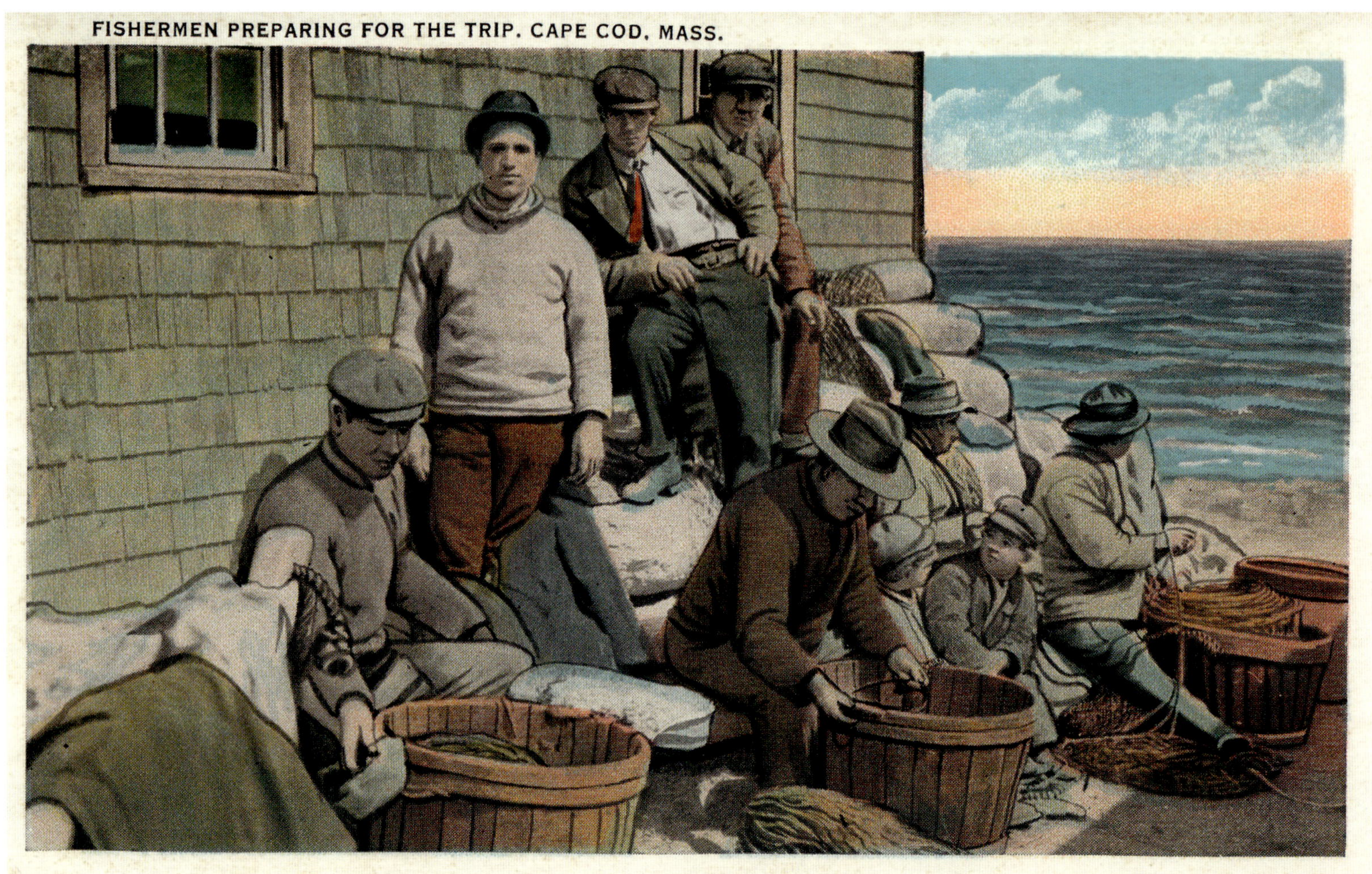

Early Provincetown explorers spoke of a harbor so thick with cod that they could walk on their backs. The fishing industry spawned other industries, such as saltworks and ice houses. Mackerel, a fall fish, was pickled in barrels. Summer brought squid and bass. Boston was the intended destination and New York also became a market for the bounty. All industries prospered until the Civil War, when bigger, more efficient ships replaced schooners.

By that point, fishermen were staying closer to home. Trap fishing, day boats, and draggers became the means by which to continue. As long as there were fish, Provincetown prospered.

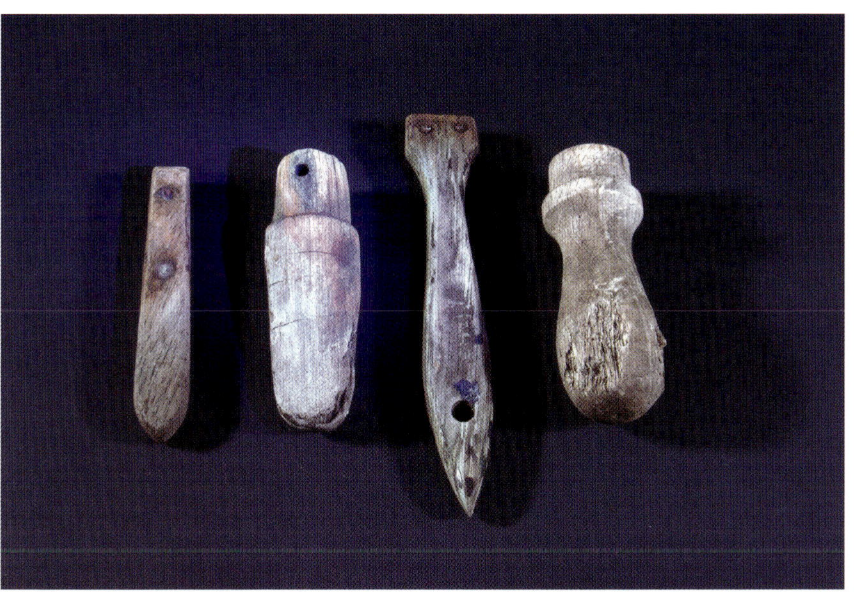

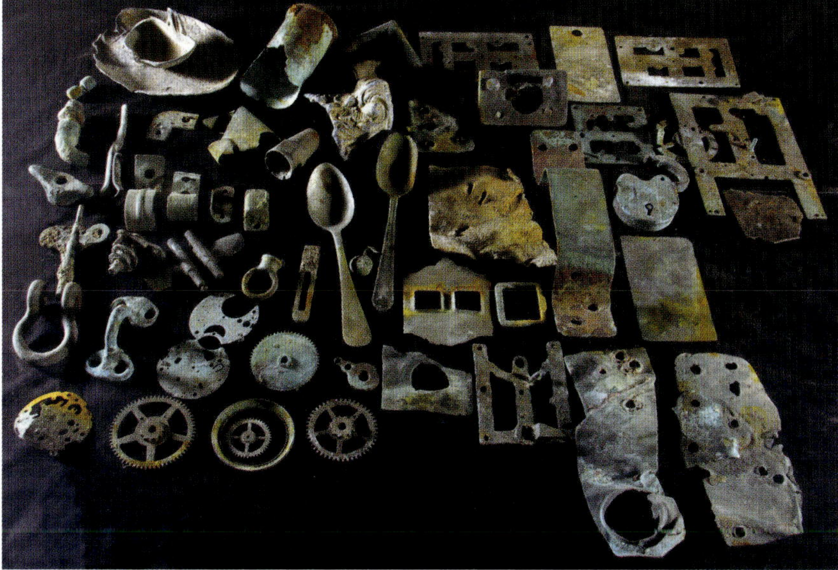

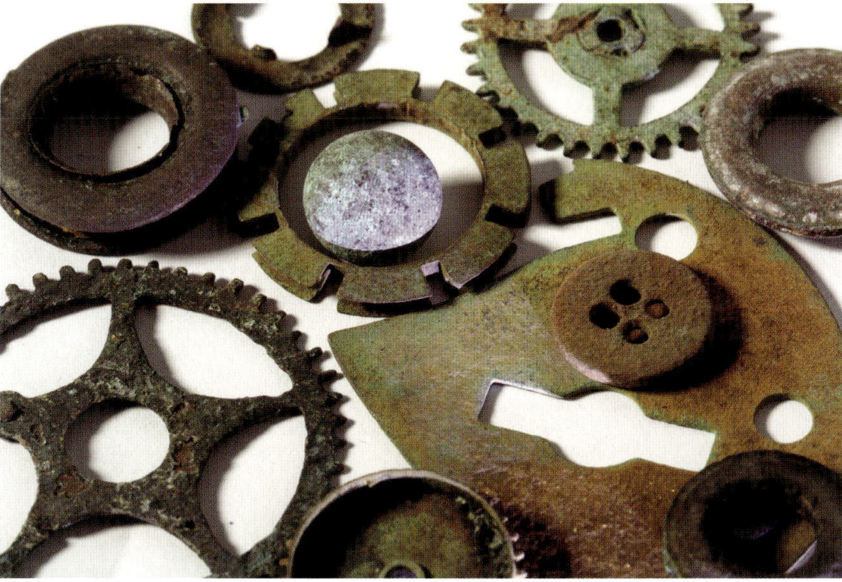

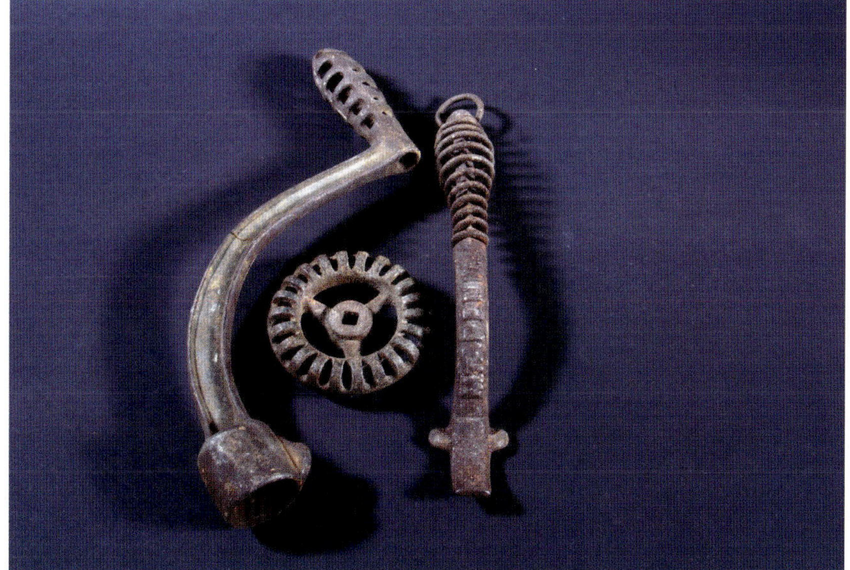

Nuts, bolts, gears, saw bits, saw blades, locks, keys, spigots, tubing, handles, grates, screws, nails, winches, turnbuckles, washers, cleats, drills, drill bits, screwdrivers, pen knives, drains, drain covers, come-alongs, faceplates, and any other fixture known to man and fisherman can and have been found in the waterfront dumps. More beautiful in their age-old patina, they live on in the adage "form follows function."

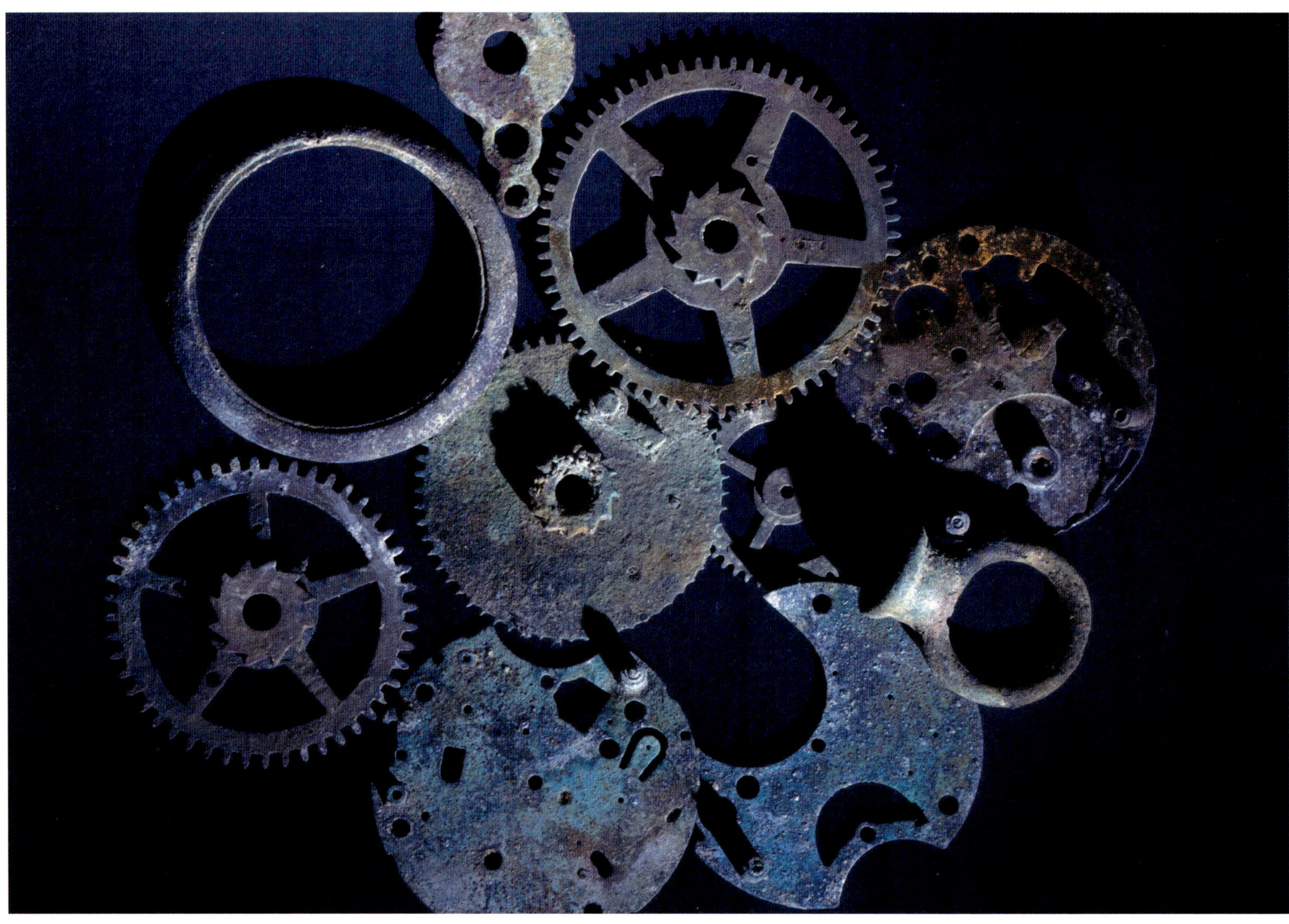

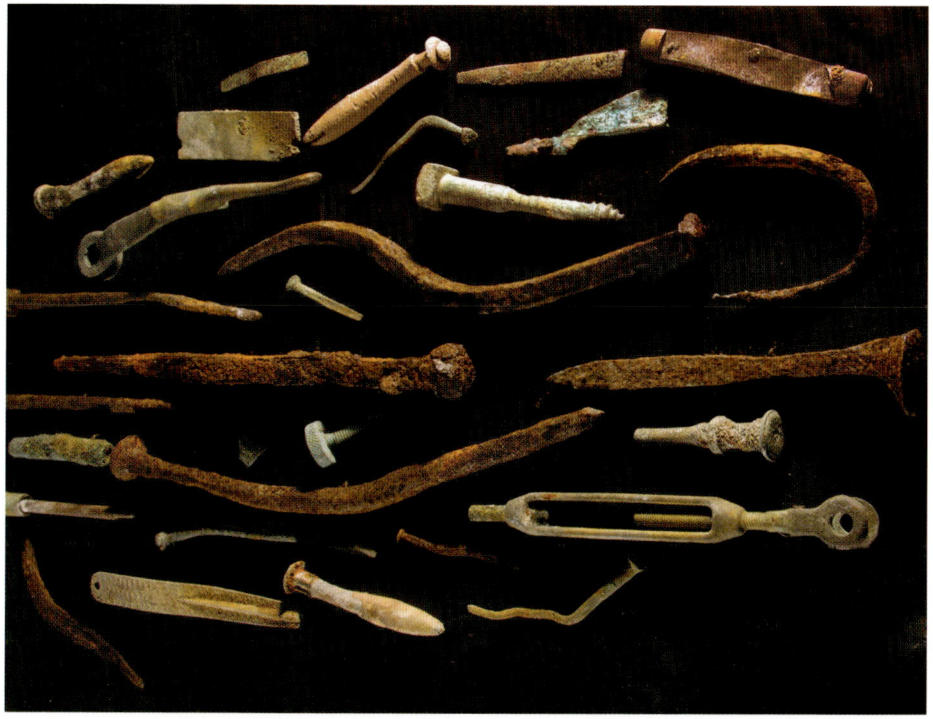

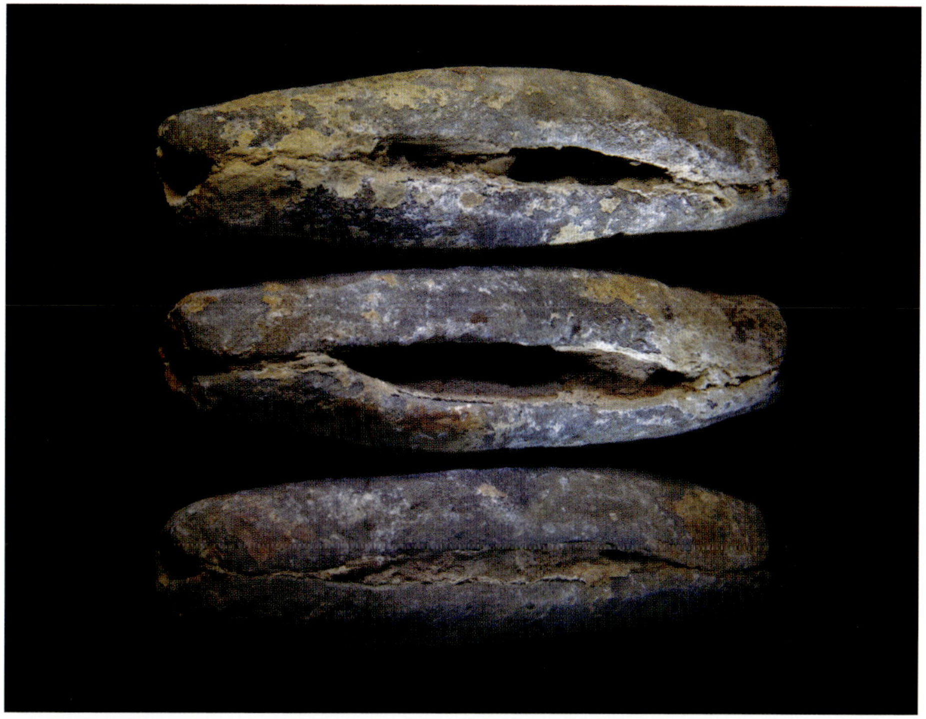

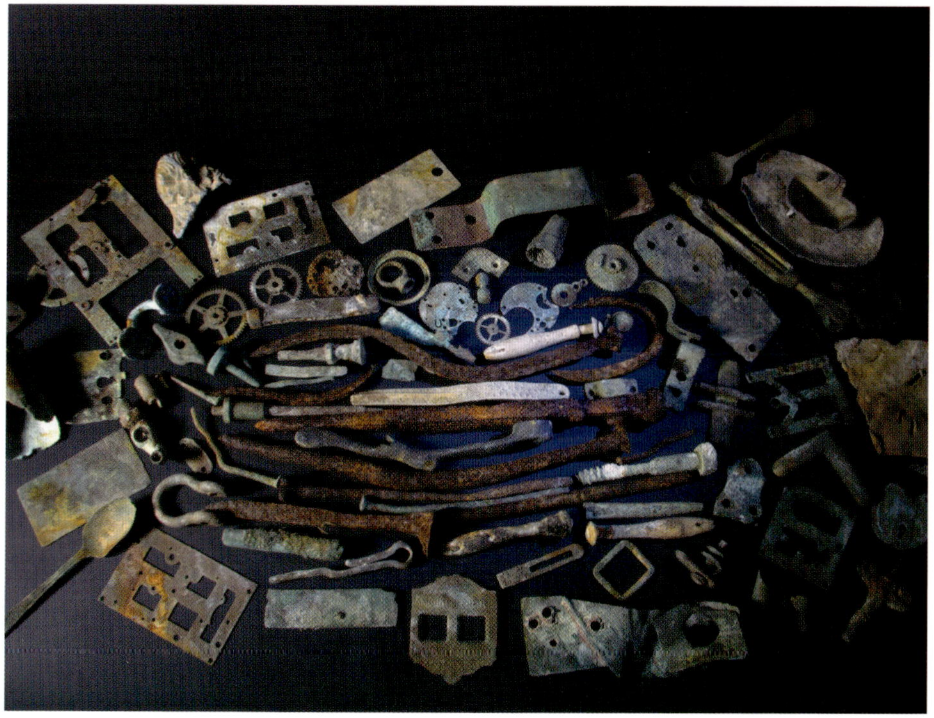

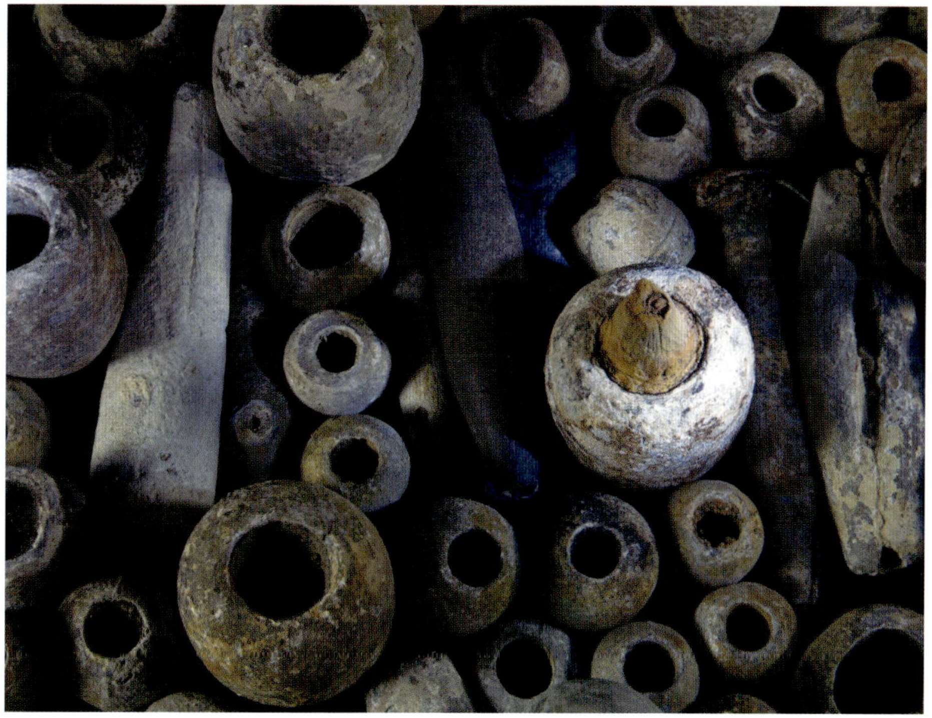

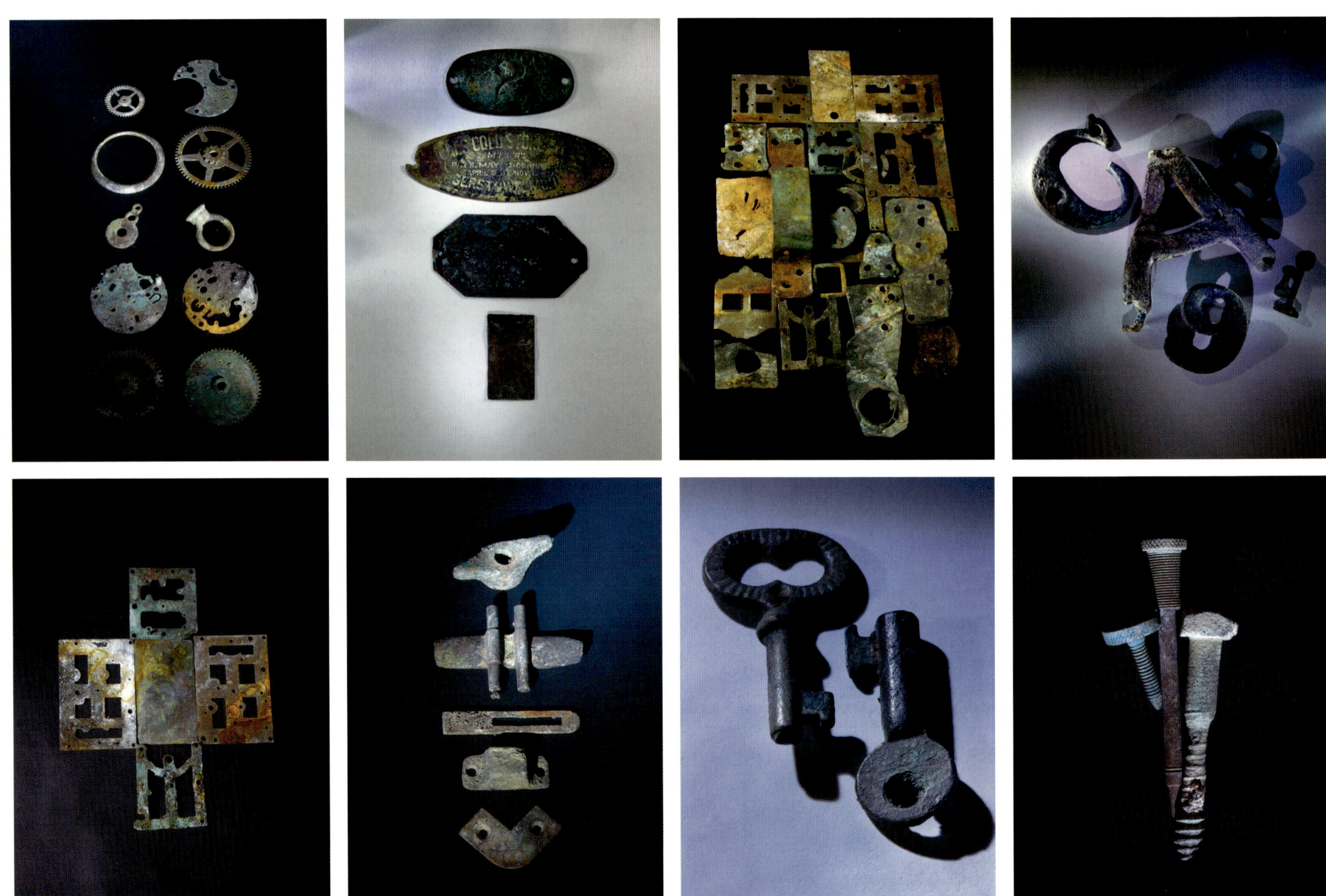

"Do you remember the storm of 1977–78? It made a cut through the Cape toward Wood End and made that part of the Cape like an island. And it undermined the Beachcombers Club. And it destroyed Boogar's studio [jeweler and bronze sculptor William Boogar, 1893–1958]. Well, the picking underneath the Beachcombers was incredible that one winter, before they fixed it all up. There was mostly stuff for sculpture, I think. . . . There was metalwork, there were gobs of molten lead. That had been a plumber's shop too . . . I think the name of the plumber was Mr. Bangs."

—Paul Bowen

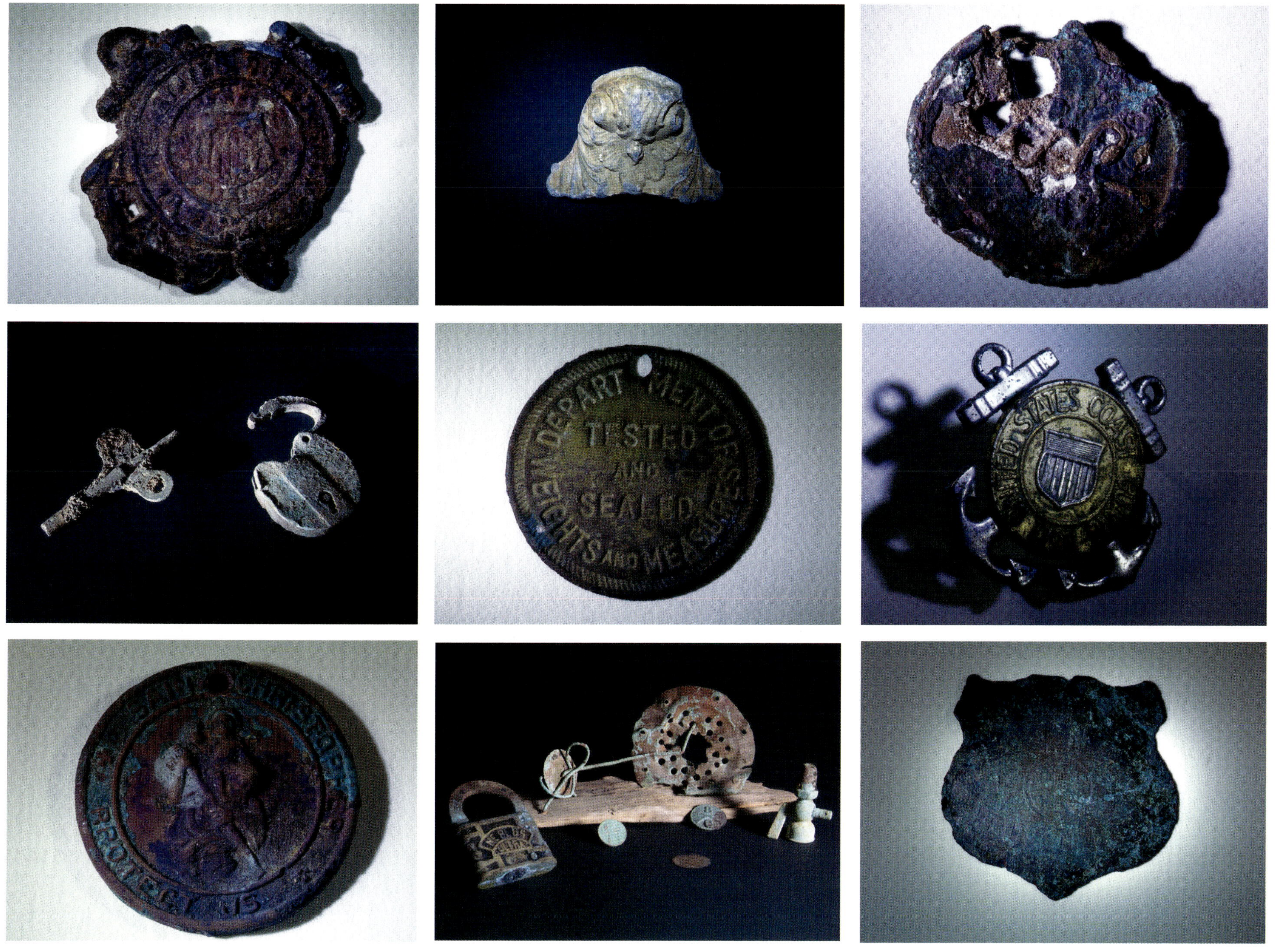
DEPART MENT OF
TESTED
AND
SEALED
STATES COAST
SAINT CHRISTOPHER
PROTECT US

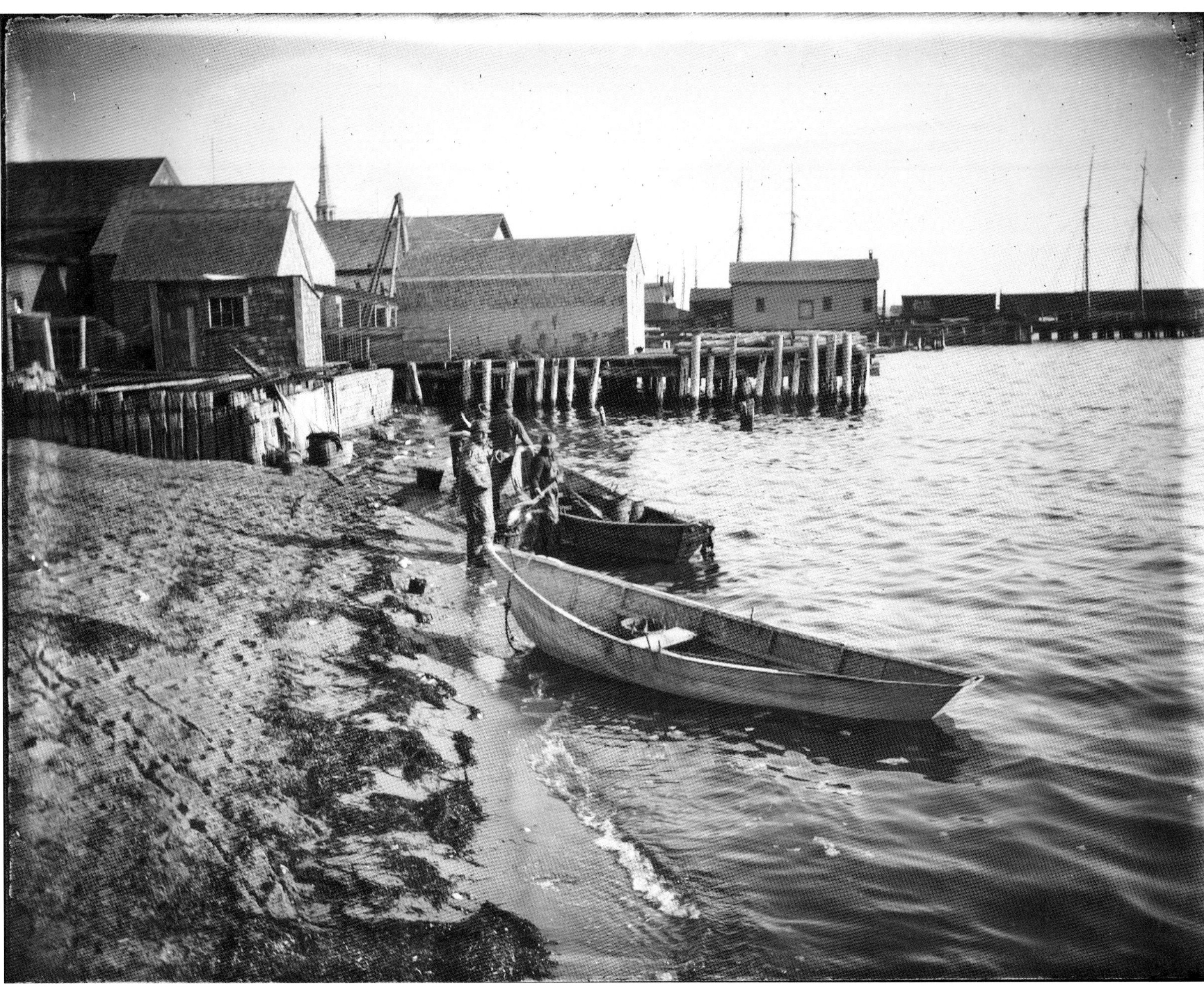

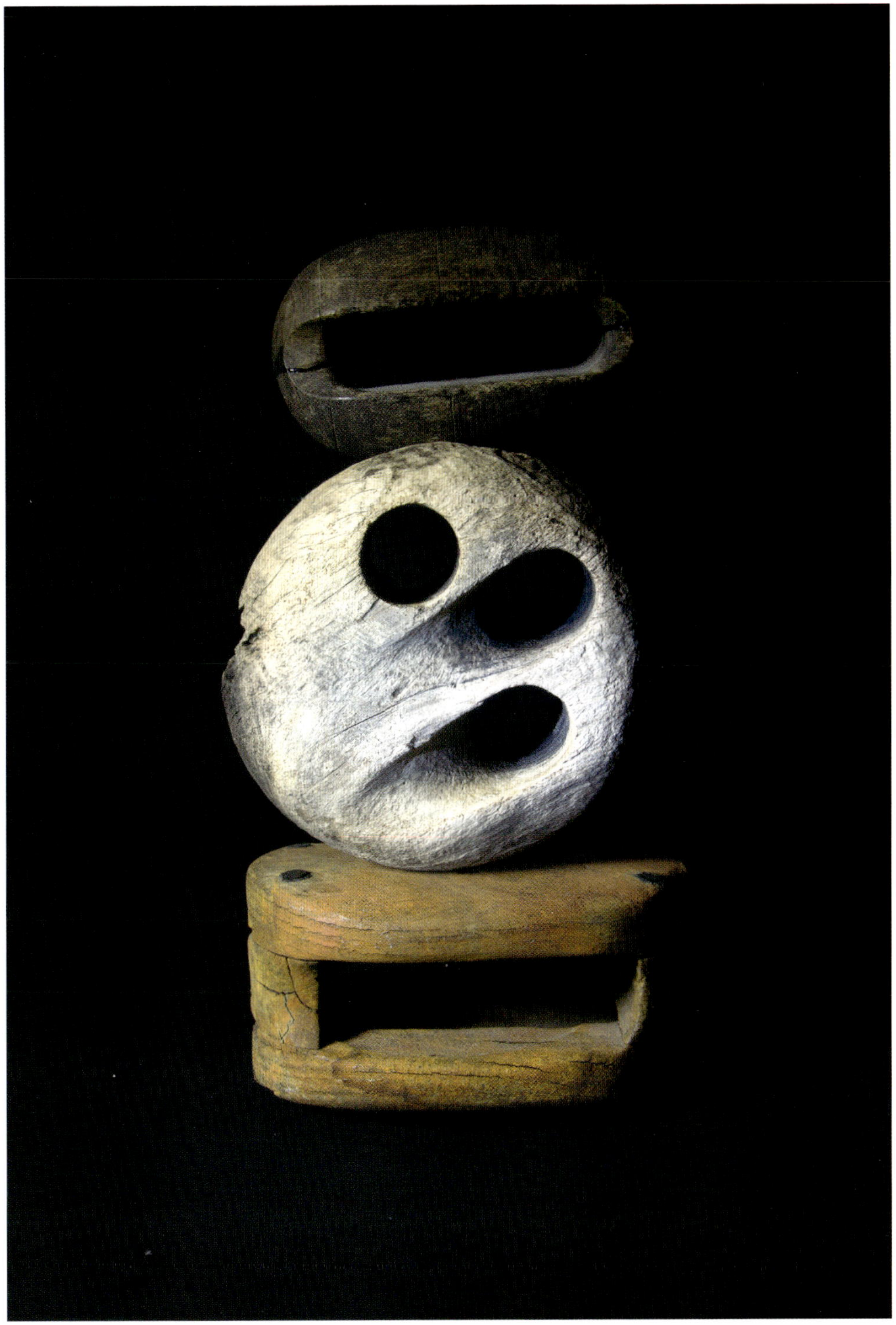

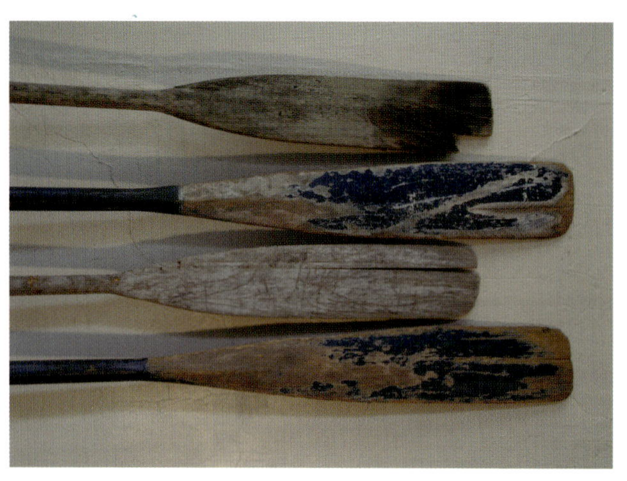

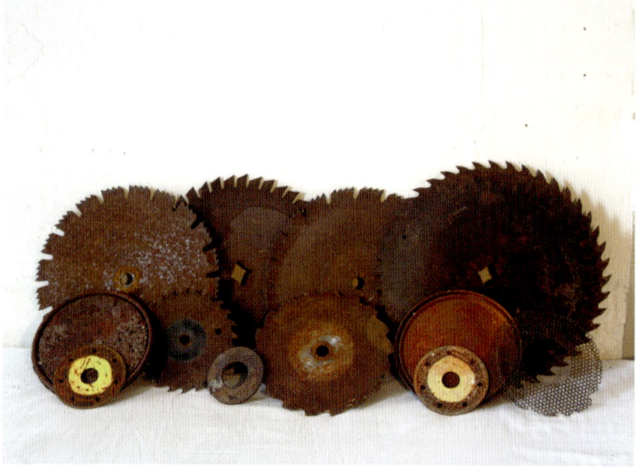

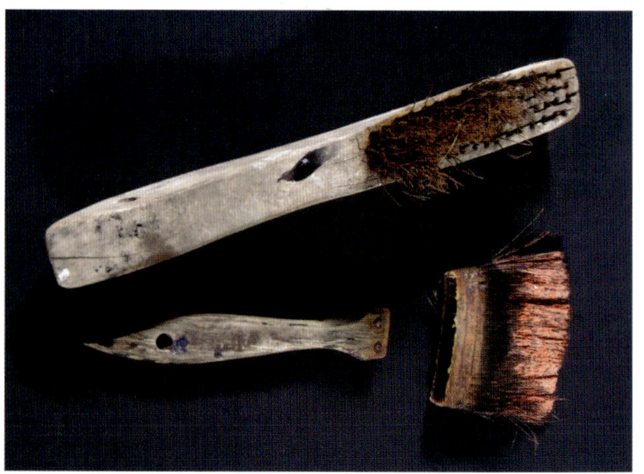

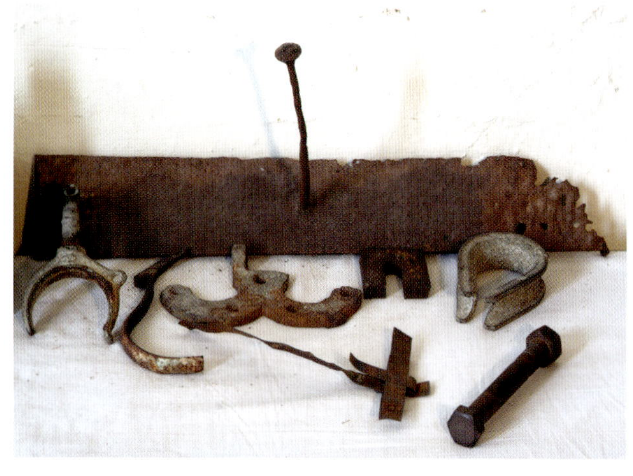

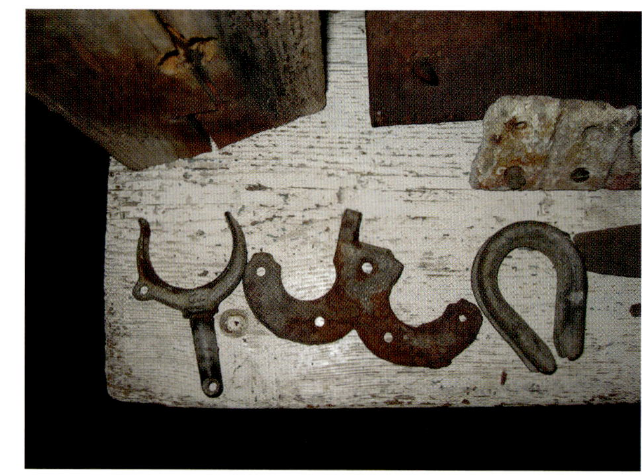

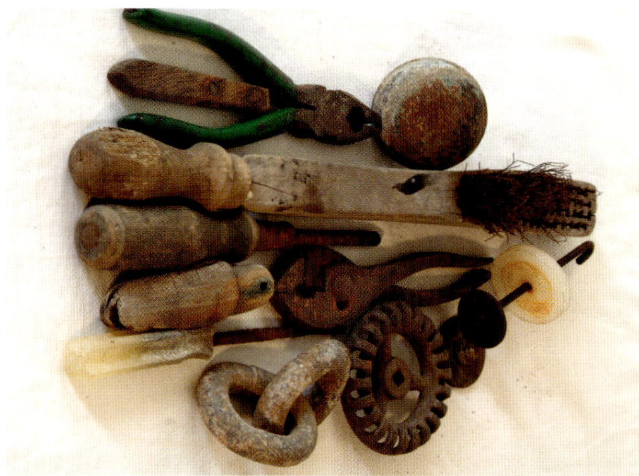

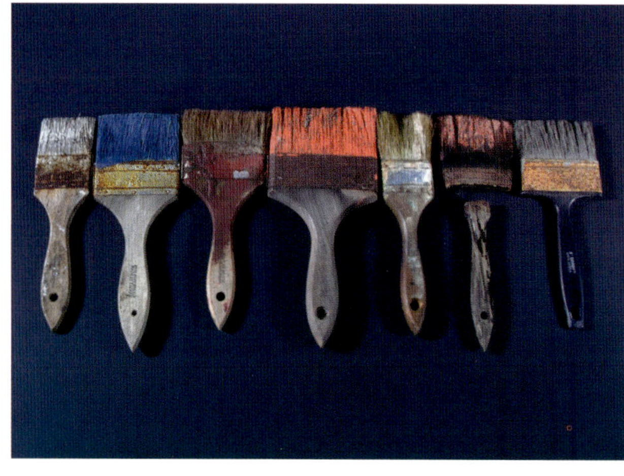

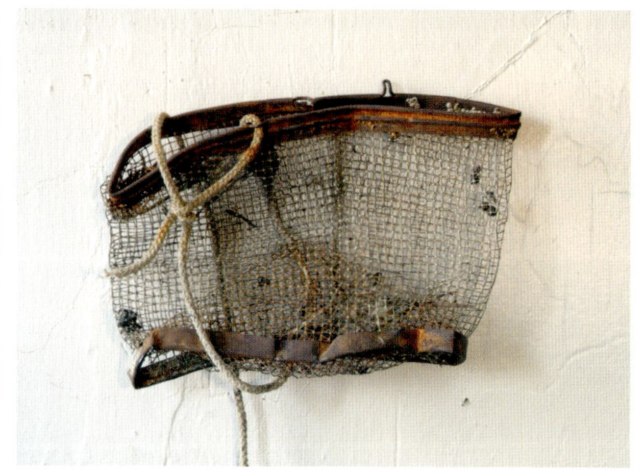

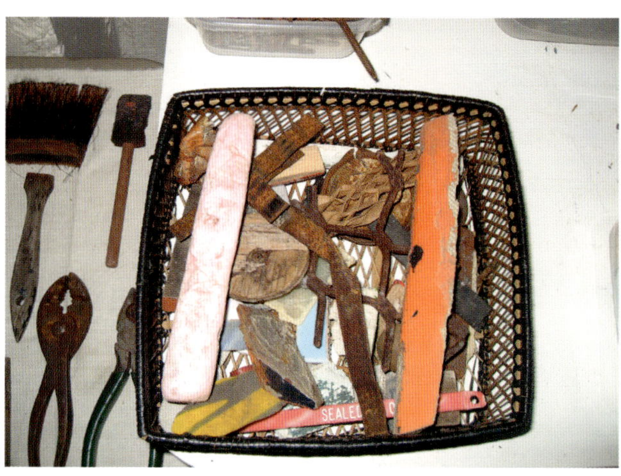

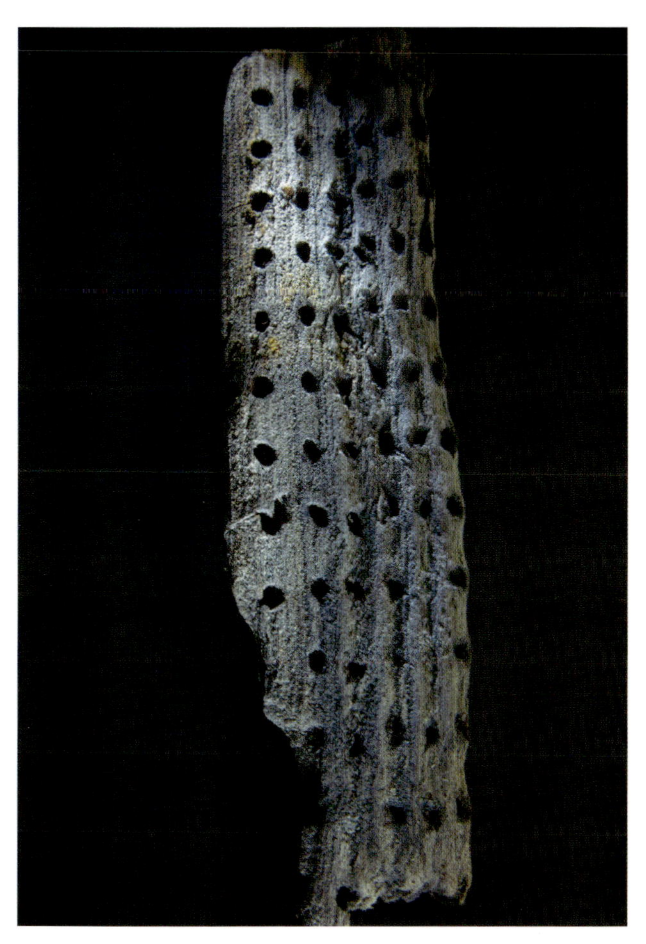

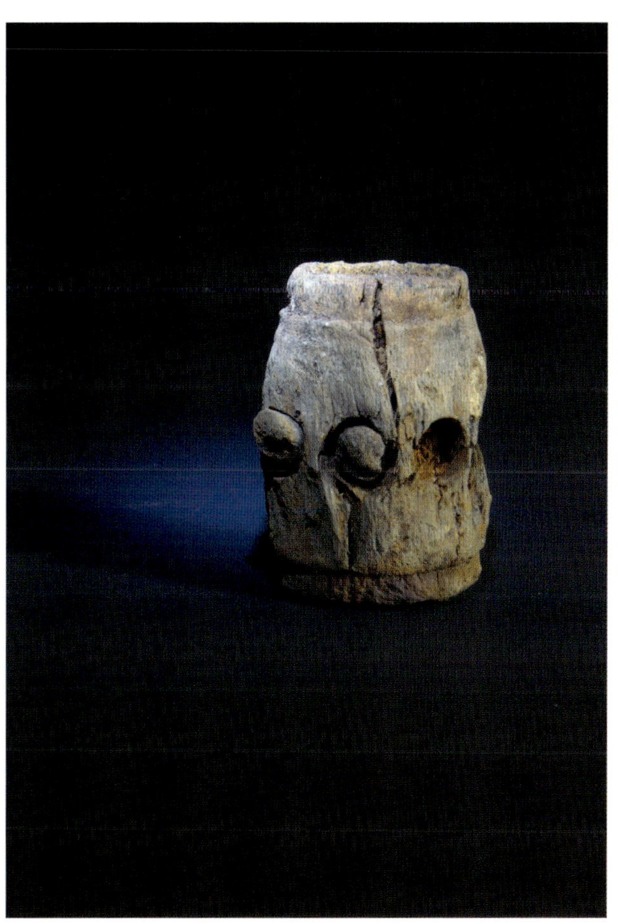

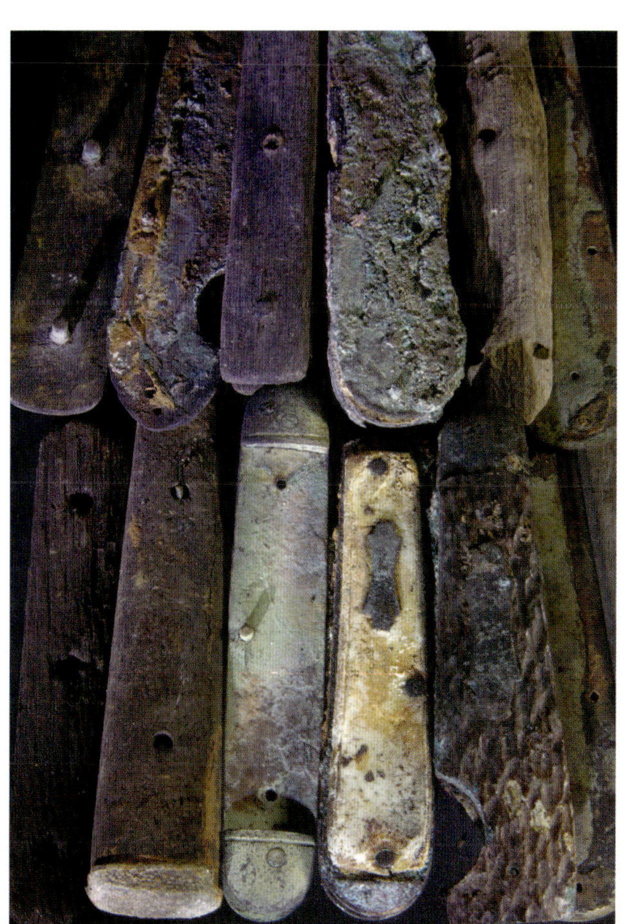

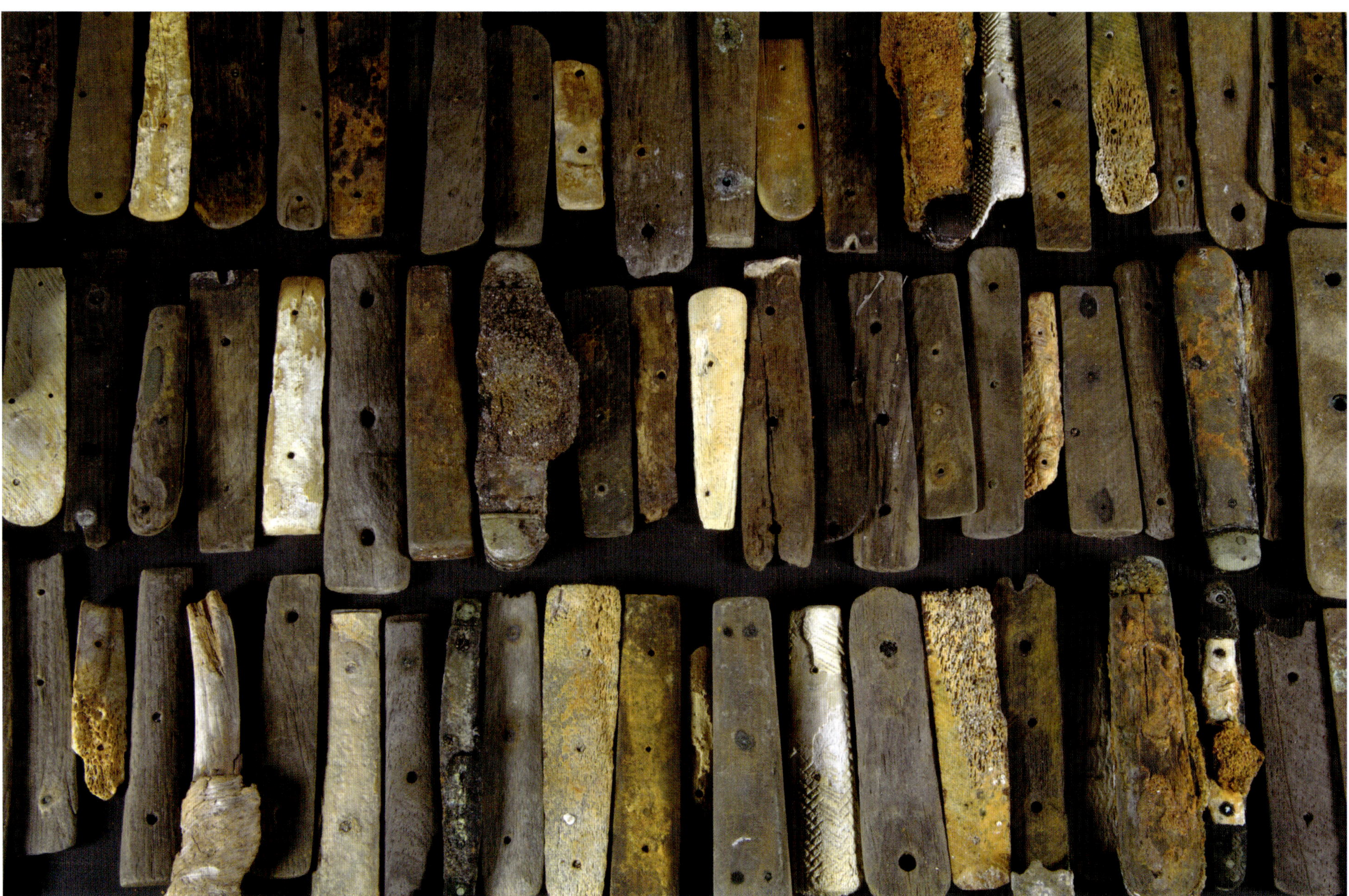

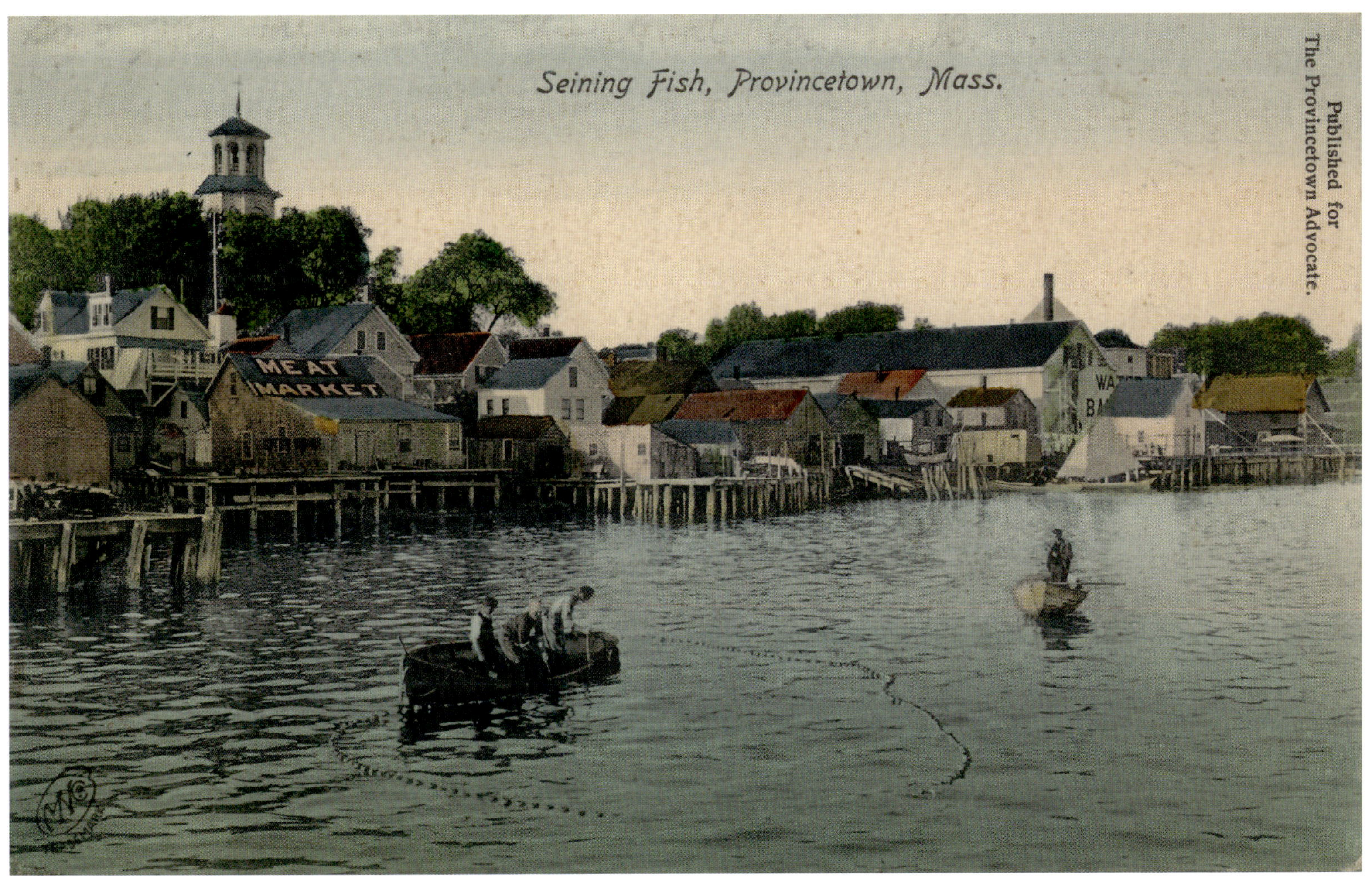
Seining Fish, Provincetown, Mass.
Published for
The Provincetown Advocate.
MEAT
MARKET

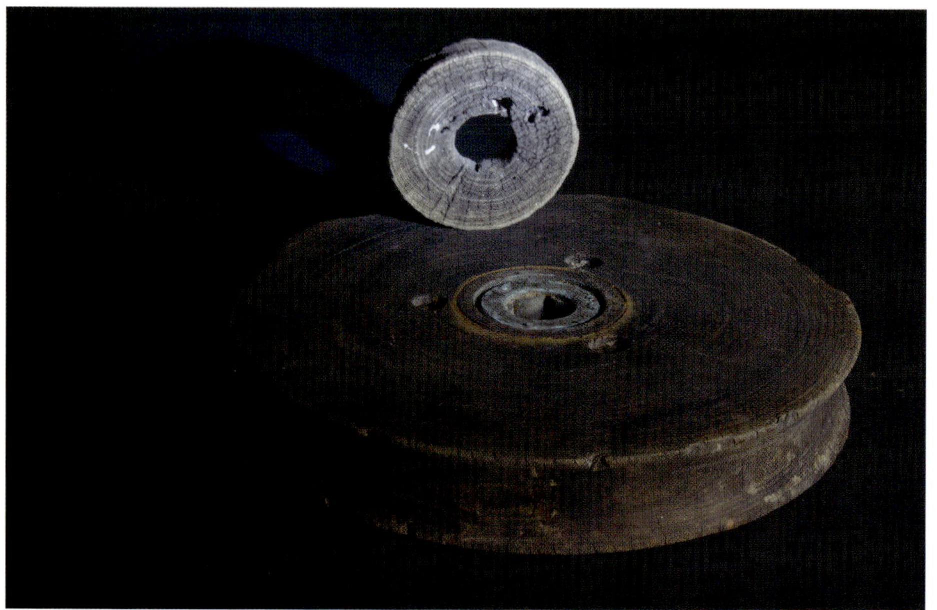

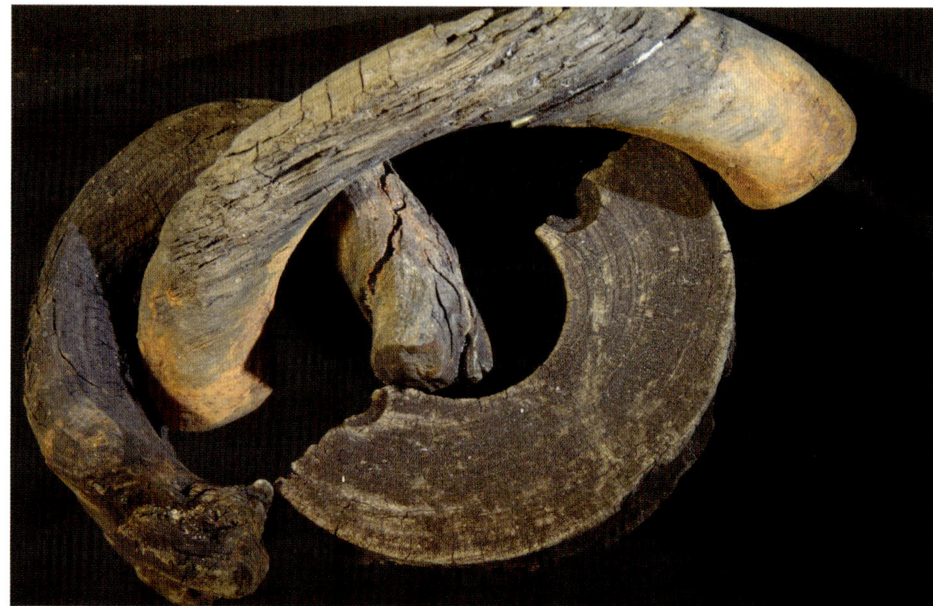

"I have made some rope pieces. . . . The rope I really like is the old natural fiber, rope that were nets you find when they used to waterproof them . . . by dipping them in paint and tar. So around some of the wharves you will see the bottom of the barrel rotting away and the remains of the tar with the rope."

—Paul Bowen

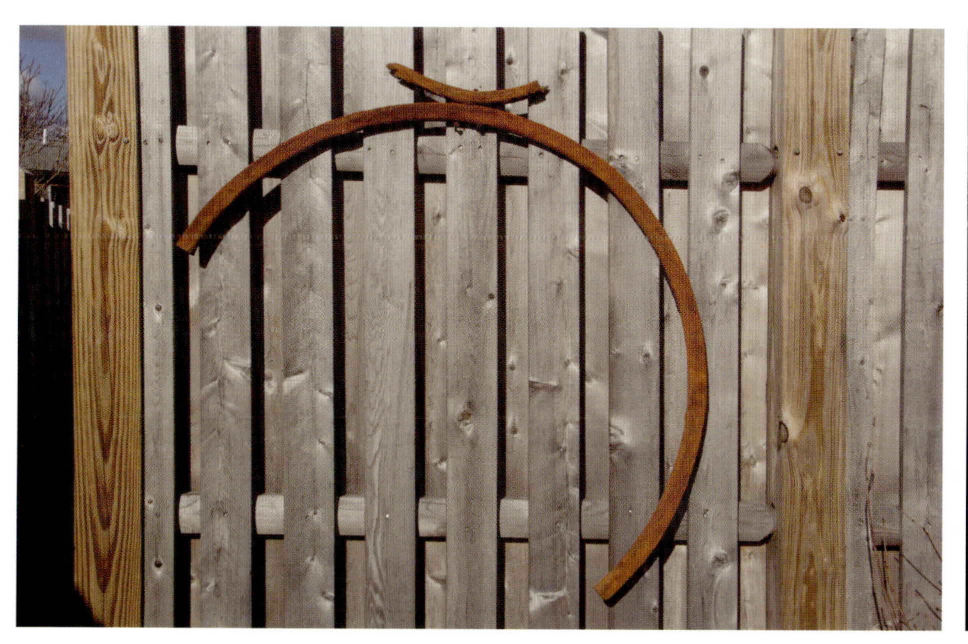

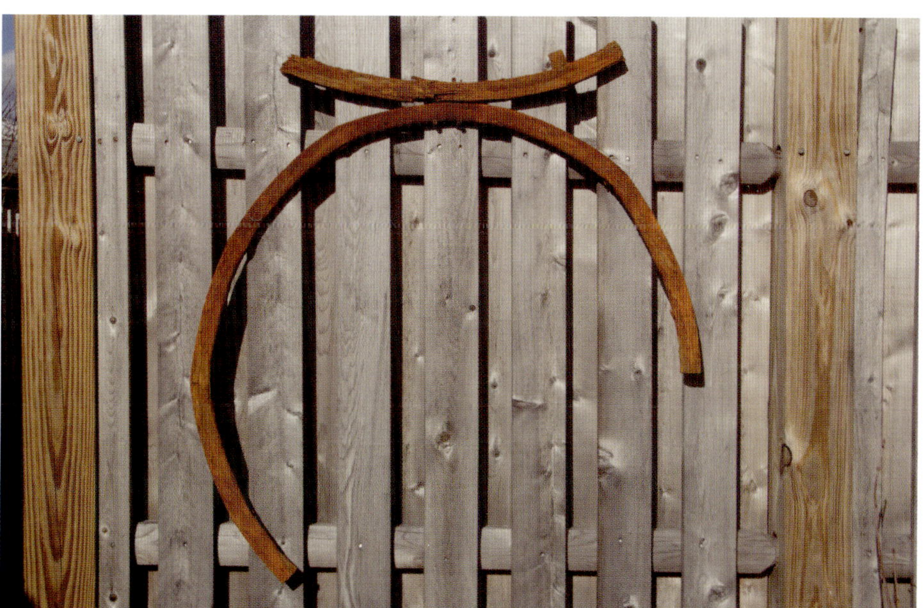

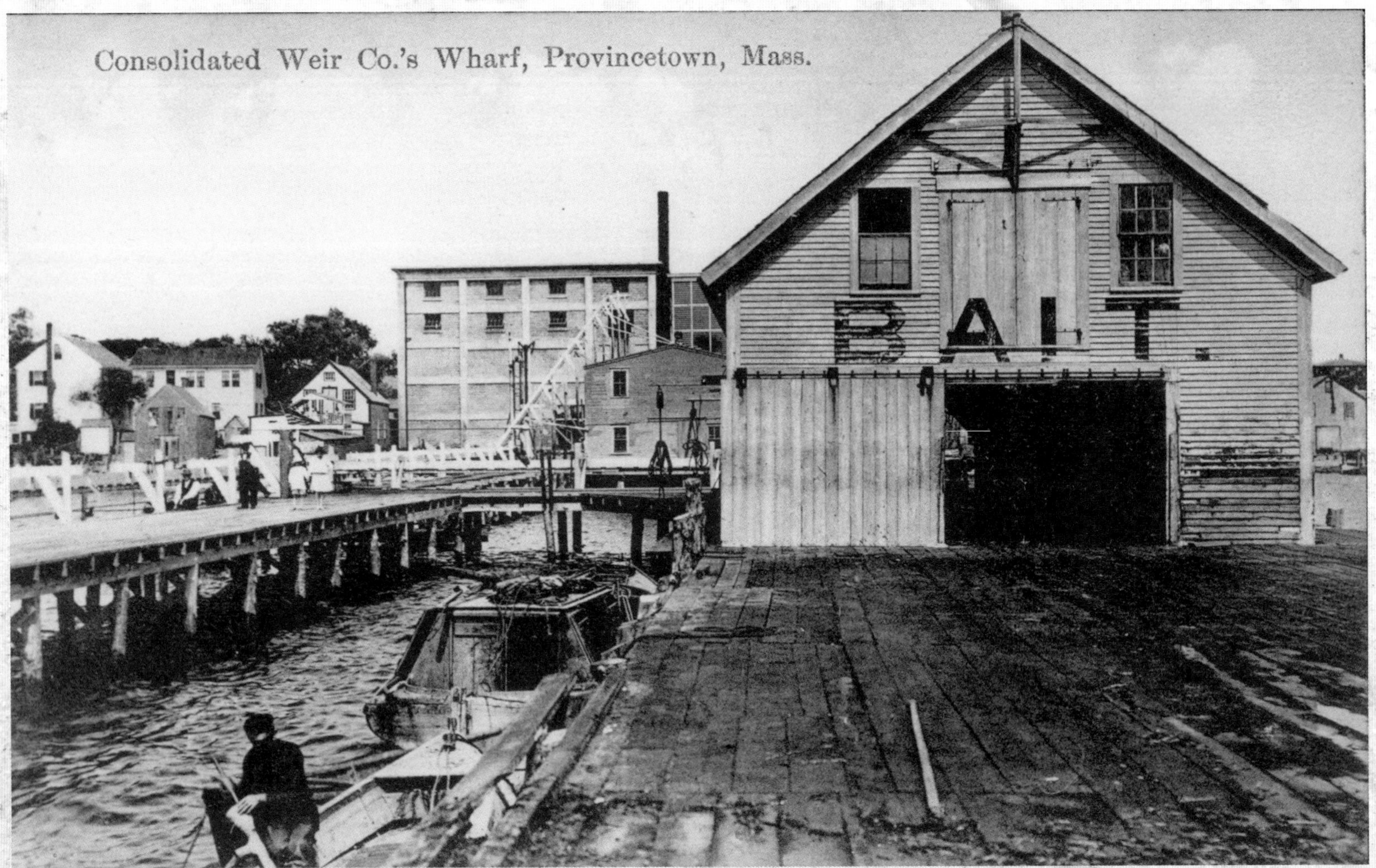

"A long, long time ago, when I lived on the East End of town, I remember George Bryant telling me one summer that he went for a quick walk on the beach . . . to the Ice House, right by the pilings. He said two women swimming found a gun on the beach, like a rusted gun, at the pilings. And I was p****d off that it wasn't me [who found it]."

—Paul Bowen

L. D. BAKER, JR.
Vice-President

W. IRVING ATWOOD
President and Treasurer

Incorporated 1900

THE CONSOLIDATED WEIR CO.

Frozen Food Fish, Bait and Ice

Herring   Squid   Mackerel   Whiting

ICE PLANT CAPACITY 25 TONS DAILY

Freezer at Provincetown

Telephone 14-2

Weirs at
Provincetown, Truro, Barnstable
Monomoy, Chatham
South Chatham

We are the Pioneers in the Frozen Whiting Business
All Our Frozen Fish are Produced by Our Own Weirs

503 COMMERCIAL STREET
PROVINCETOWN, MASS.

House Telephone of Manager, Provincetown, Mass.

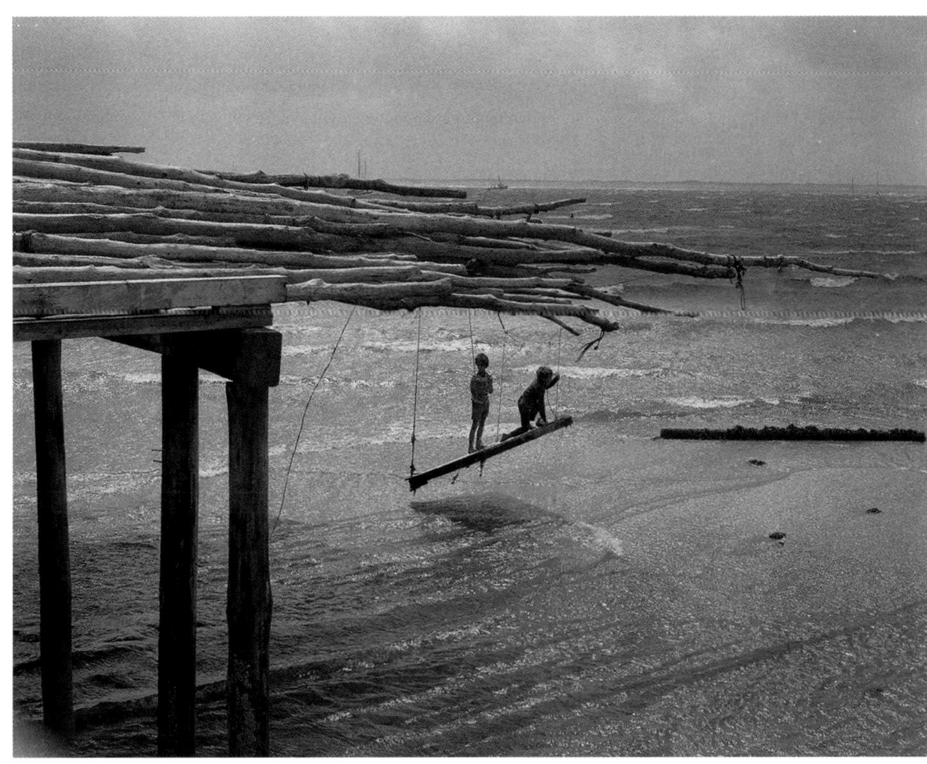

Indigenous peoples taught the settlers weir fishing, also called trap fishing. Tall poles were set in a large circle with an offset opening. At high tide the poles were barely visible and were wrapped with nets. Fish became trapped inside, unable to access the opening. Low tide was harvest time.

Mooncussing, Piracy & Lifesaving

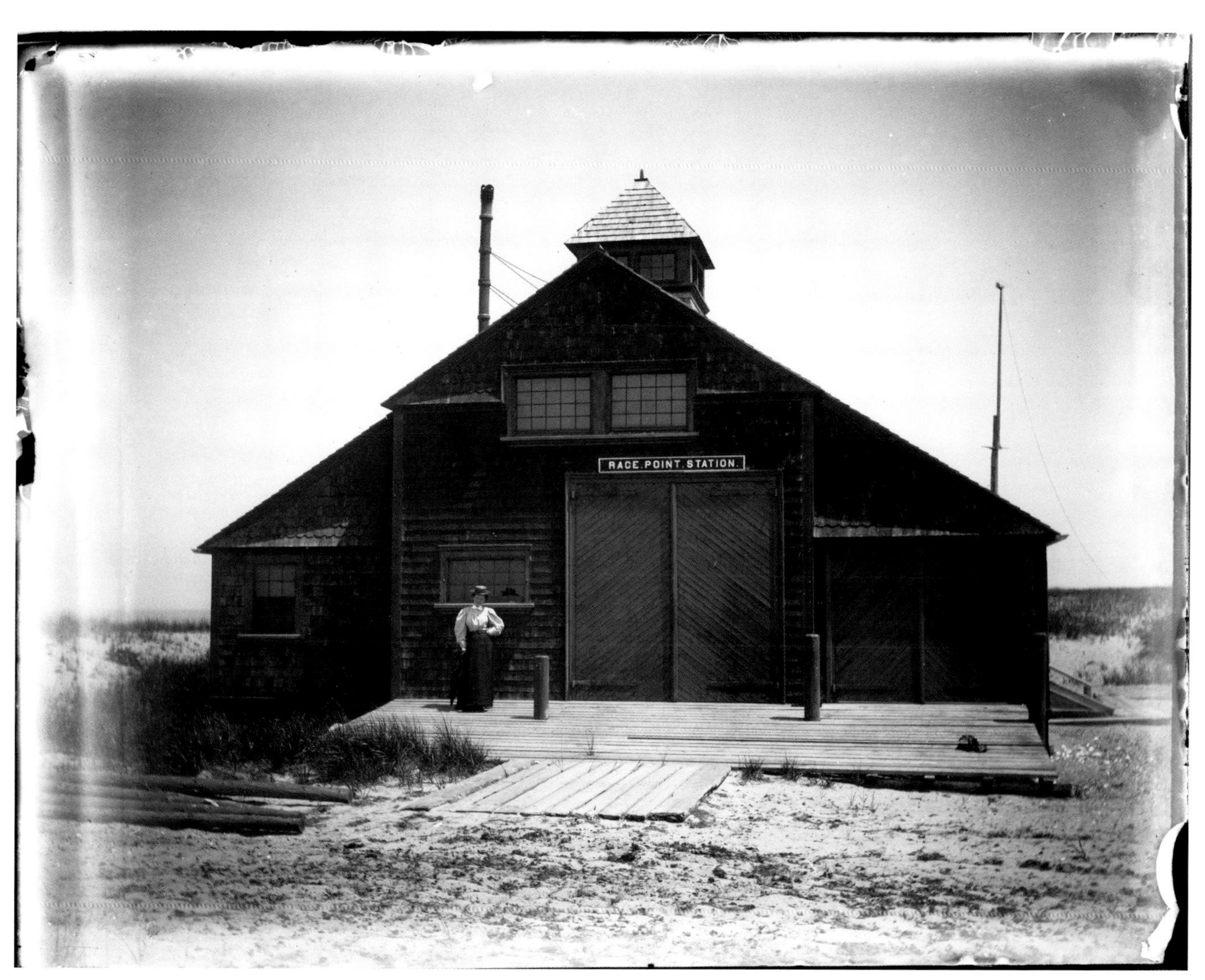

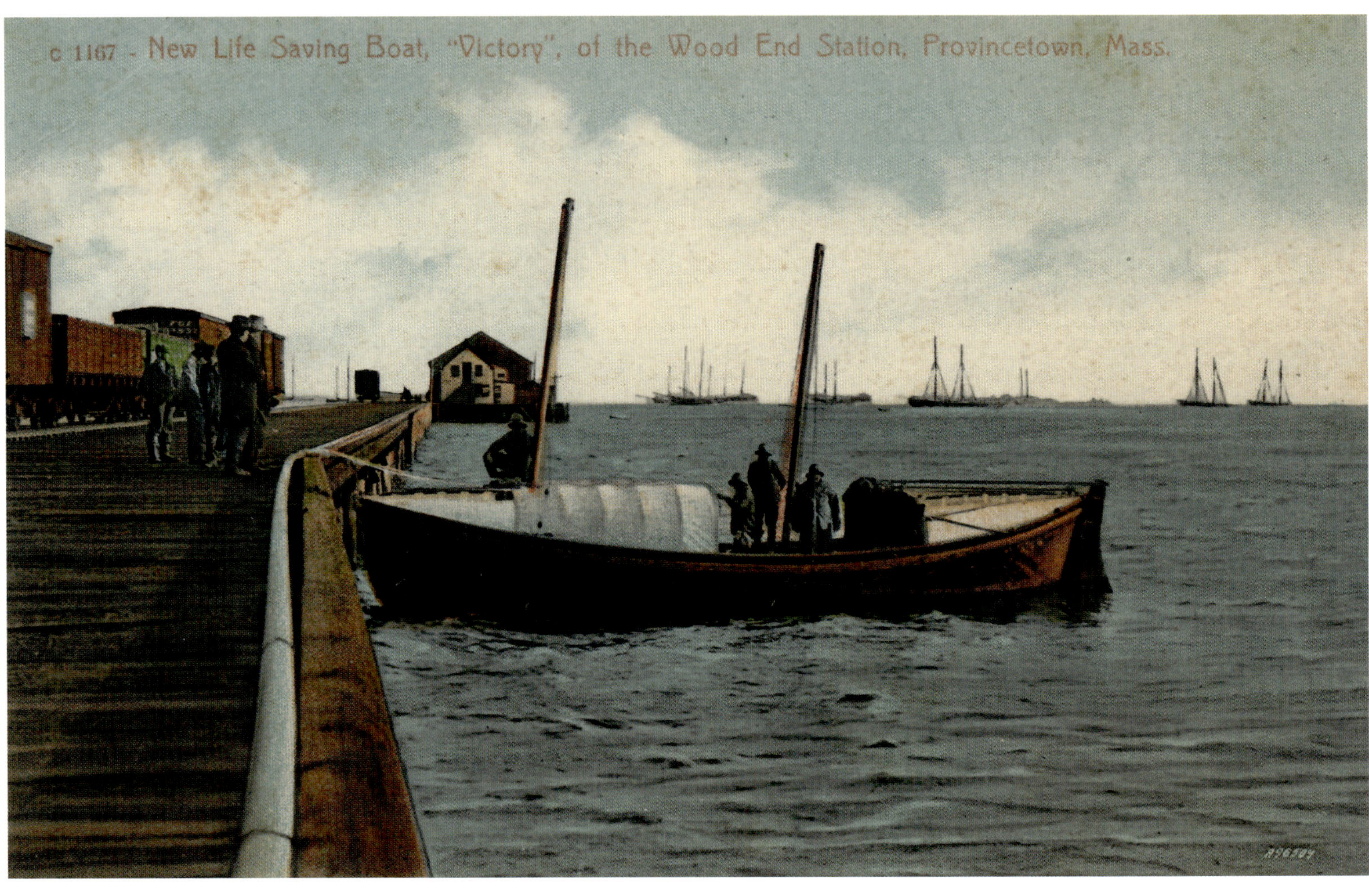
c 1167 - New Life Saving Boat, "Victory", of the Wood End Station, Provincetown, Mass.

The area we refer to as the Backside (from Race Point to Highland Light) was a mile and a half inland when indigenous peoples were here. Traces of their presence can be found in the middens (trash heaps) that became exposed in the face of the cliffs.

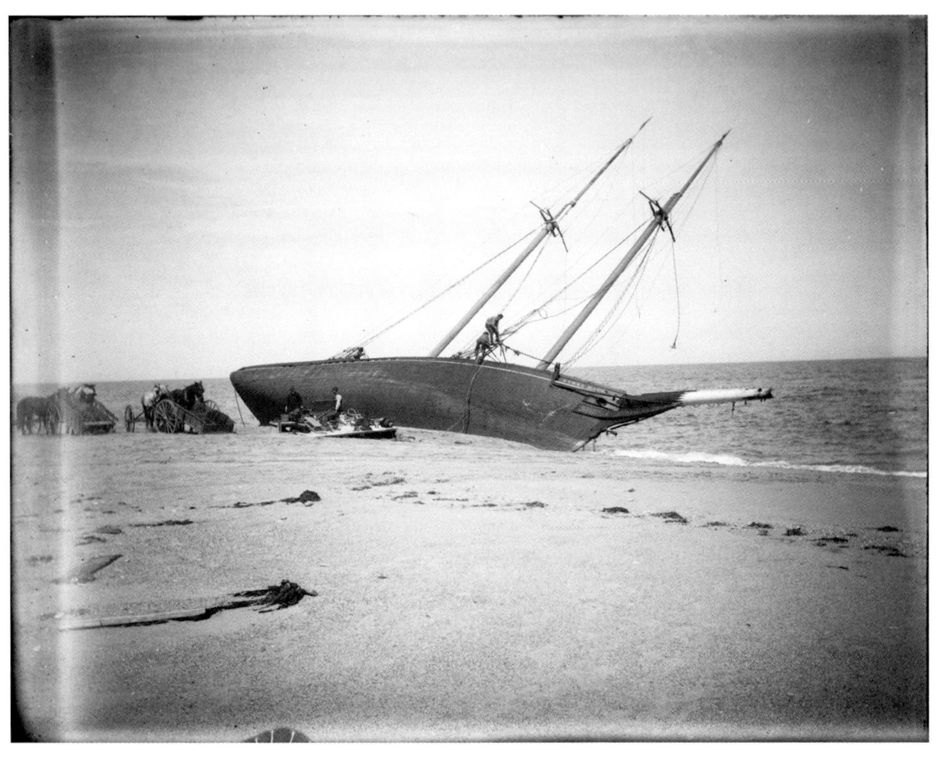

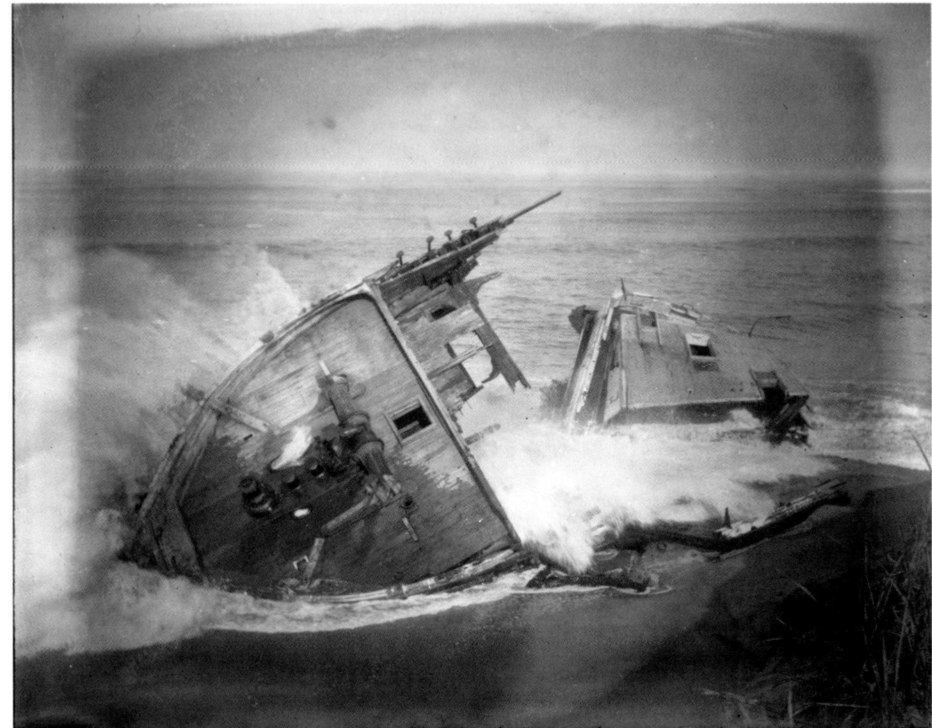

With the passing of time and steady erosion, the Backside shoreline developed dangerous sandbars and underwater gullies. By the eighteenth century, offshore whaling and the shipping industry were in high gear. When the ships came too close to these underwater bars, all was lost.

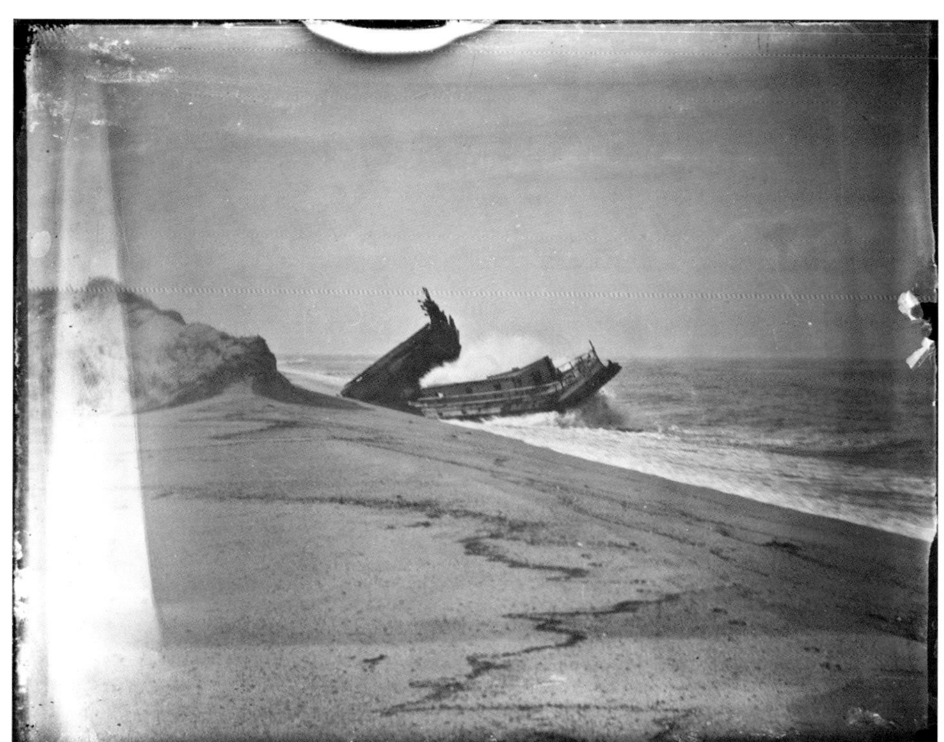

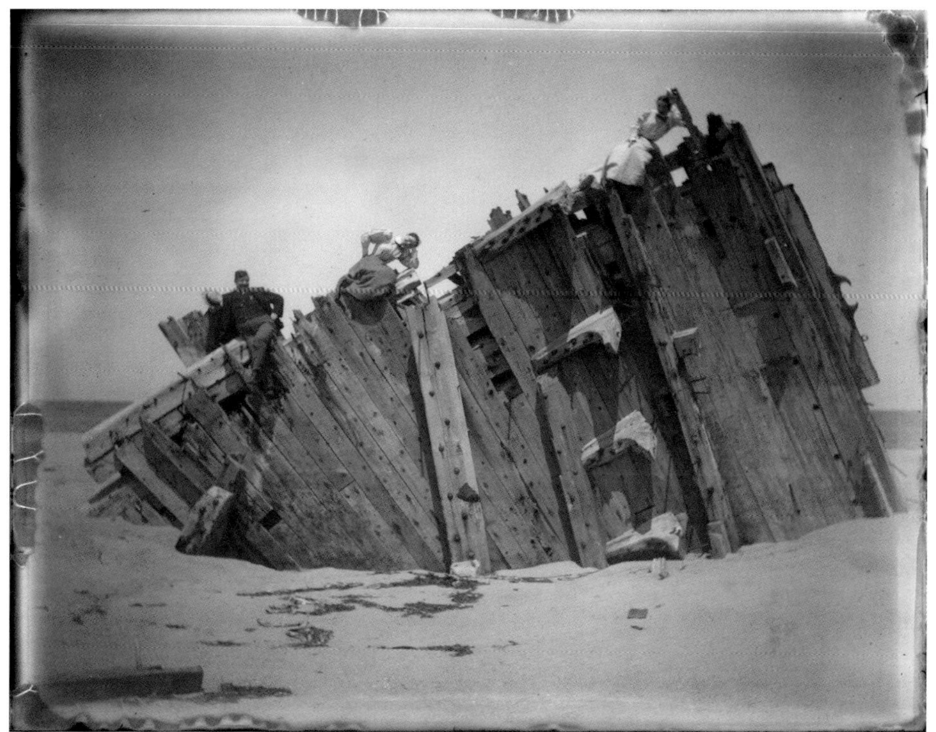

According to Provincetown lore, "mooncussers" capitalized on this tragedy. The term suggests lunacy, howling, and irrational behavior. It is all that and something more: an act of betrayal. On moonless nights, scoundrels would swing lanterns onshore that captains mistook for safe harbor, leading them to run aground on shoals and sandbars. These incidents were usually fatal for ship and crew, and the salvaged profits were enormous.

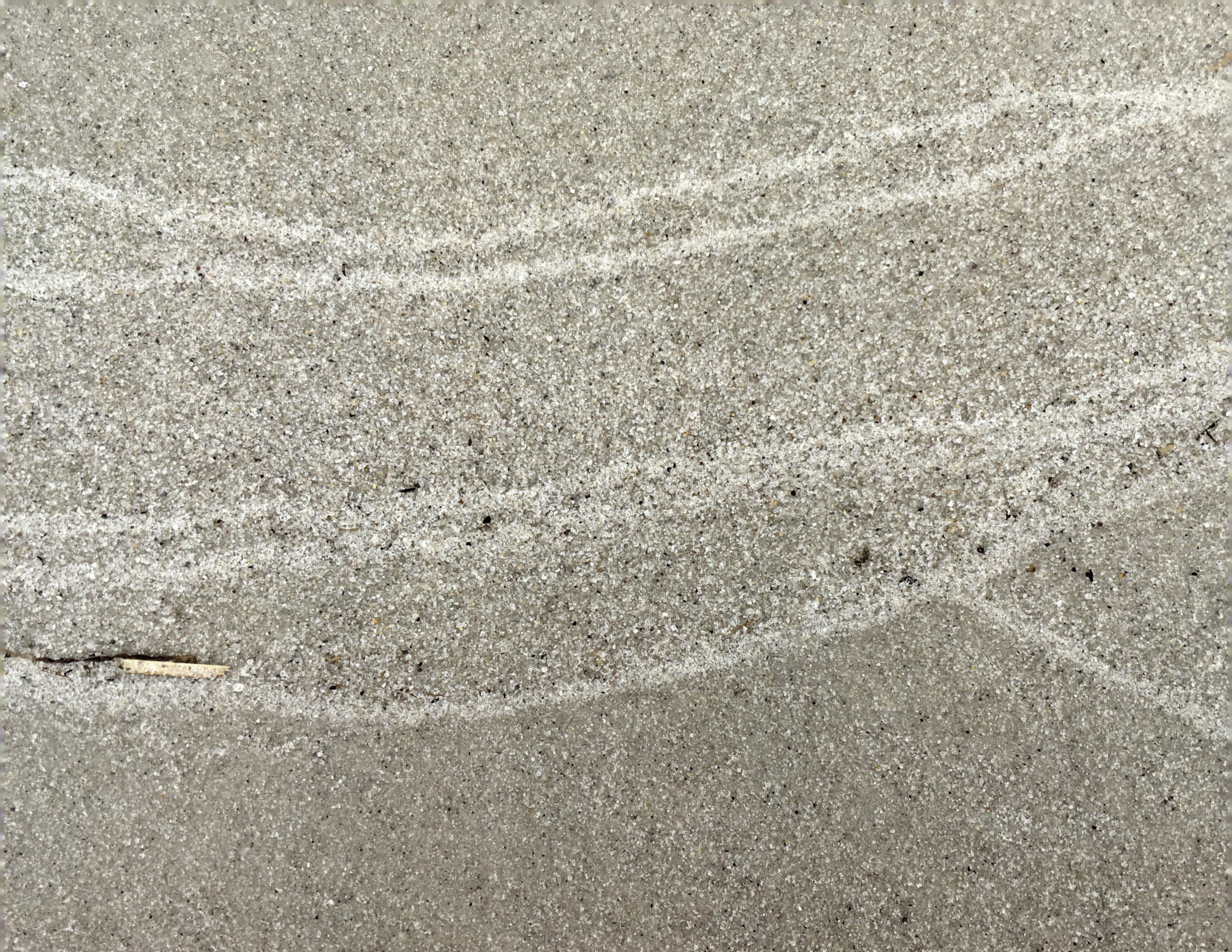

At the End of the Day

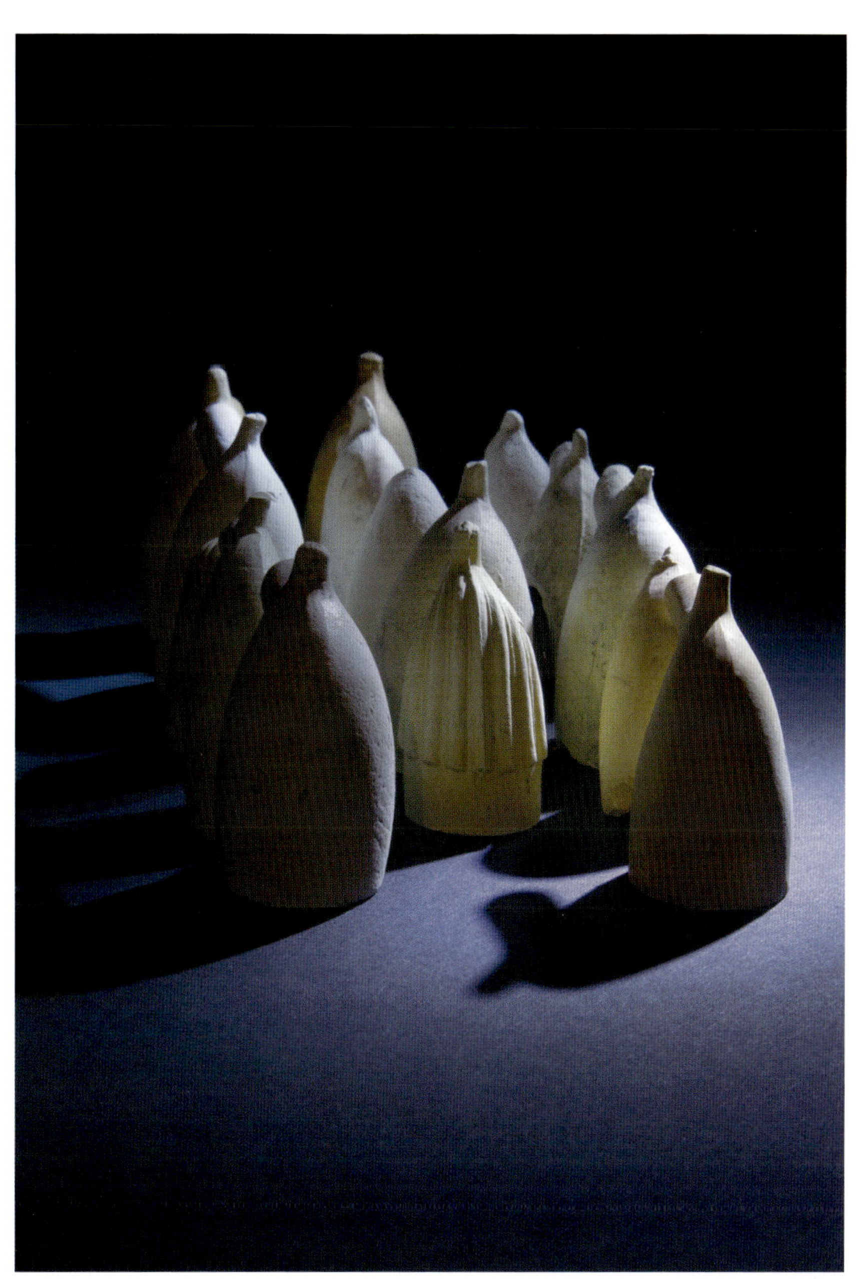

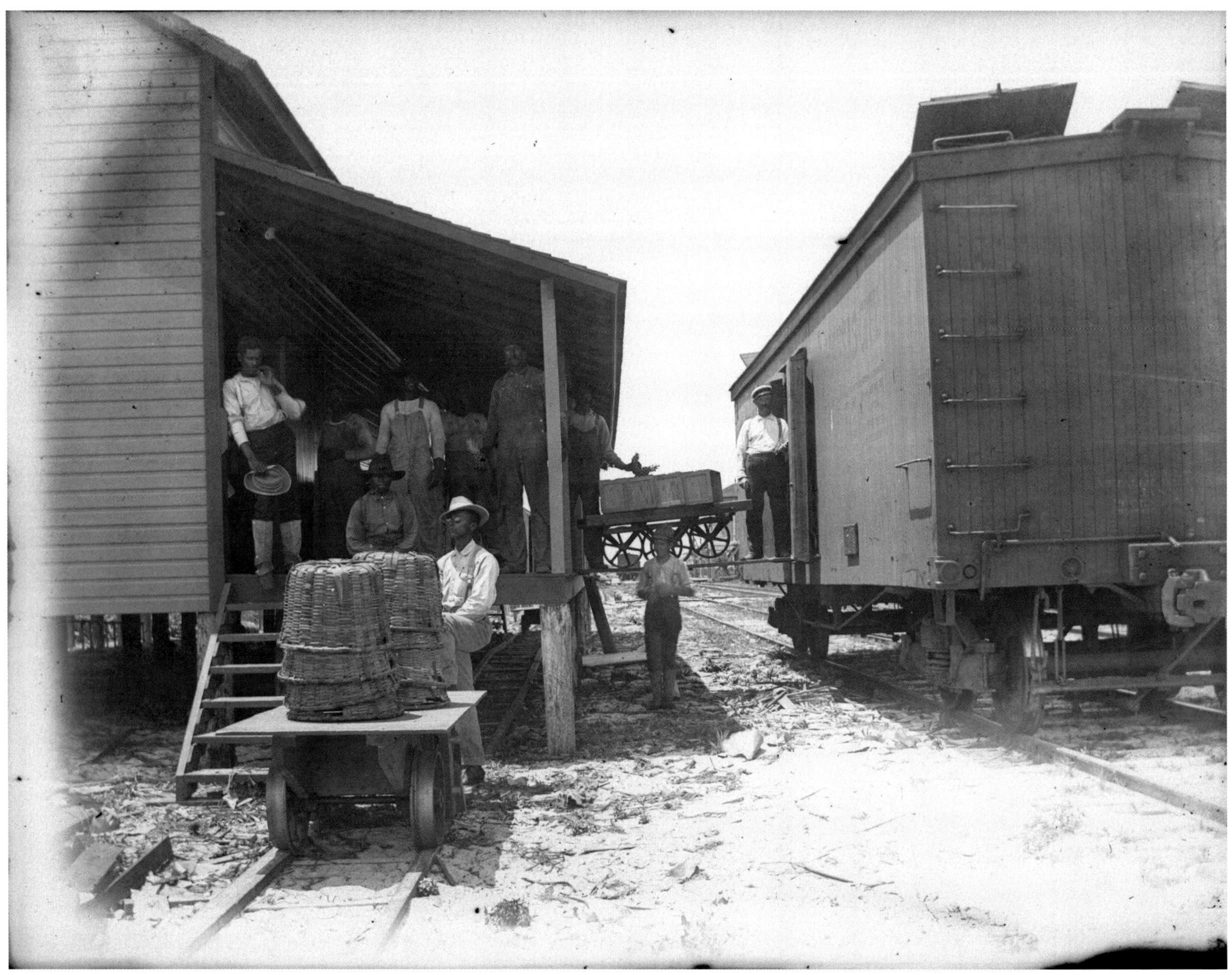

And for the reward at the end of the day: after the ropes have been tarred and the fish gutted and iced, it was time for a drink and a smoke, judging by the countless pipes, pipestems, and bottles that have turned on up the beach.

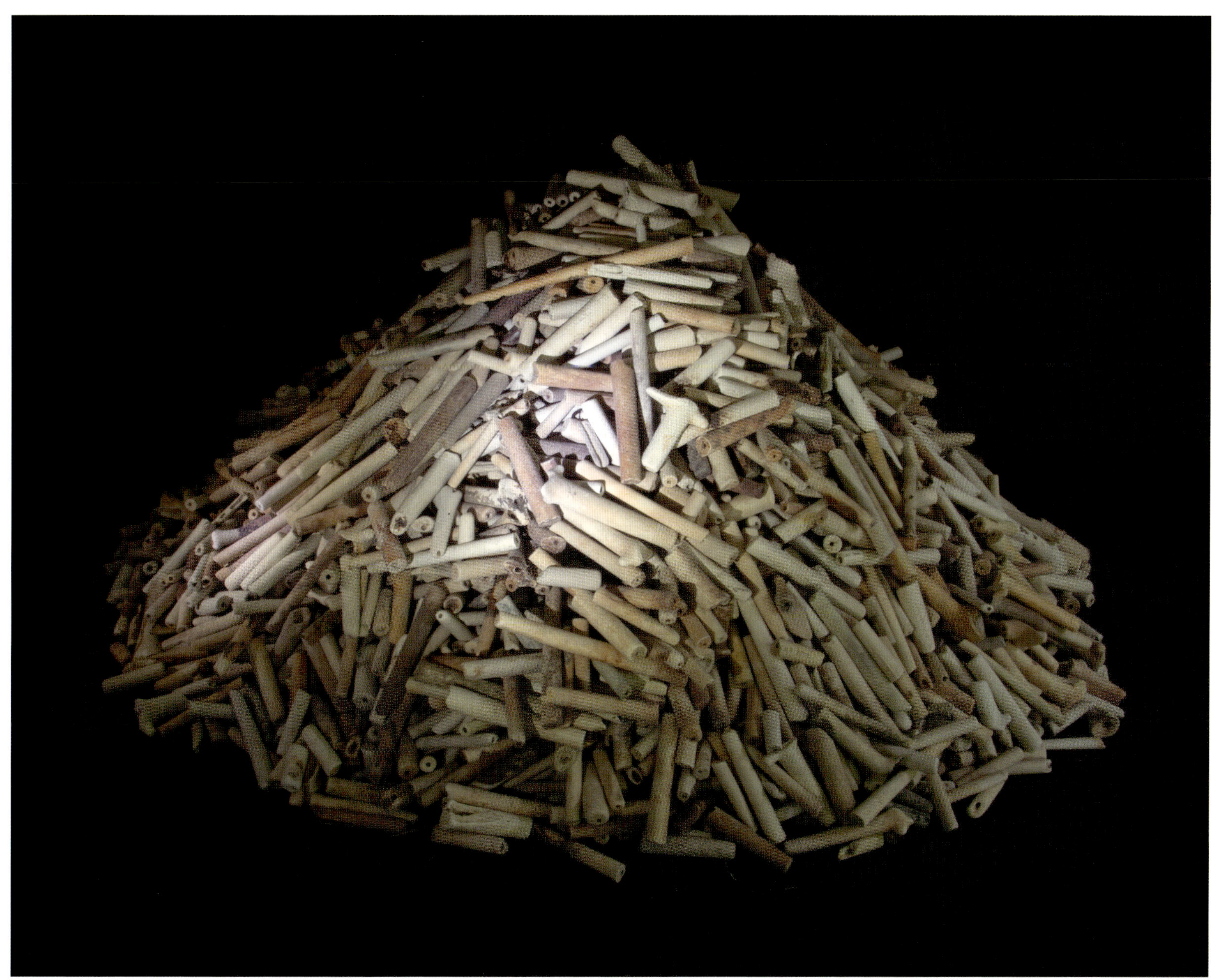

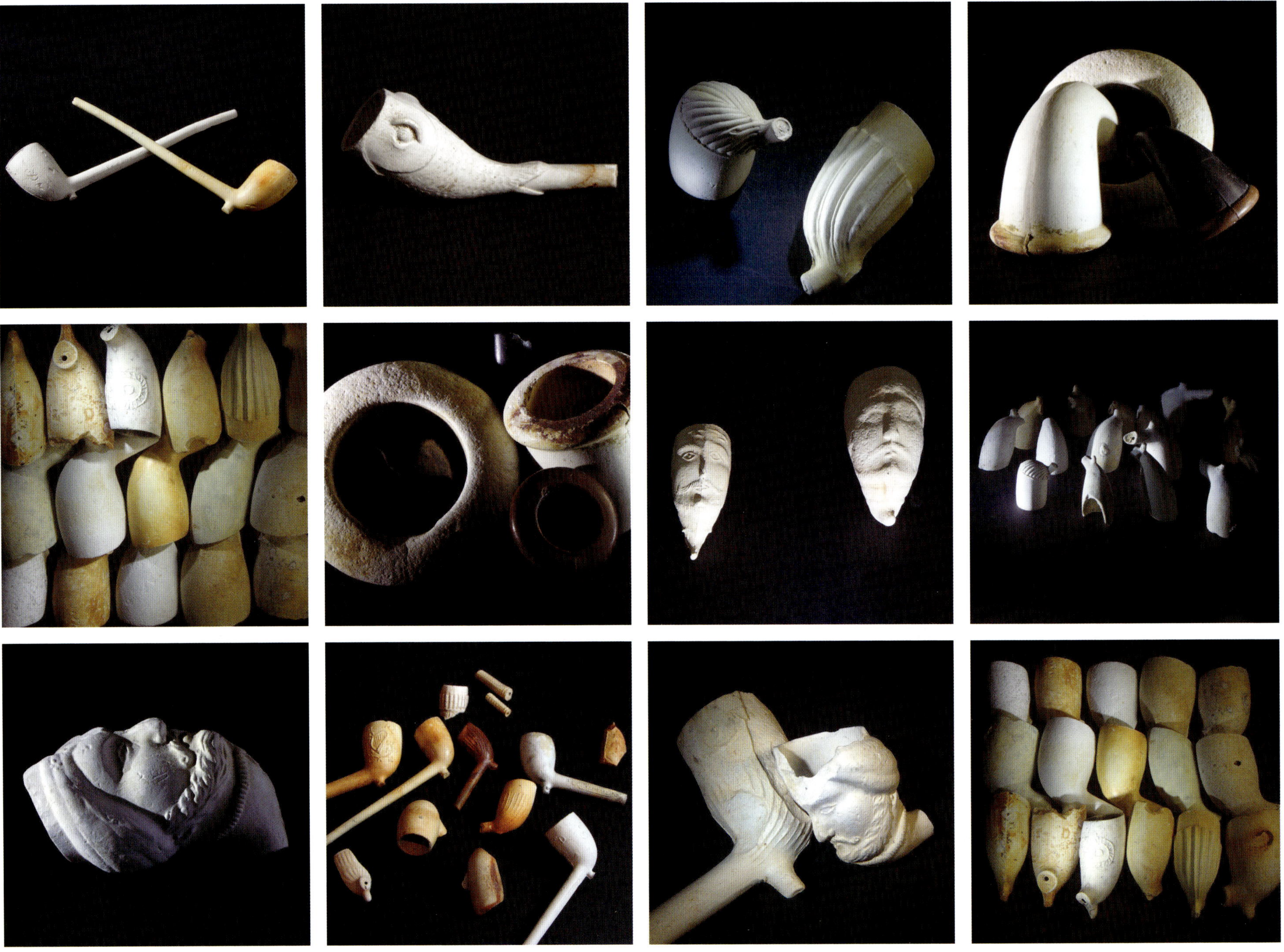

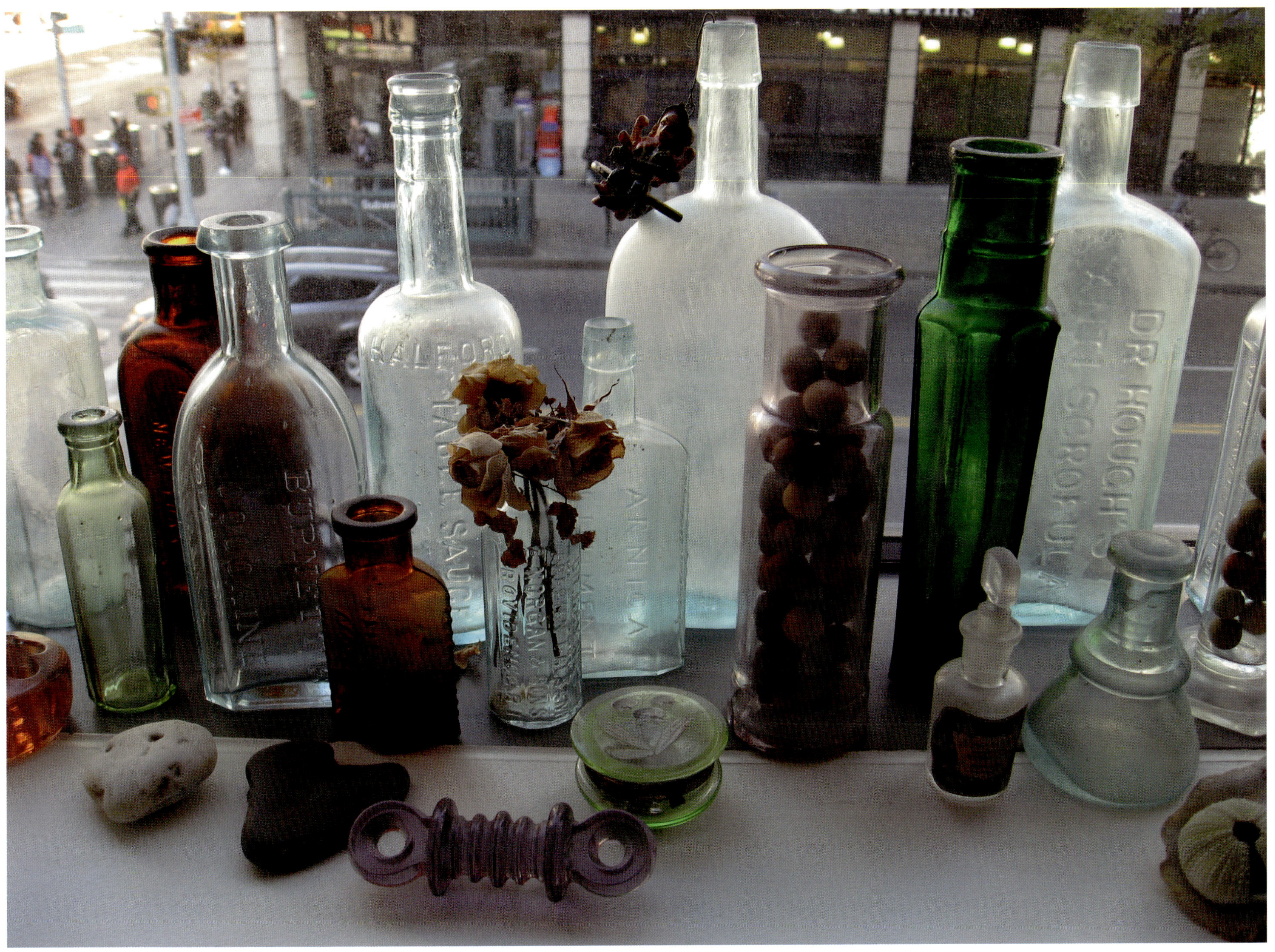
HALFORD
TABLE SAUCE
ARNICA
DR HOUGH
SCROFULA

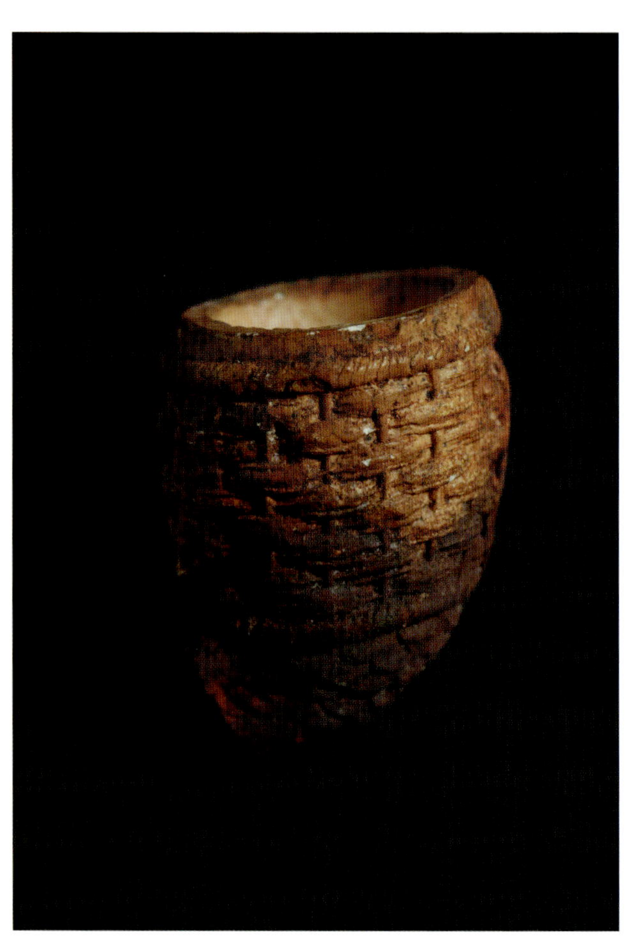

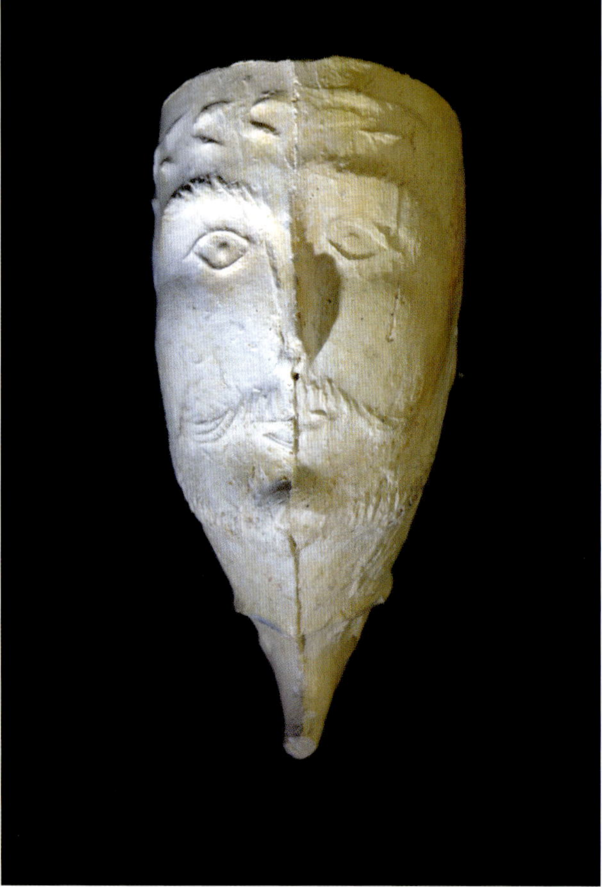

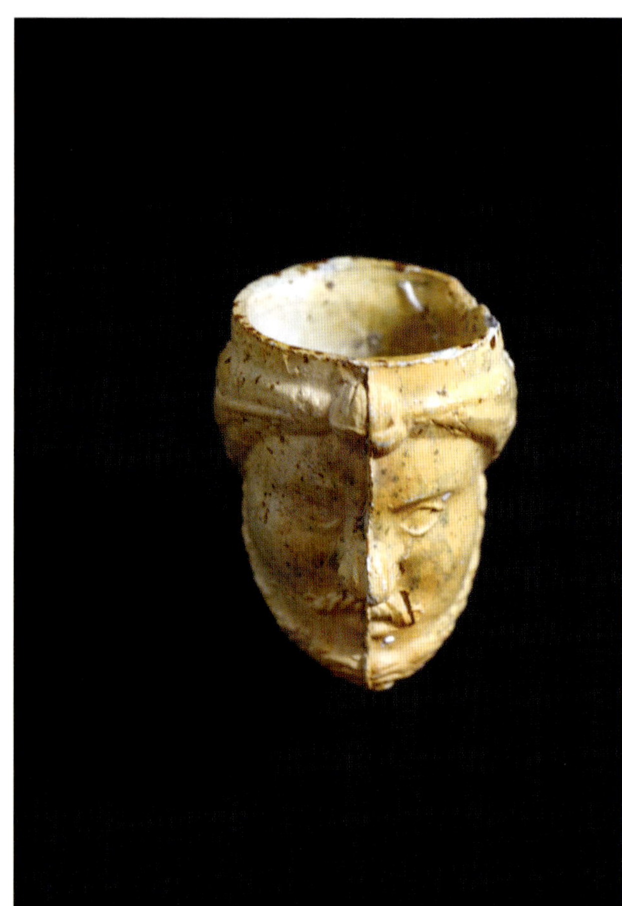

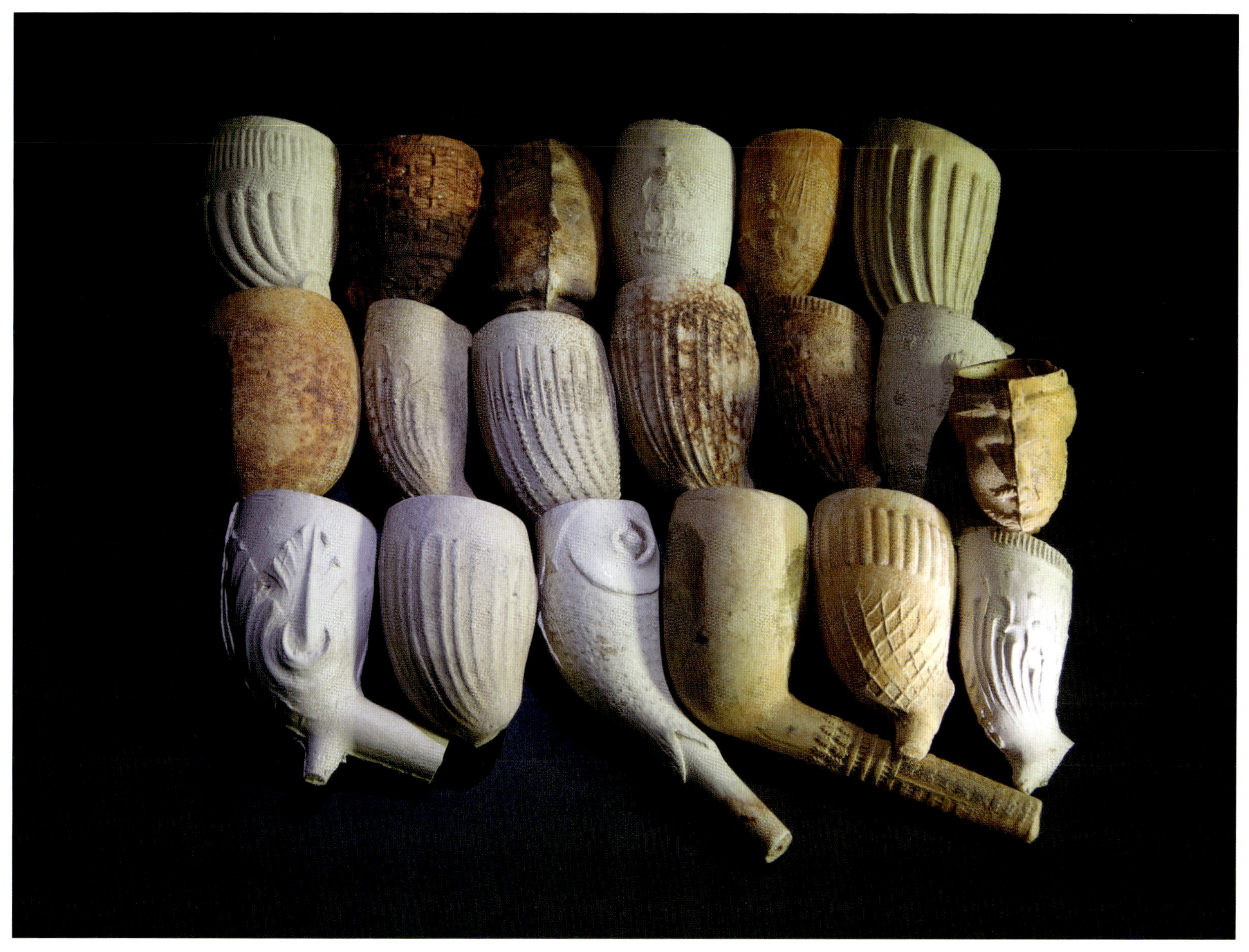

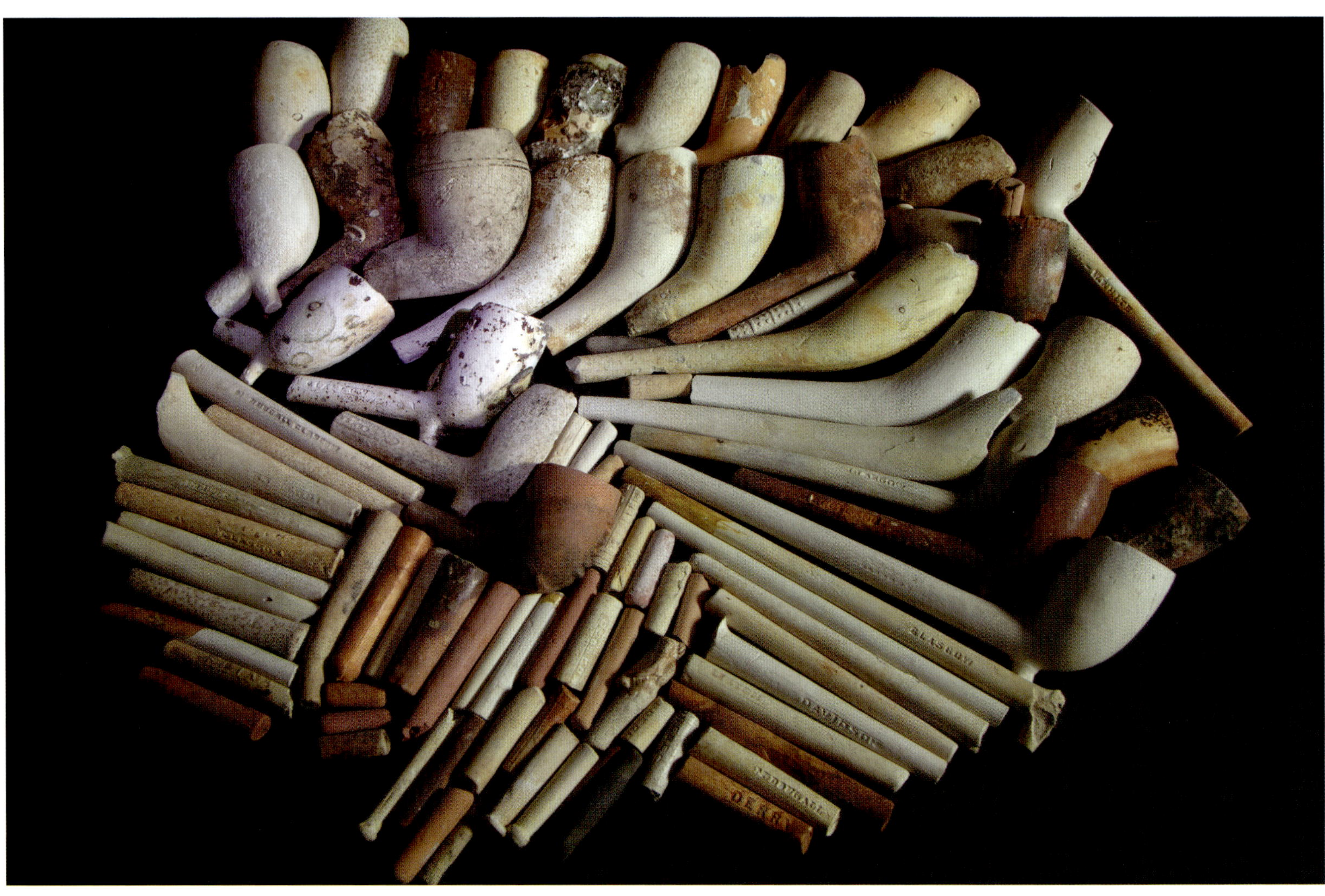
GLASGOW
DAVIDSON
DERRY

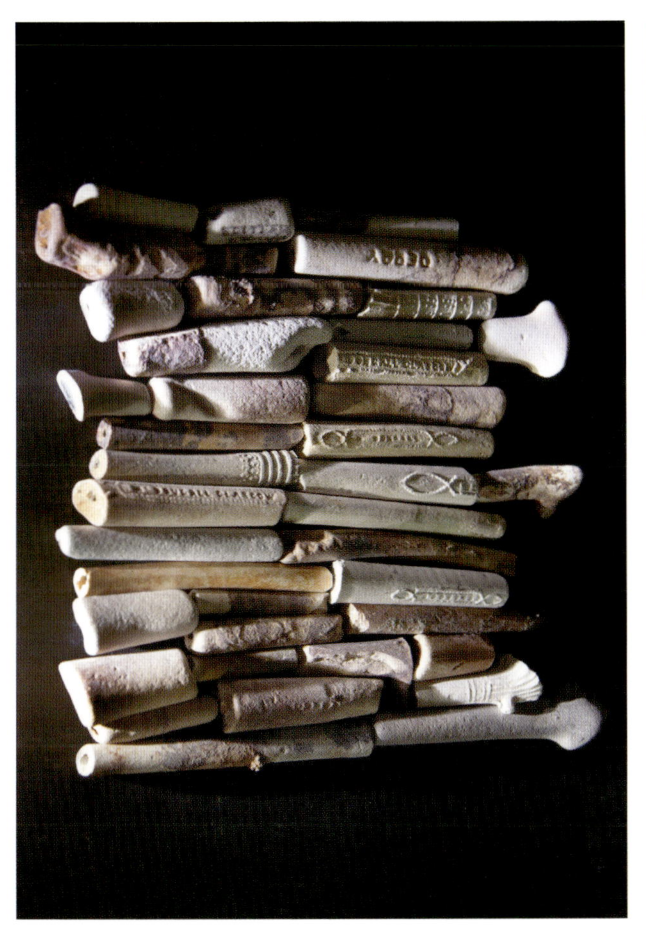

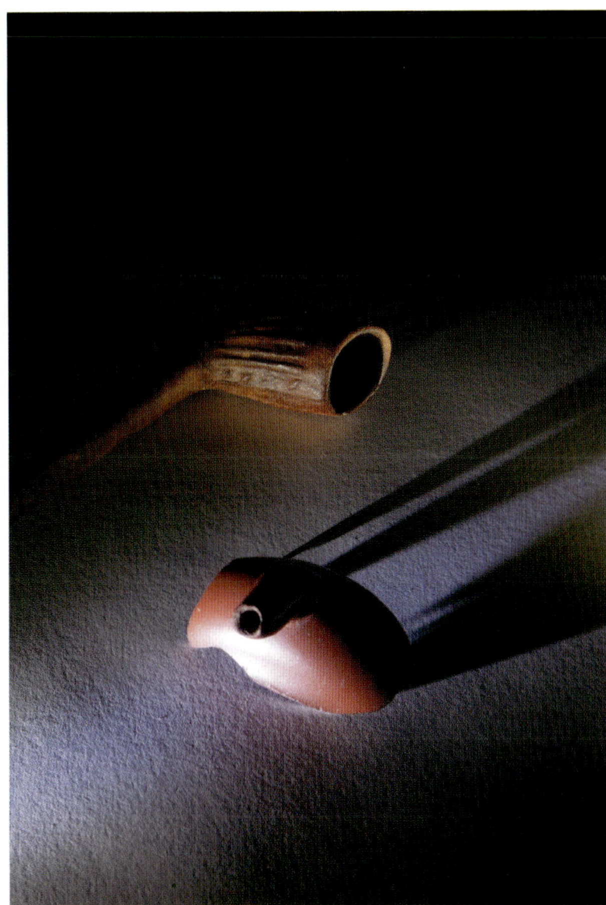

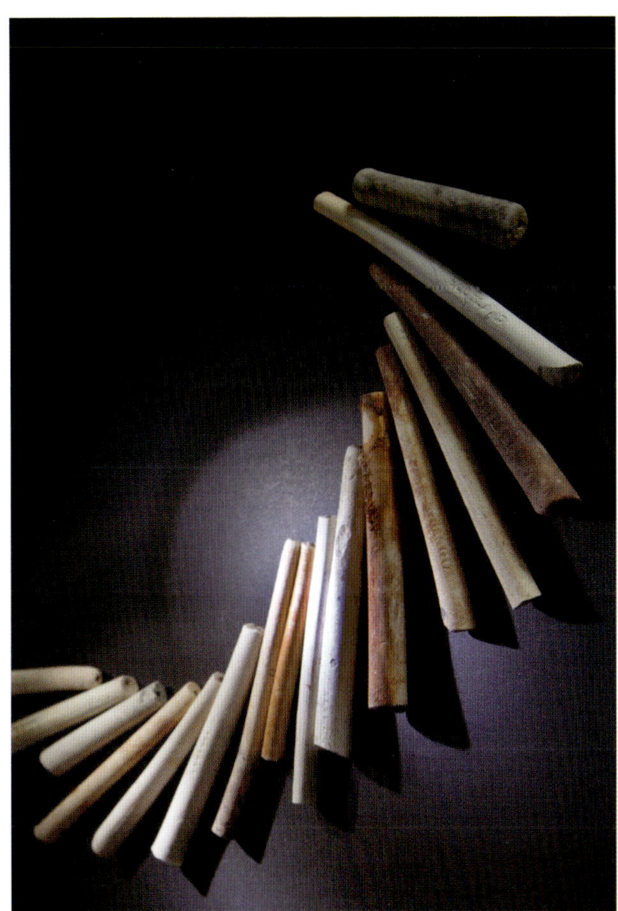

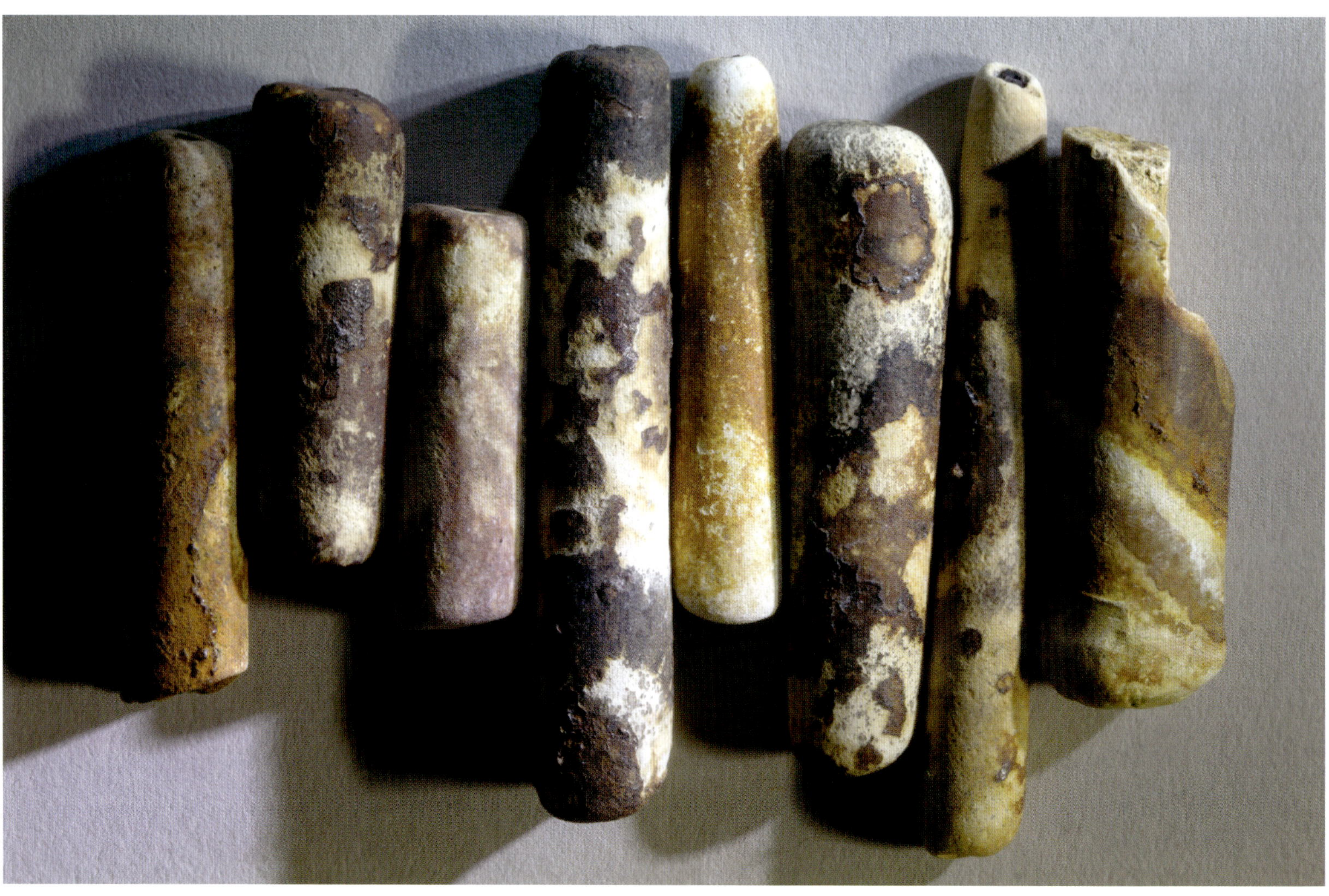

May 23, 2005

Hello Gail,

I'm writing to you from my kitchen table with my collected plates next to me. How are you doing? Summer is coming fast. My family is coming to the Cape, we are going to be there July 9–16. Has the Winter Season brought new treasures to the Surface? Have you found any new pieces of plates? I would like to go plating with me? See You Soon. I drew a picture for you on the back. Oh yeah Gail I got a new puppy named Lexie she is a German Shorthair Pointer.

Sincerelly Alex Frechette

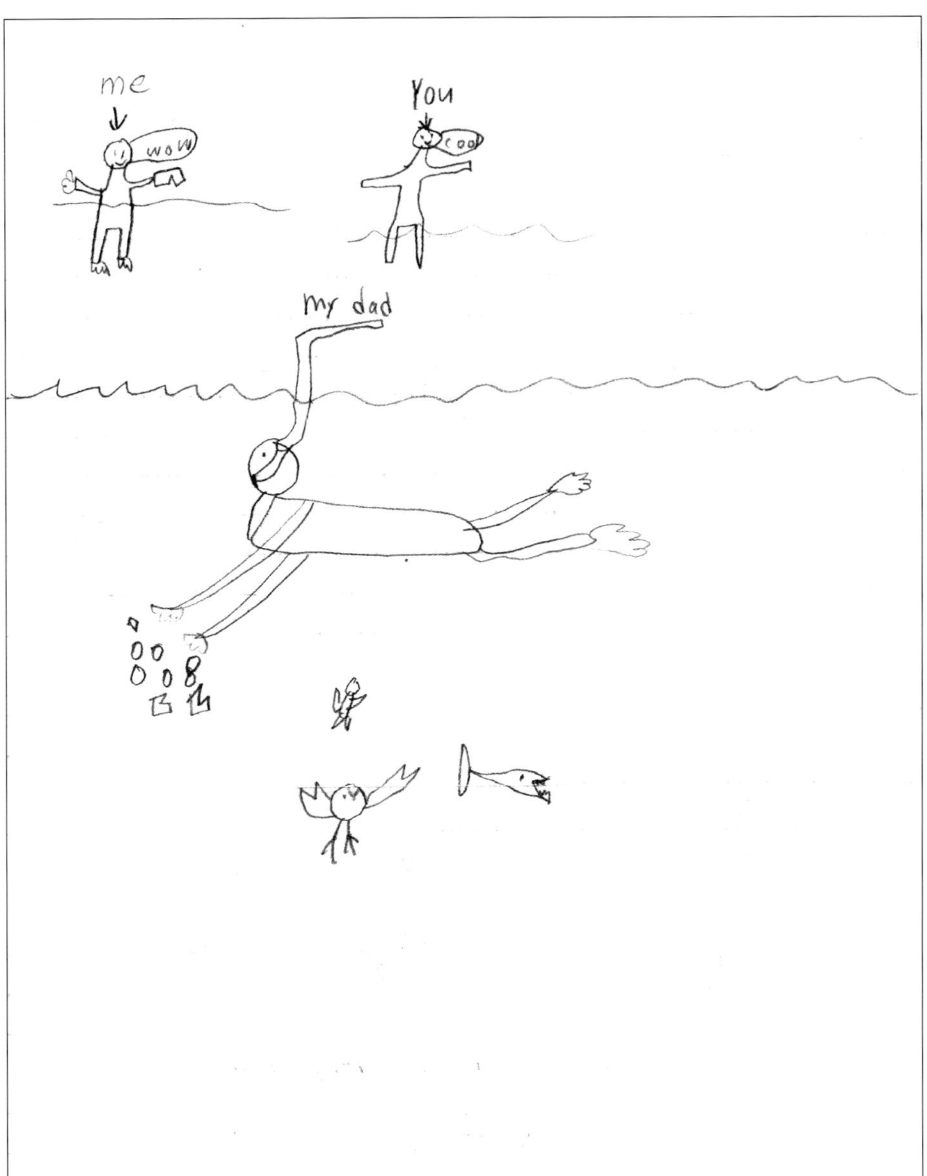

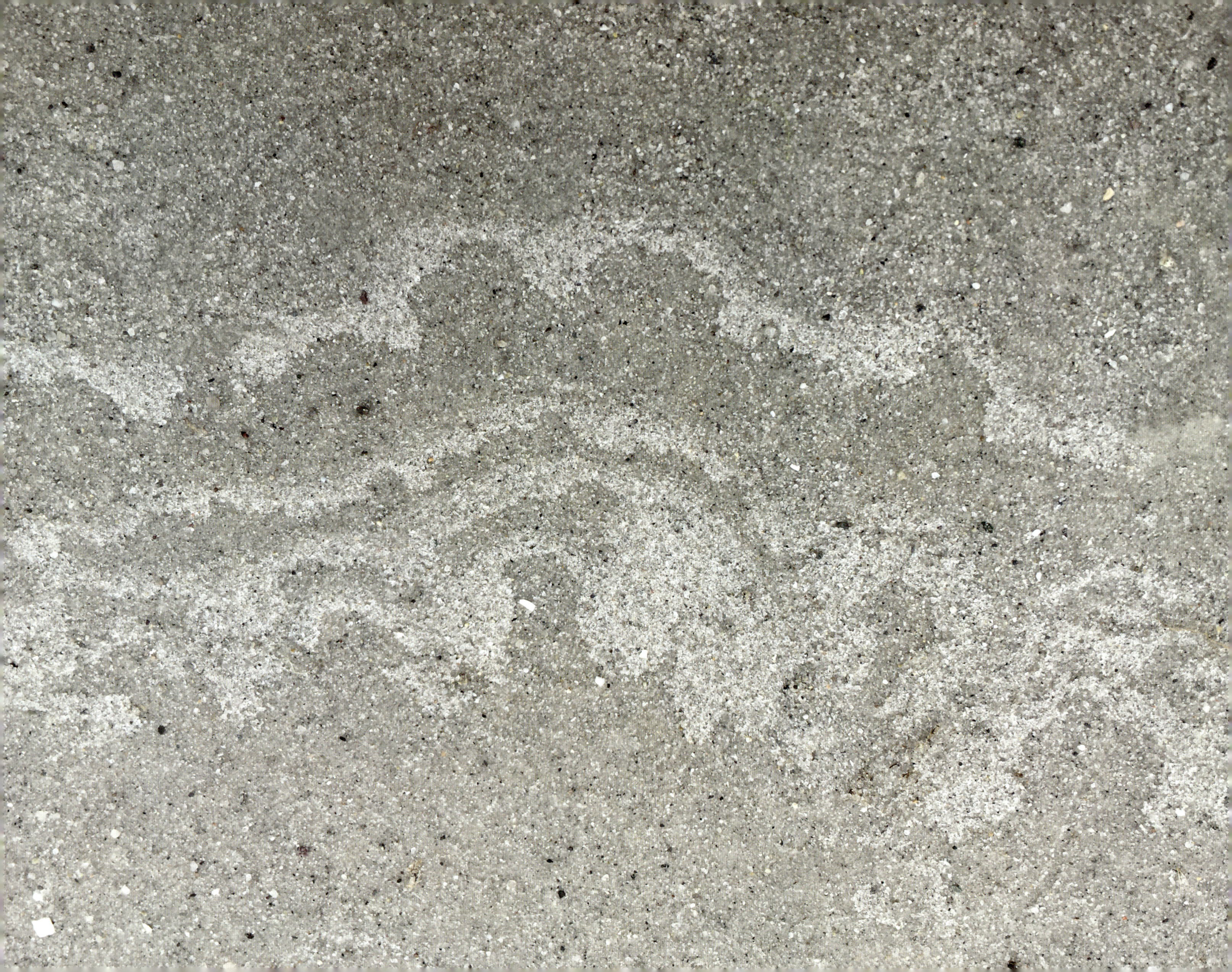

Toys

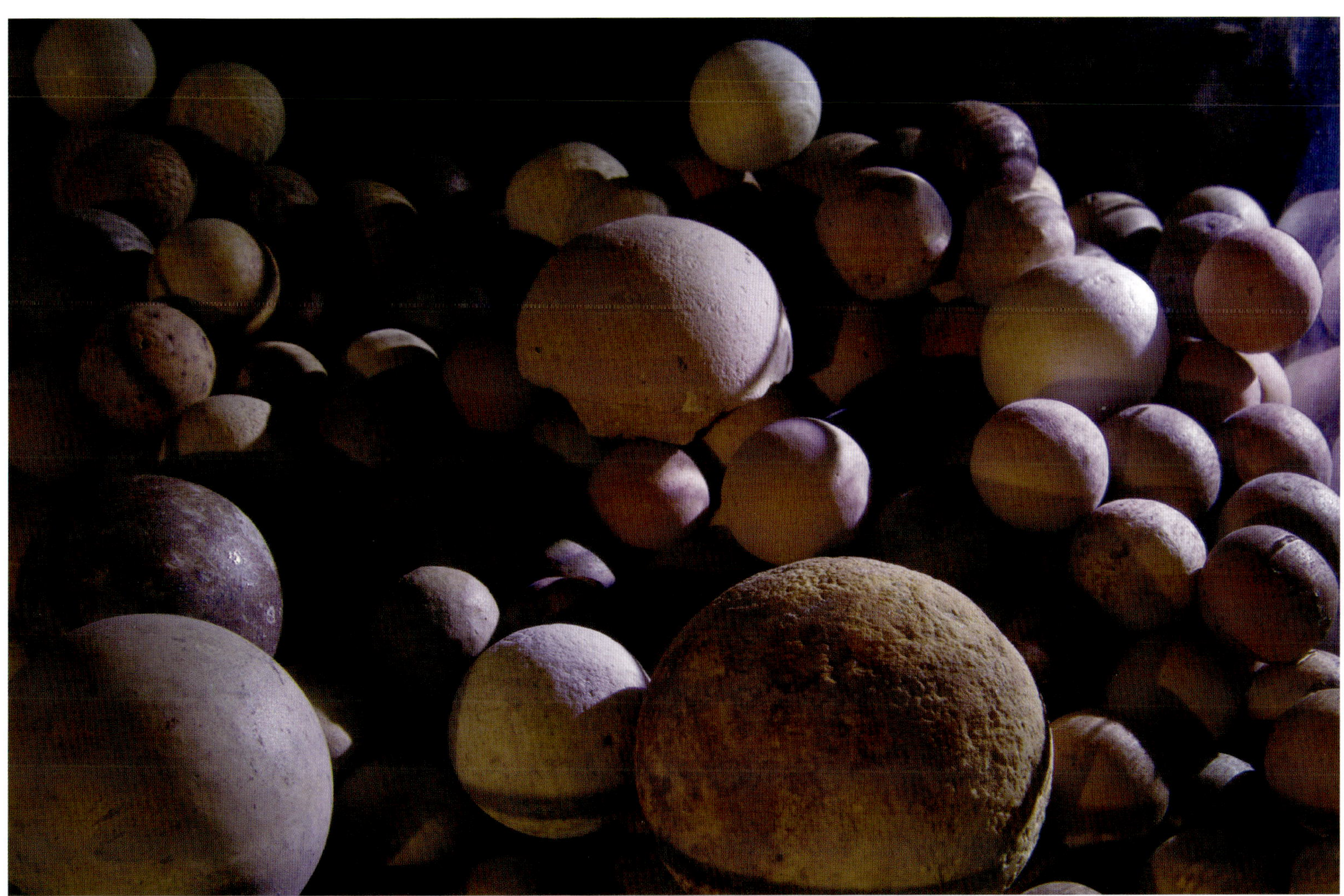

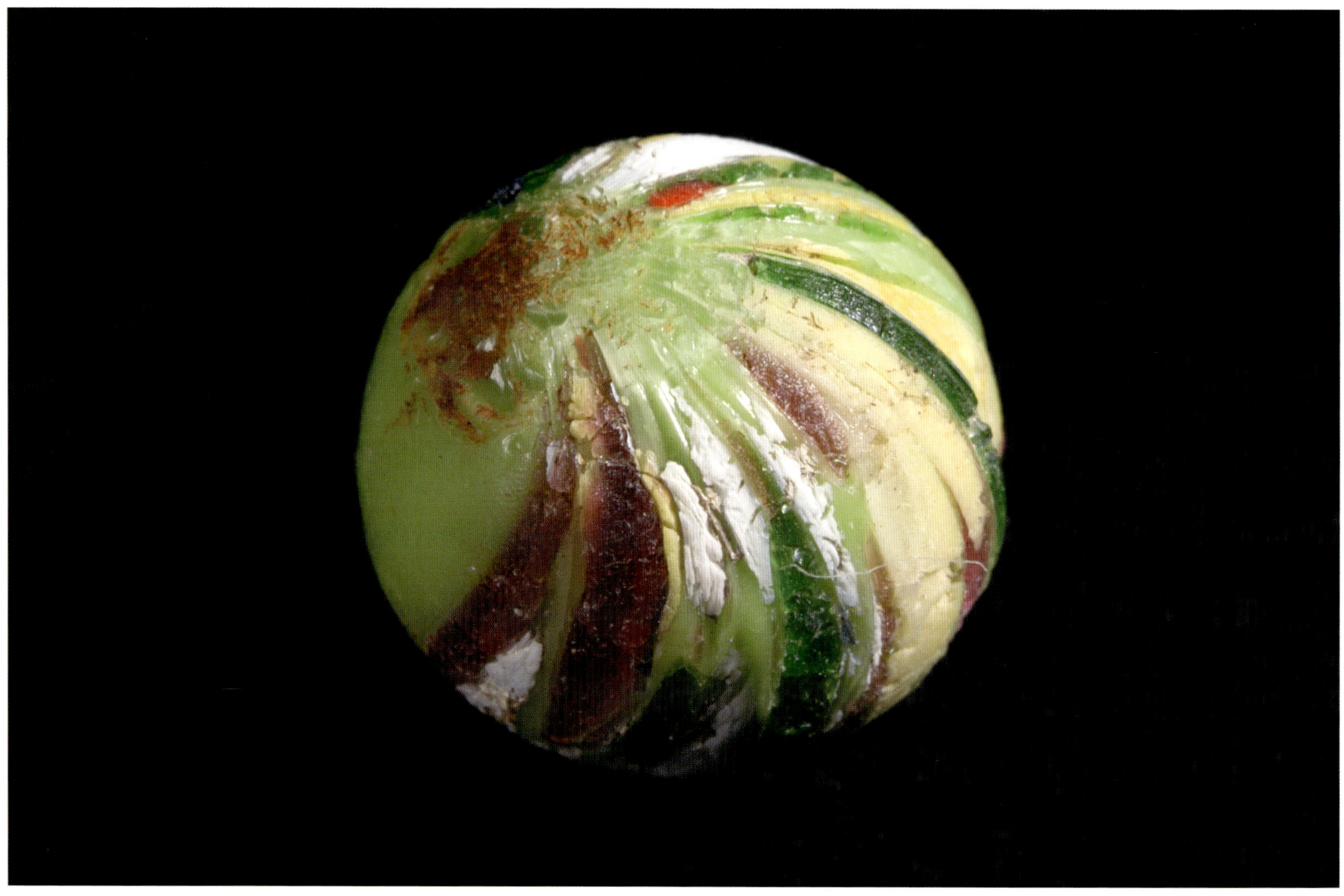

"There was a man who lived around Cook Street, and he had everything just so. He had a nice small boat he was heading out to, and he came up to me and asked if I was looking for food. And I said no. He said, 'What are you looking for?' I said, 'To find old things like clay pipes and bottles, but they are really hard to find.' And he looks down and finds a marble between his two feet and says, 'Like this?'"

—Betty Bodian

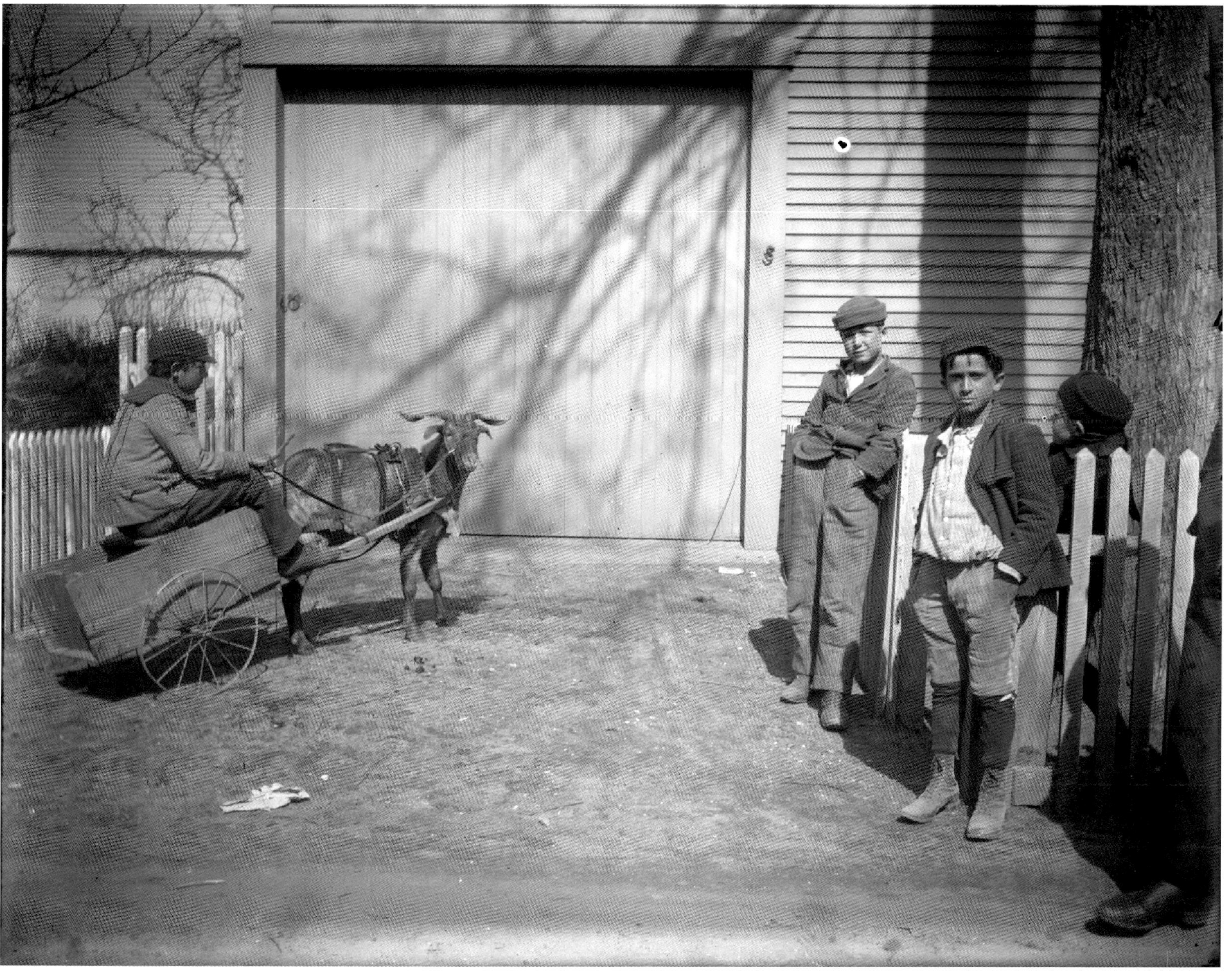

Before the twentieth century, children had few toys; many were roughly the size of a quarter and made of ceramic. Finds include pieces such as dogs, cats, horses, baby dolls, tea sets, soldiers, and, of course, marbles. Limited resources encouraged children to be creative with everyday objects and natural resources.

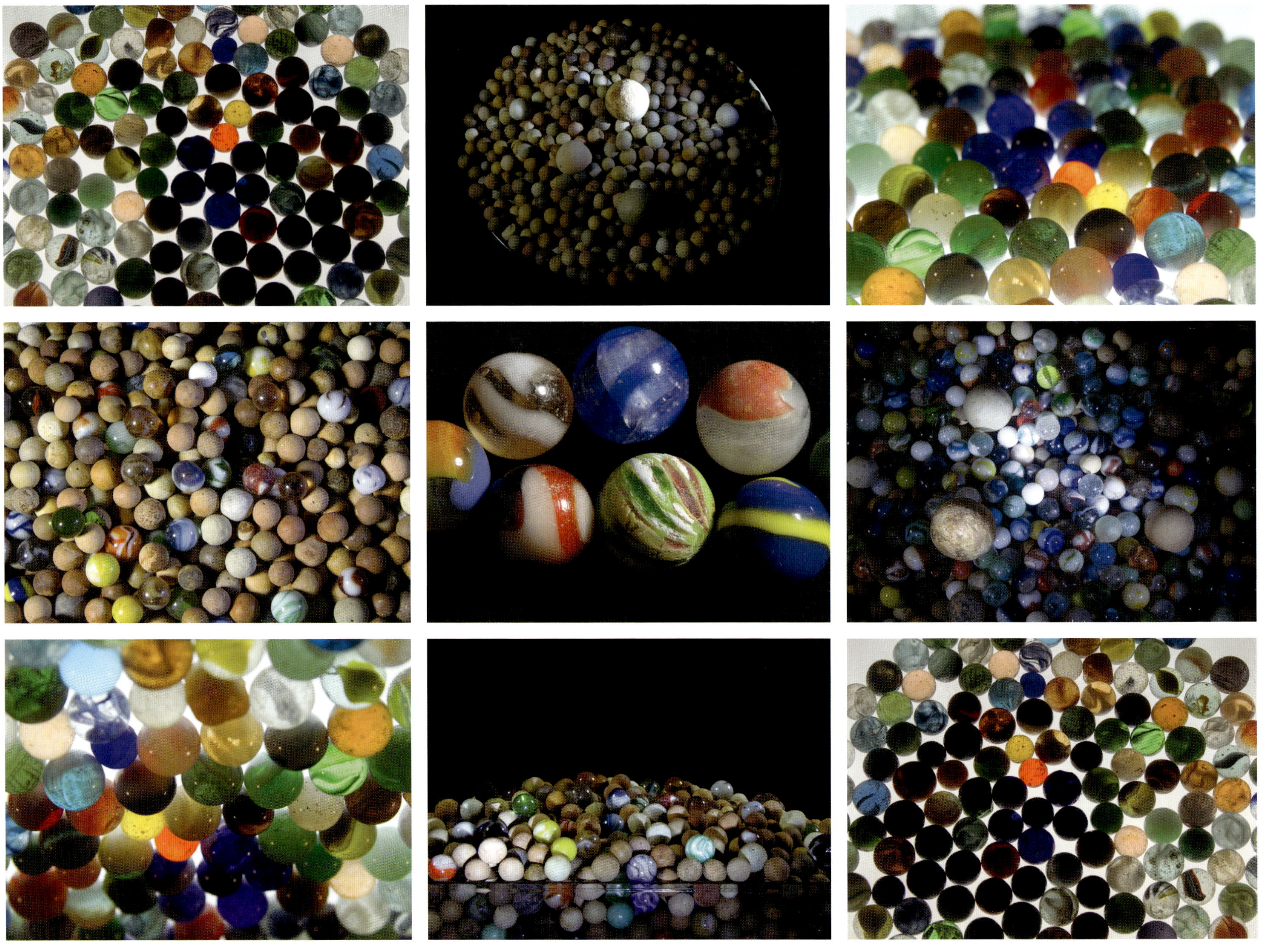

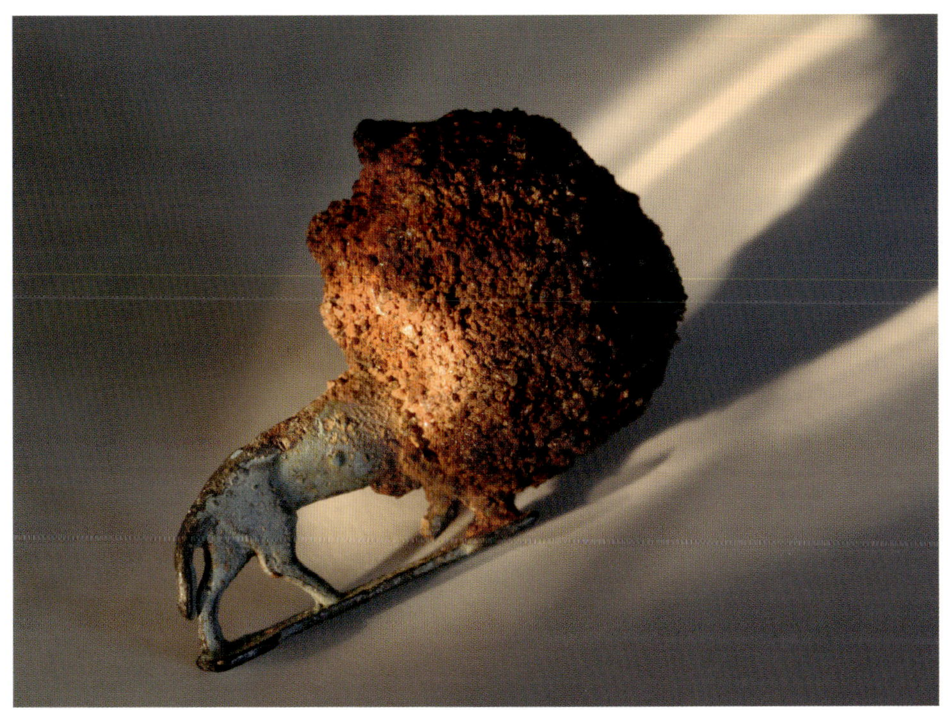

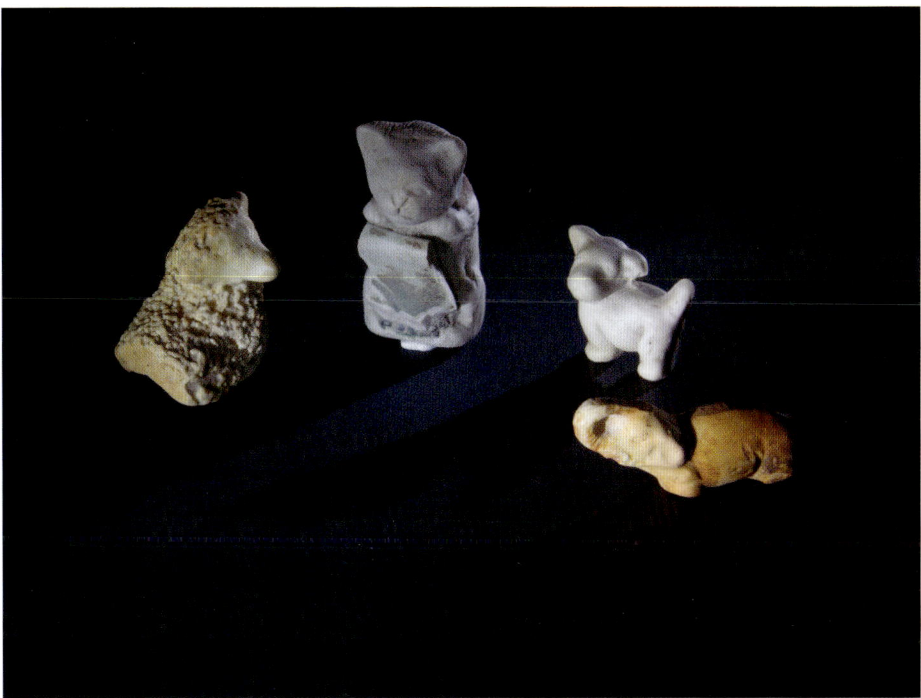

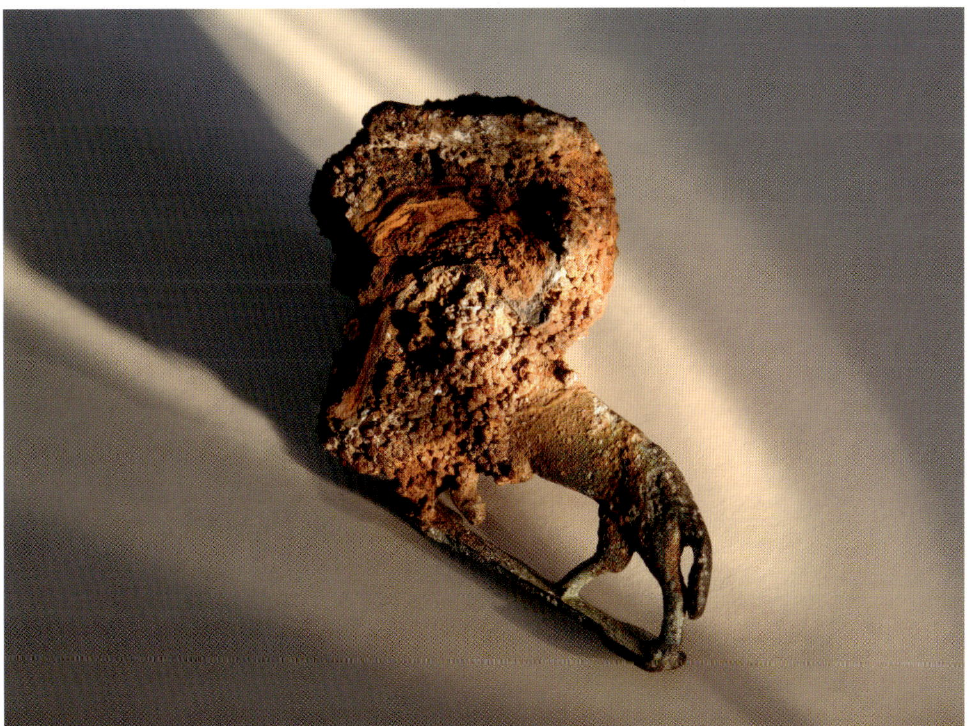

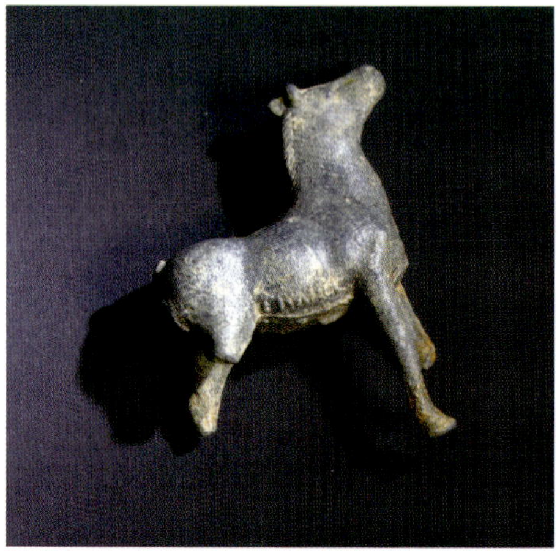

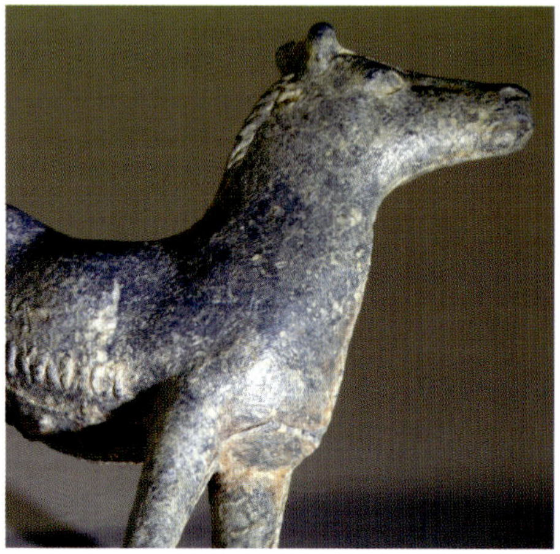

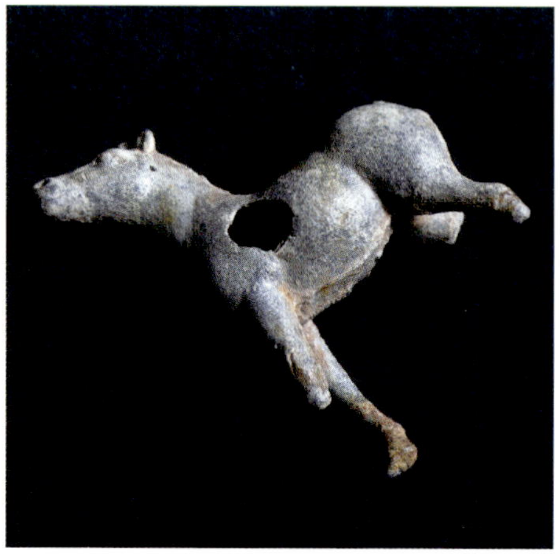

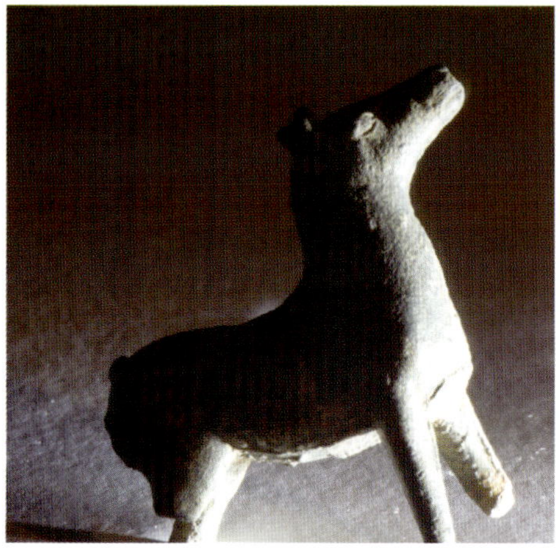

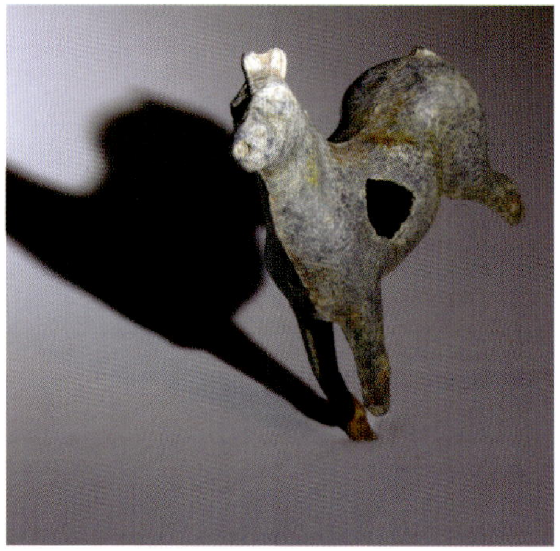

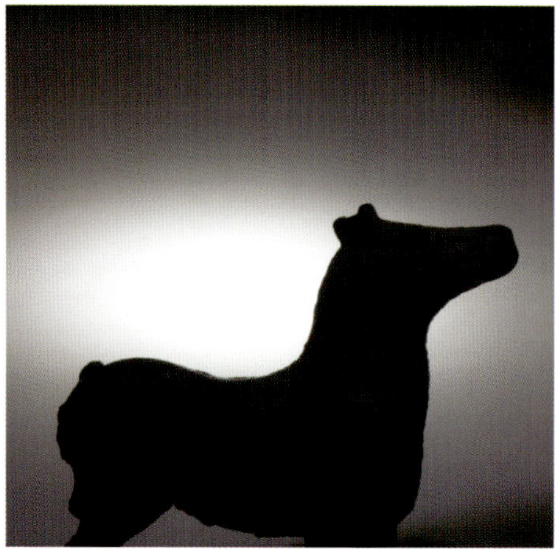

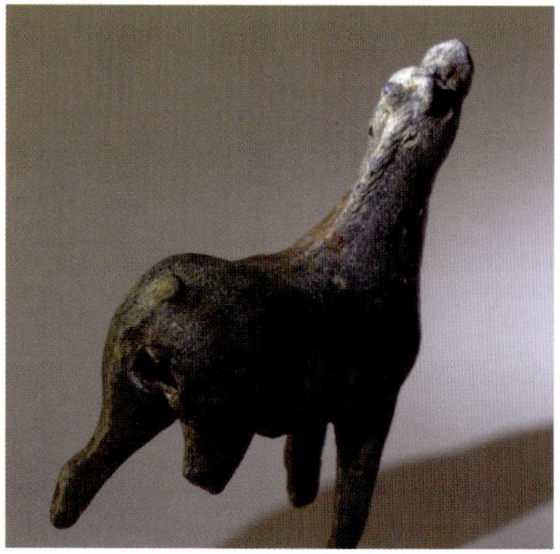

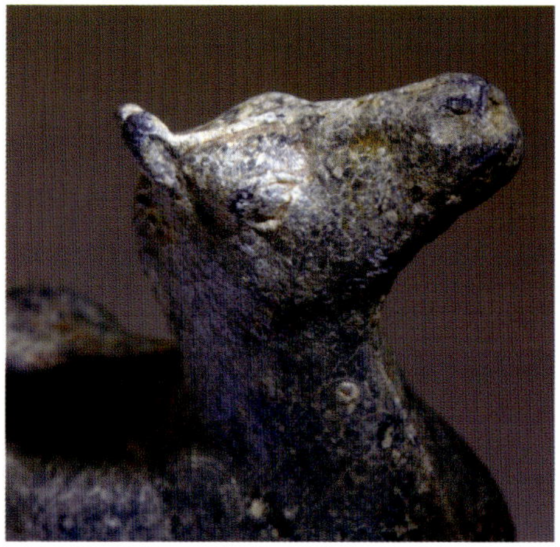

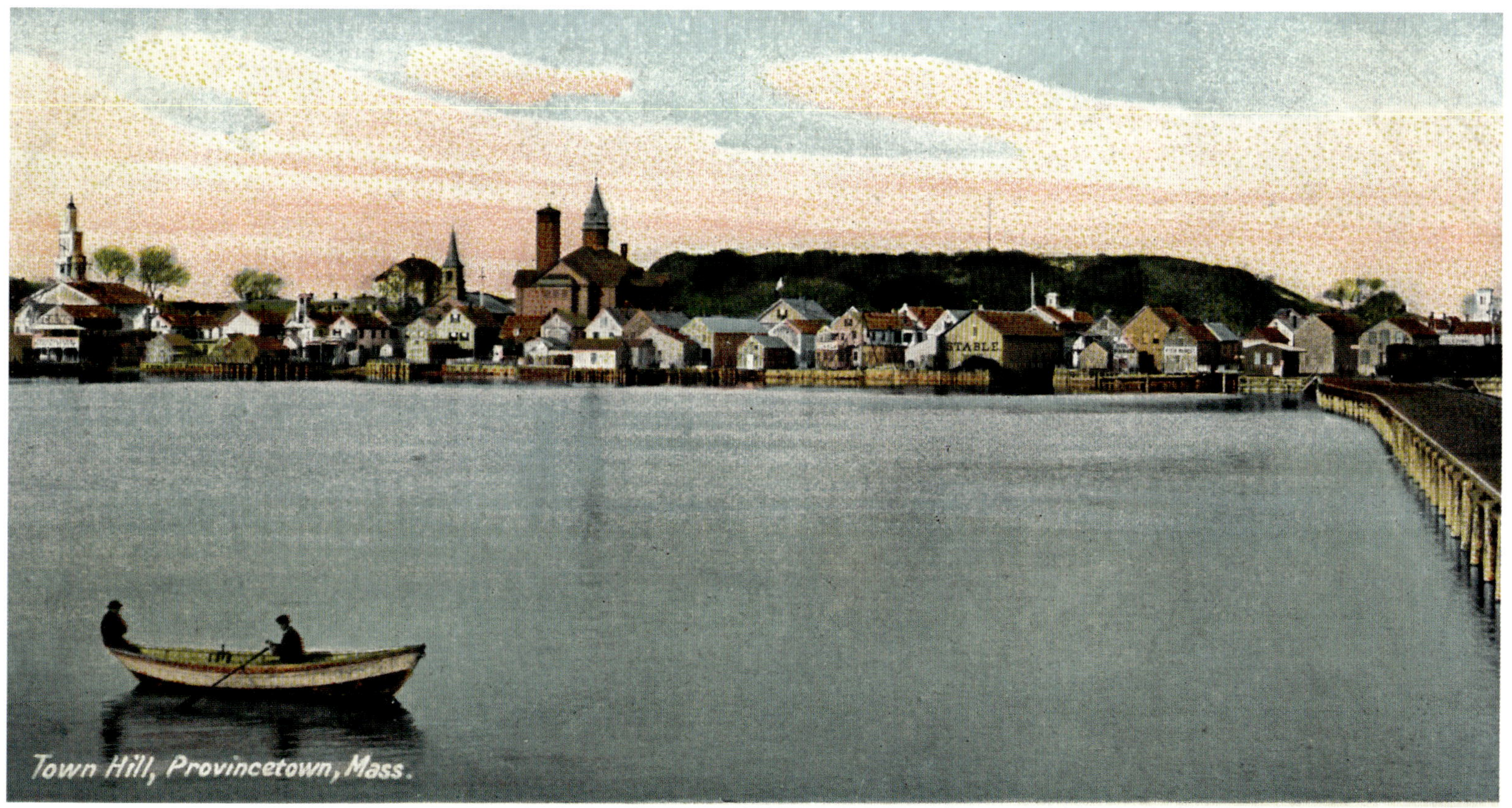

Town Hill, Provincetown, Mass.

"I was out wading in some of those holes and eel grass bends, which are a little bit scary, but on the other hand, you do find good stuff," Paul Bowen says. "I always think that some massive eel is going to come out and bite my leg off. I put my foot on something rectangular and I ducked down in the water, and there was a digital camera. I was able to find the switch that penned up the card slot and the card popped right out! It was perfectly dry." With a little research, Paul and his wife found the owners. You could say it was a twenty-first-century message in a bottle.

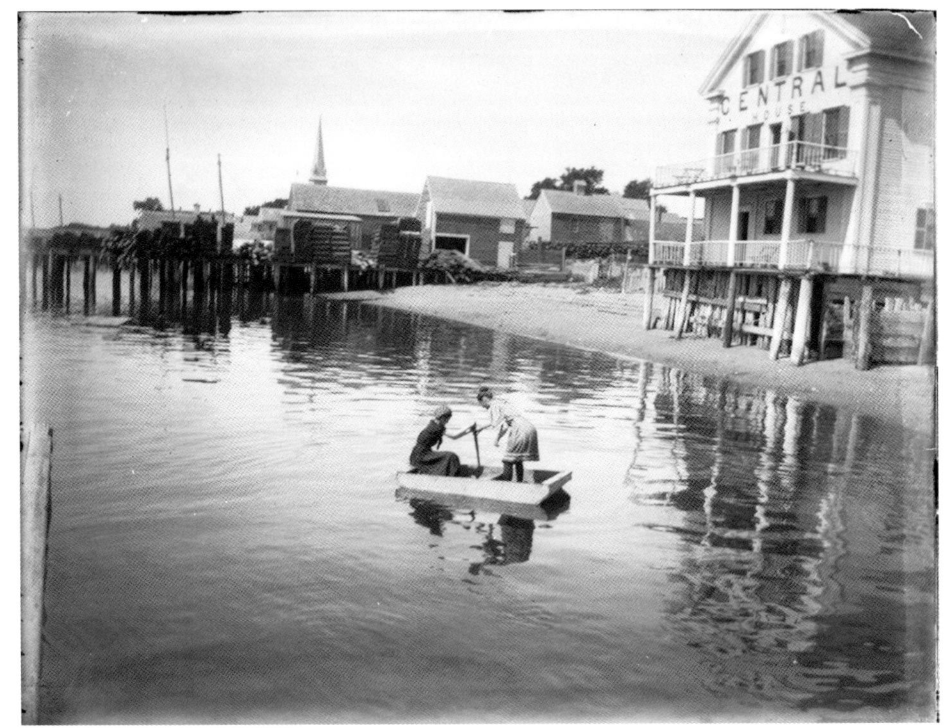

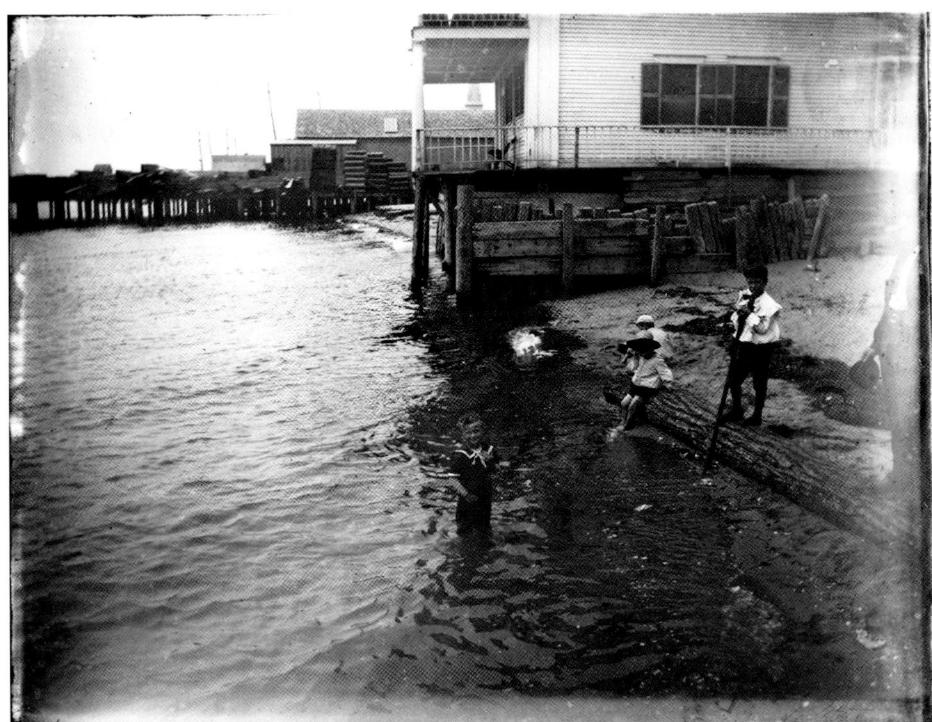

As the waterfront industry was developing, people living on the harbor did not prioritize the water view because of the sewage and the practice of dumping trash and burying dead animals there. Water views weren't valued until the 1930s, when the establishment of a legitimate town dump put an end to these practices.

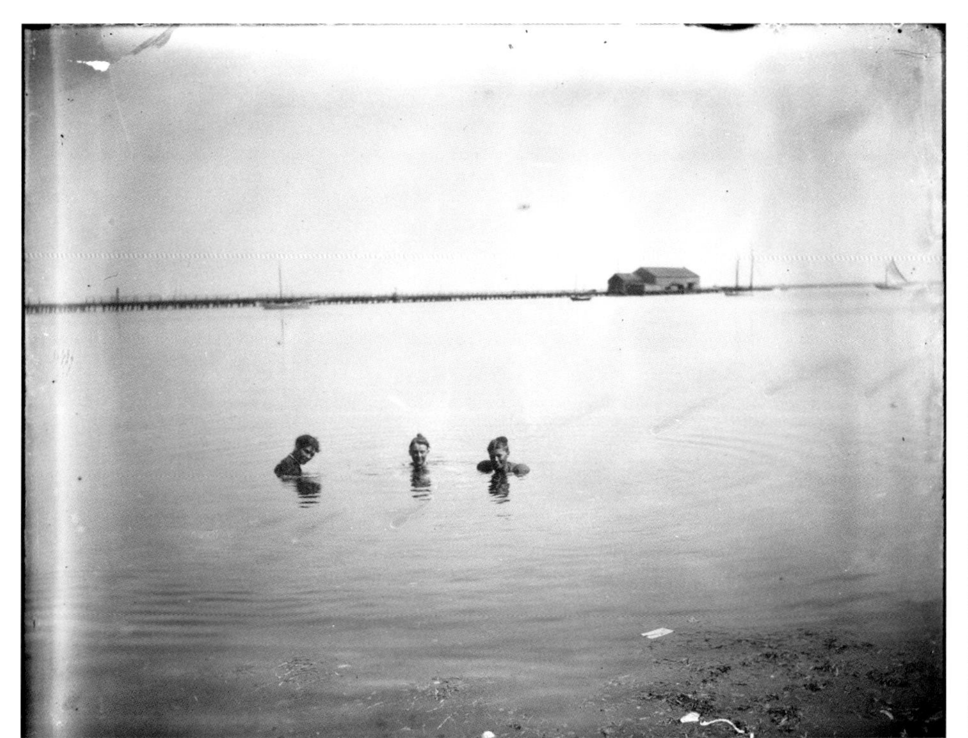

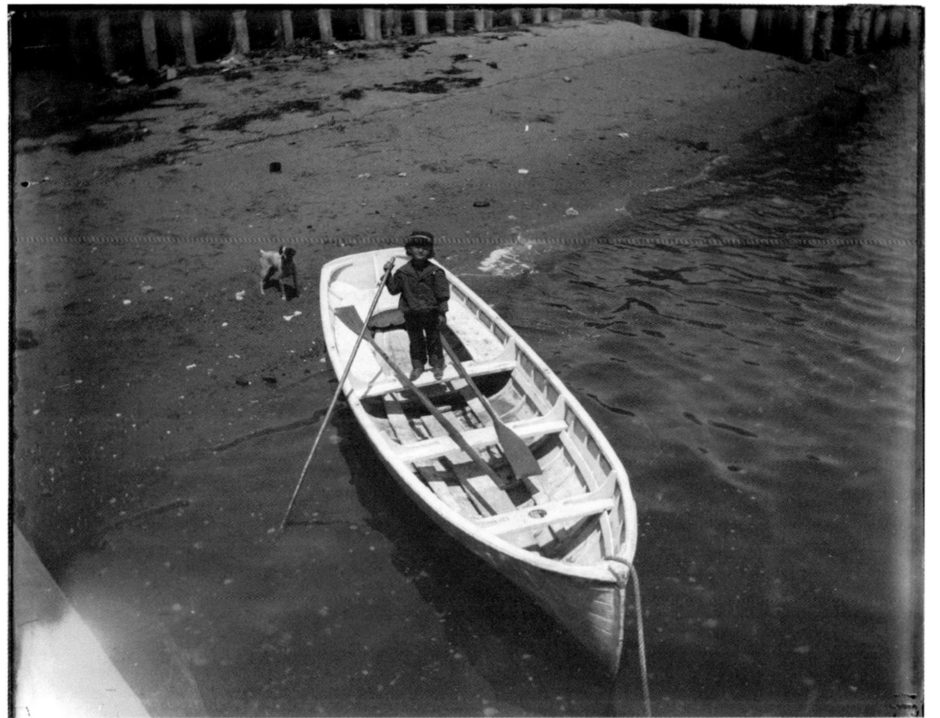

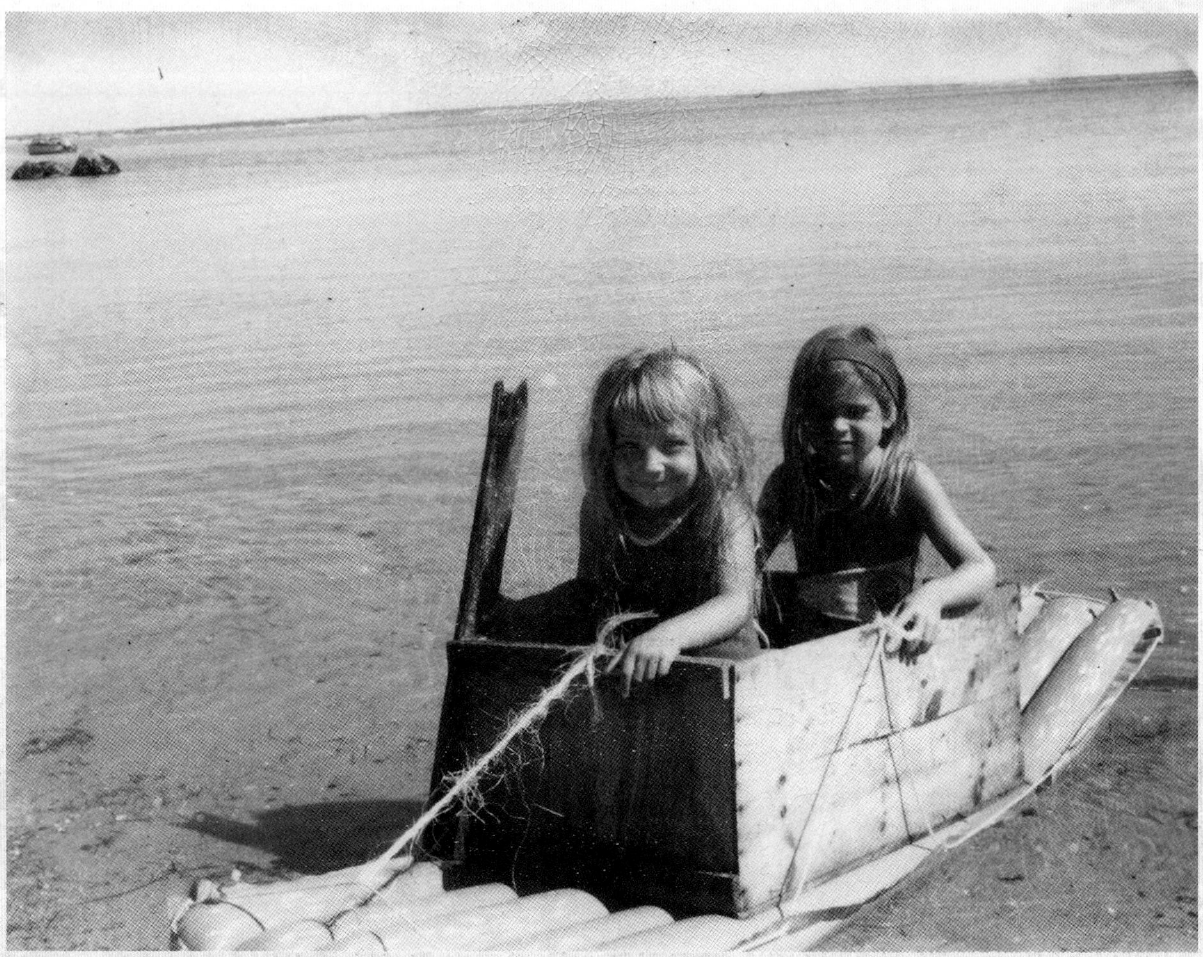

Five-year-old Amy Heller *(left)* gives her friend a ride in her handmade boat on the East End of Provincetown.

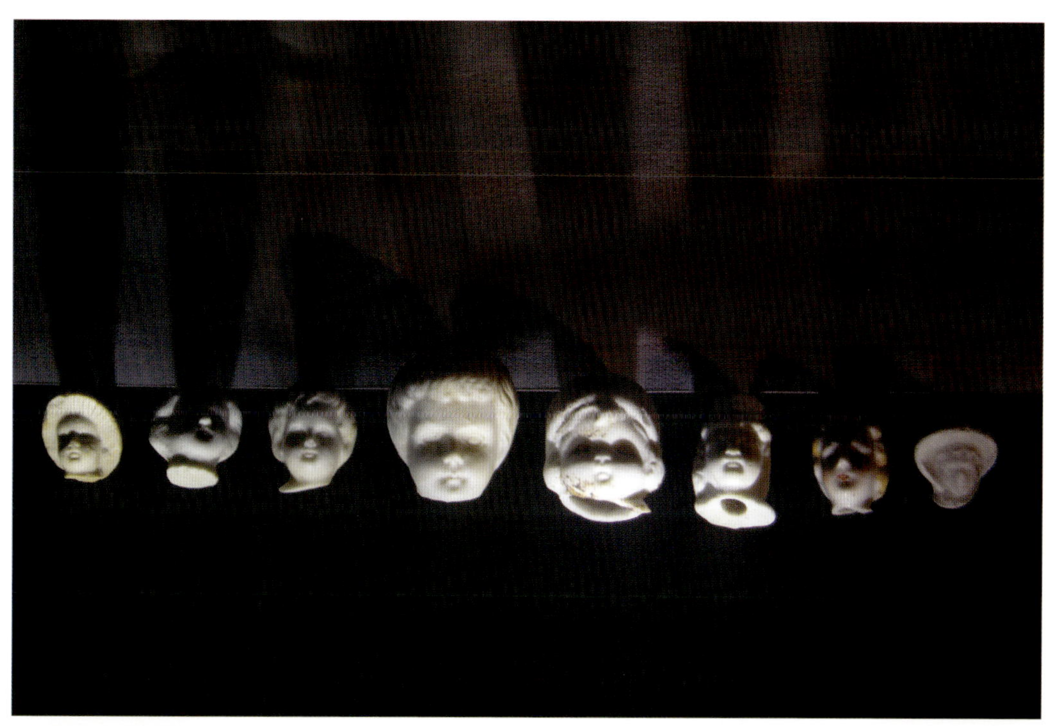

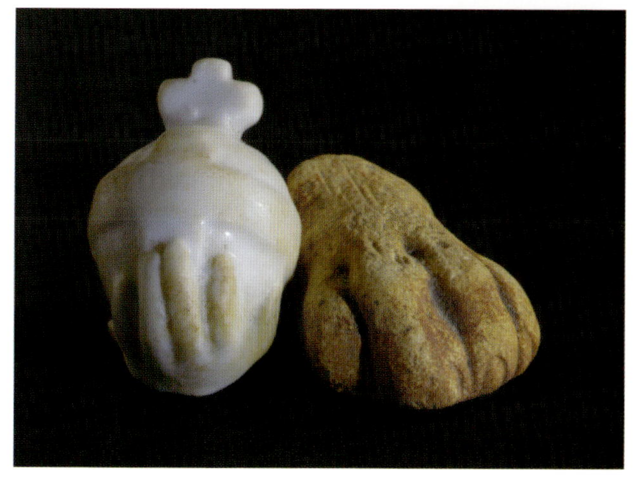

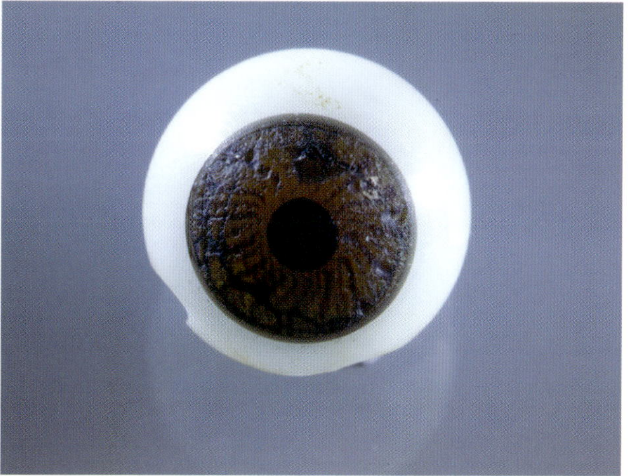

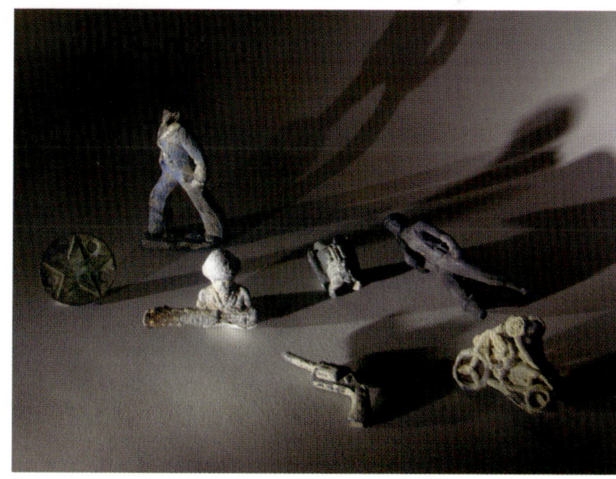

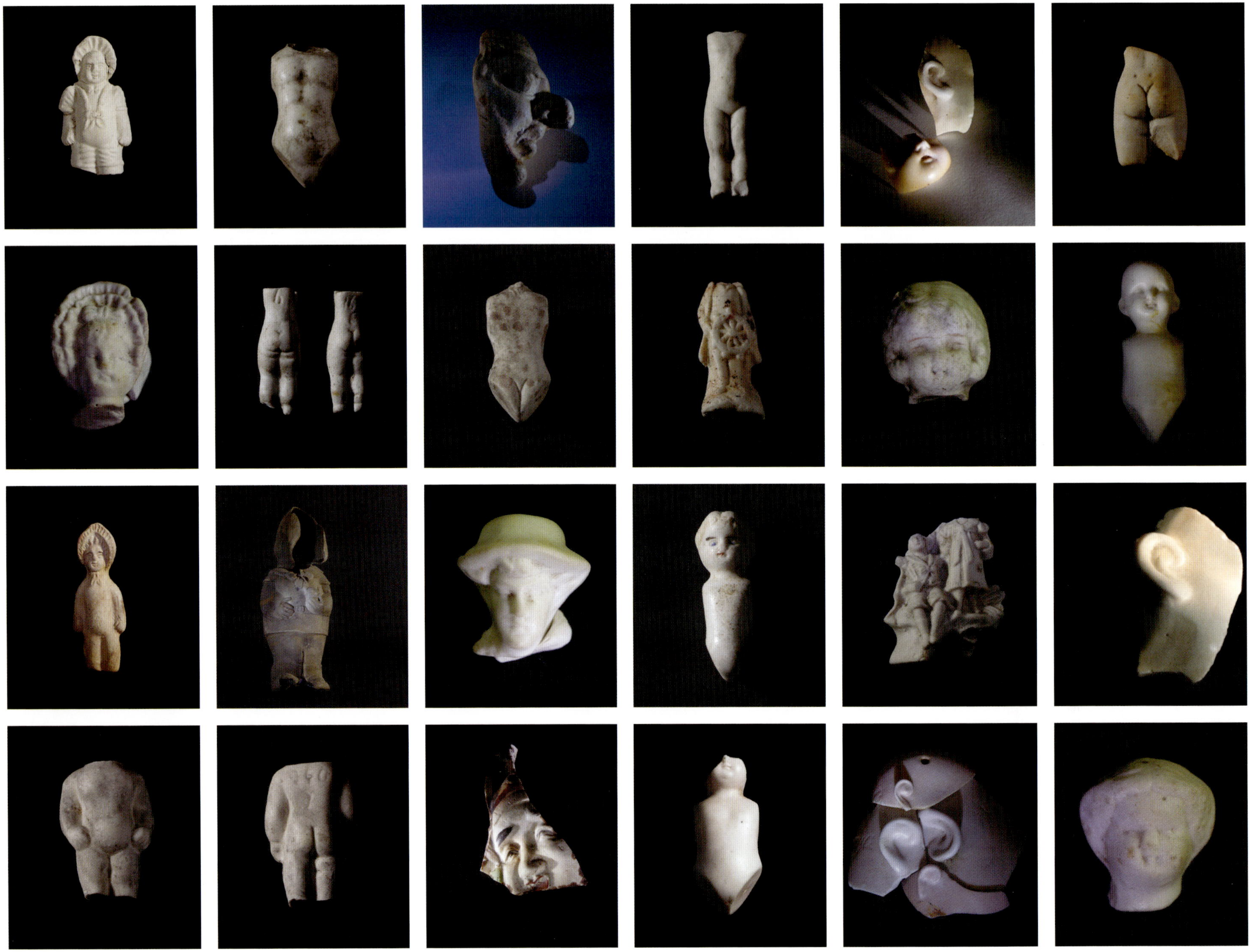

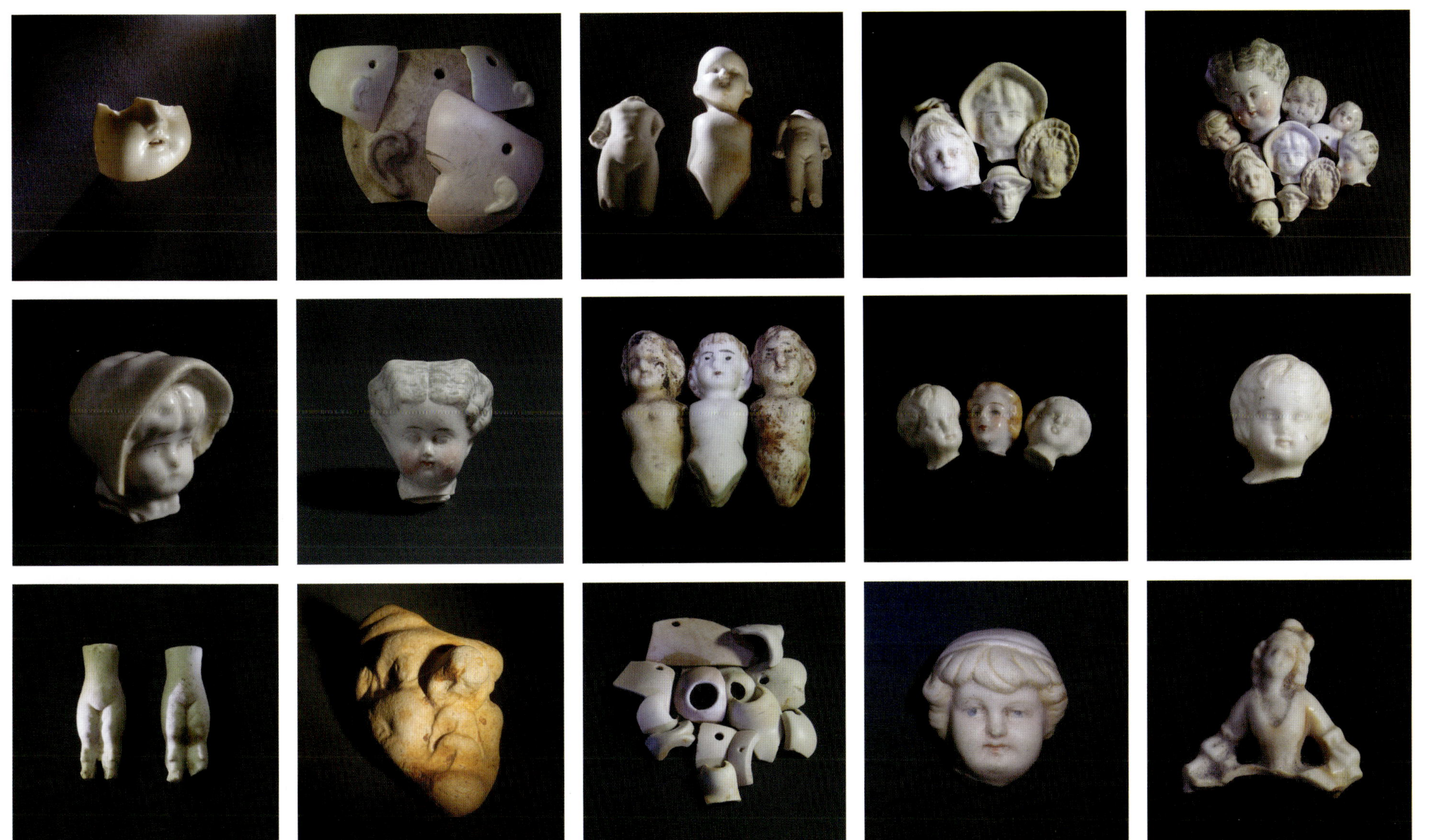

Many years ago, a five-year-old girl explained to me her theory on the abundance of ceramic dollies on the beach: "Once upon a time a little girl got very mad at her mother, so she packed up all of her dollies in a paper bag and ran away from home to the beach. She didn't know there was a hole in the bag. The end."

—Gail Browne

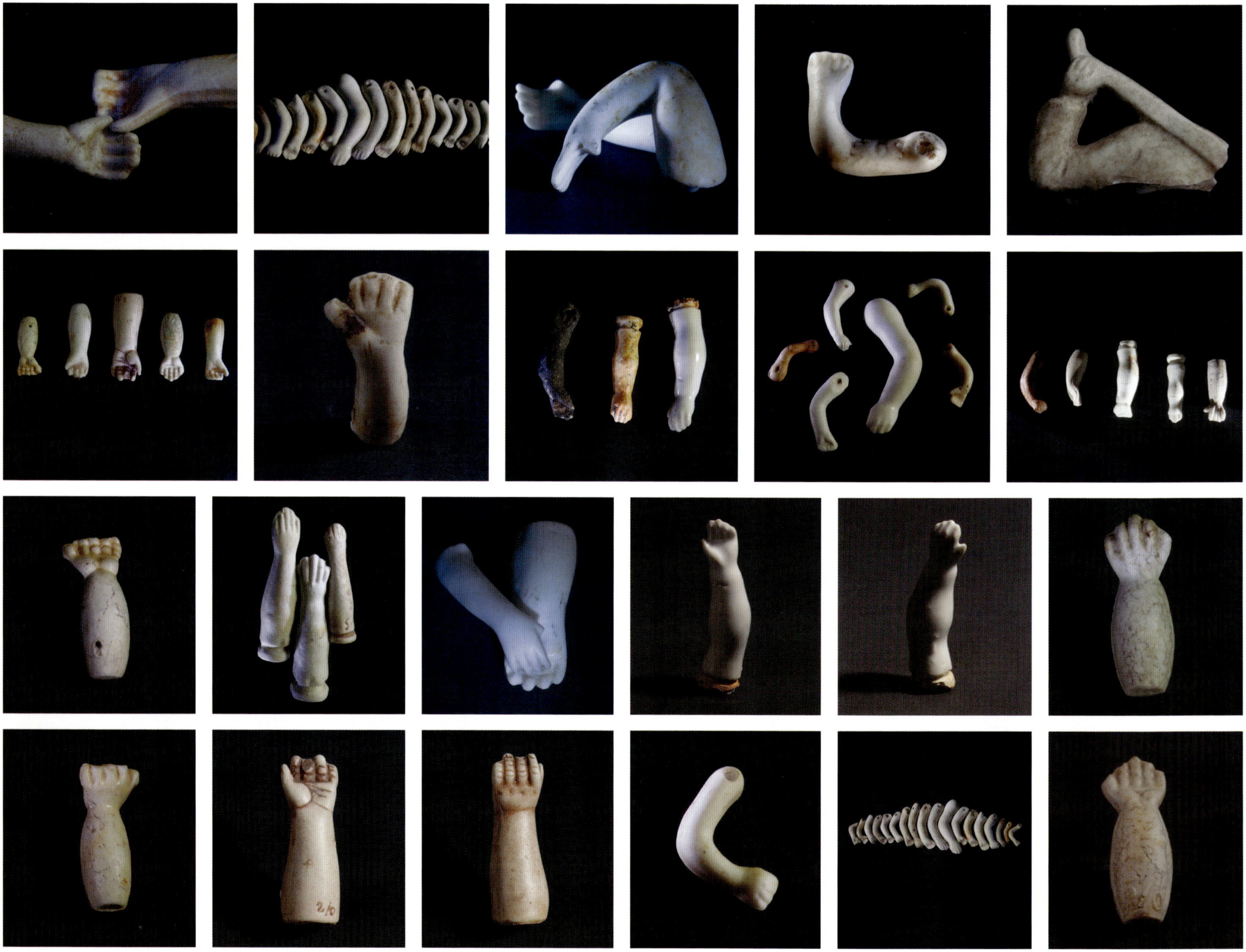

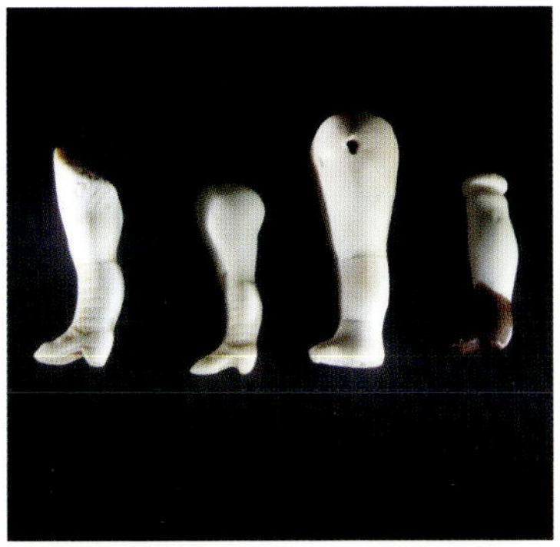

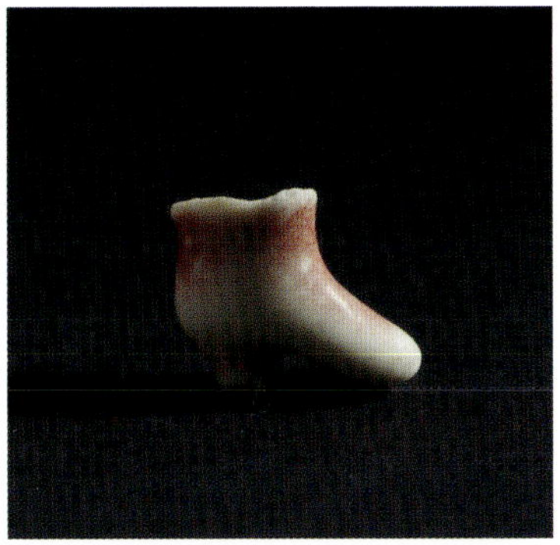

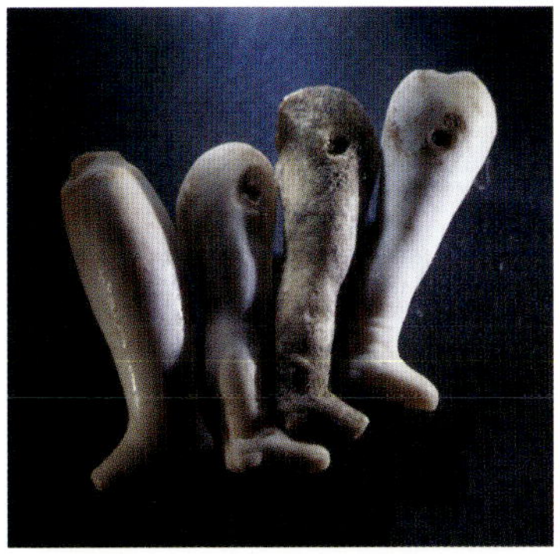

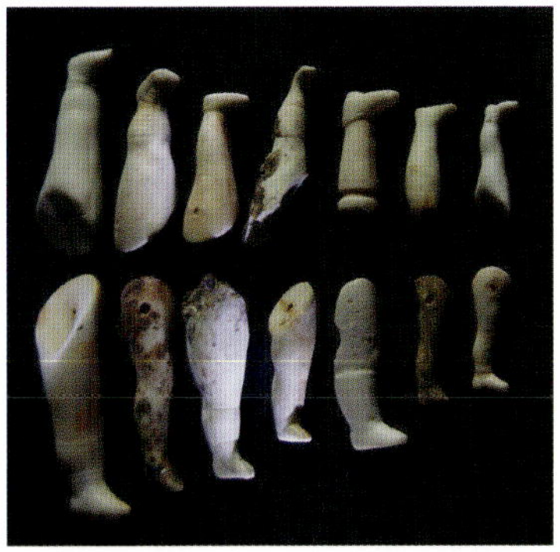

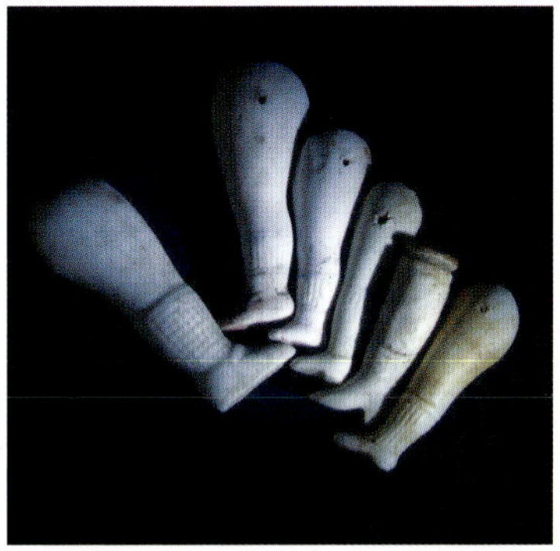

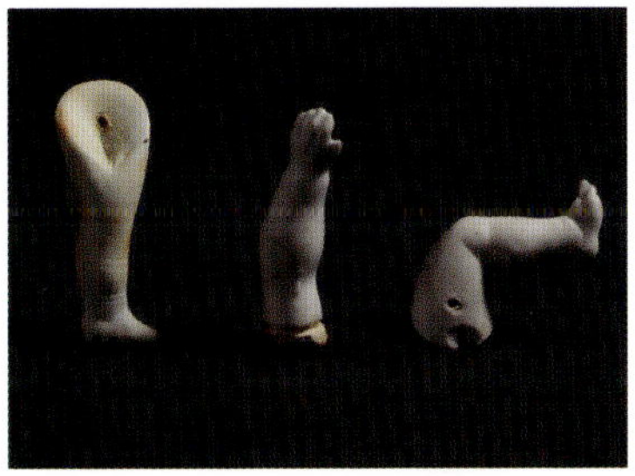

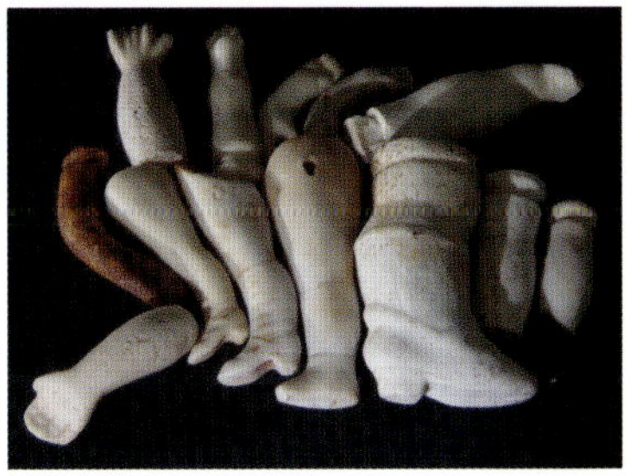

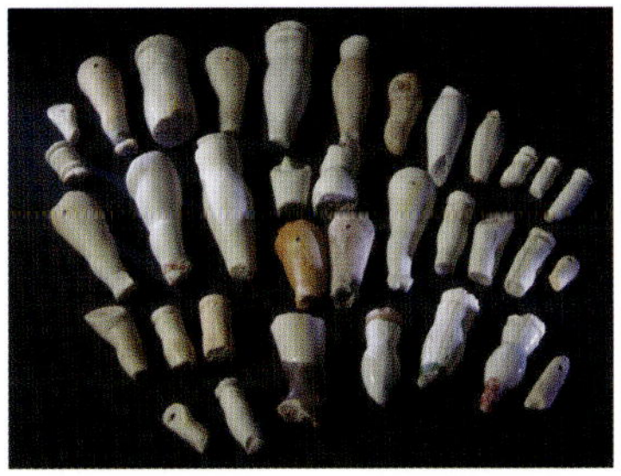

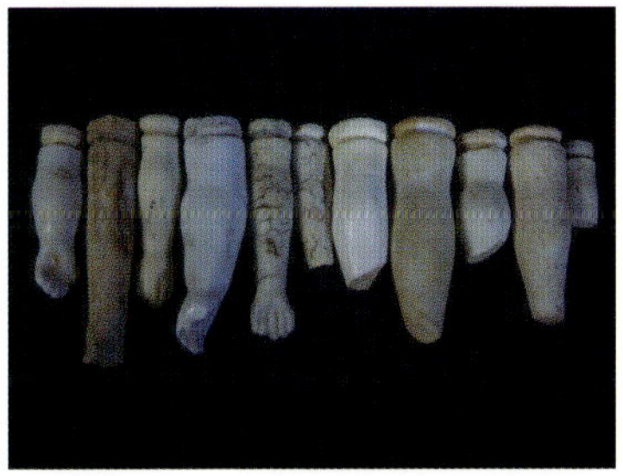

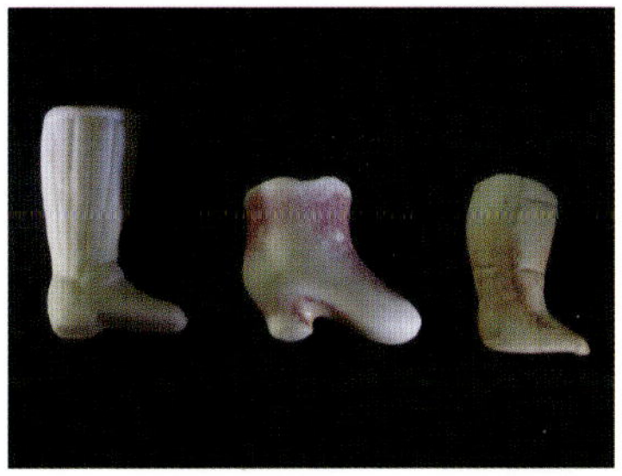

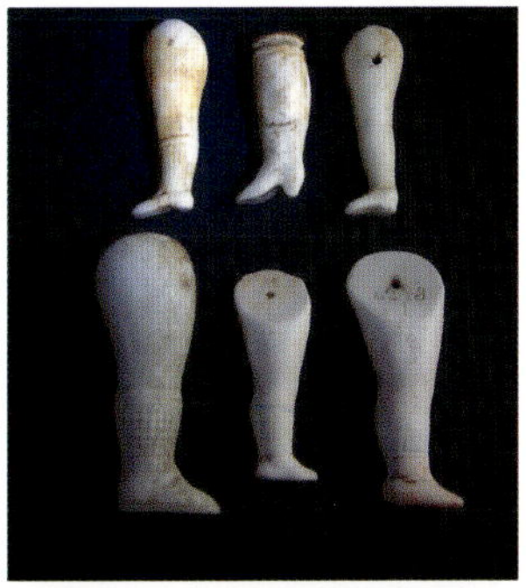

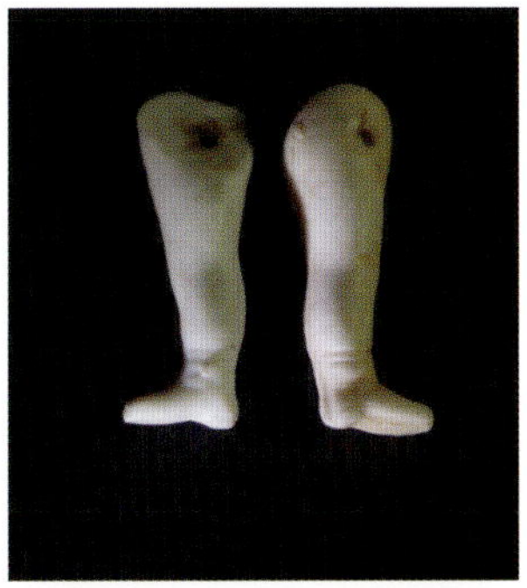

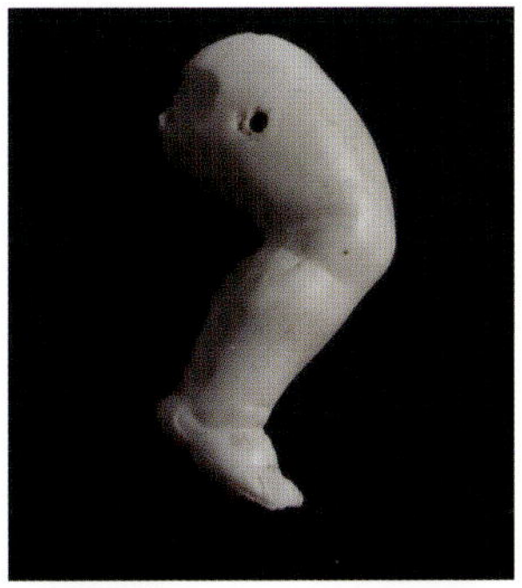

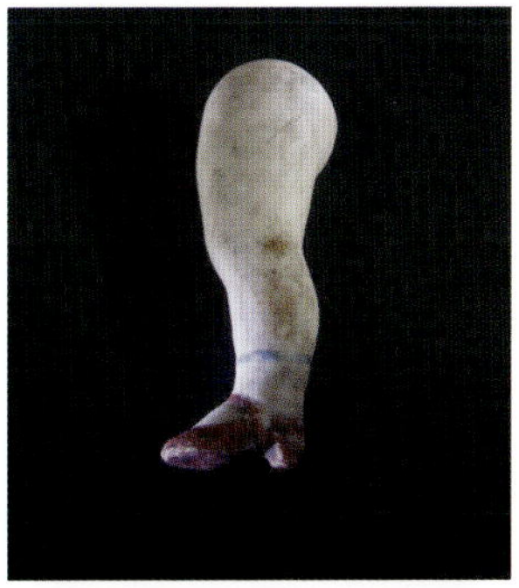

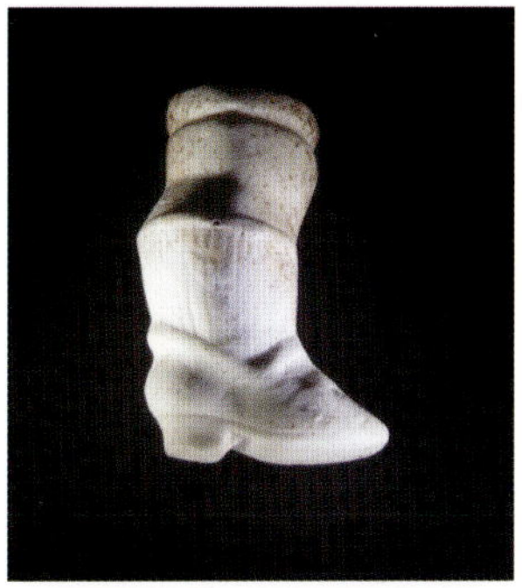

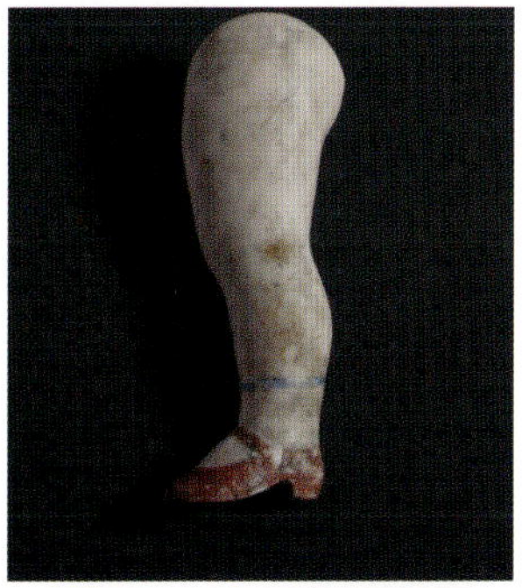

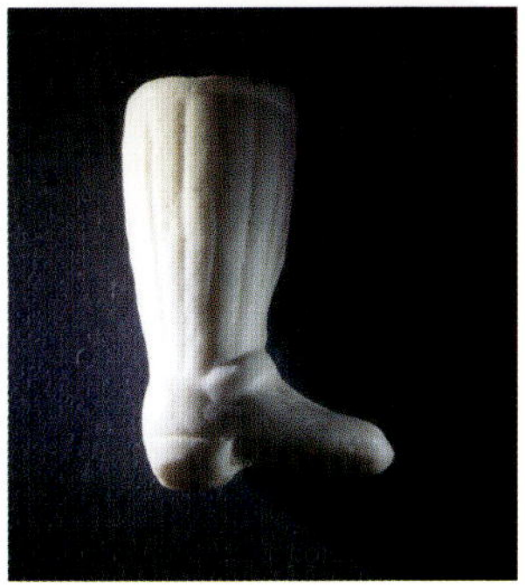

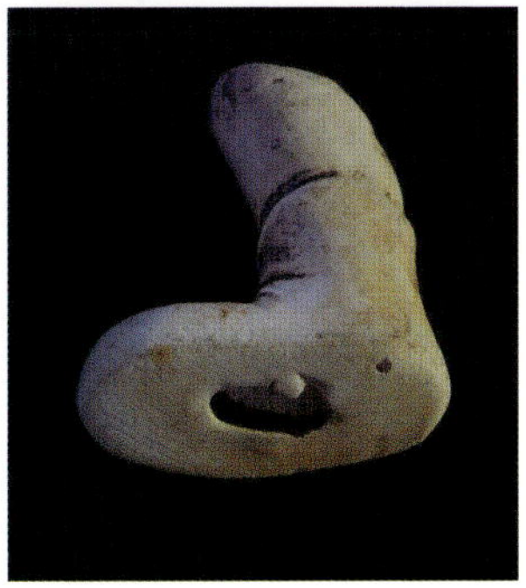

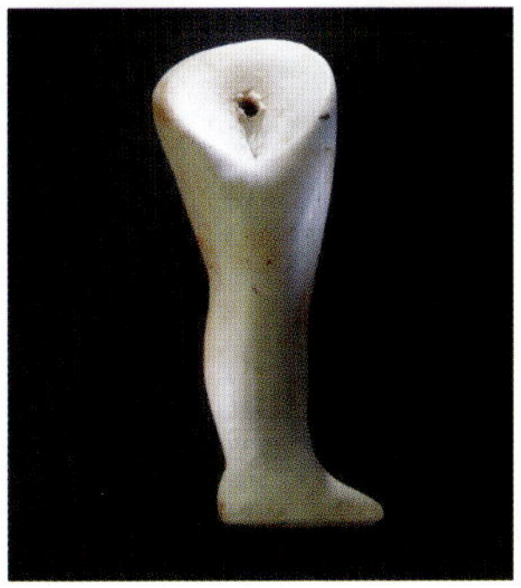

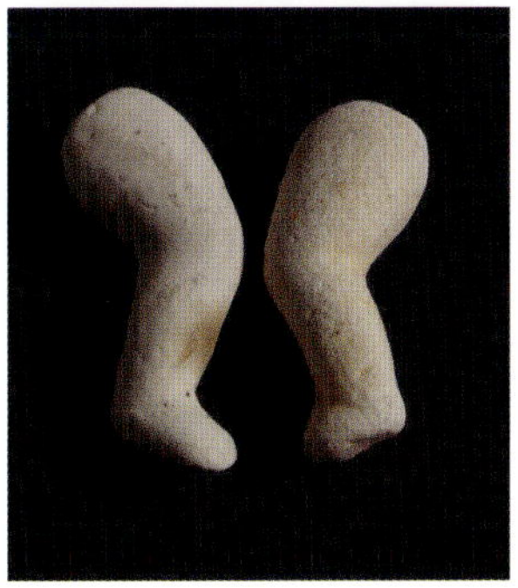

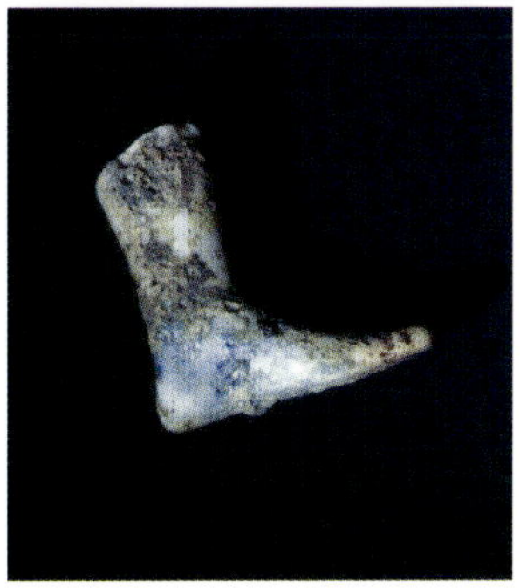

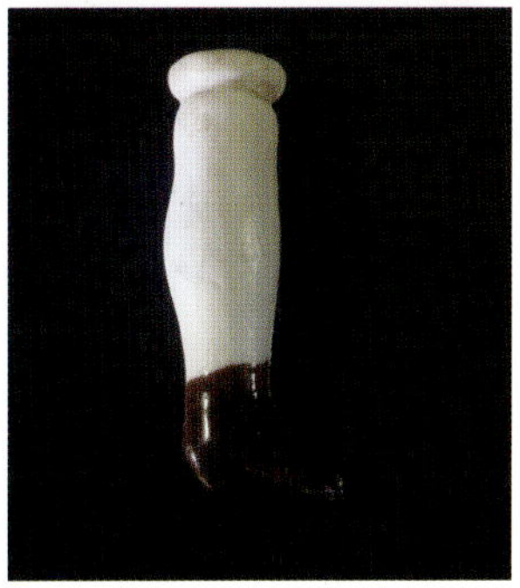

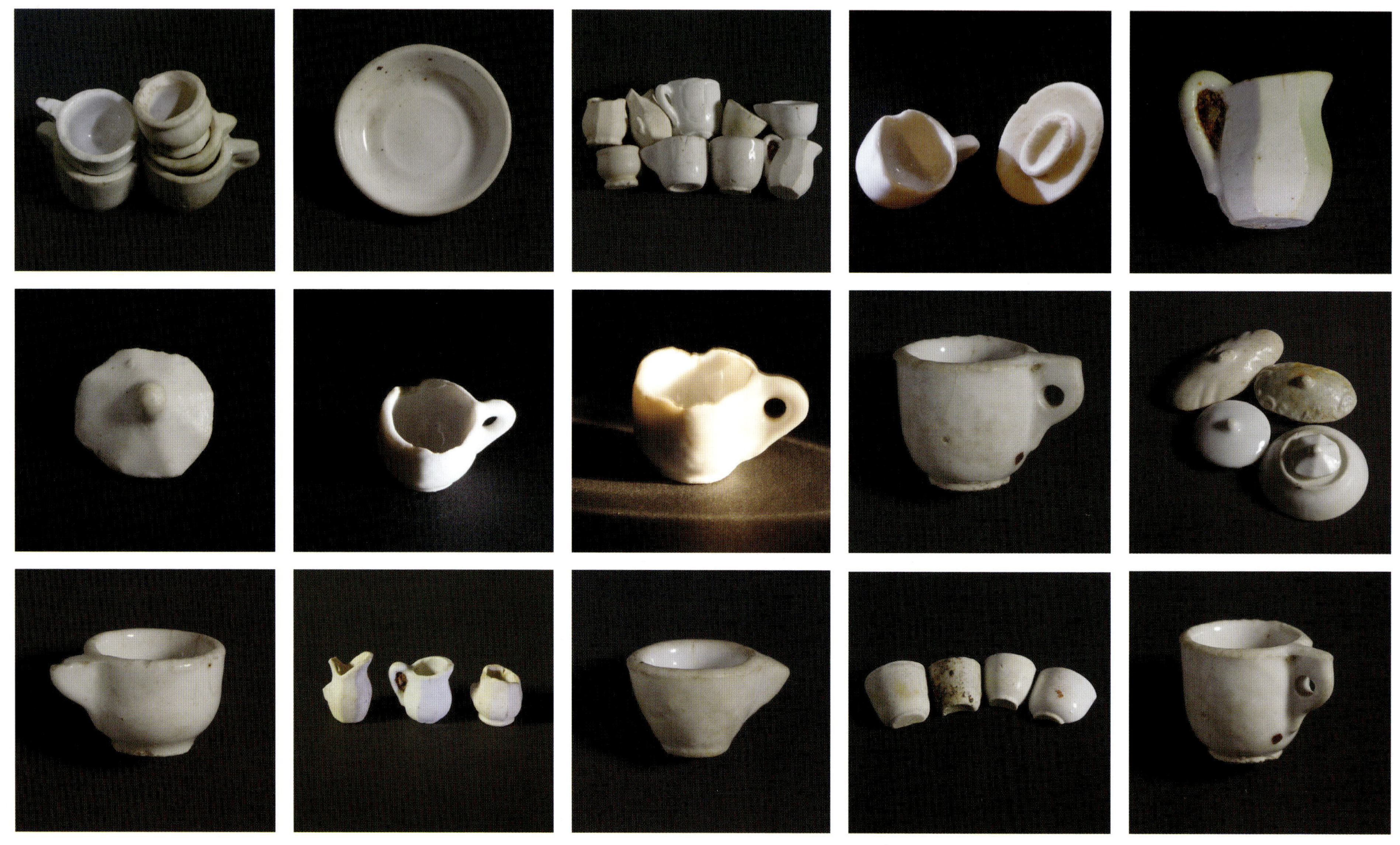

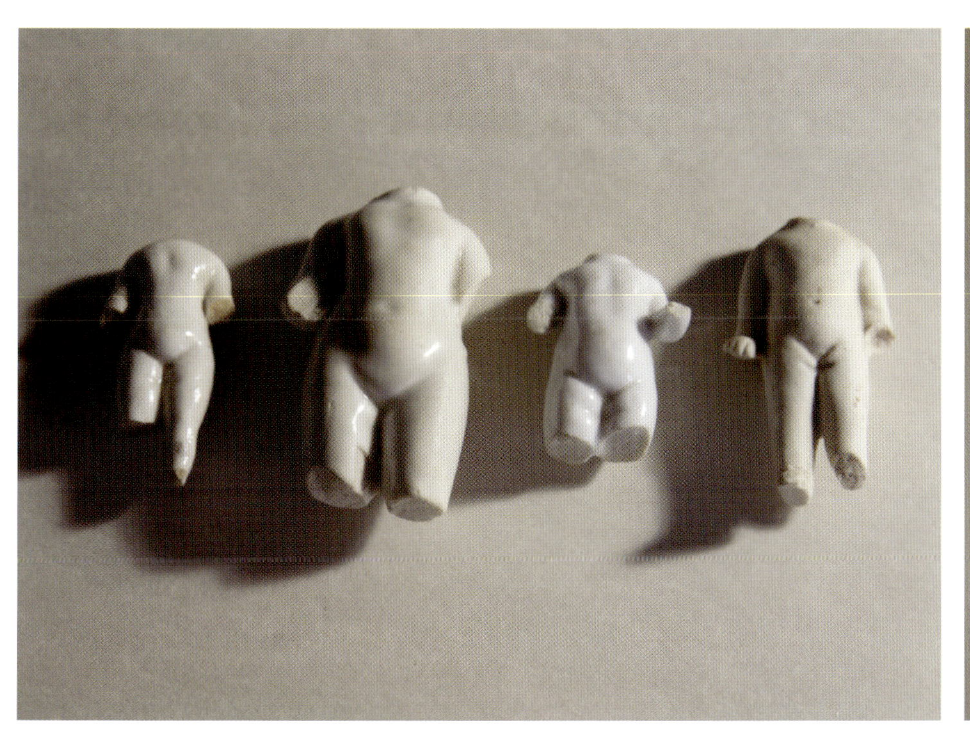
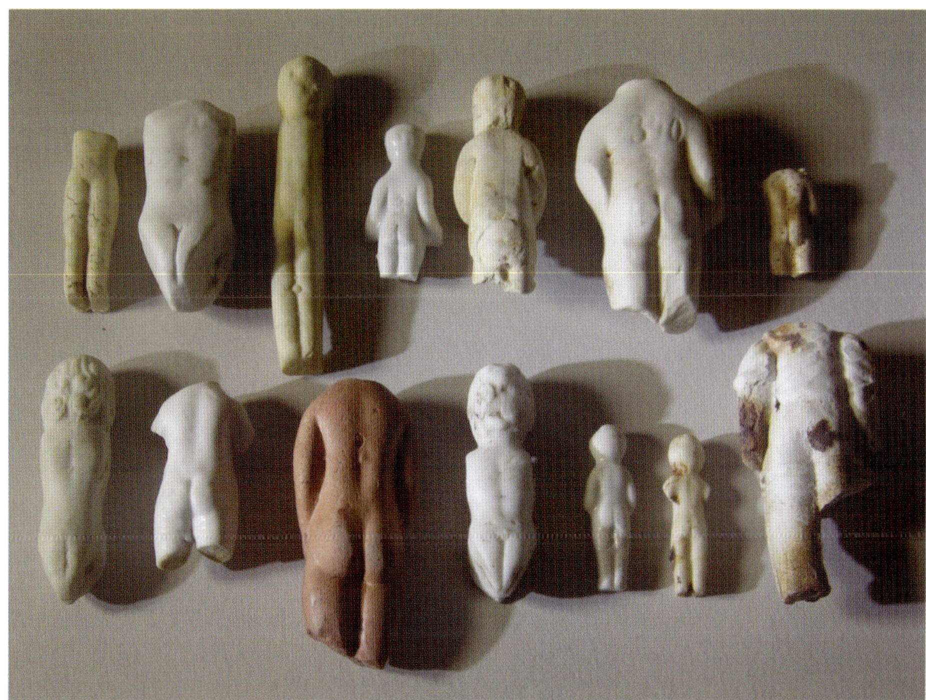

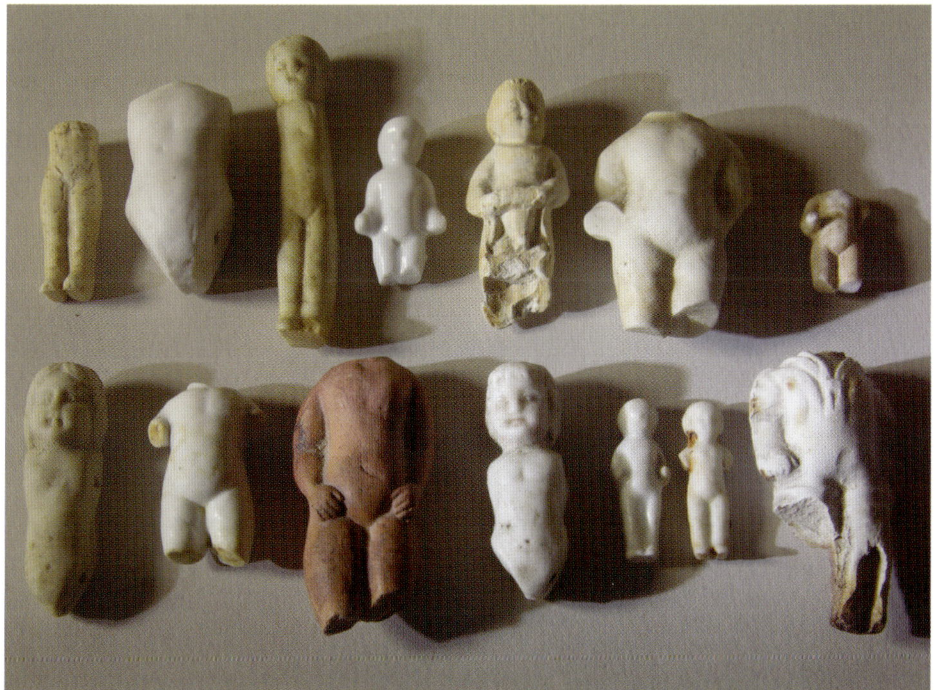
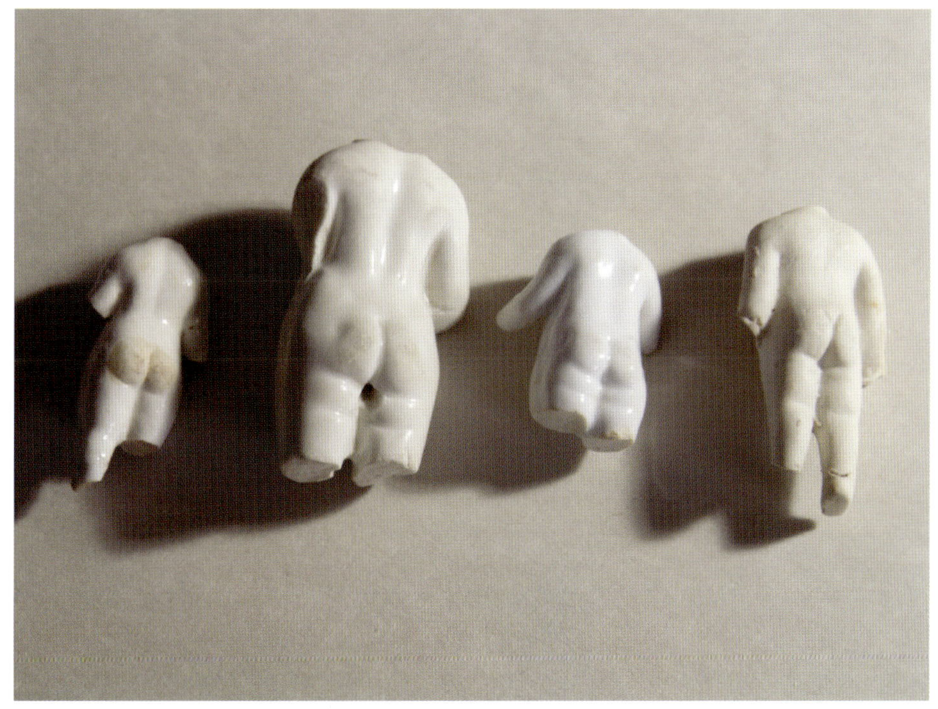

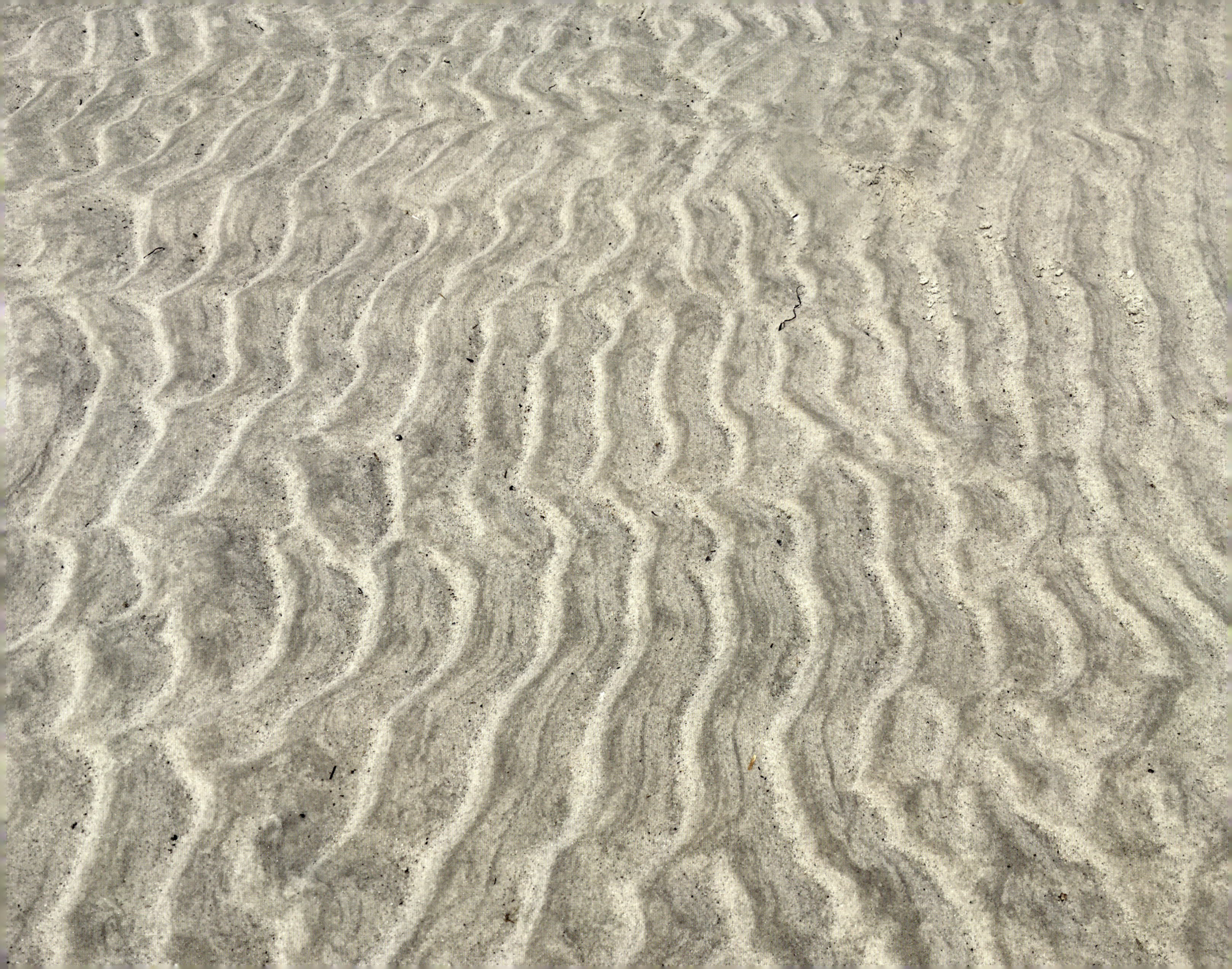

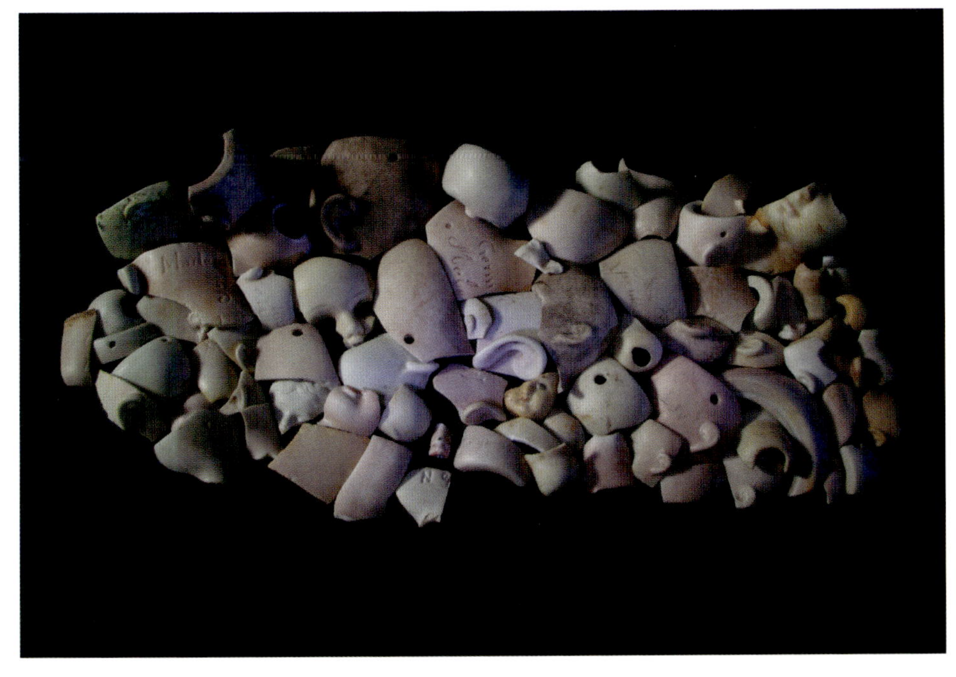

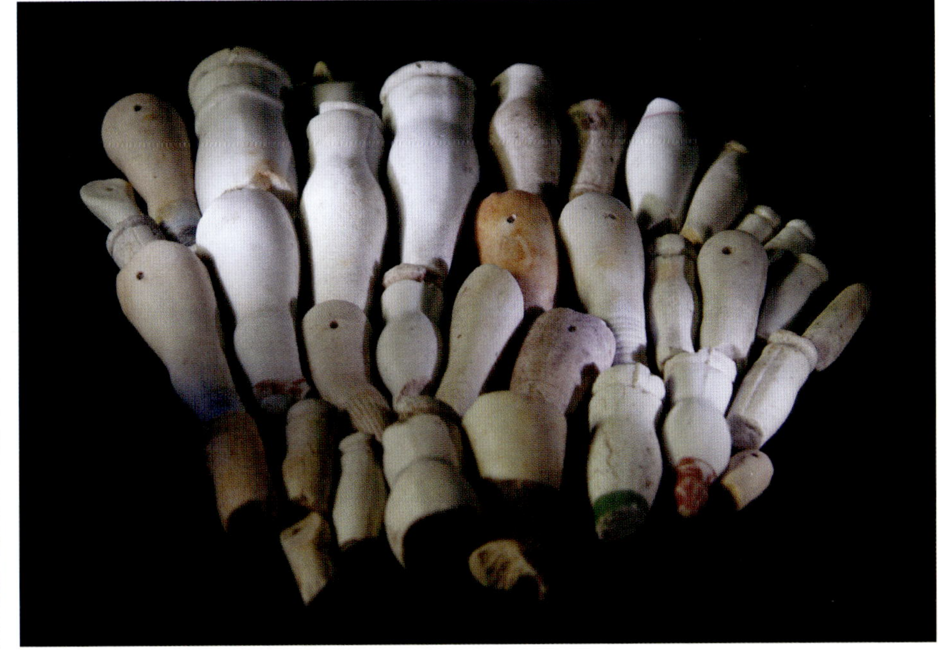

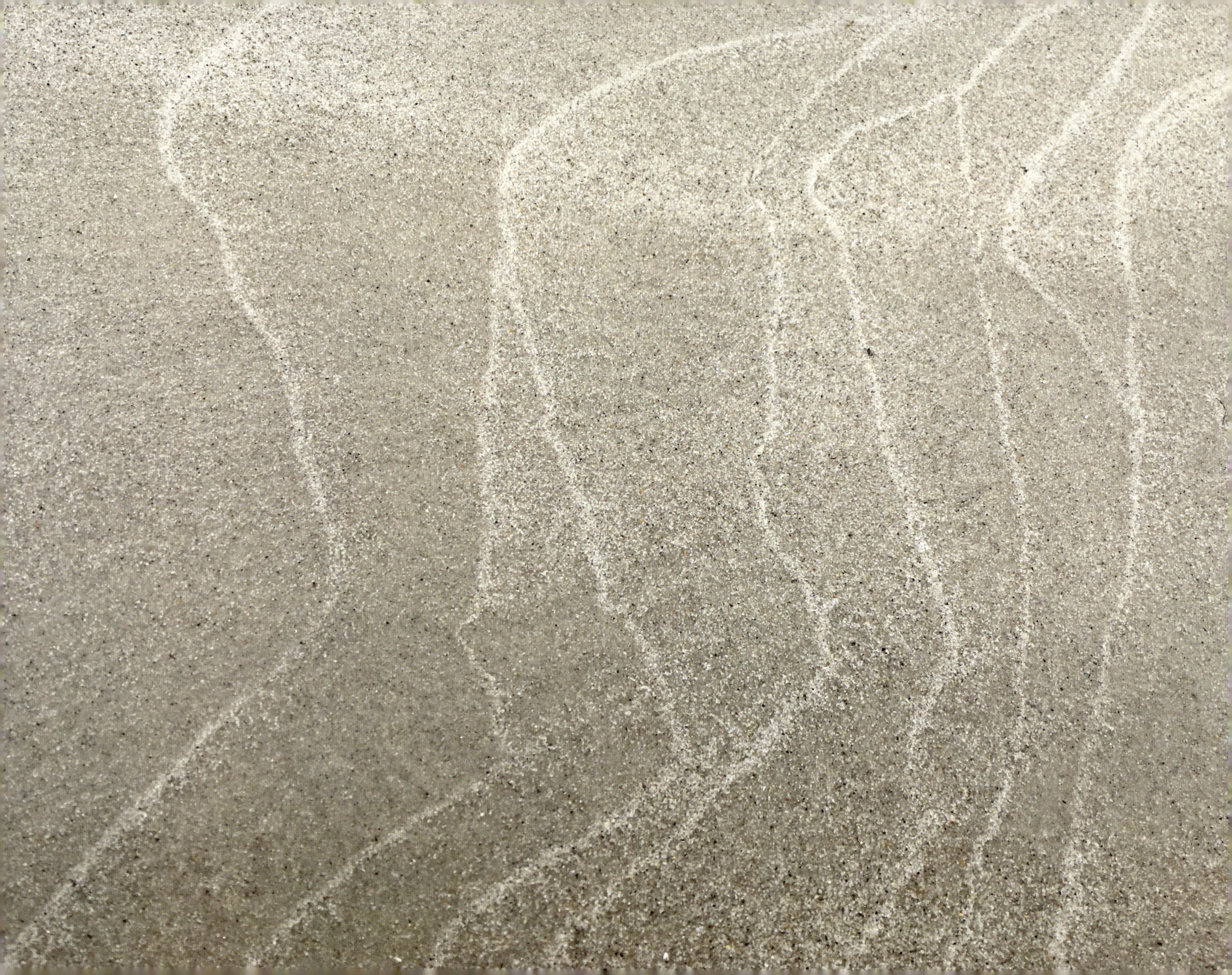

CERAMICS

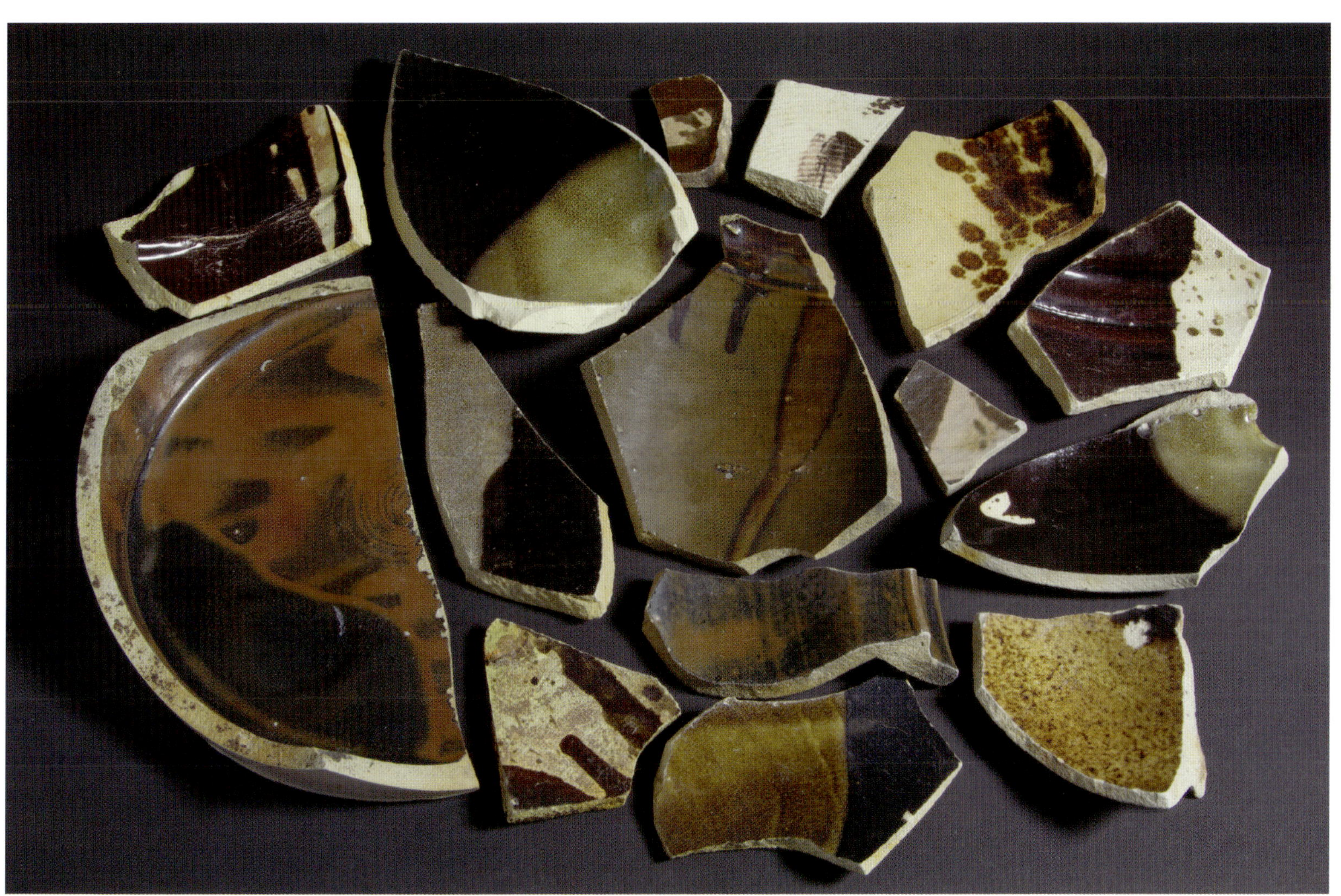

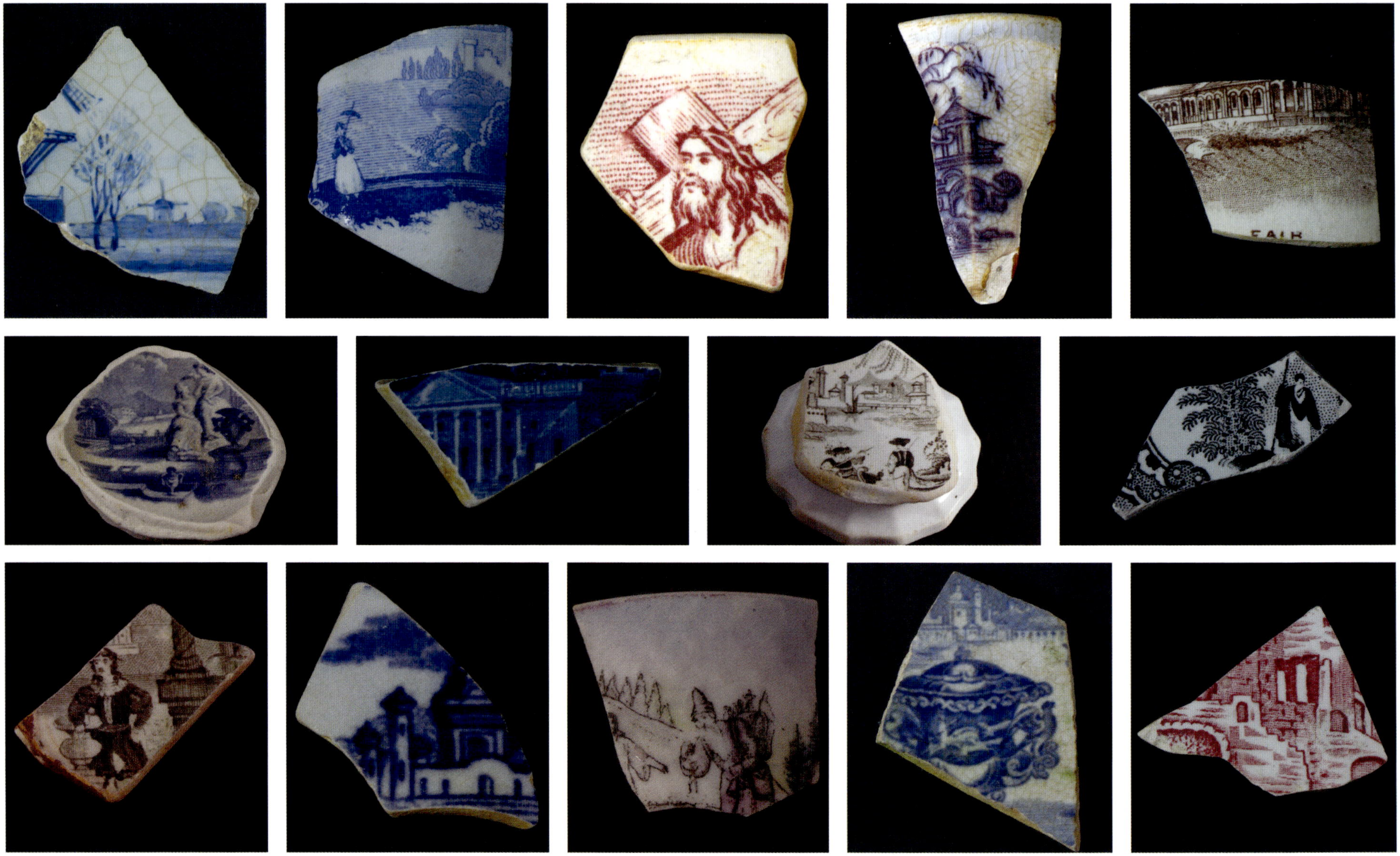

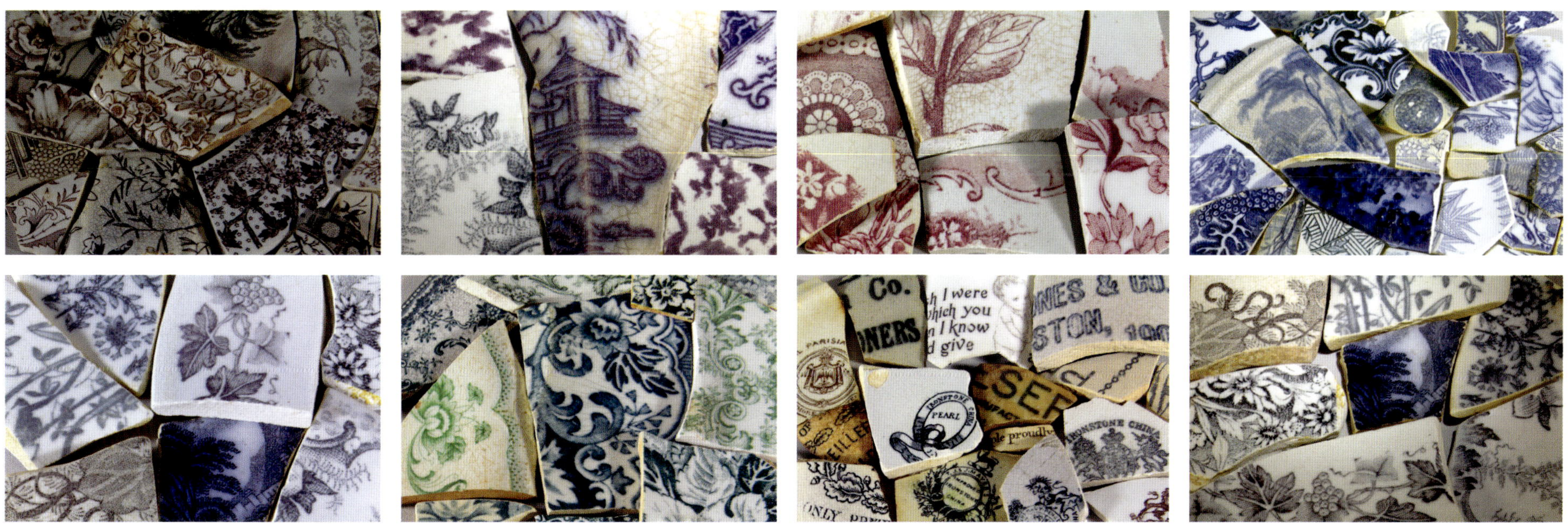

Provincetown does not have a solid clay base for producing domestic earthenware, and initially imported items for basic needs. However, Vermont to the north was rich with clay deposits and waterpower, and in 1785 a Revolutionary War soldier named Captain John Norton founded Bennington Pottery. The factory provided housewares such as teapots, crocks, doorknobs, dishware, and more.

As early as the 1750s, England began producing and importing tableware made with a new technique called transferware. An engraved copper or steel plate created a monoprint on paper that was transferred to the ceramic surface and fired. The emerging American middle class provided a ready-made market for this more decorative approach.

Mochaware also appeared around this time. This economical yet decorative technique produced a softer, less stable pottery that was widely used in taverns, homes, and slave quarters. "Dip't" ware, as it was called, was dipped in a watery ceramic glaze, then coated with a mixture of tobacco juice, turpentine, hops, and urine. This acid solution reacted with the alkaline base to produce feathering, blooming, and marble veining.

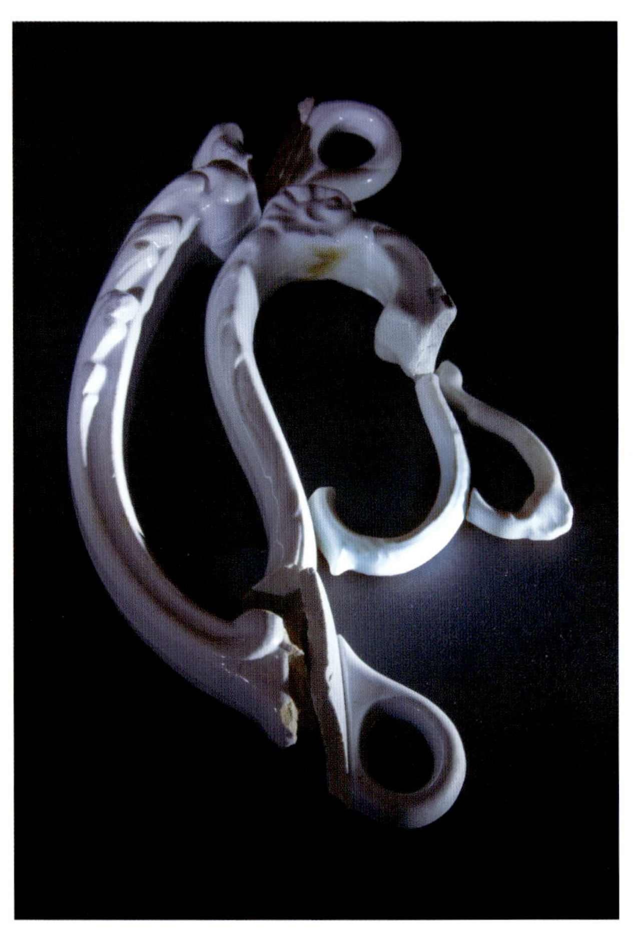

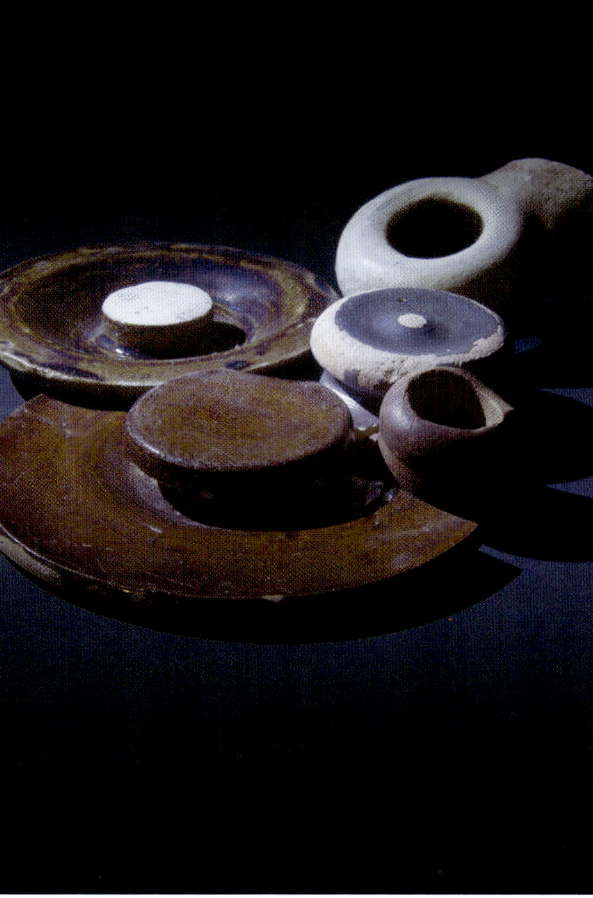

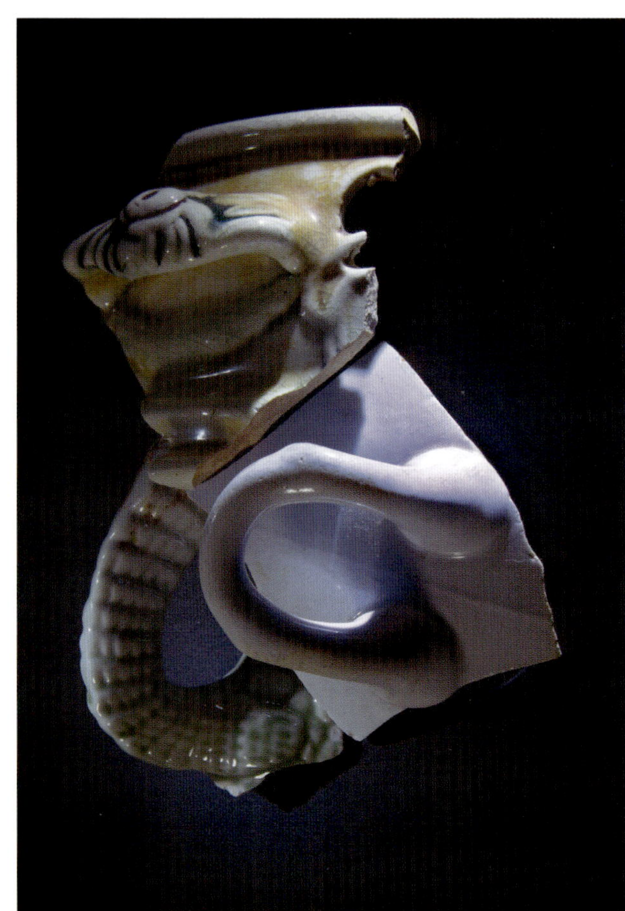

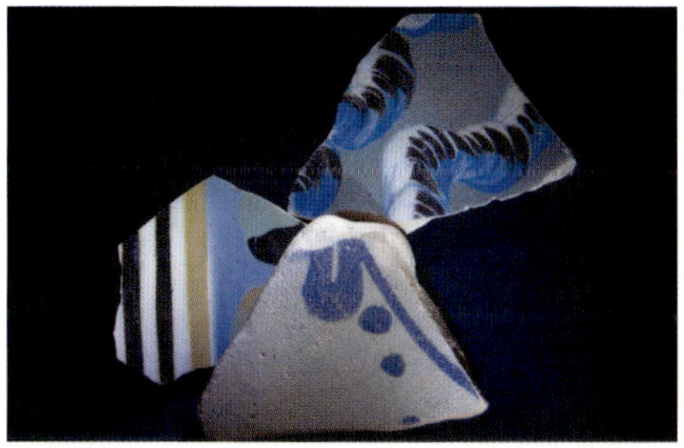

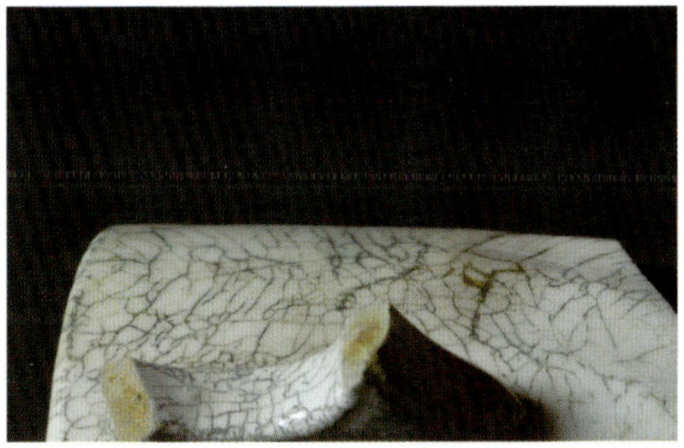

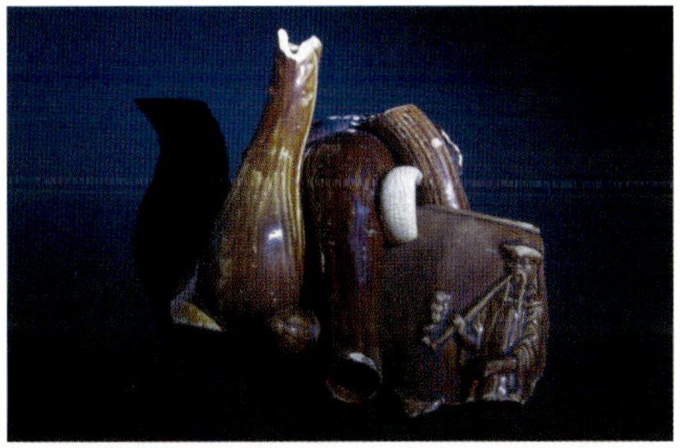

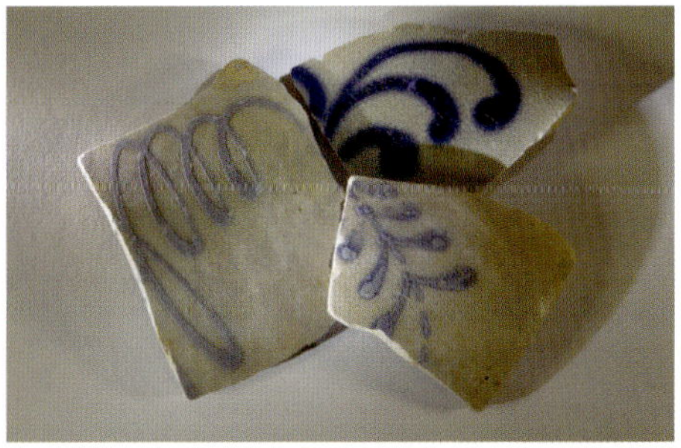

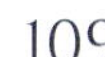

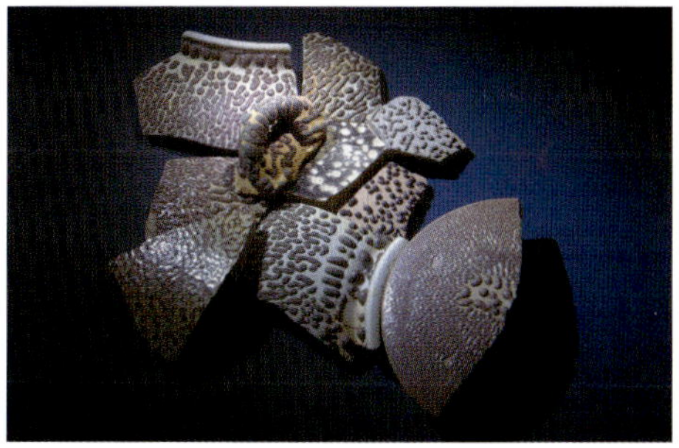

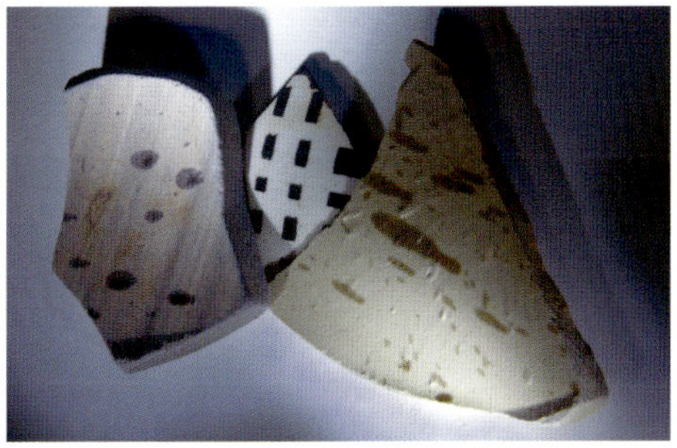

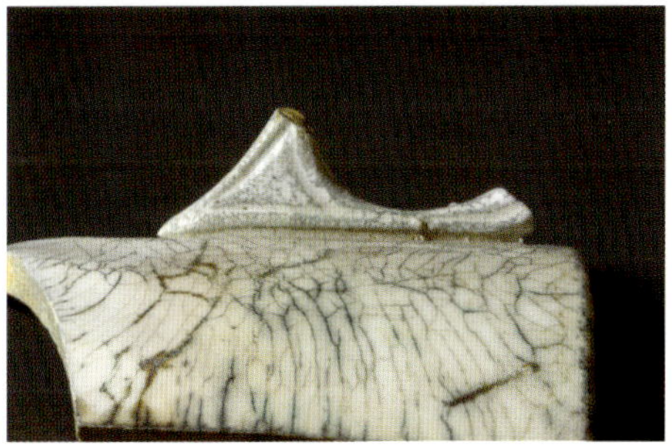

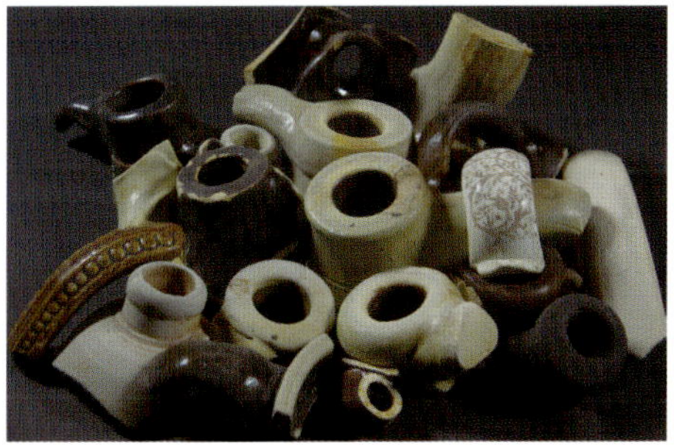

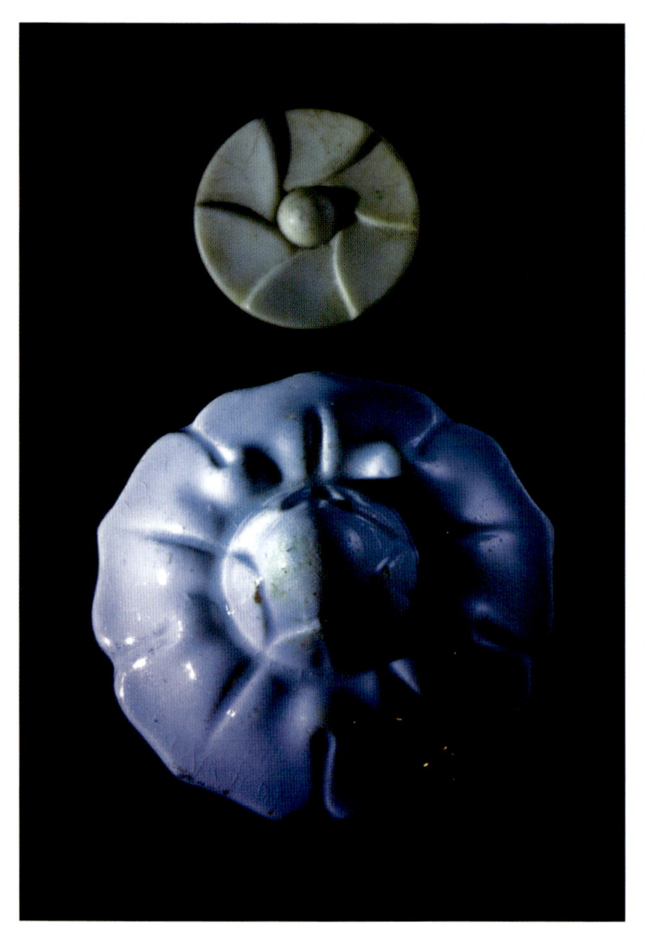

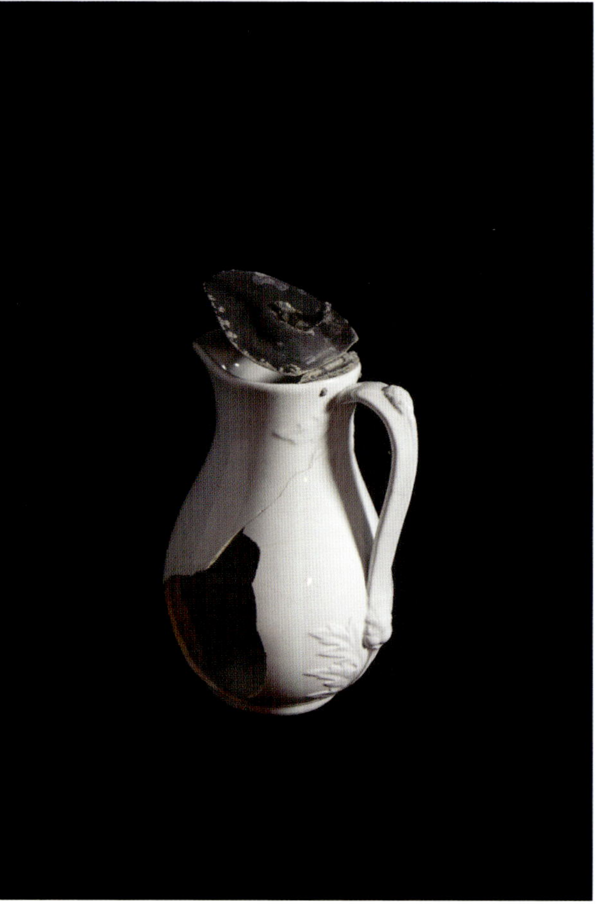

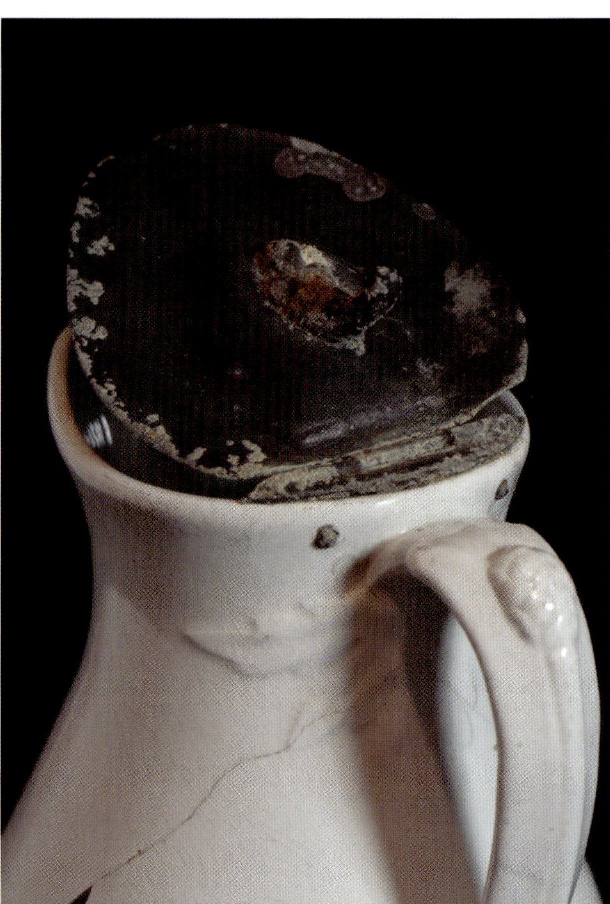

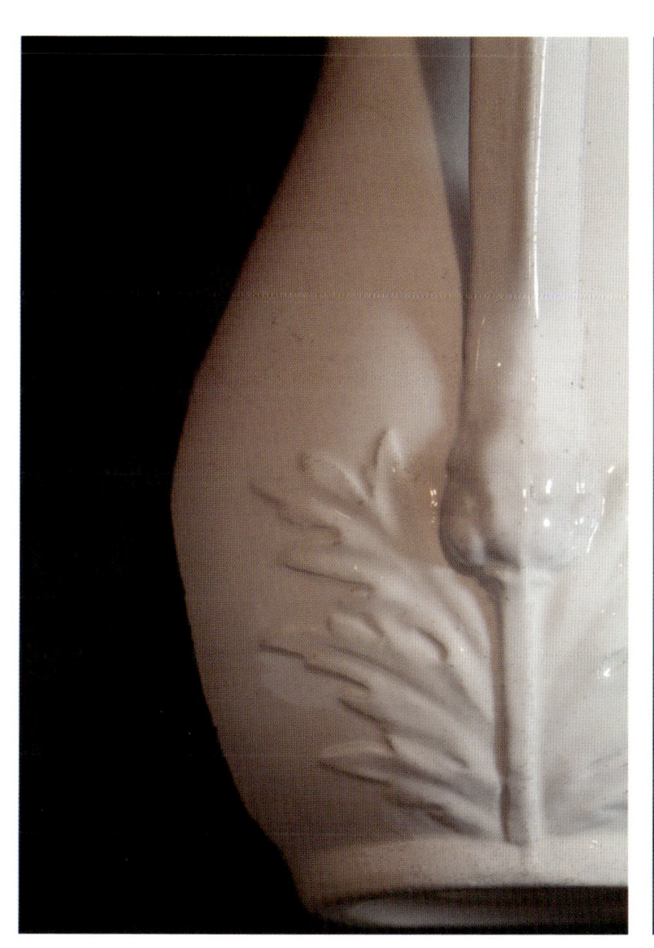
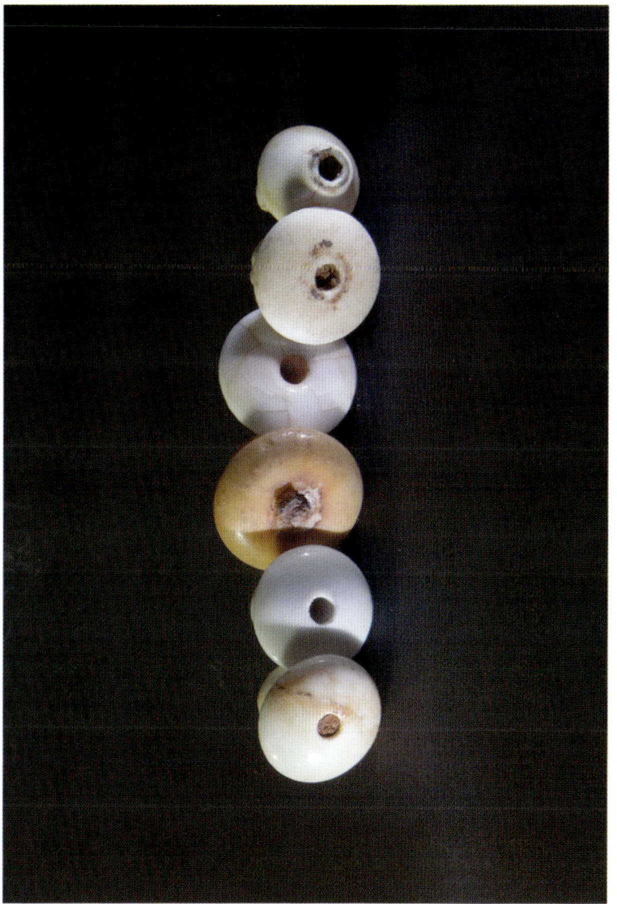
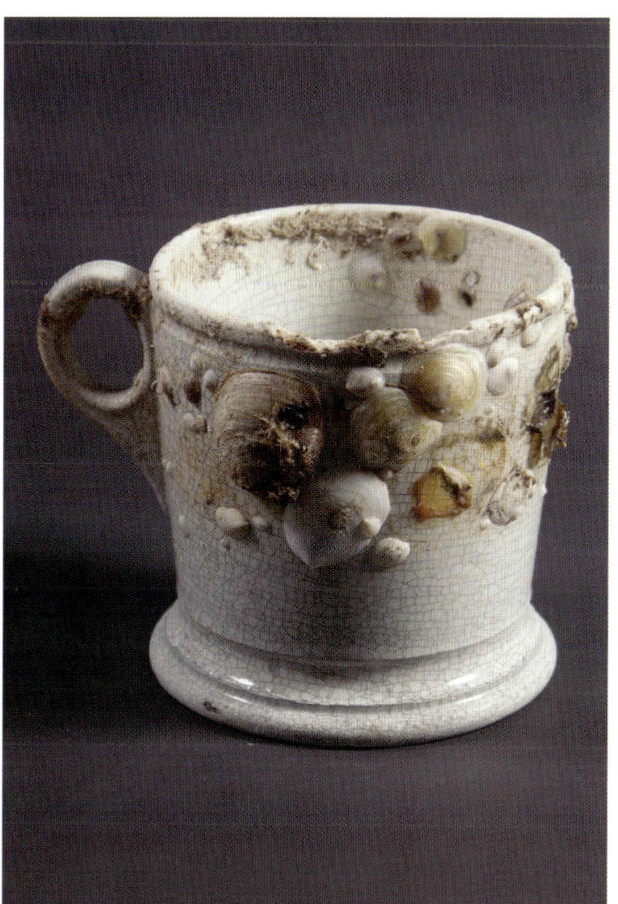

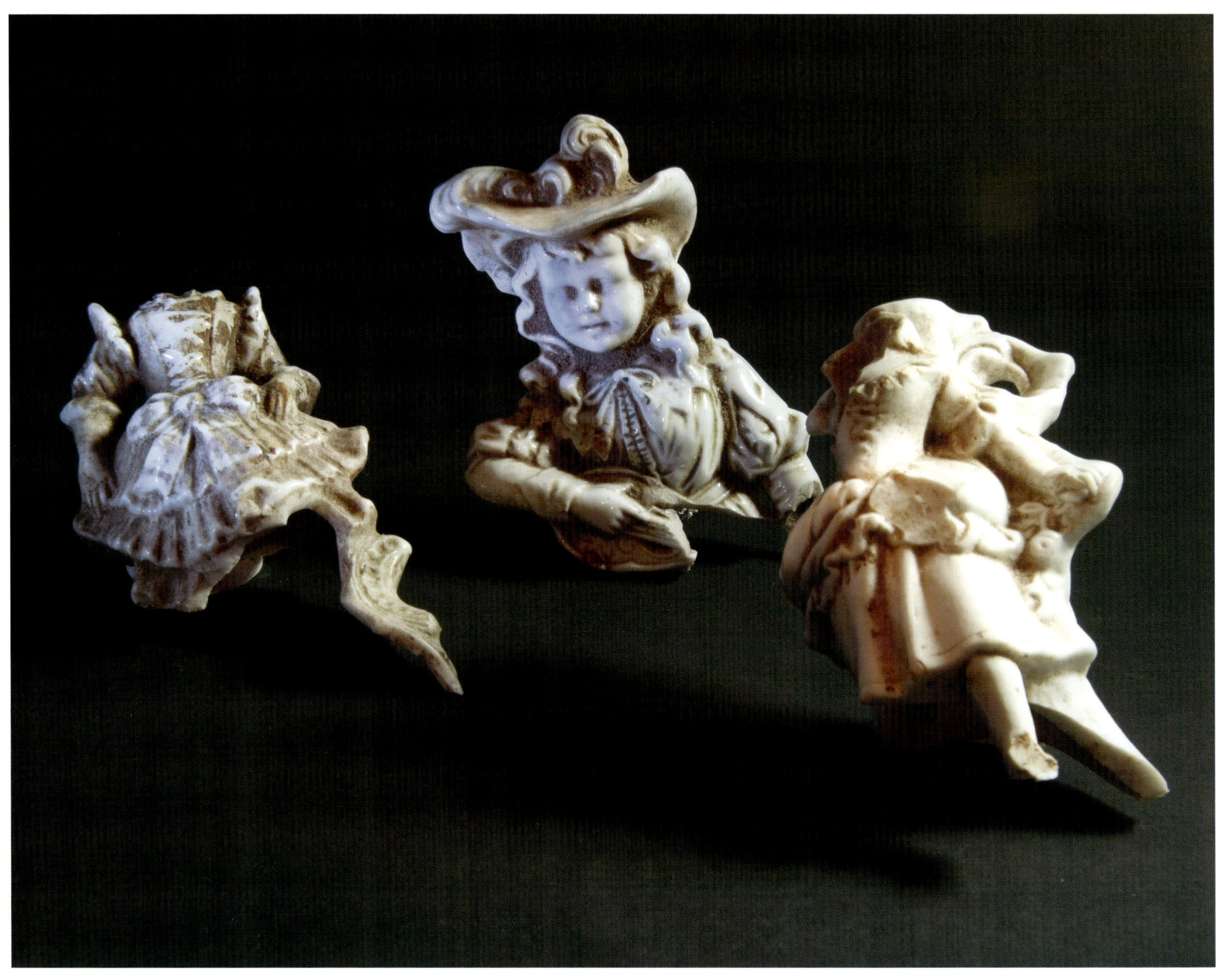

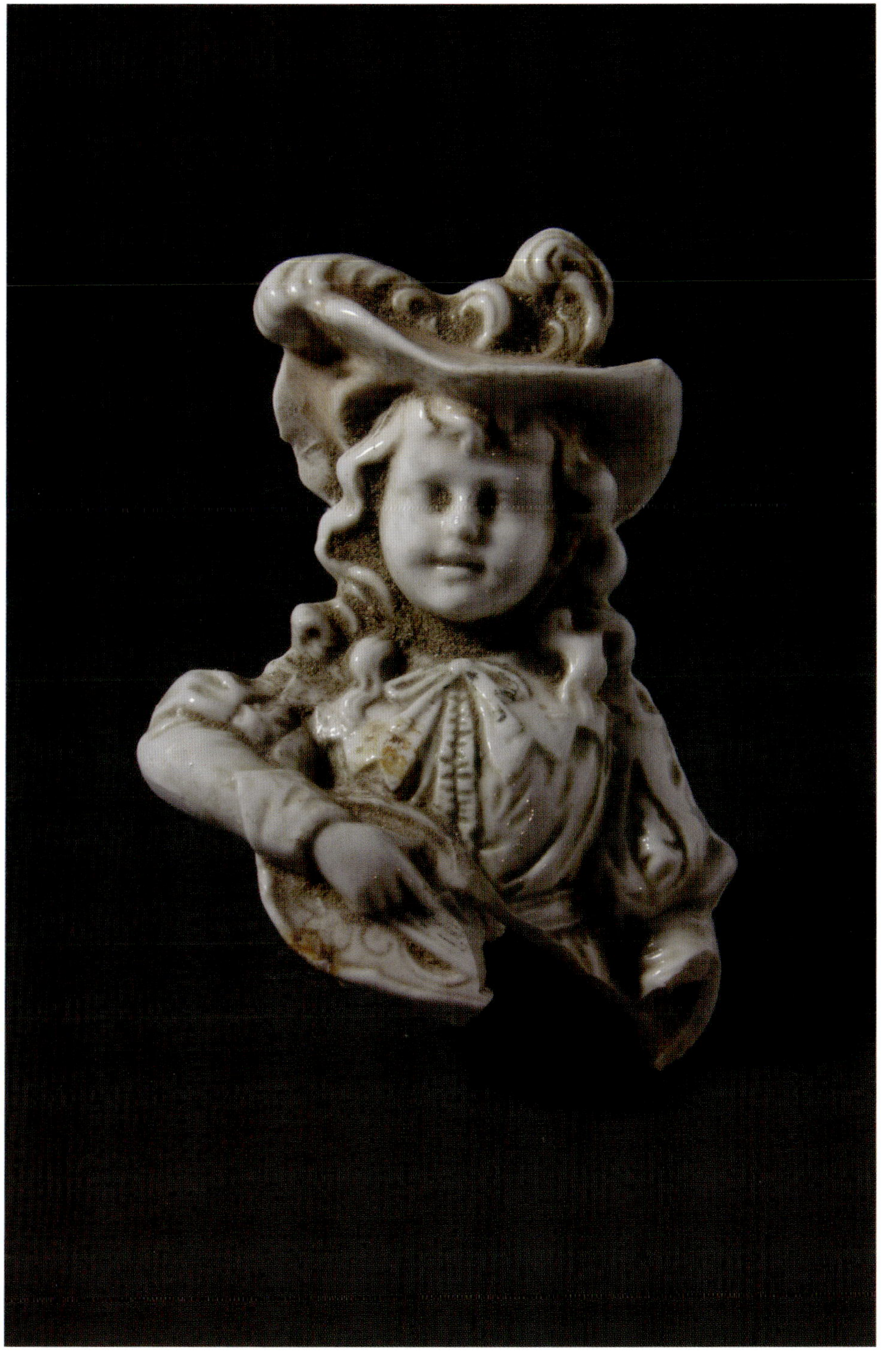

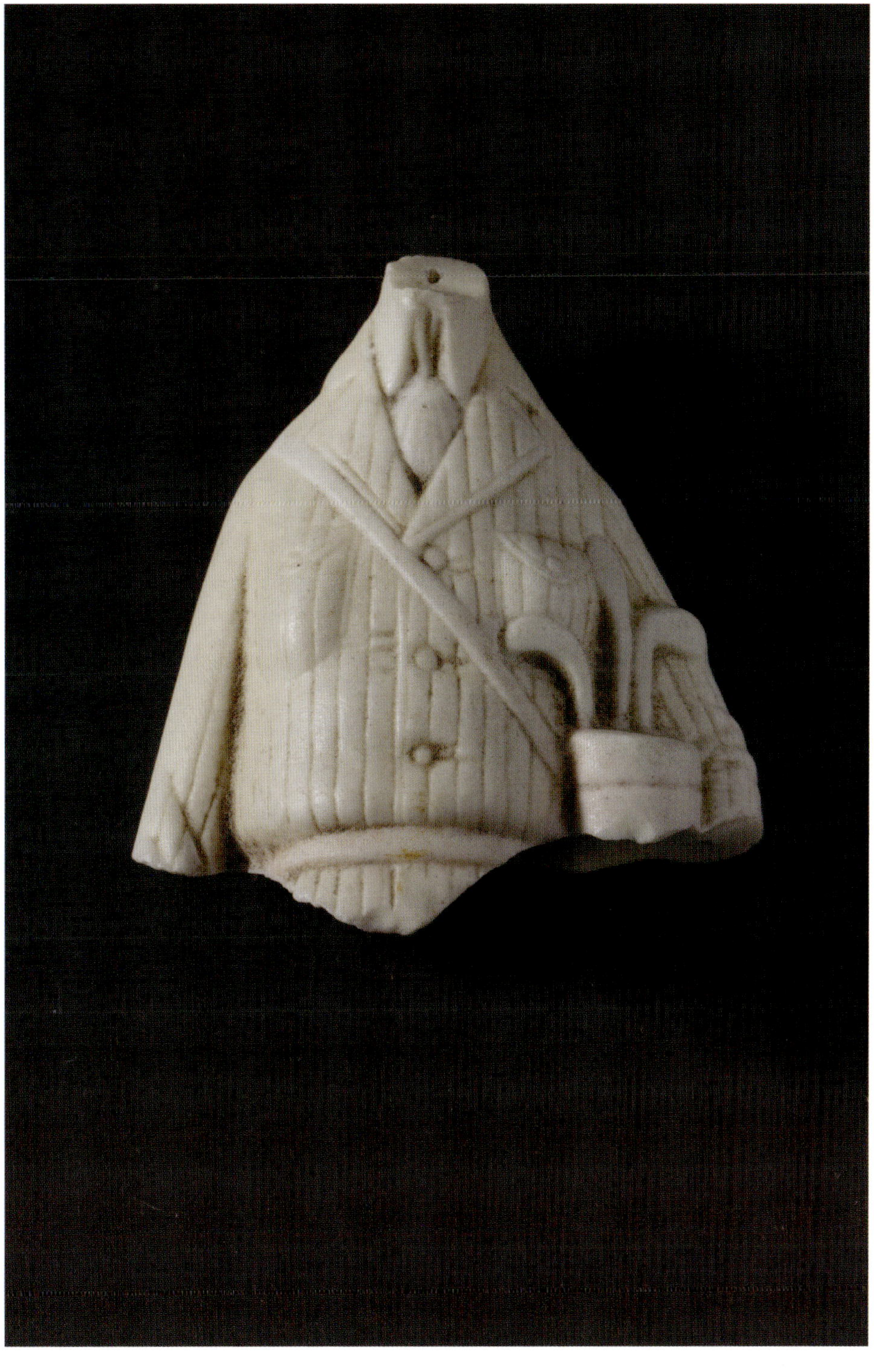

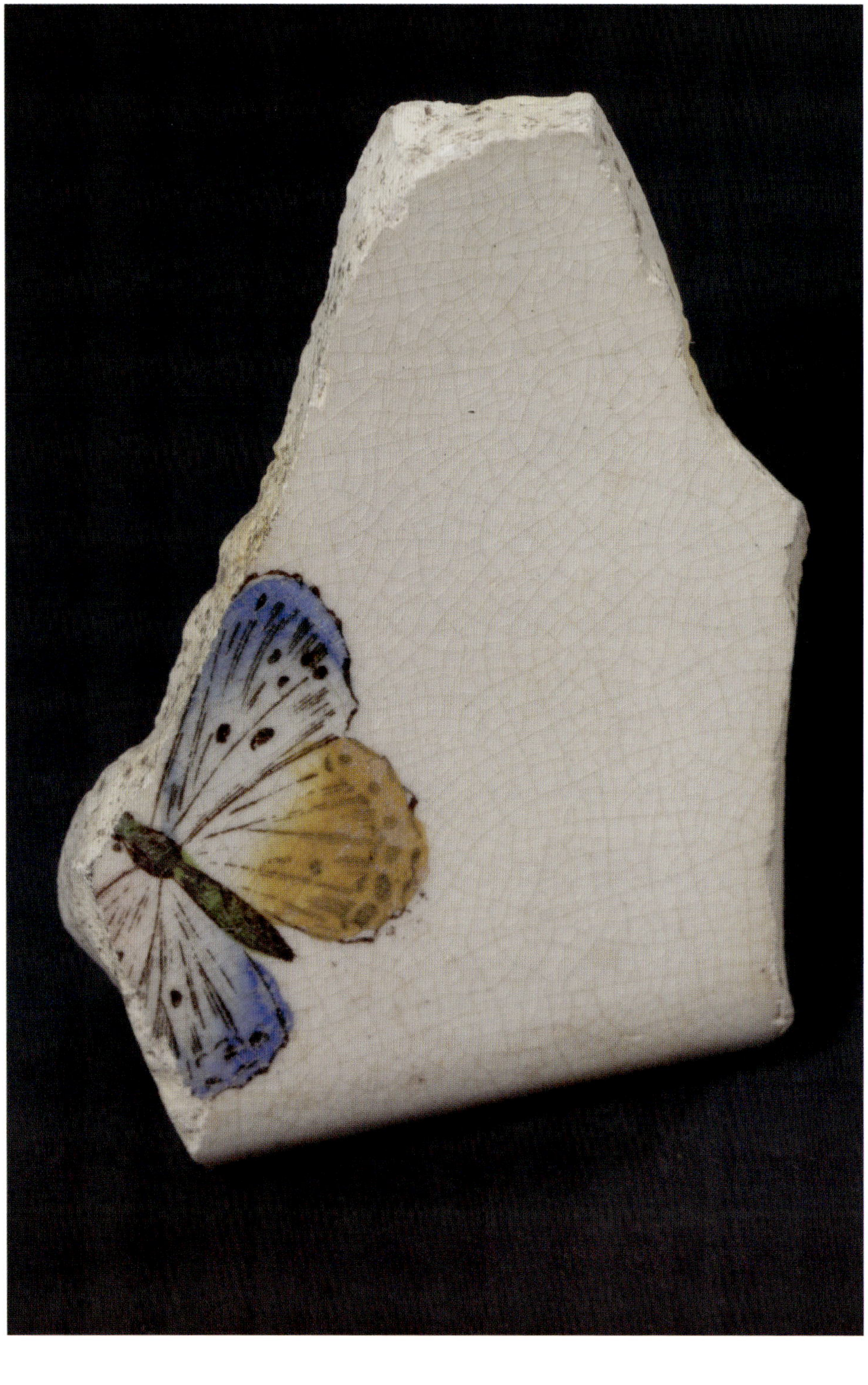

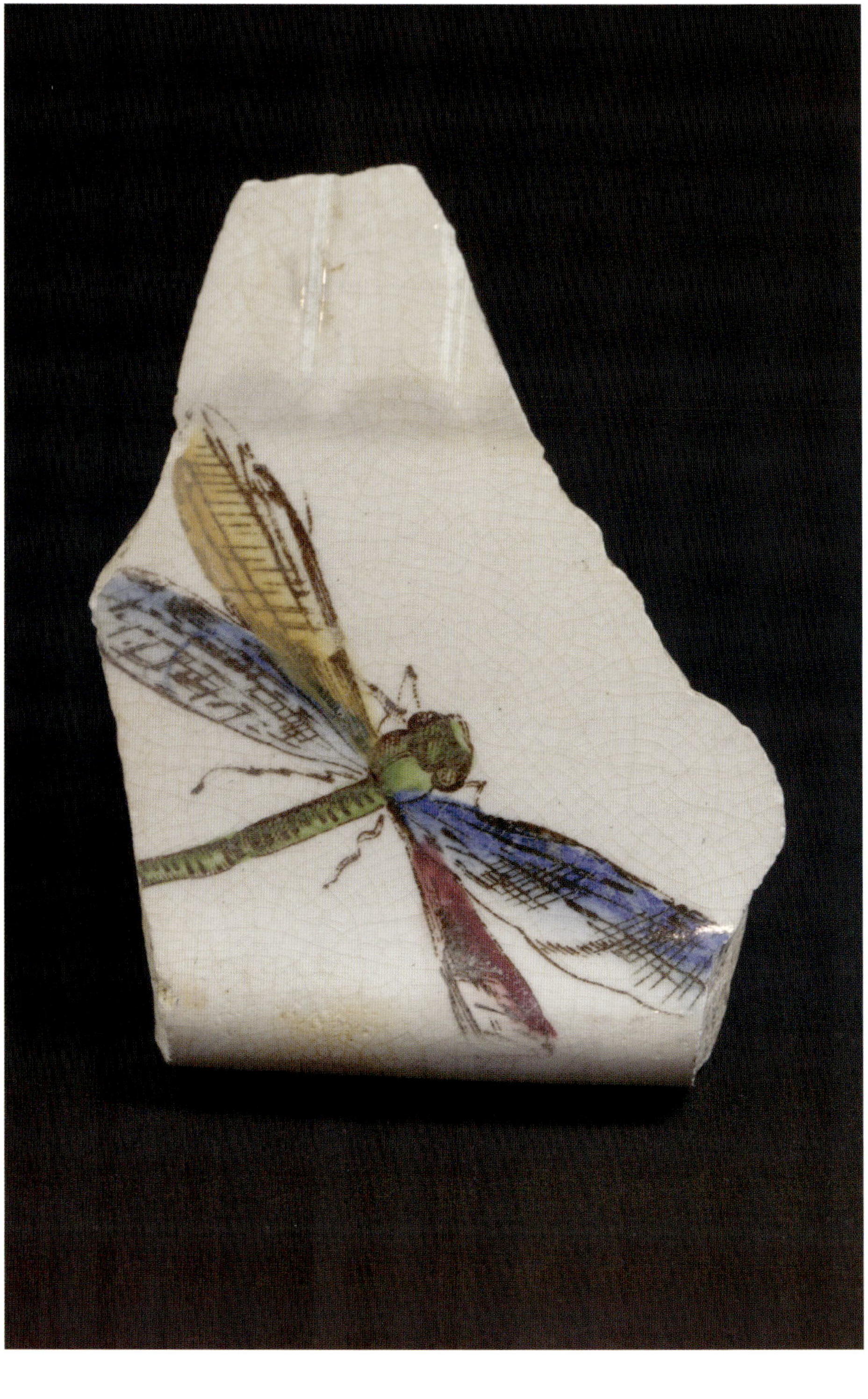

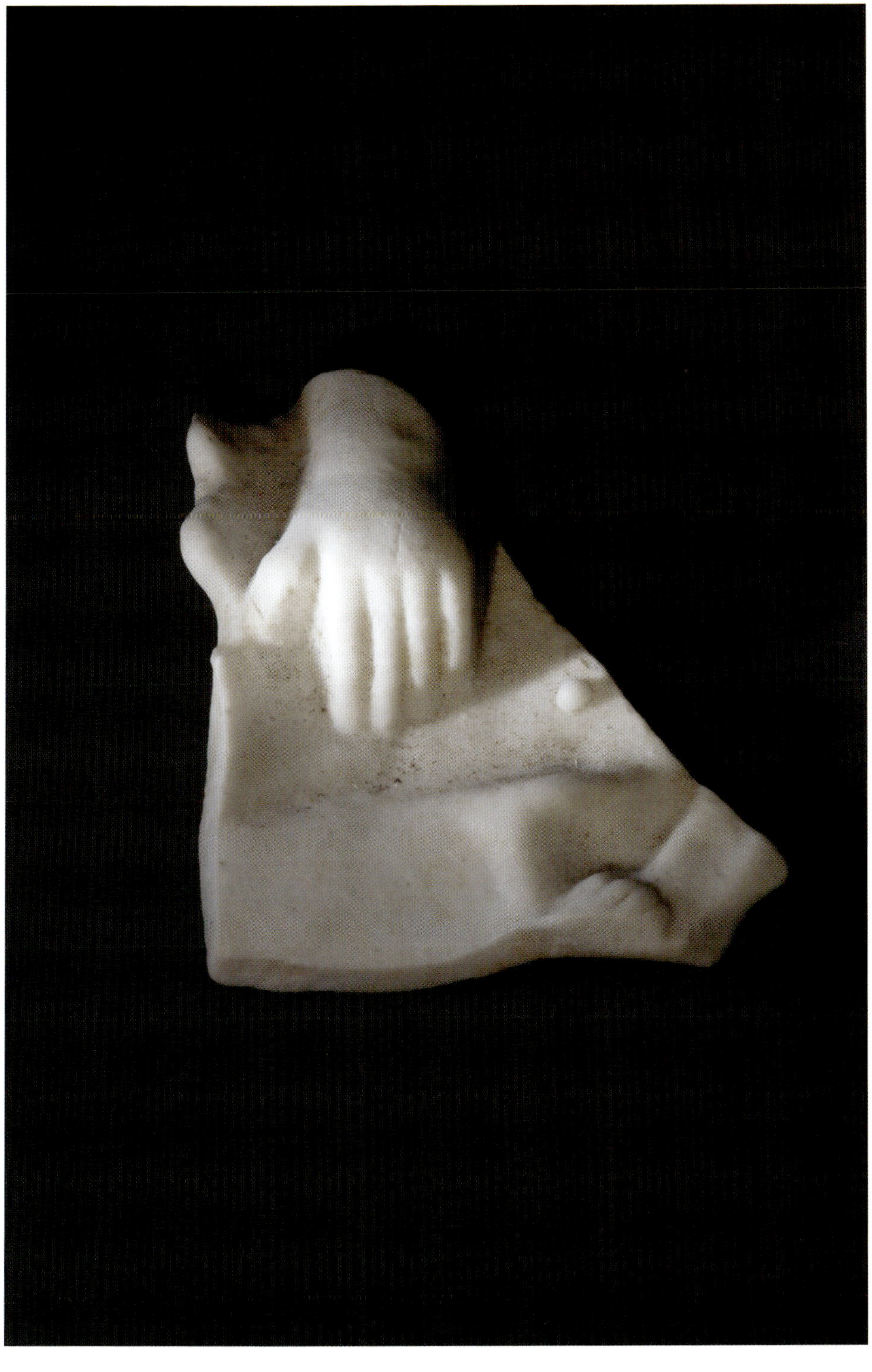

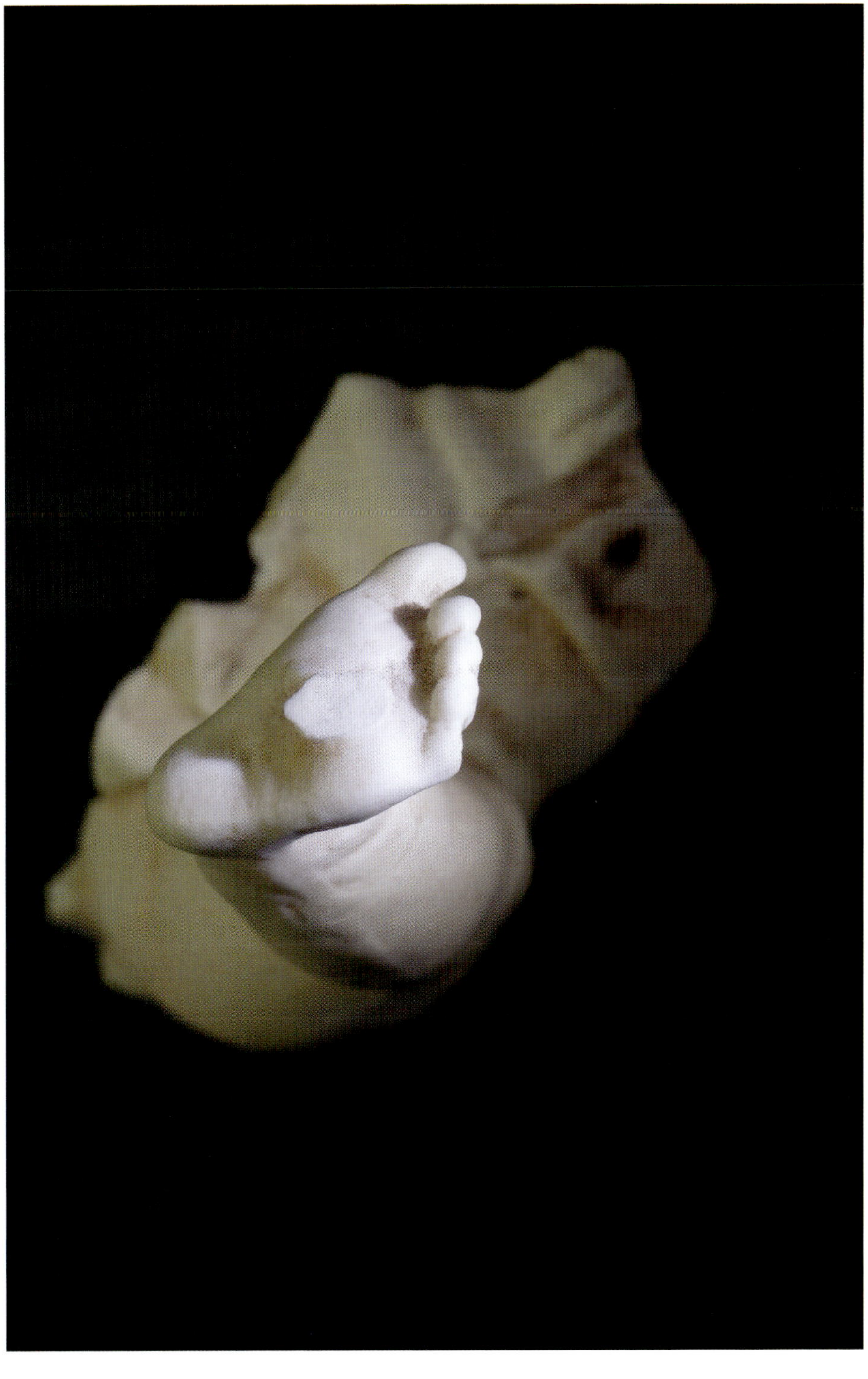

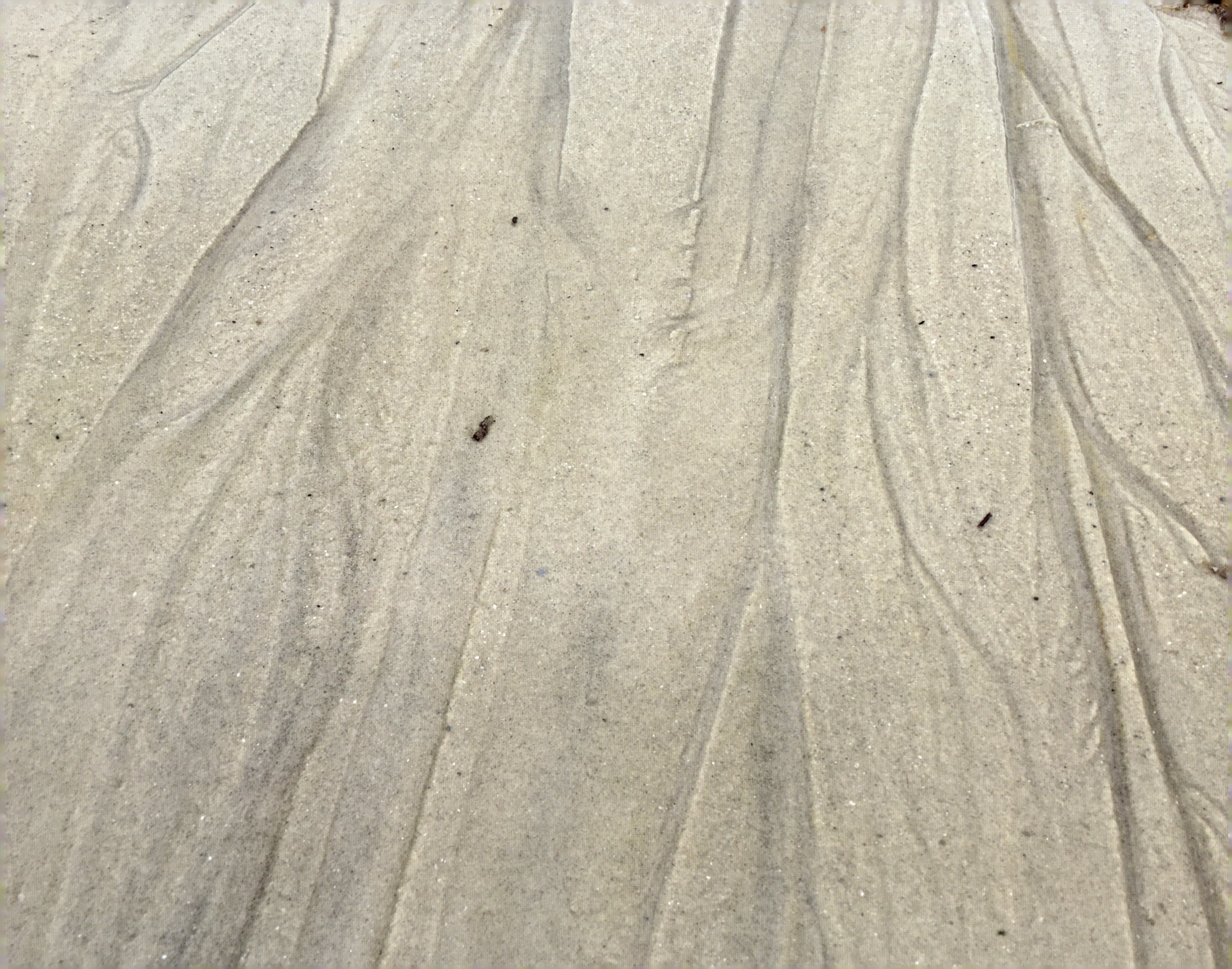

GLASS

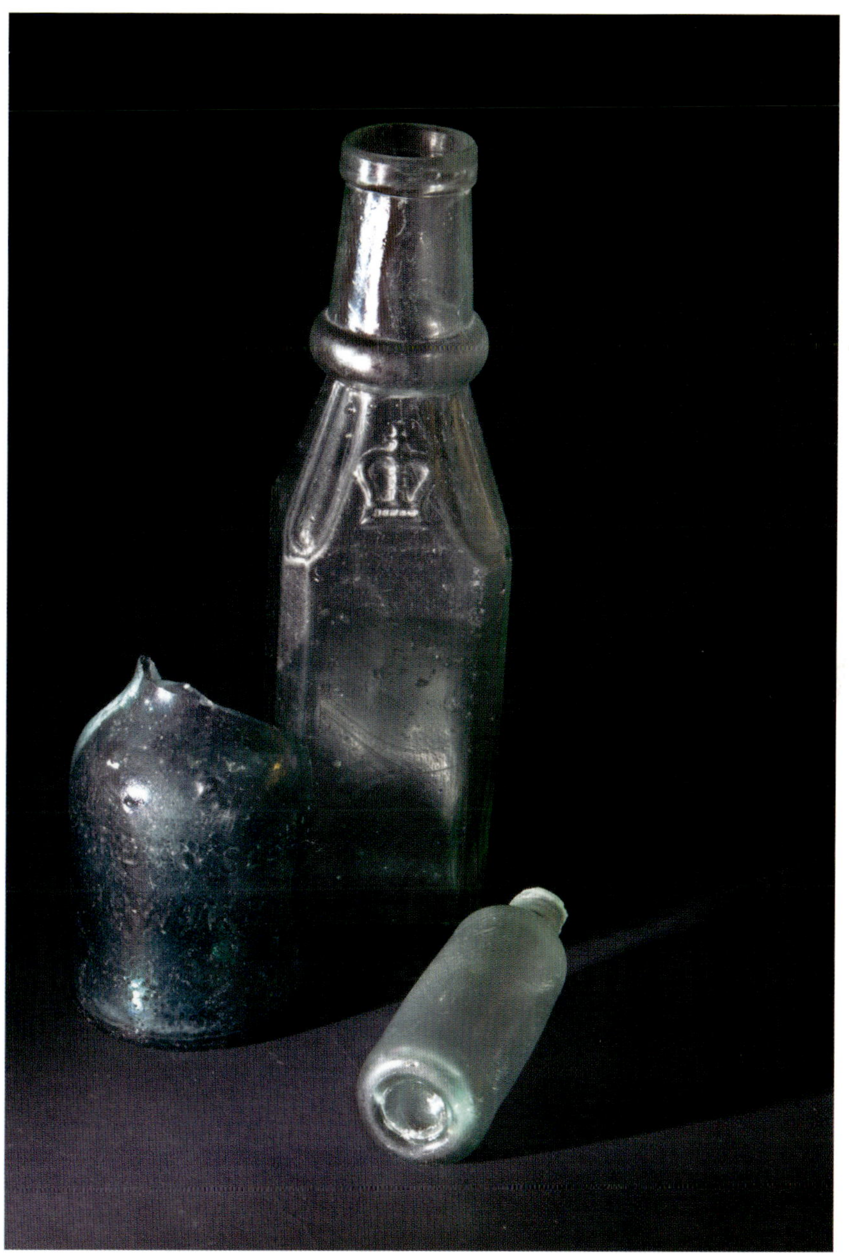

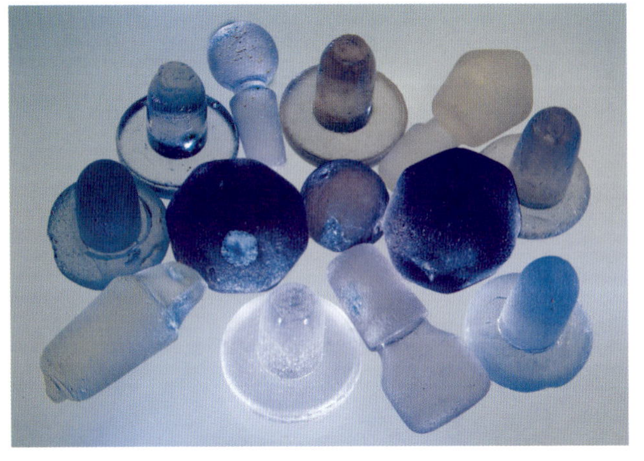

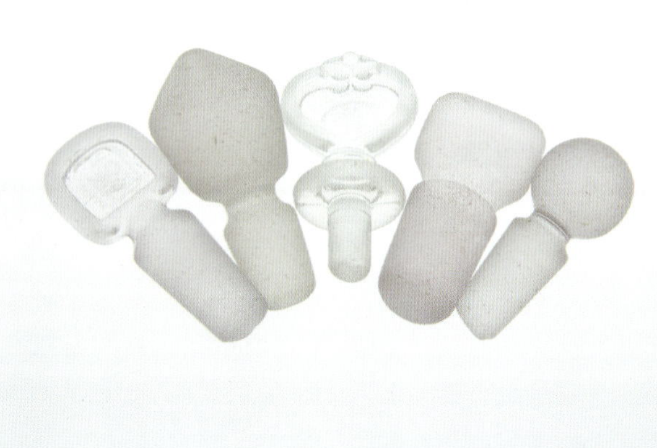

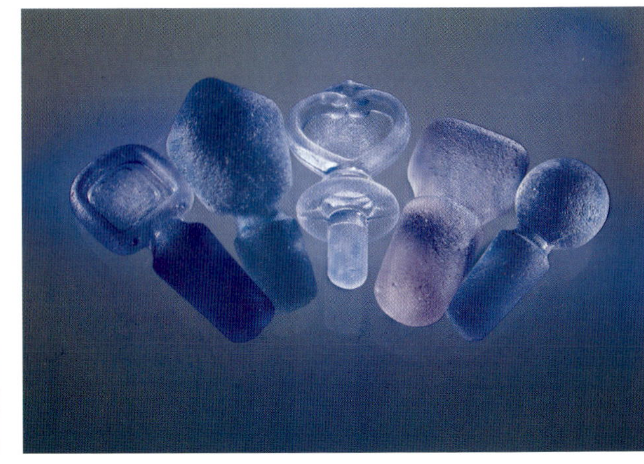

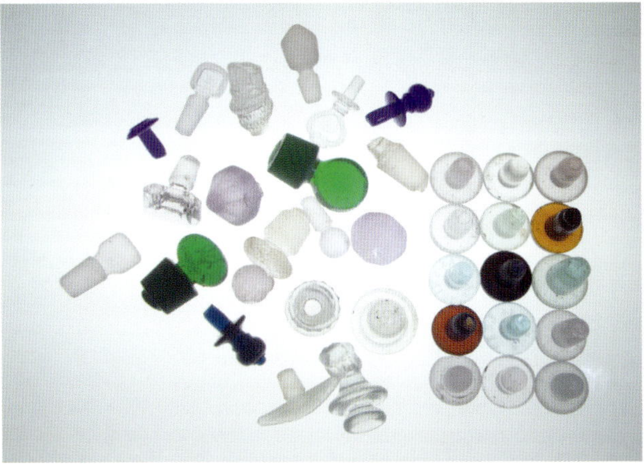

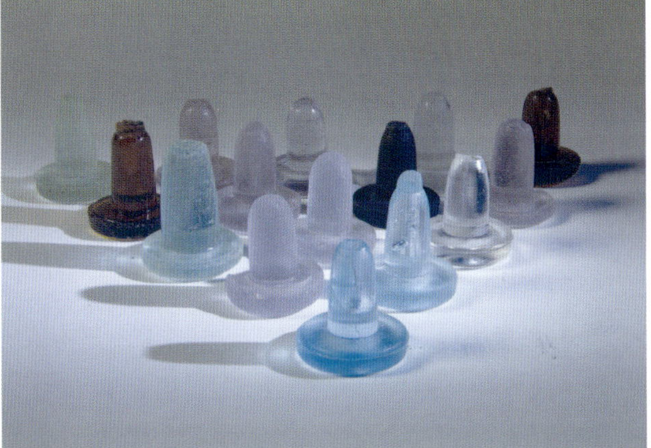

Sea glass has universal appeal and the cachet of a semiprecious gem. Glass is made from humble natural ingredients: sand, soda, and lime, and the colors were initially modest greens and browns due to the iron oxide in the sand. These naturally darker colors protected the contents from sun exposure. Later, bolder, more-expensive colorants were used.

Local naturalist John Alexander often walked the dunes looking for treasure. He found bones and driftwood and could recognize the natural occurrence of petrified sand, called fulgurites, formed when lightning discharges into the sand.

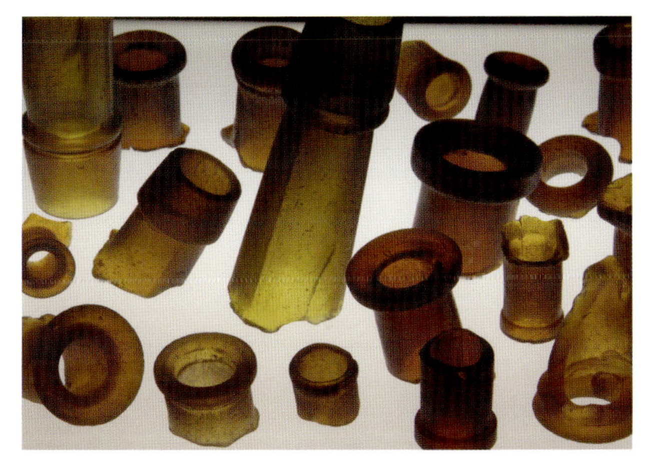
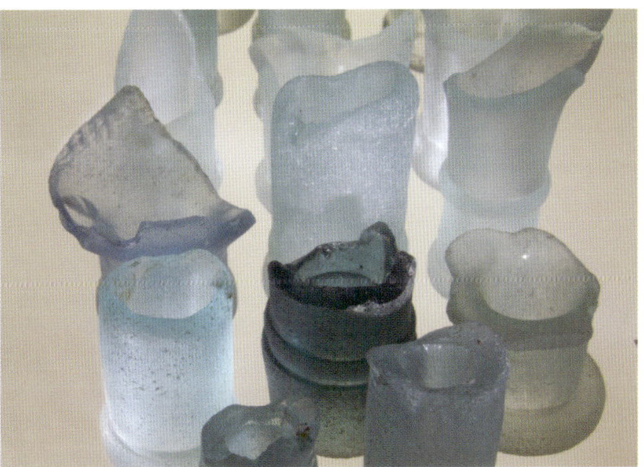
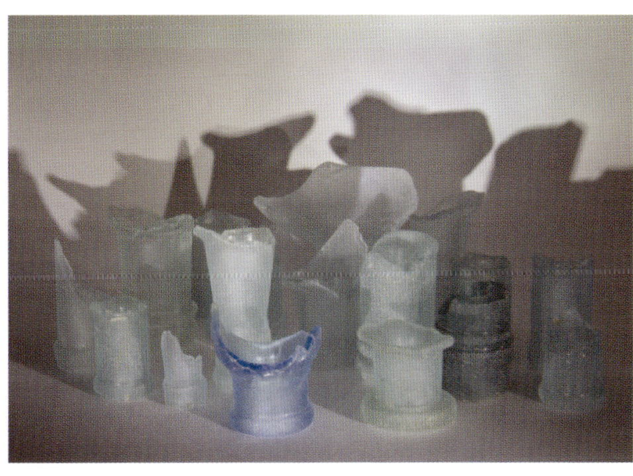

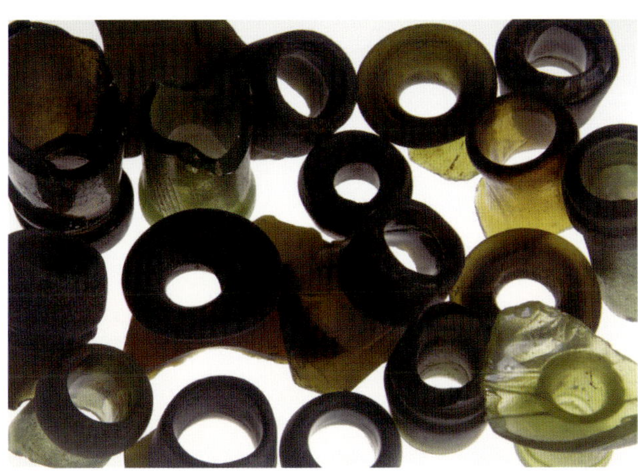
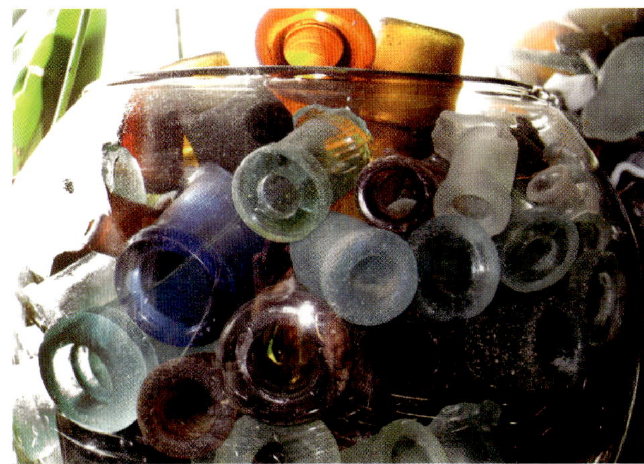

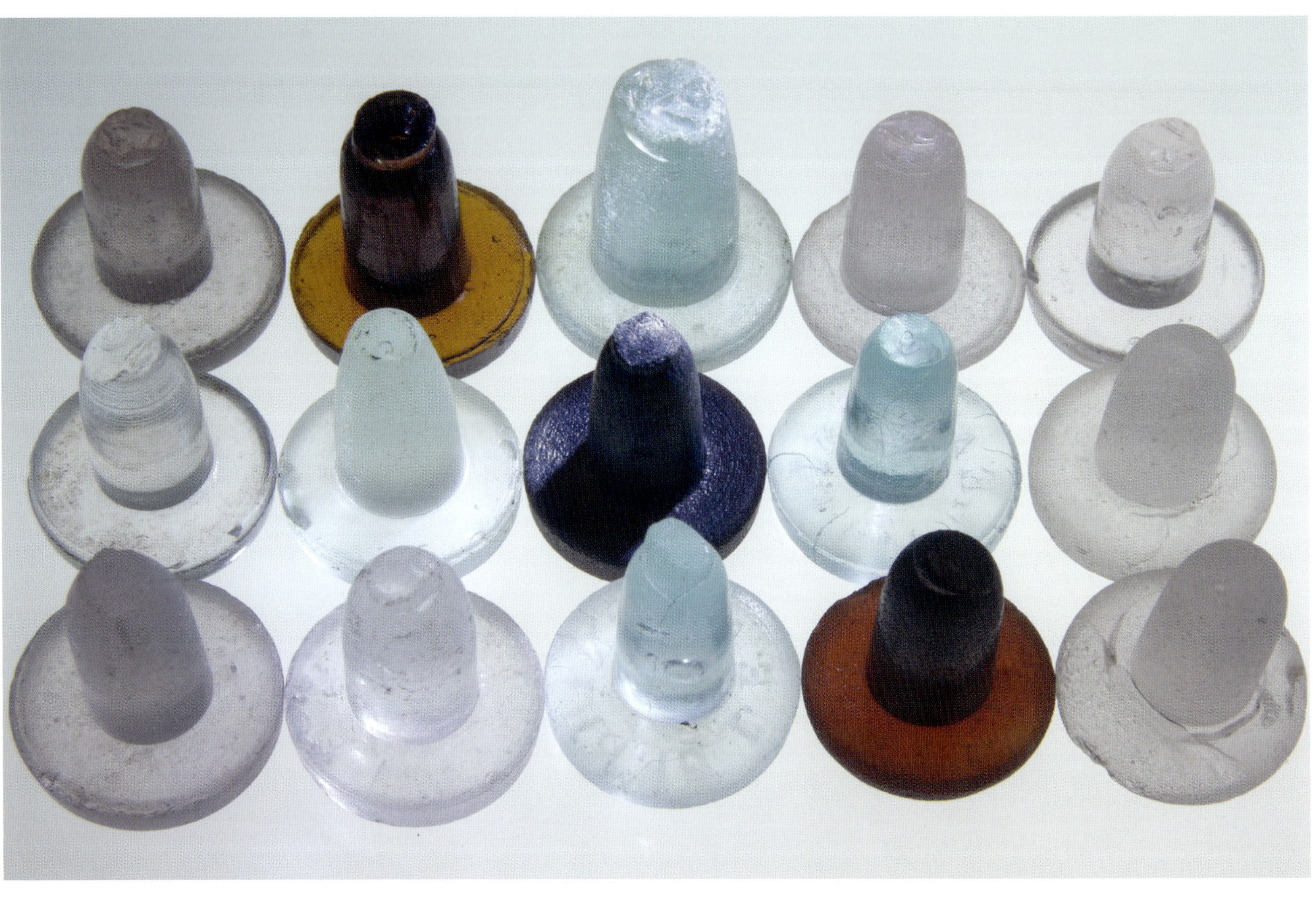

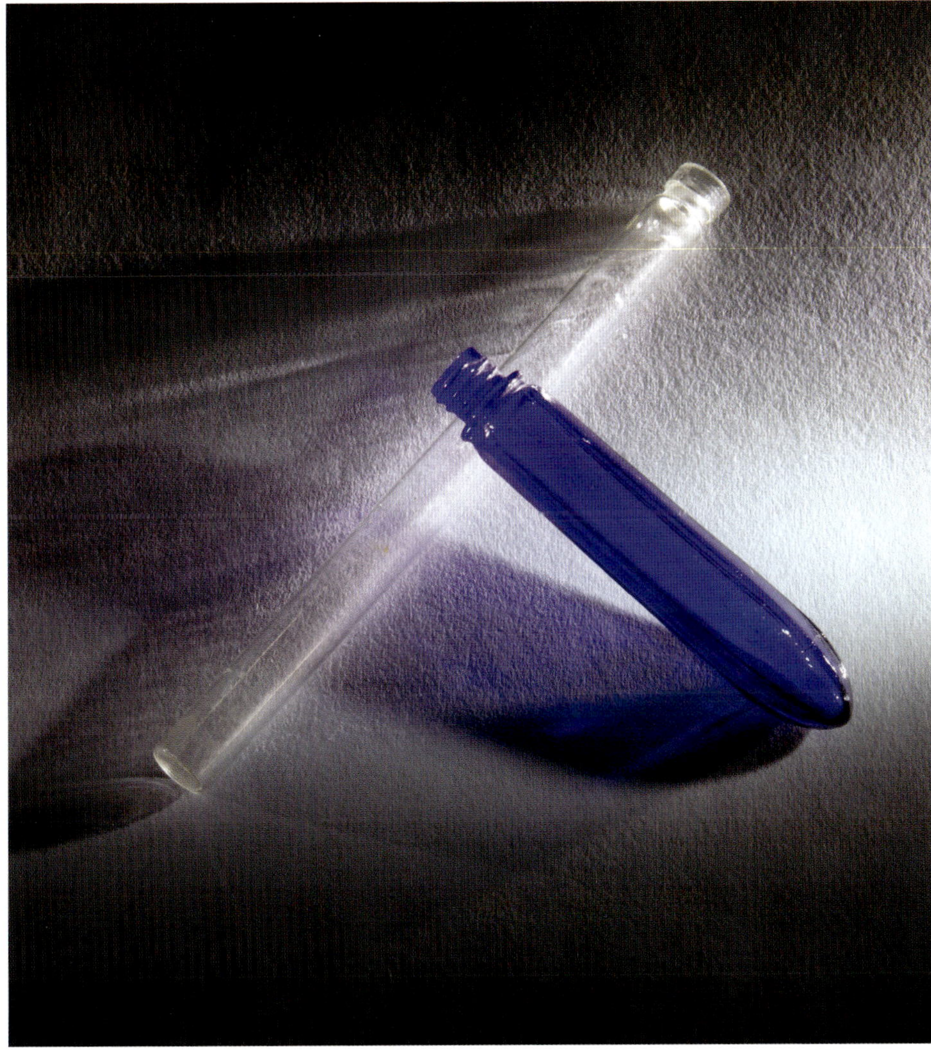

Small, narrow glass bottles, or vials, are referred to as Victorian tear-catchers or lachrymatory bottles. It was believed that their purpose was to catch the tears of a mourning person to keep the dearly departed close. When the tears evaporated, the mourning period ended. Bottles of this nature have been found in Greek and Roman tombs. In modern times, scientists have tested the residue in these bottles, leading them to conclude that the bottles held perfumes and unguents.

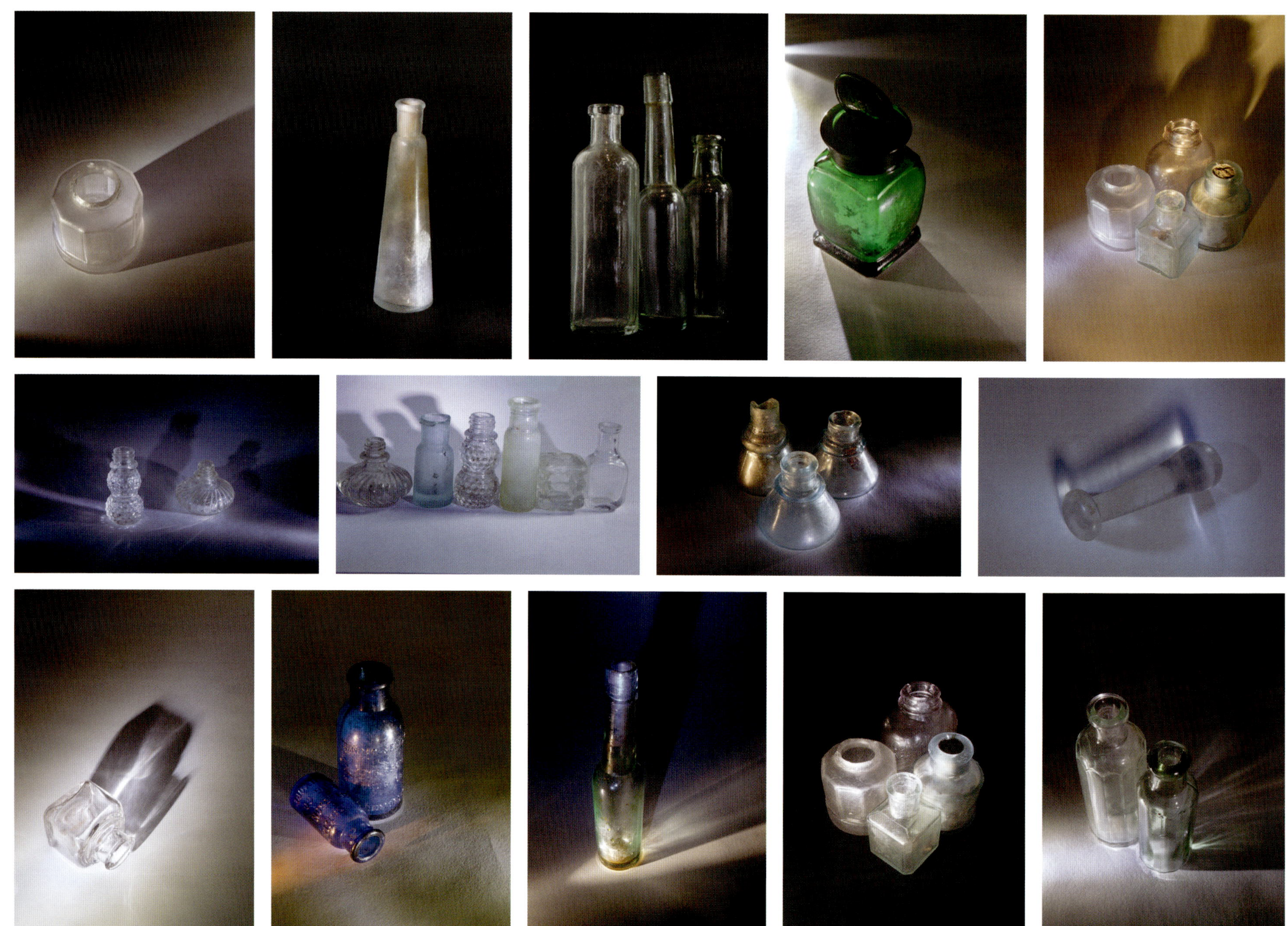

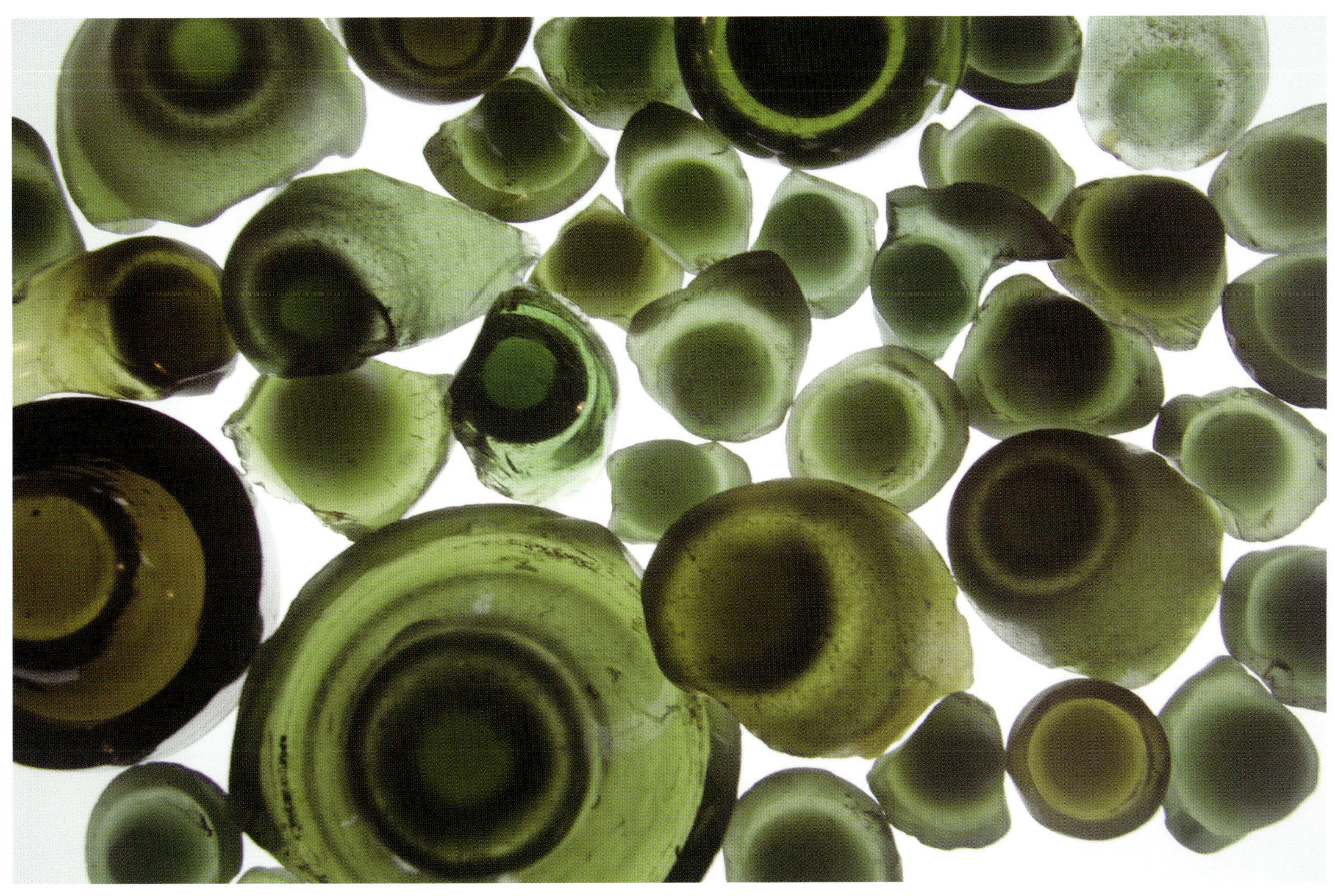

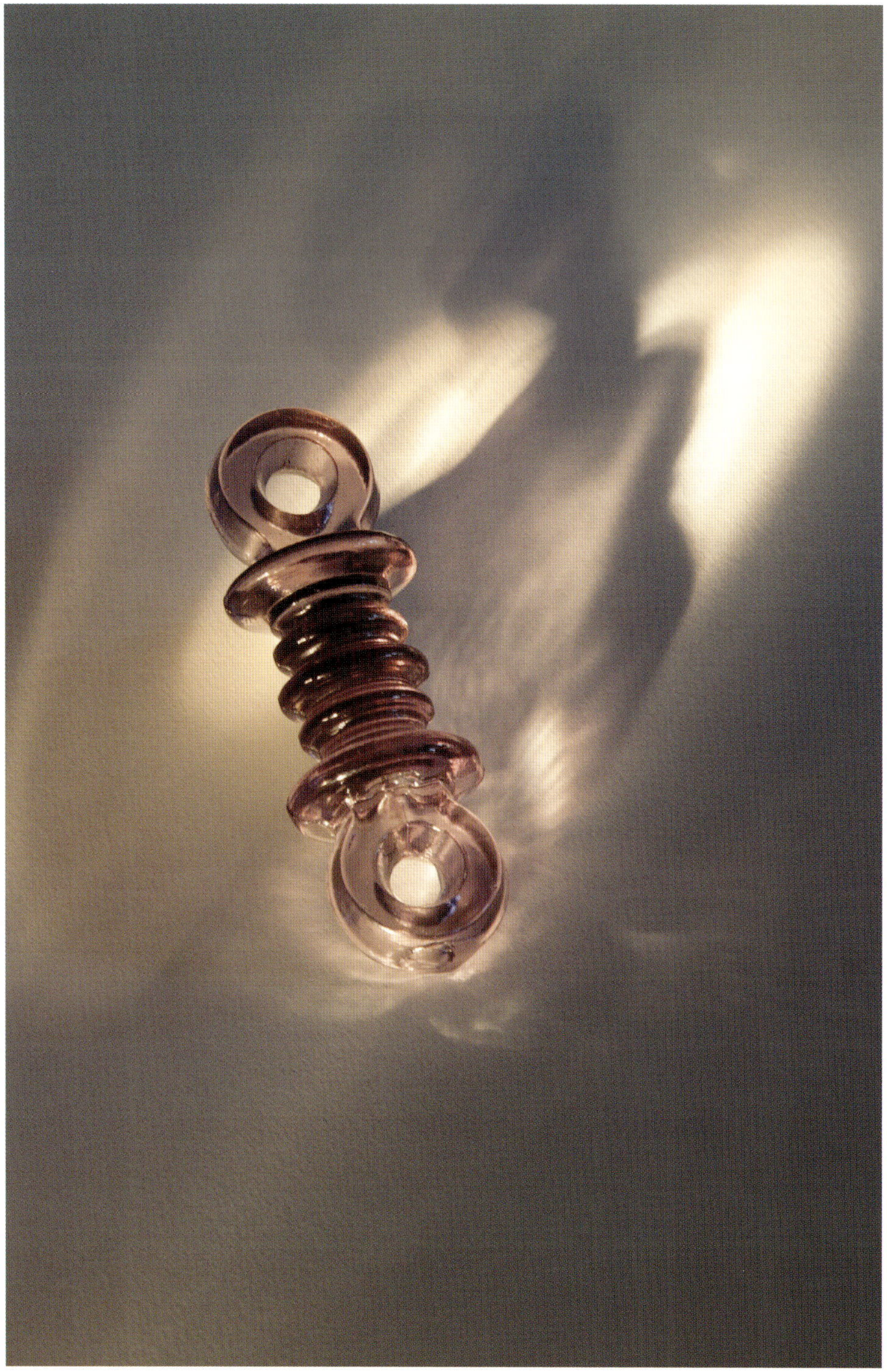

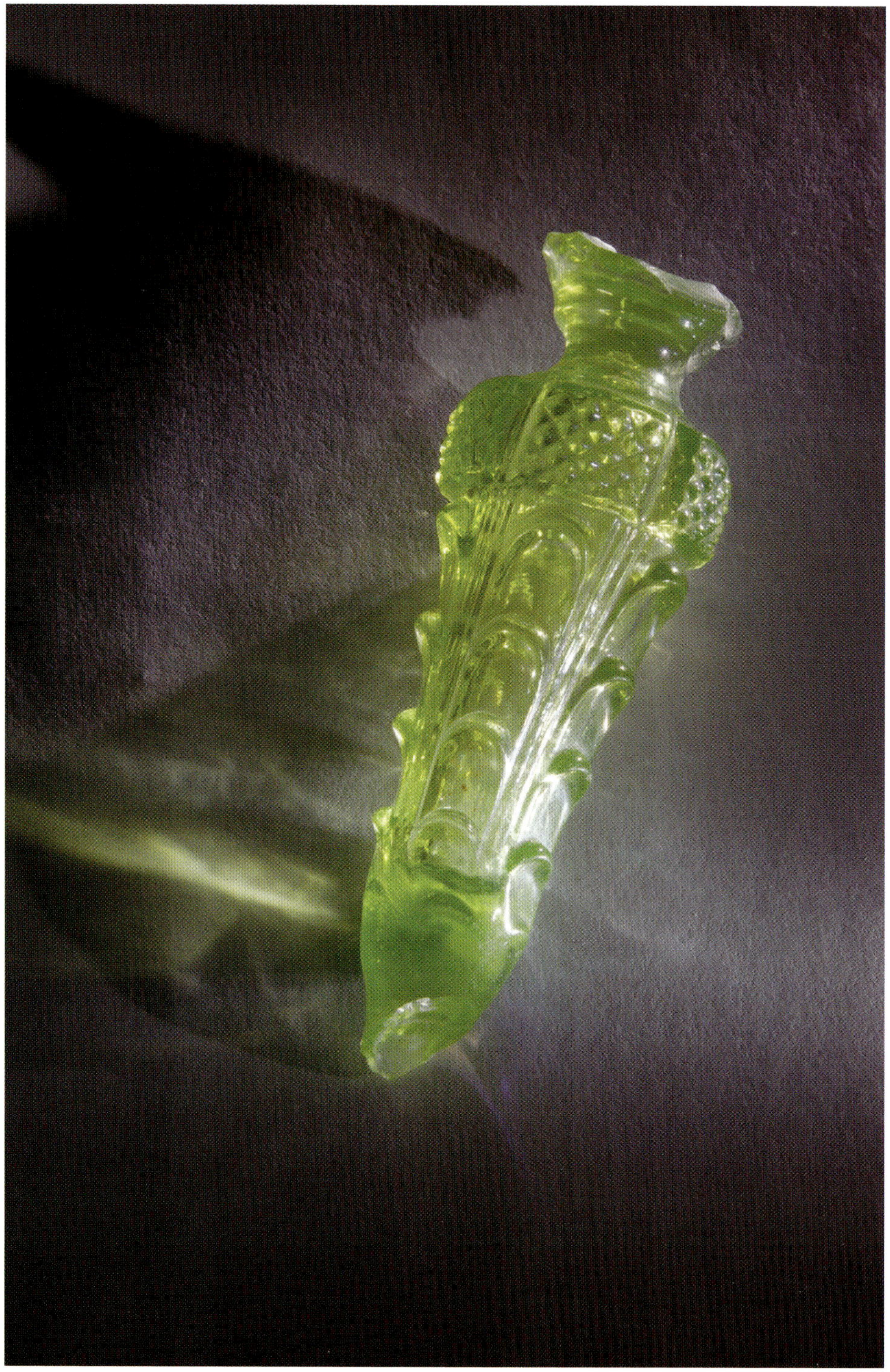

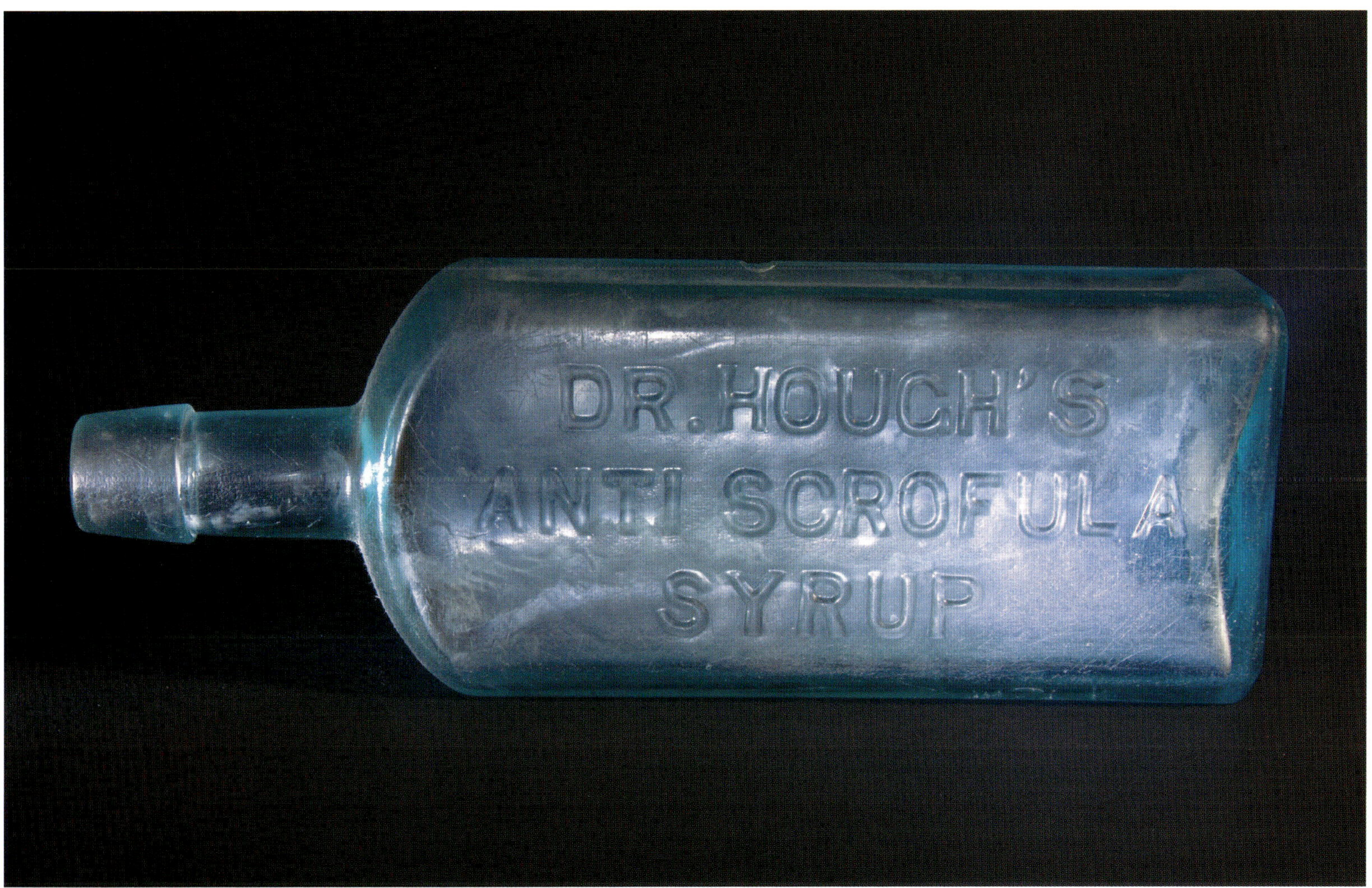

Conversation between Betty Bodian and Amy Heller:

Amy: "You said that back here is the pièce de résistance?"

Betty: "I probably didn't find it in the water, but I thought you'd want to see it. This is my real pièce de résistance because it was one of the first bottles I found. And you have to read it!"

Amy: "Doctor Hough's Anti-Scrofula Syrup? What is Scrofula?"

Betty: "It's a form of tuberculosis. And it sounds like it was something that would have a scab or a rash, but it wasn't."

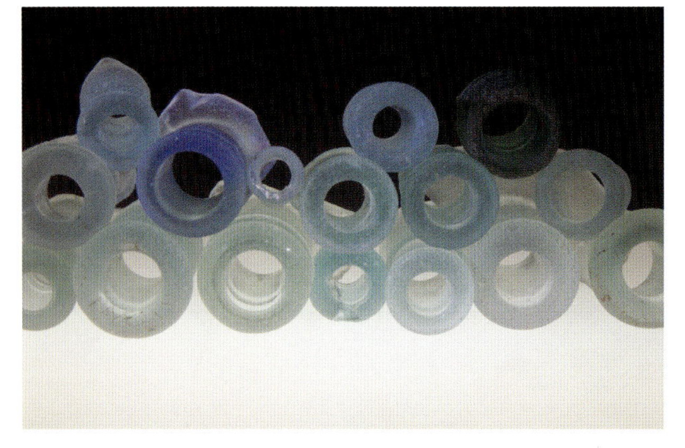

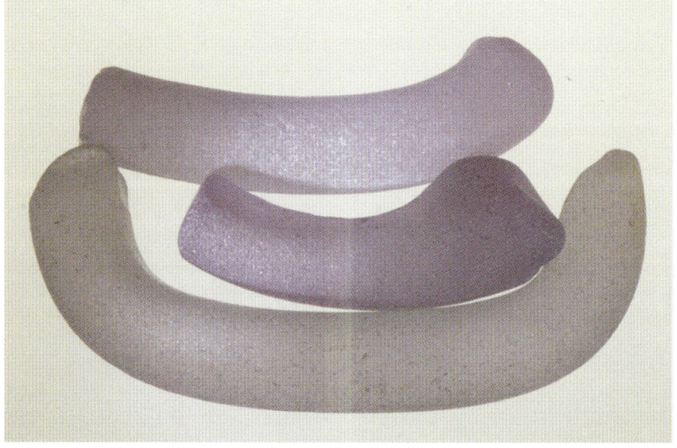

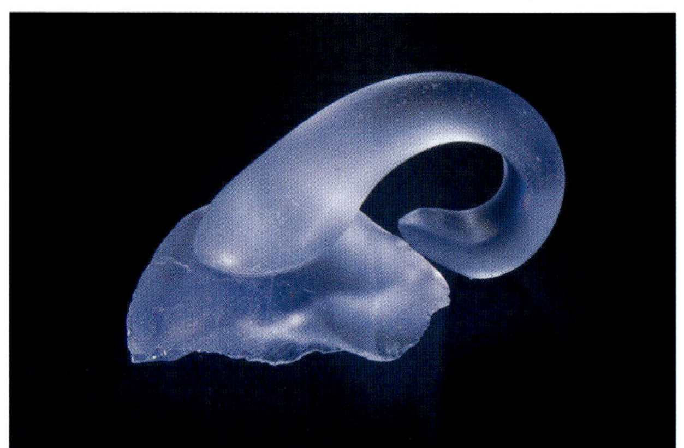

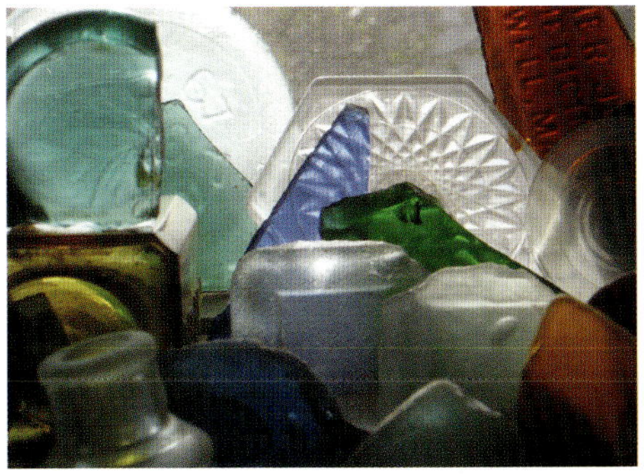

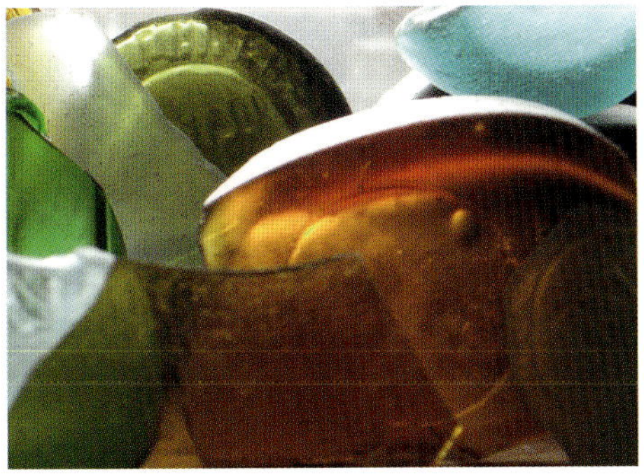

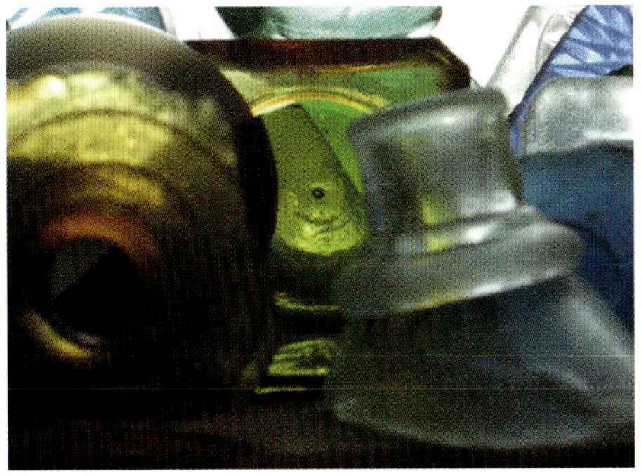

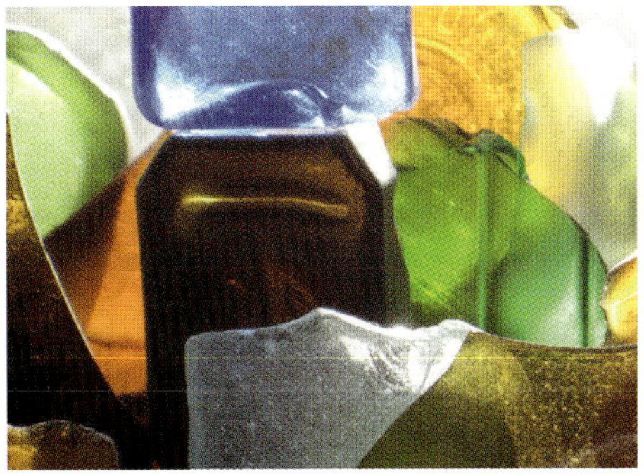

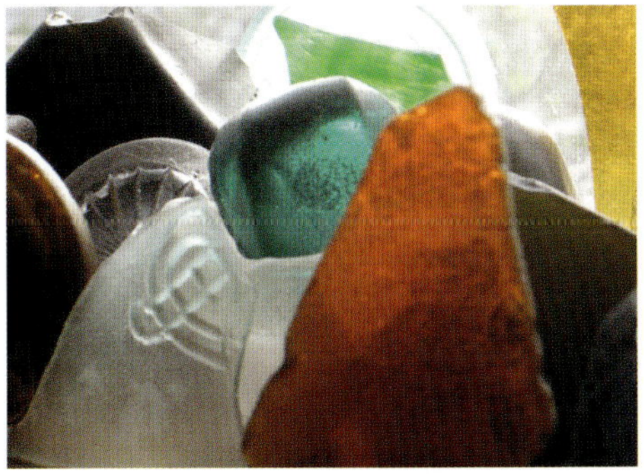

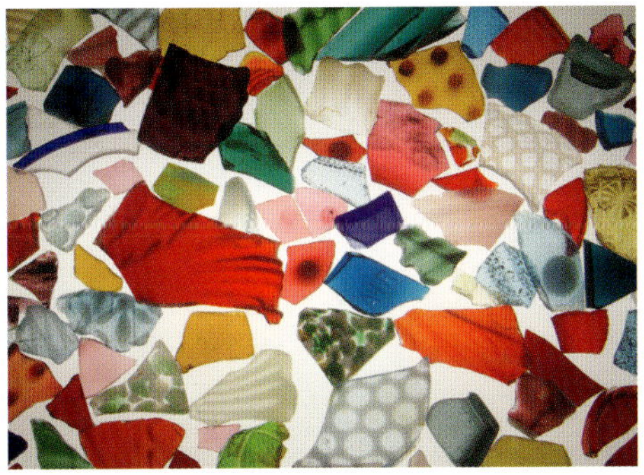

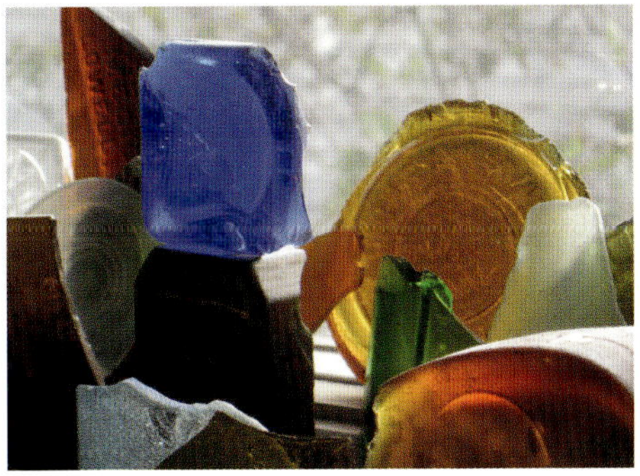

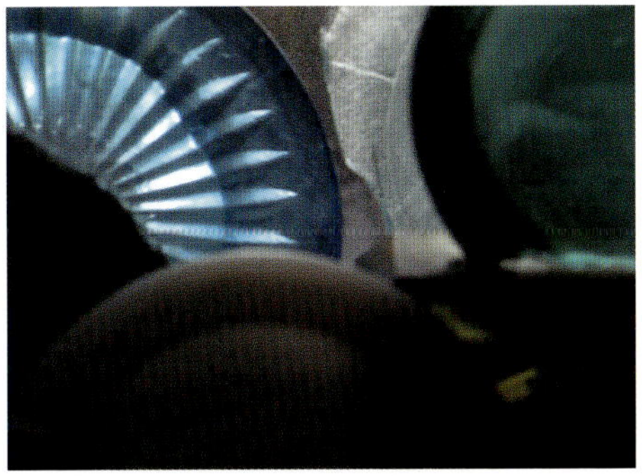

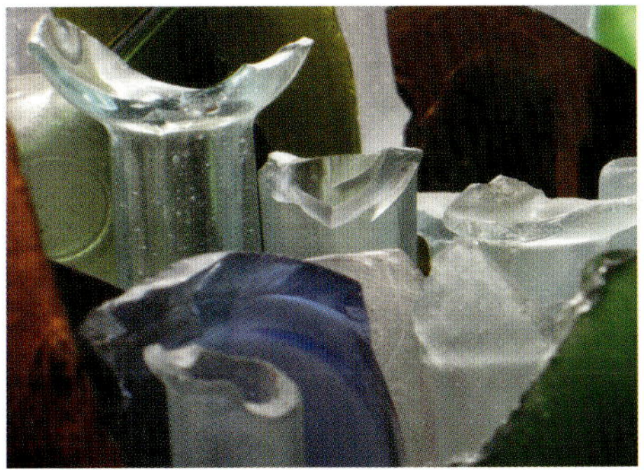

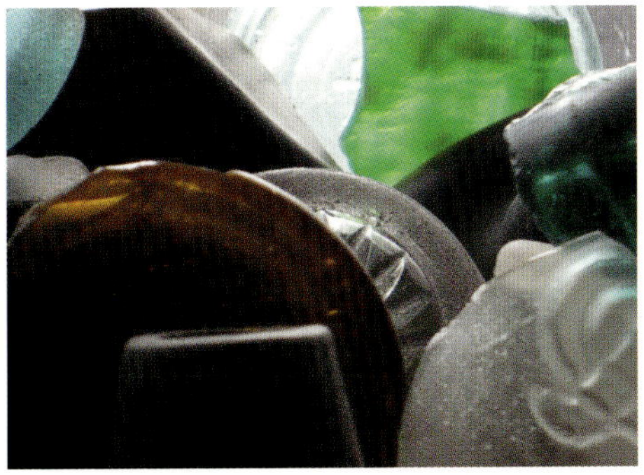

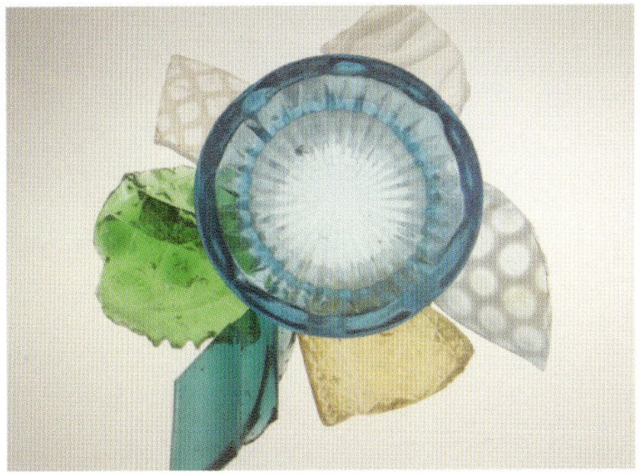

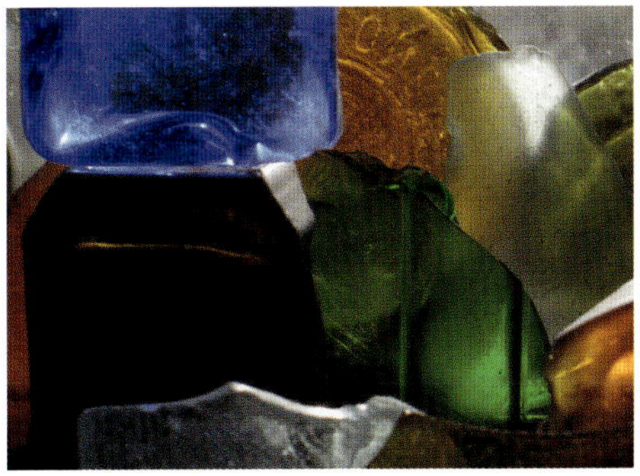

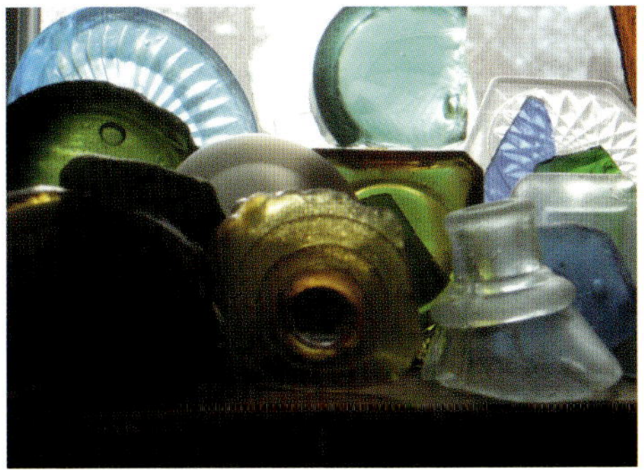

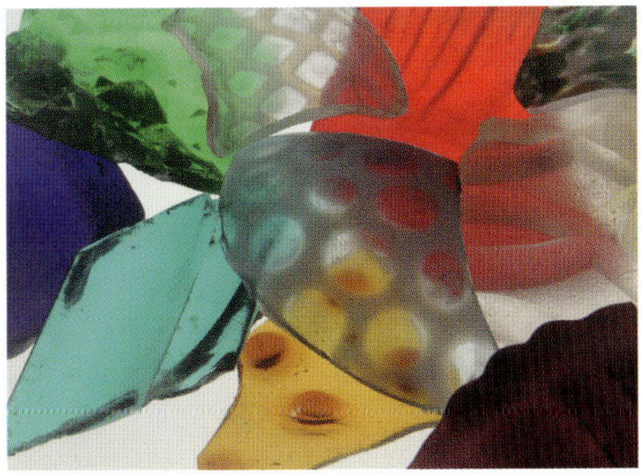

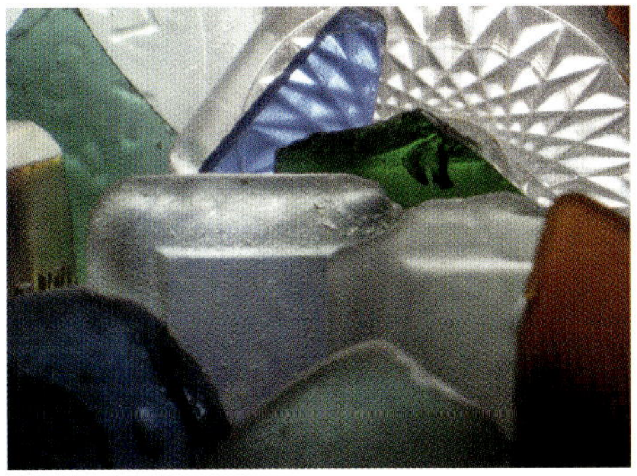

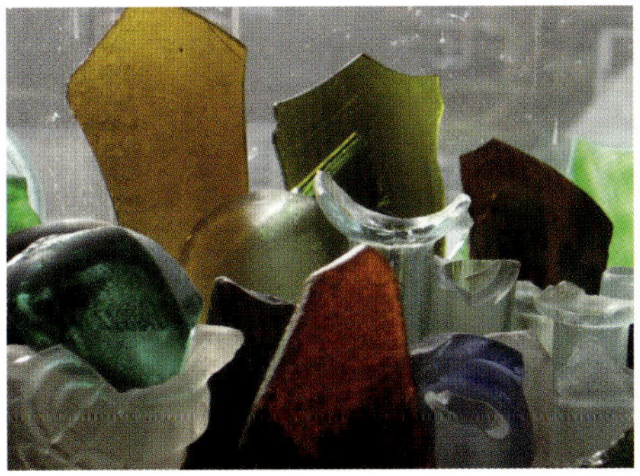

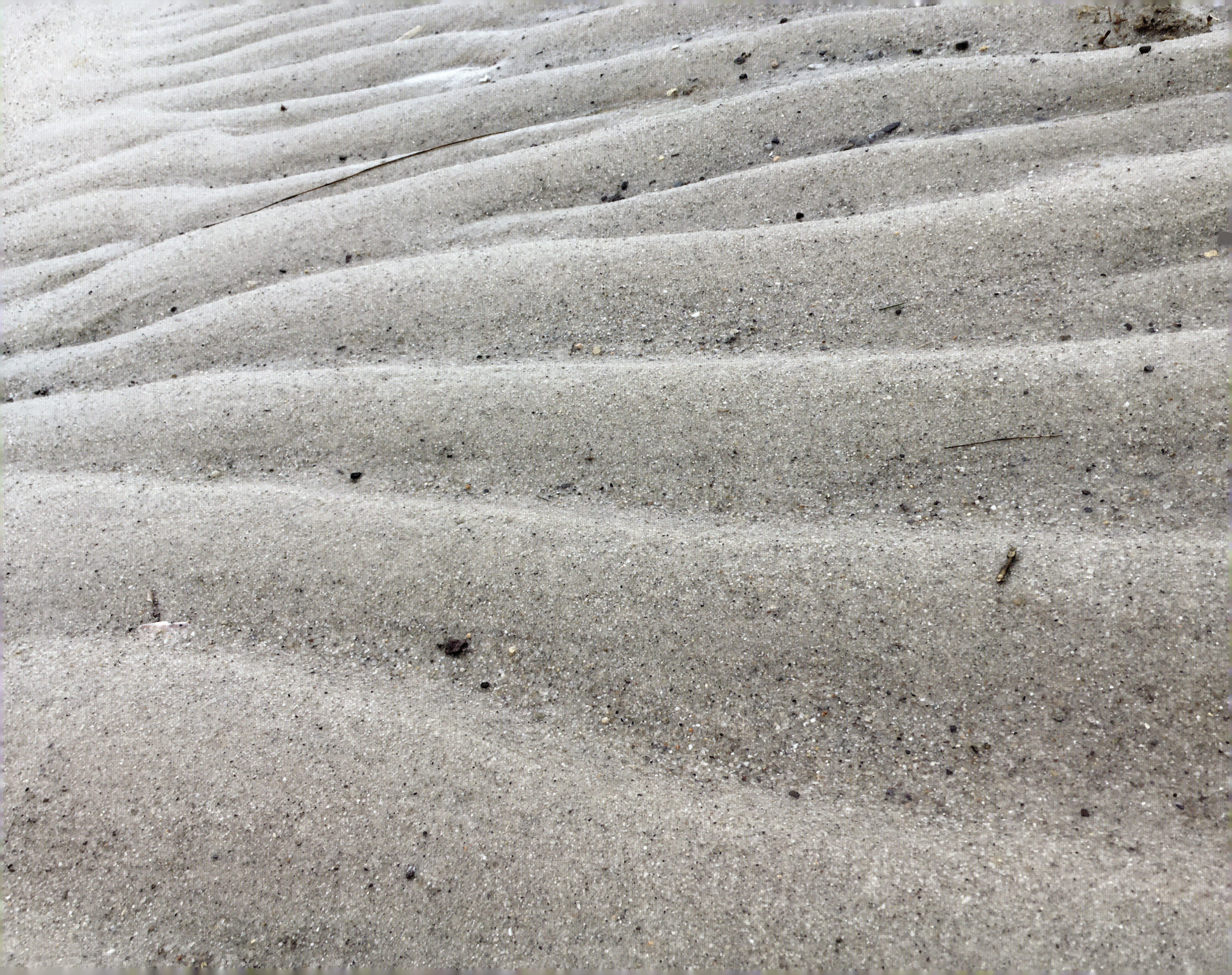

JEWELRY

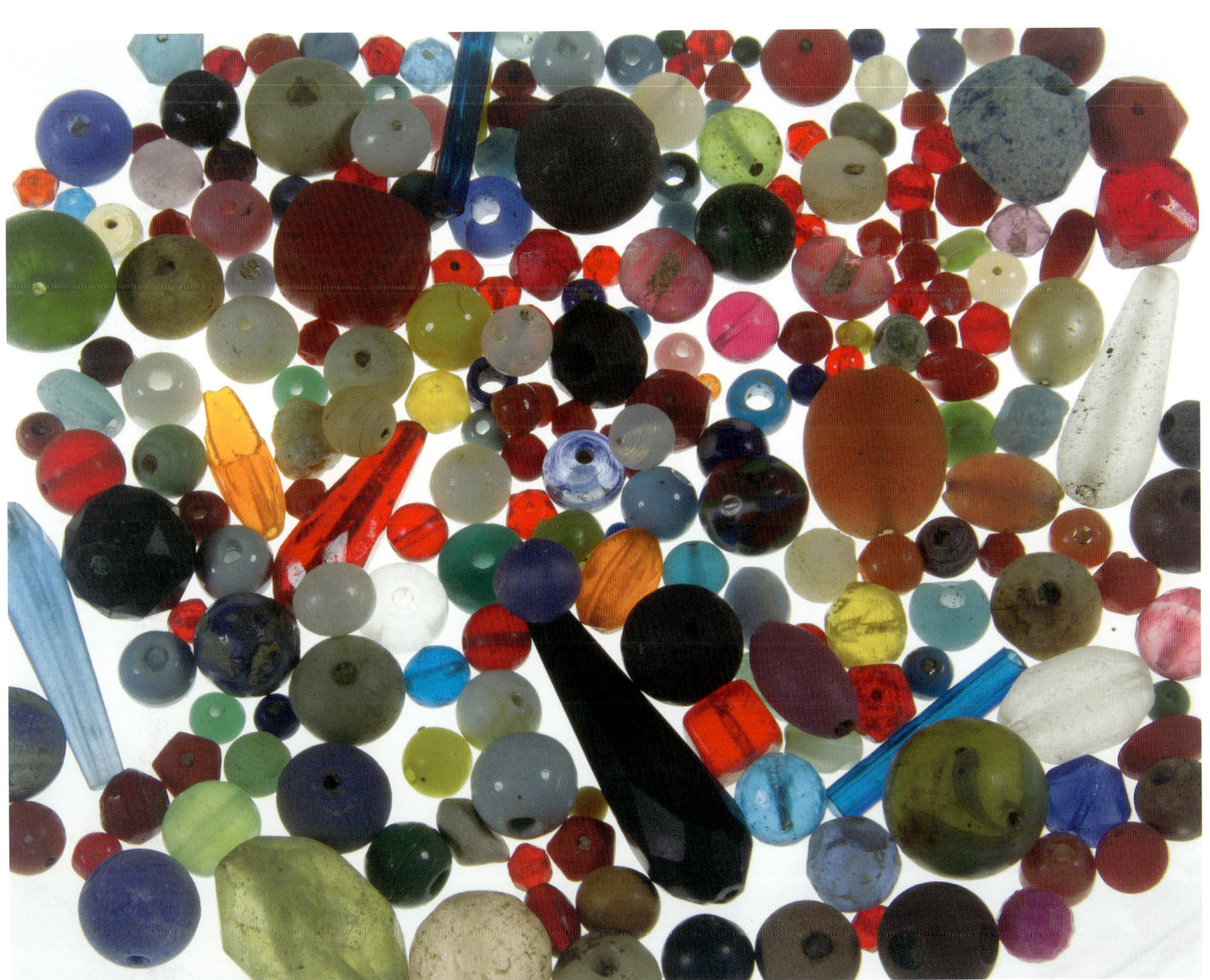

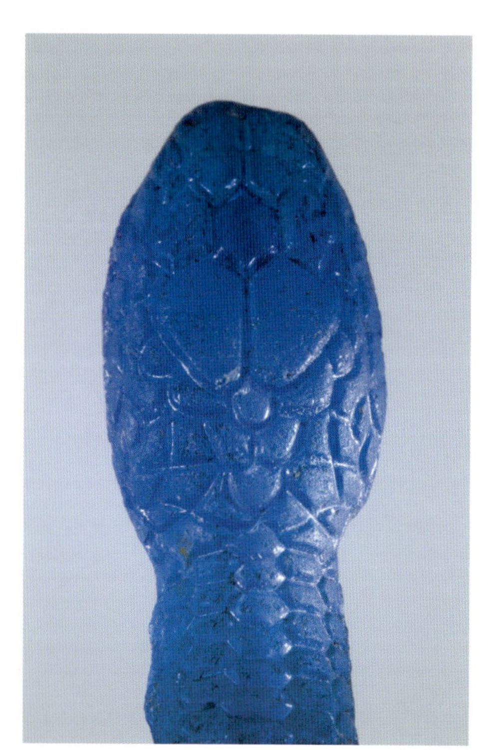

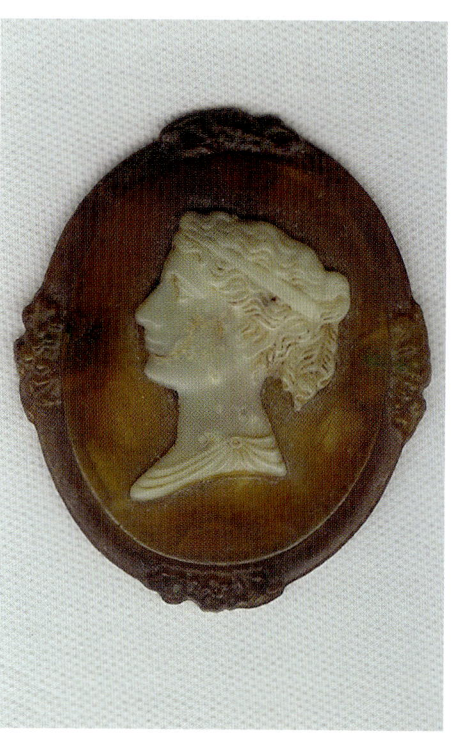

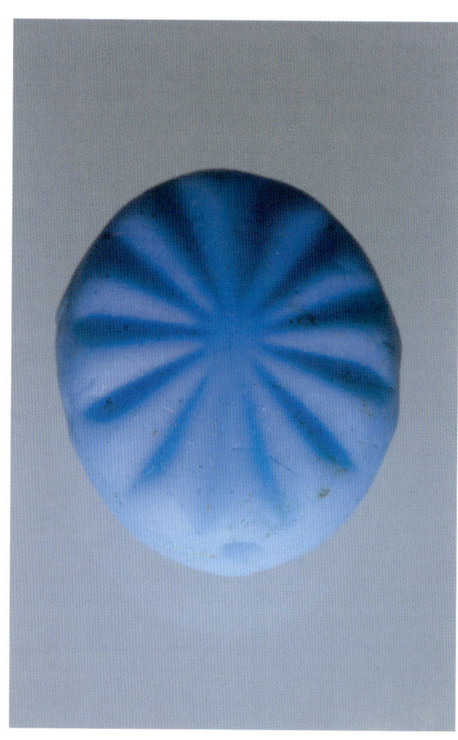

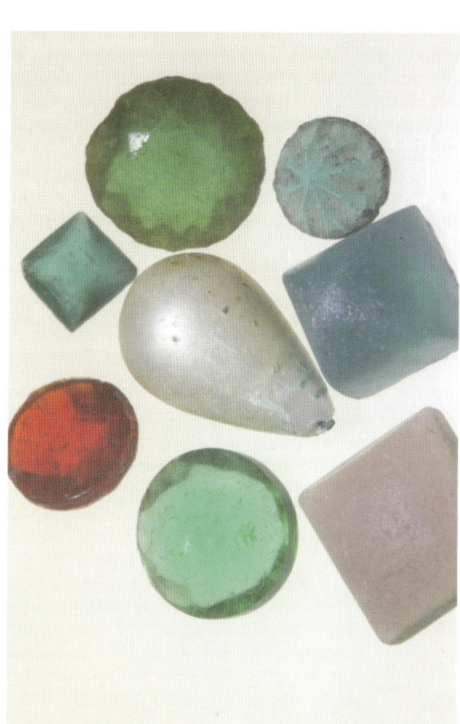

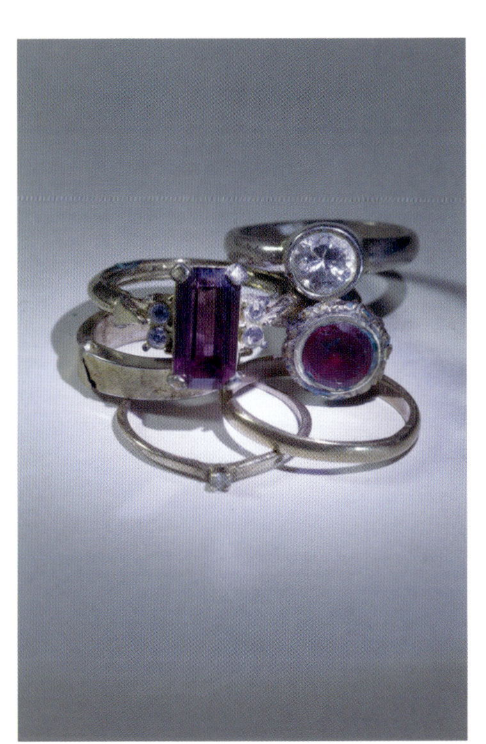

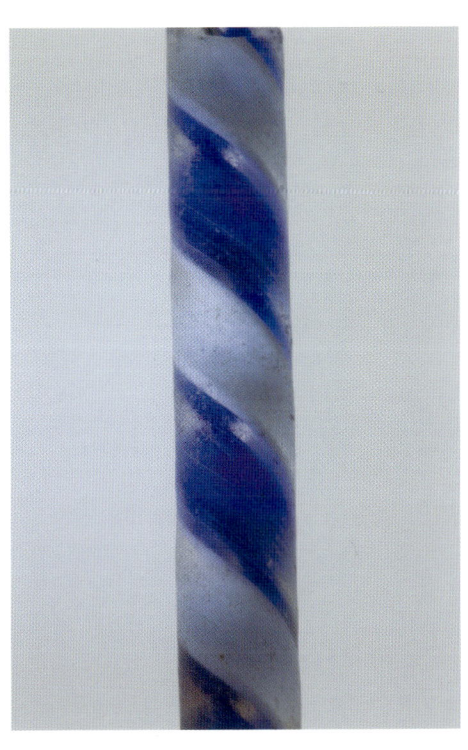

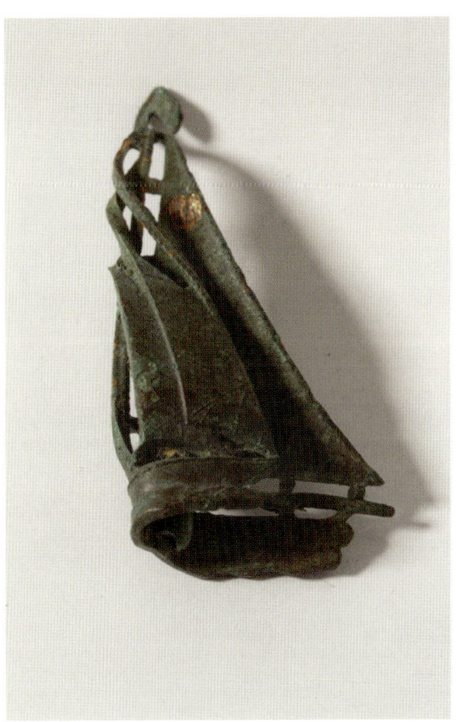

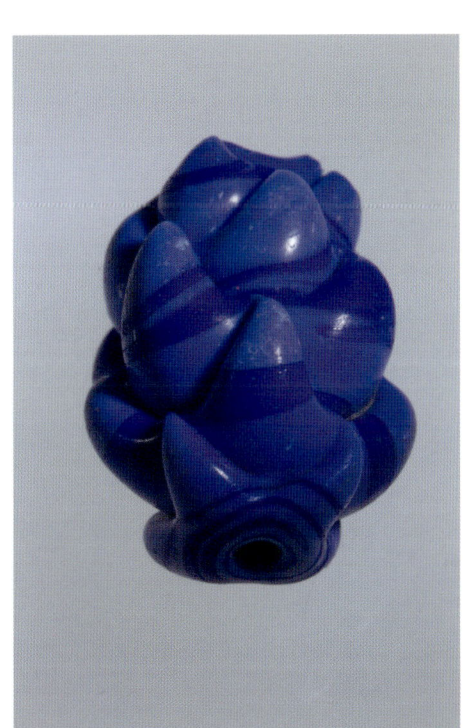

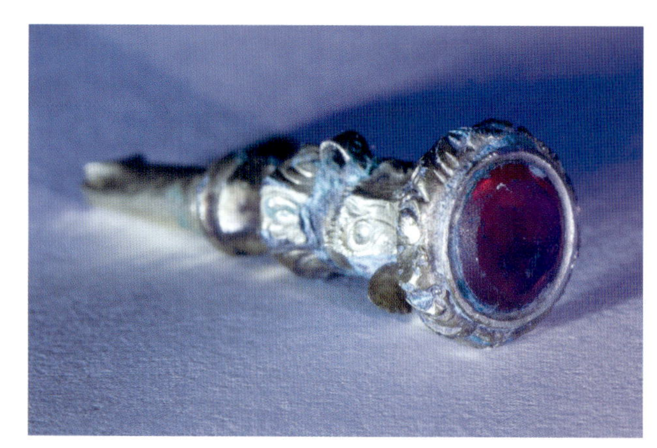

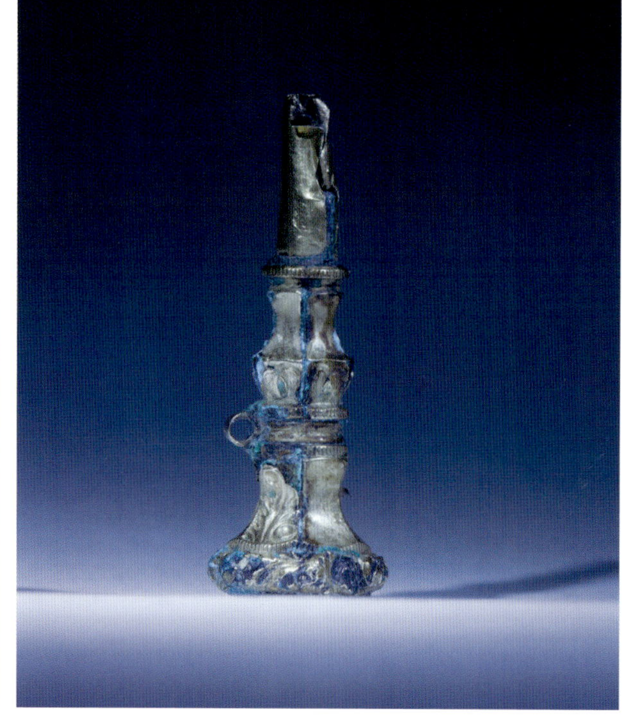

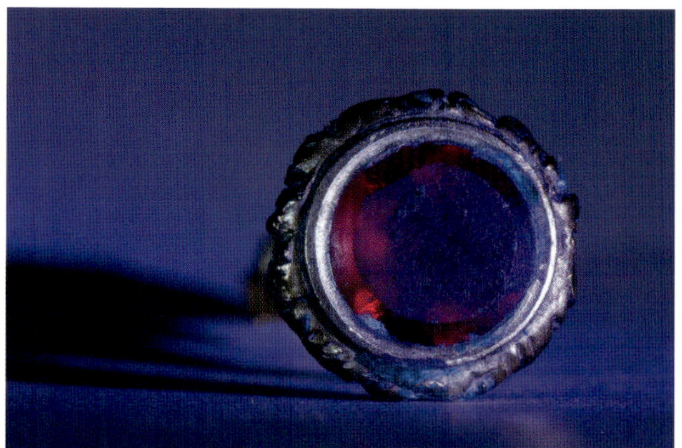

RUBY STICKPIN

If you were to head down to the beach in Provincetown to find shells and pebbles, you might also find old nails, screws, and various other unidentifiable metal objects in shades of rusty oranges and greens, remnants of a bygone industry. The most astute eye would recognize personal metal objects as well. Most of these items are encrusted in concretion, a green mass that results from a chemical reaction of minerals and salt water.

Knowing this, I was never one who passed up a green mass. But one summer morning I surprised even myself. Picking up a green mass, I carefully flicked off a grain of sand or two, expecting to reveal a common nail. What peeked through the encrustation was a glimpse of gold. I tucked it in the safety of my jeans pocket and tried to walk casually home, but my heart was pounding with excitement.

I went upstairs to my studio, closed the door, and slowly began to peel away the grains of sand, revealing an engraving of symmetrical swirls and patterns of braiding around the perimeter of a dark-red jewel. The setting was about an inch long, and the object was later identified as the tip of a stickpin.

Throwing aside my Zen attitude and spurred on by thoughts of a jewelry case gone overboard, I made sure I caught the next low tide. Not wanting to attract attention, I sauntered to the same area of discovery. To my wonder, another green mass was peeking out of the sand, revealing its identity as a man's gold filigreed ring. Unfortunately, the ring was held together by the concretion and fell apart once it dried. But I still have the gold foil oval from the ring, along with the ruby stickpin.

Through research I discovered why women used stickpins in their hats: These could be used as protection against an assault, piercing the heart without a trace. And her virtue, highly valued in those times, would be intact. I prefer to think perhaps there was a midnight tryst or a midnight swim.

—Gail Browne

BOOTLEGGING

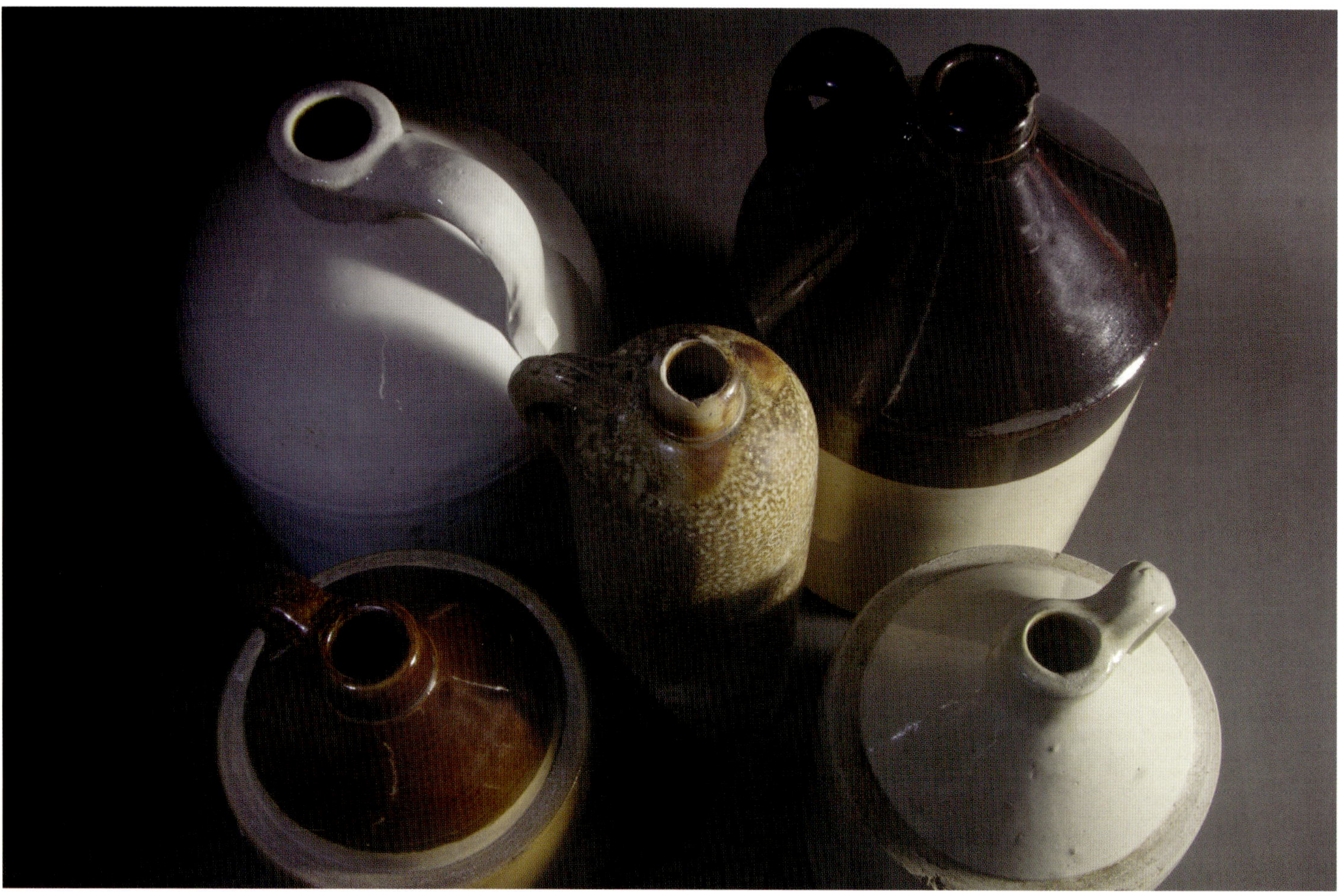

In the early 1980s, I was sea clamming on the far East End flats. At one point my rake hit something with a different feel and sound, and I yanked up a fifth of whiskey, cork and seal still intact. The bottle held a place of honor in my refrigerator. And as word spread, occasionally an old salt would stop by for a shot on the way home.

—Gail Browne

Provincetown has always been segregated from society by virtue of its geography—a condition that encouraged entrepreneurial spirit. Liquor was often used medicinally and as payment for services. Prohibition, which lasted from 1920 to 1933, was an economic boon to the town. Not only did liquor provide a shadow economy, but residents were occasionally rewarded with a cache that had sunk or been jettisoned overboard and washed up onshore.

Fortunes were also made by rum-running. As a matter of fact, it was a third-generation patriarch married to a second-generation restaurateur who headed the largest operation in Provincetown. In his seventies, the family "retired" him to golfing. But some form of the occupation persisted well into the 1980s, and speculation exists to this day.

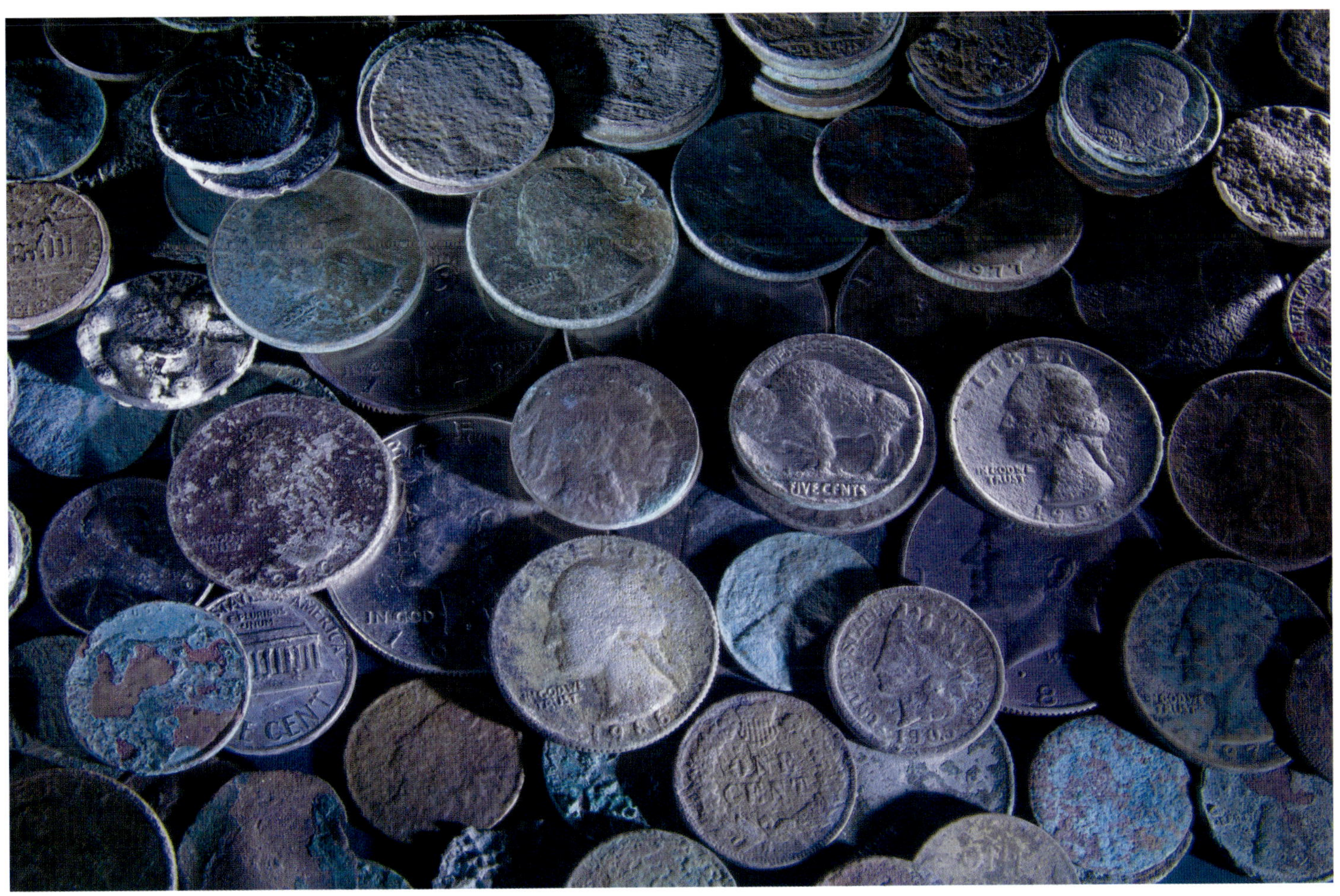

In a related vein, in the mid-1970s, bales of pot washed up on the Backside beaches. To the disappointment of many, the salt water had a detrimental effect on the product.

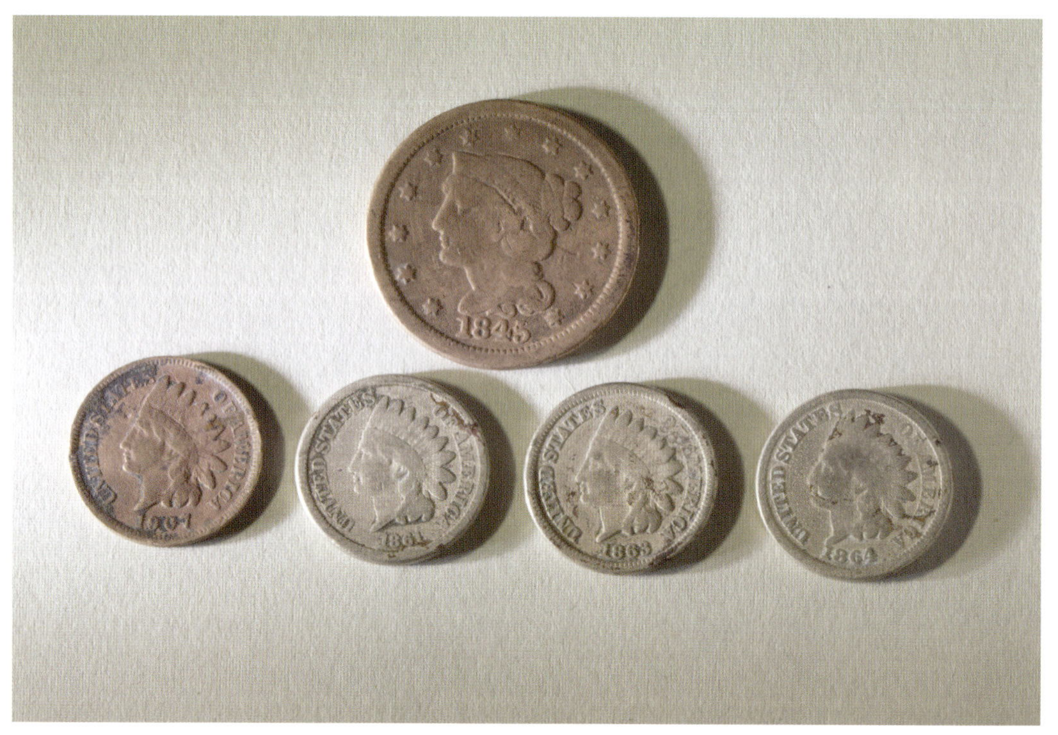
1845
1861
1863
1864

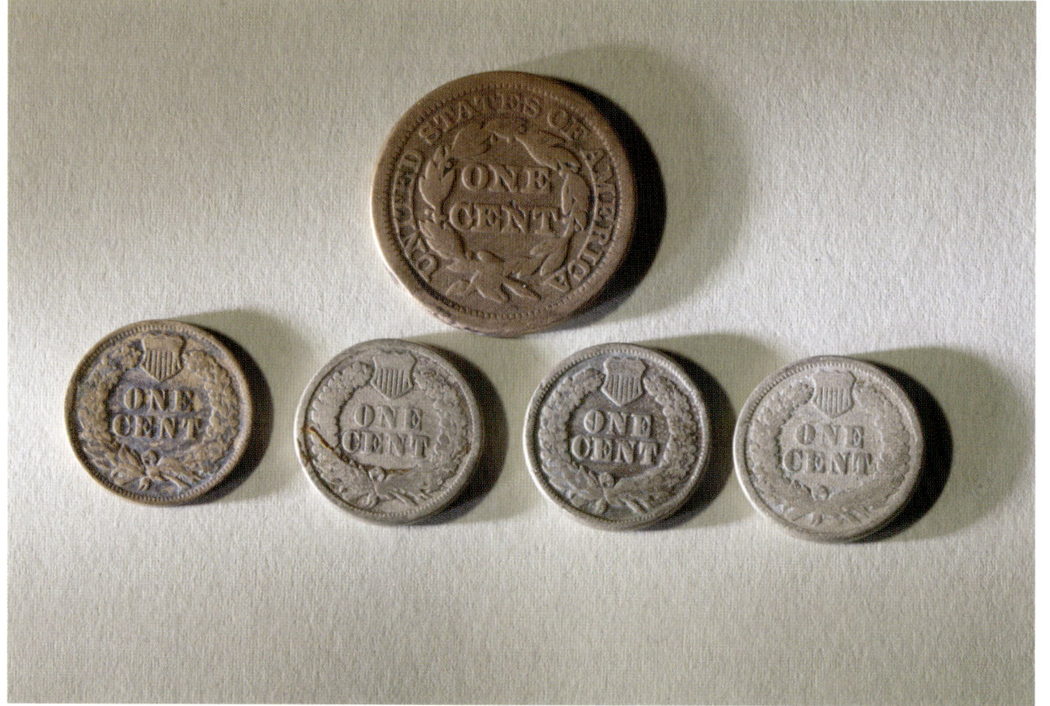
UNITED STATES OF AMERICA
ONE CENT
ONE CENT
ONE CENT
ONE CENT
ONE CENT

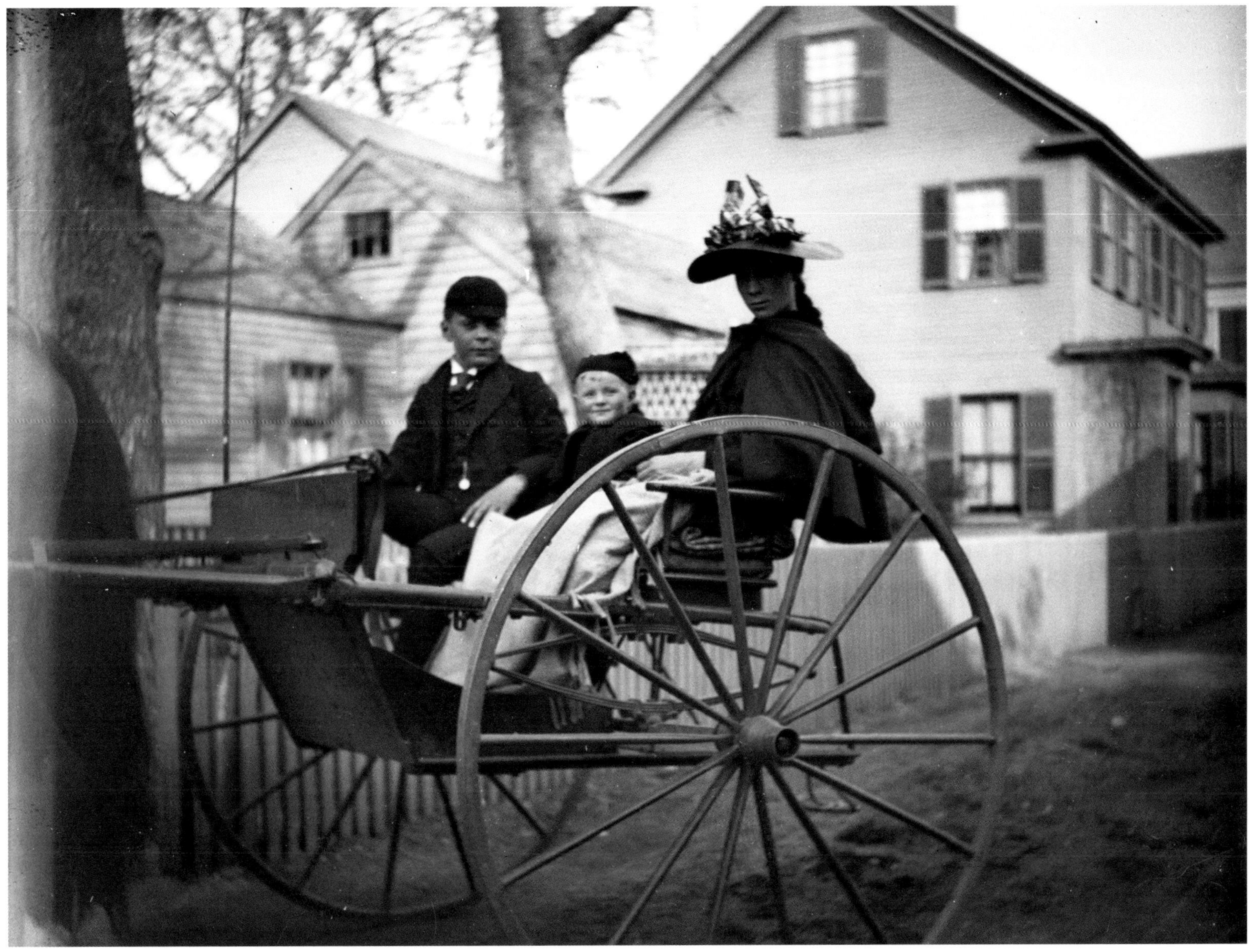

Provincetown developed into an interdependent society. Hard work was the norm, and everyone shared in the spoils to varying degrees. Some people had fine woven rugs on their floors, and some had painted floors. But it was a nonclassist society, and no one went hungry. The catch of the day could be had by meeting either the incoming boats at day's end or your neighbor over the back fence.

THE MAGIC CARPET

On a still January afternoon, I headed out to beachcomb at sunset, which is usually spectacular in the winter. As usual for that time of year, there was no one else around. I wasn't planning on staying long because it was so cold I could see my breath. After a short walk, I decided to return to the Town Landing.

Just then, my eye caught sight of an unusual texture at the shoulder of the sandbar: Fringe! A rug! The sun was going down and the tide had turned, so I knew I didn't have much time. Frantically, I began digging with my hands and kicking sand with my feet. I tugged and pulled and kicked and dug until I could see patterns of red. I ran to my house, grabbed my car keys and my two children, and headed back to the beach.

We tugged and scraped and dug until we pulled it free, this sand-and-water-soaked hunk of heaviness. Rolling it up as best we could, we dragged it to the waiting station wagon. I felt as though we were in a movie, having created the perfect crime and disposing of the evidence!

It took about a month to wash out all of the sand and dry the rug by the wood stove. For about eight years, the rug served as a centerpiece in my Commercial Street gallery.

—Gail Browne

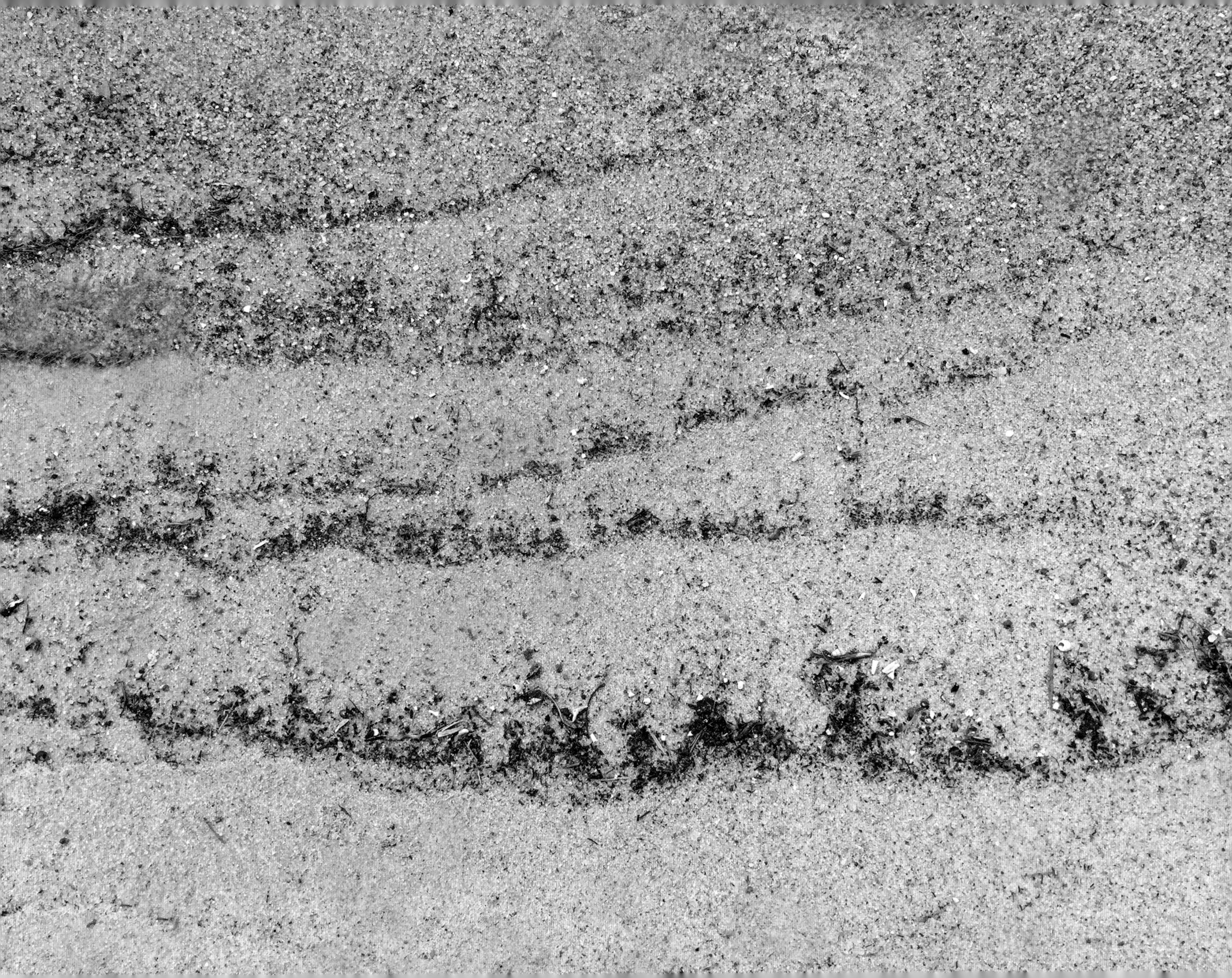

Domestic Livestock

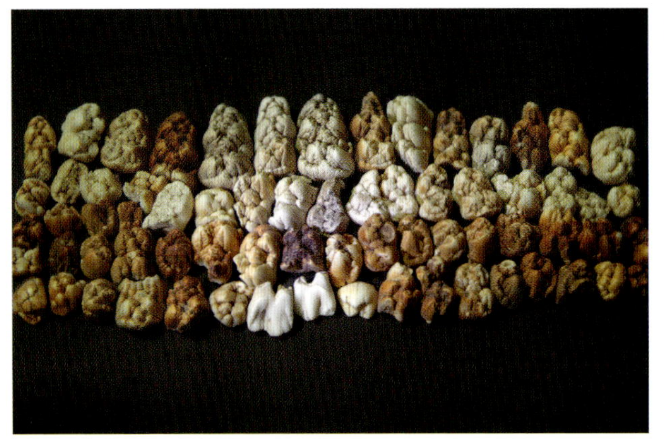

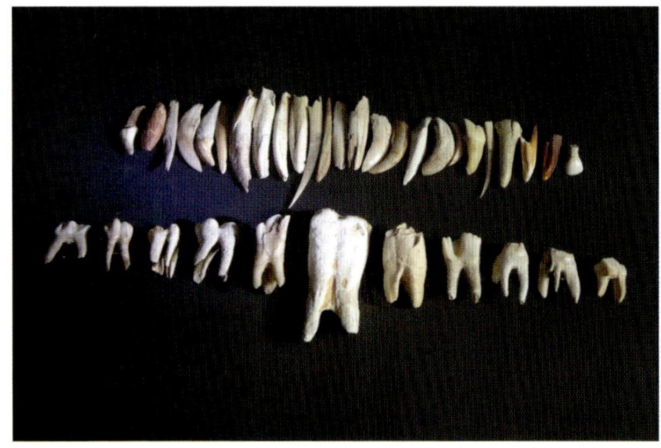

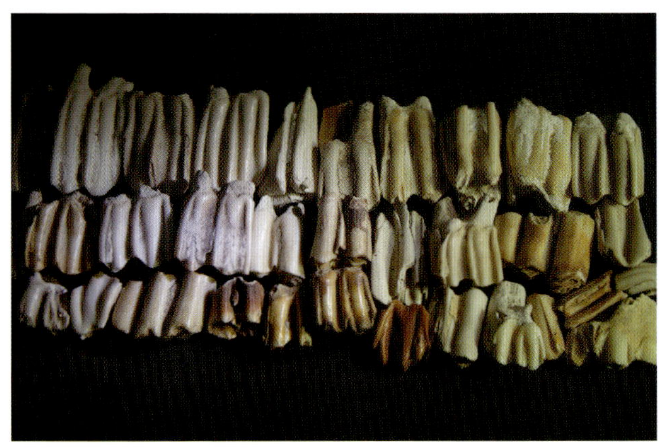

The working class typically tended vegetable and herb gardens (which often included medicinal marijuana) and domestic animals: chickens, pigs, cows, and horses, the remains of which were often buried in the sand at low tide or in backyards. Their bones and teeth still turn up today.

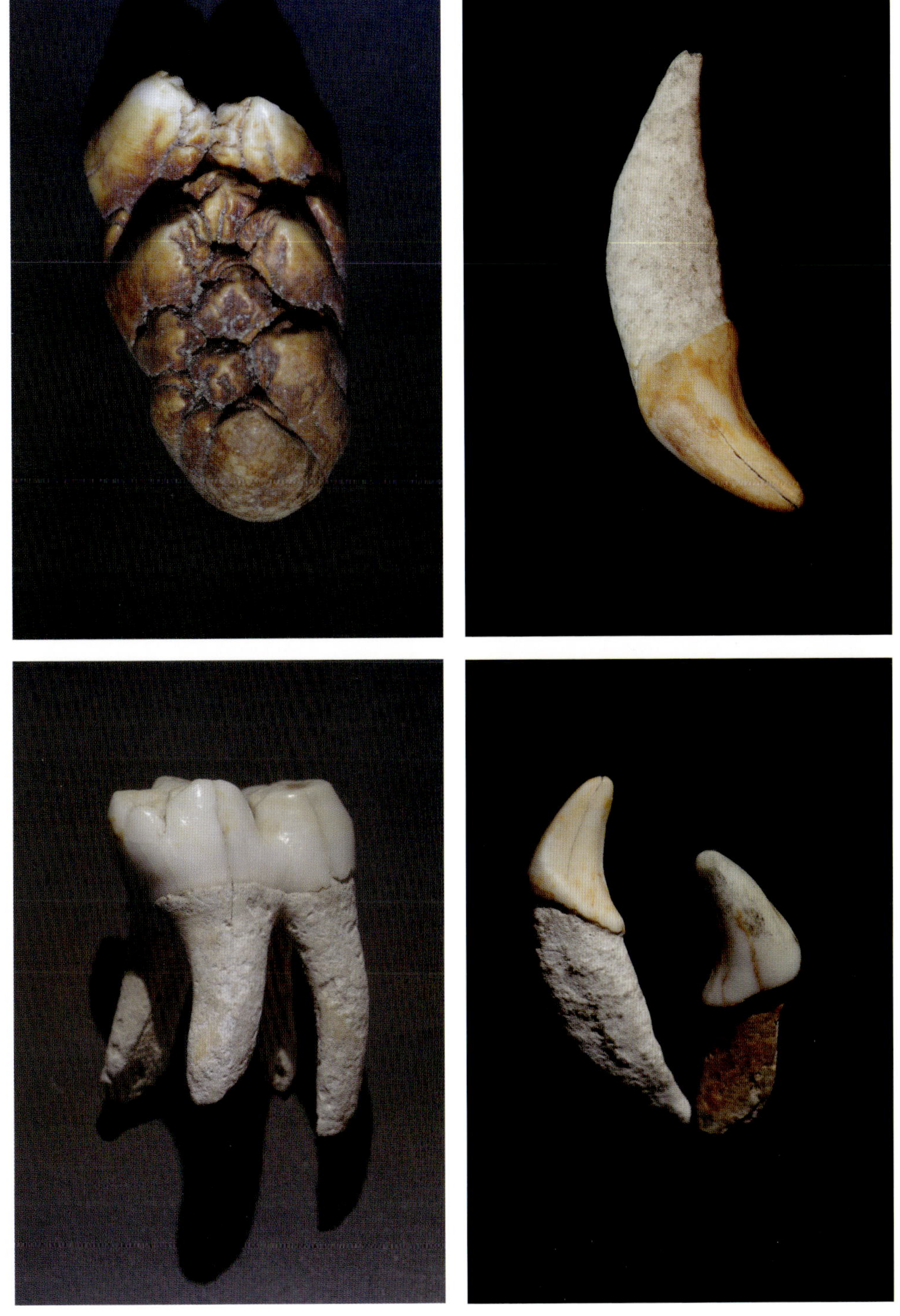

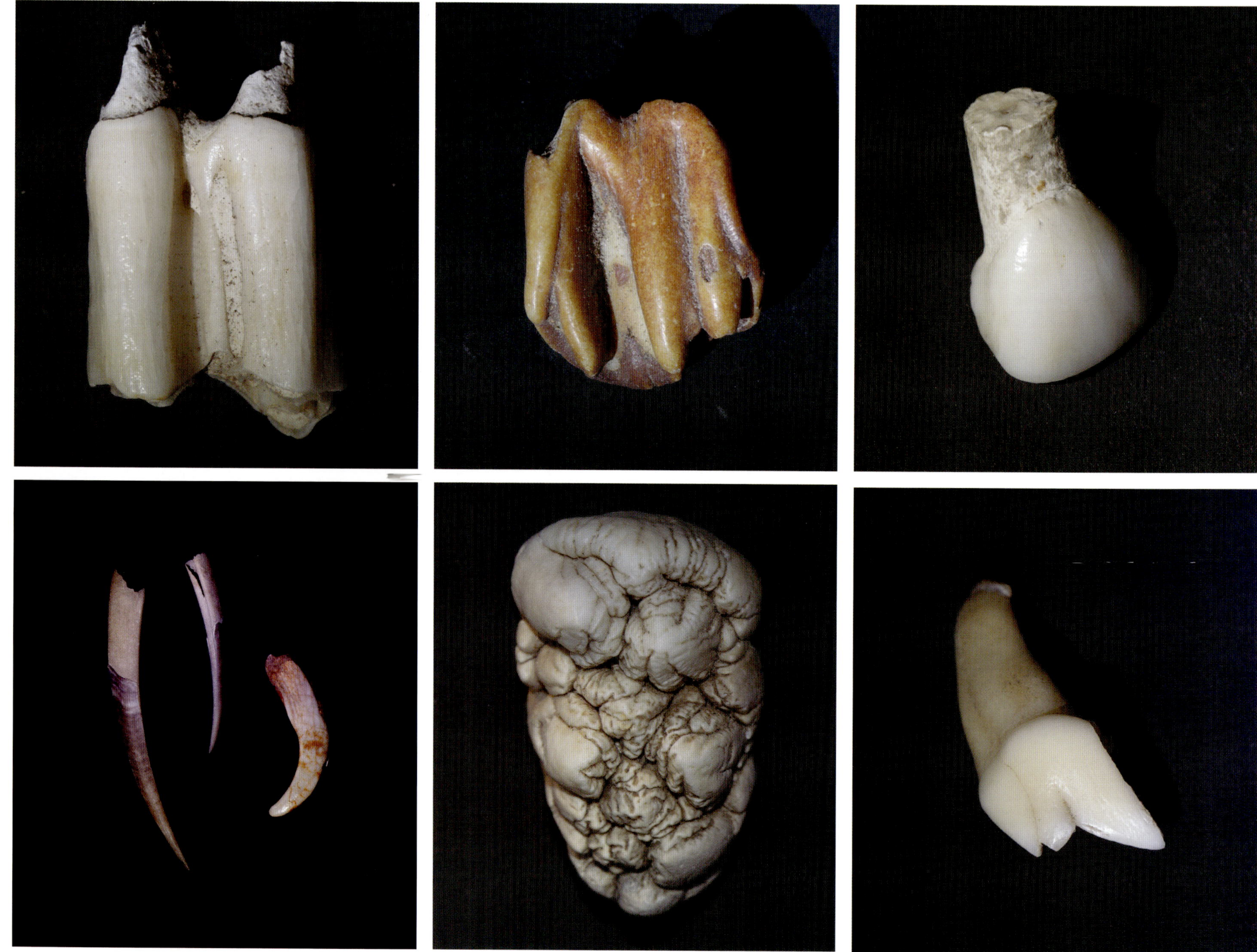

142

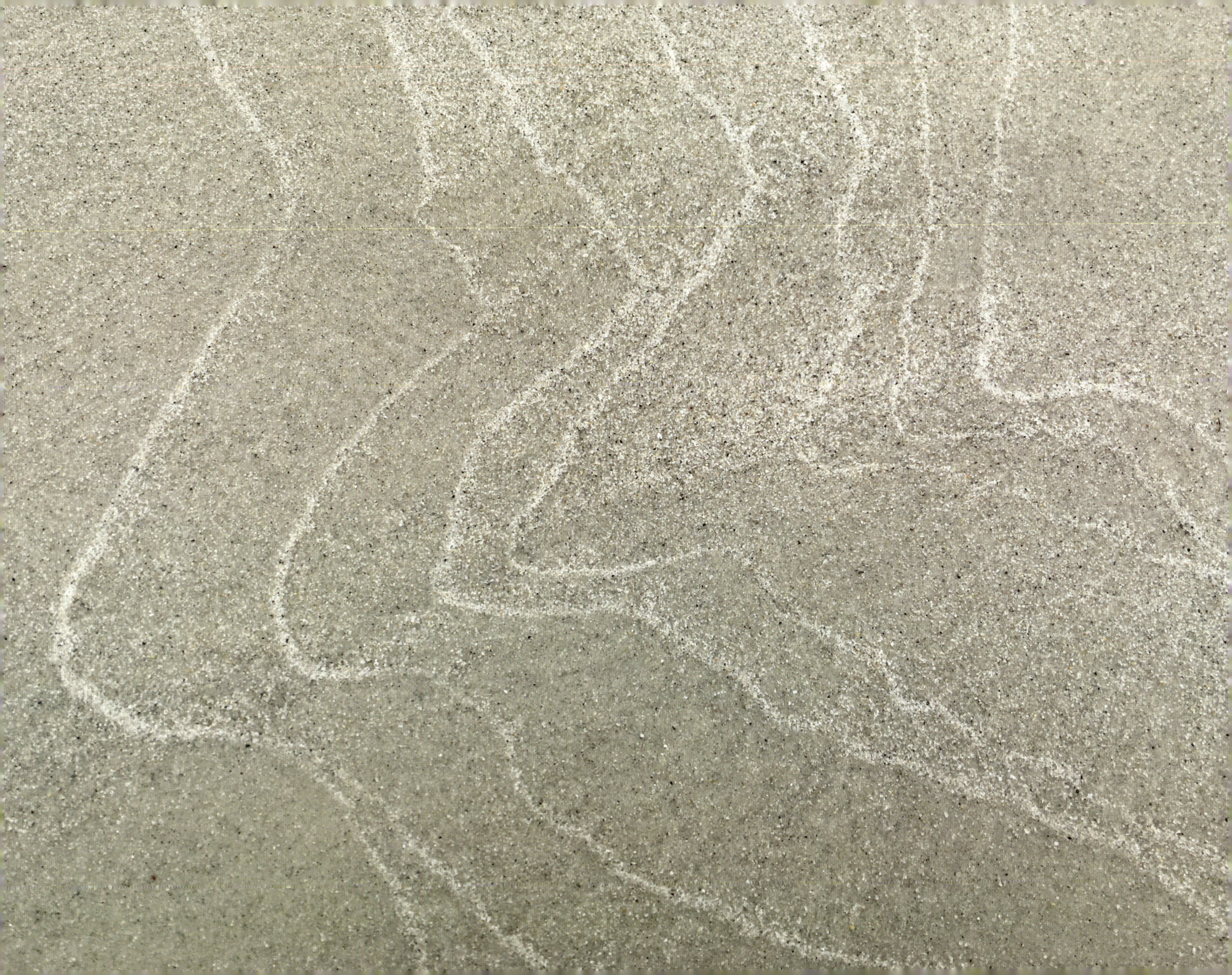

TOURISM & CULTURE

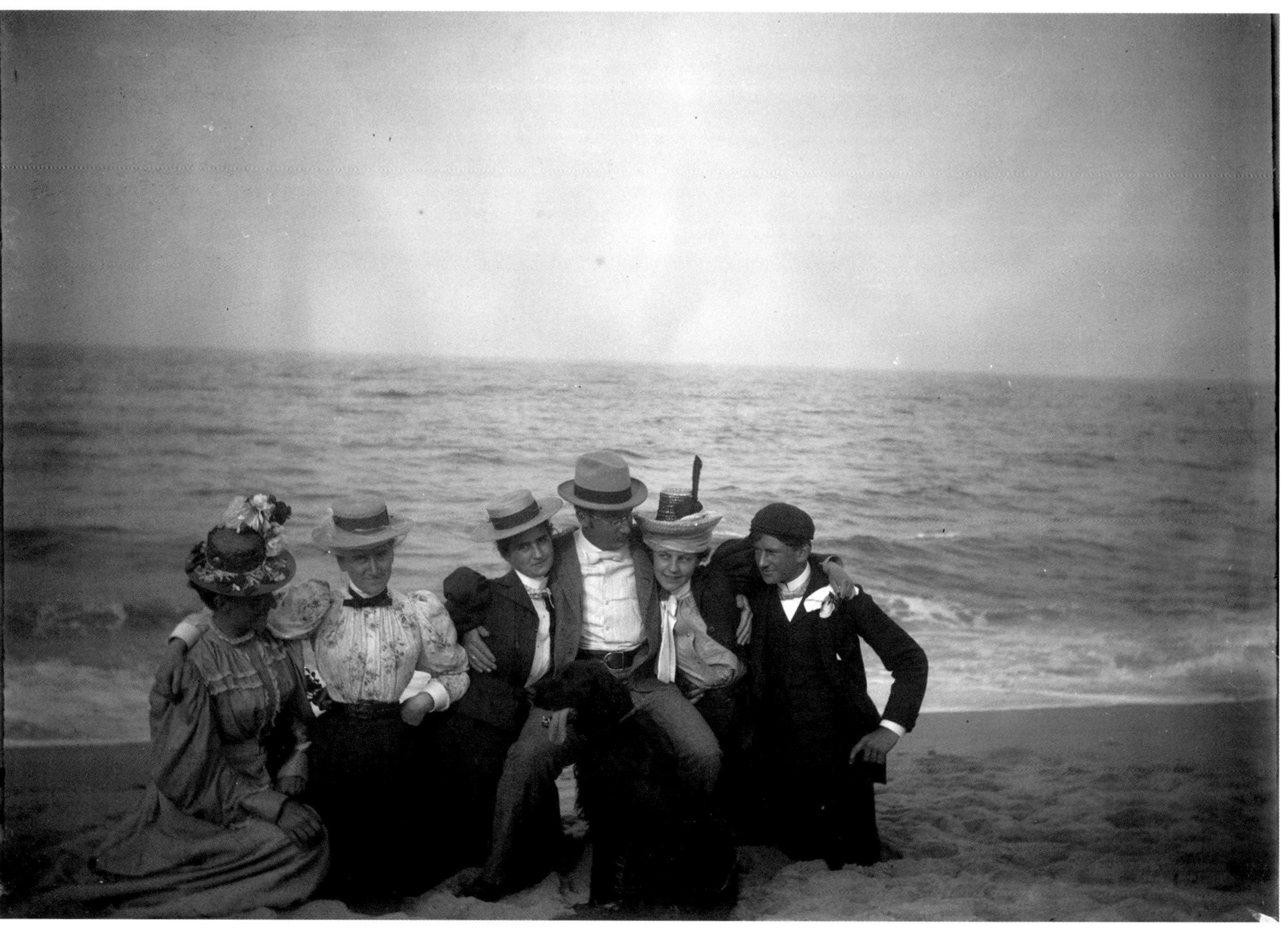

While studying painting in Provincetown, Varujan Boghosian took a job as salad man and dishwasher at Pablo's Restaurant, across the street from what is now Spiritus Pizza. One day he stepped out into the alley for a smoking break just as Elizabeth Taylor and Mike Todd sauntered by, arm in arm. Liz was "thin as a rail" in high heels and a bathing suit, he recalls.

As the whaling and fishing industries waned, tourism grew, attracting writers and artists. In 1899, Charles Hawthorne founded the Cape Cod School of Art, providing an environment to inspire and nurture new artists. As the school's reputation grew, the Provincetown Art Association, founded in 1914, provided meeting and exhibition space for the artists. In 1915, Blanche Lazzell and others studying in Paris migrated back to the United States, bringing with them a new printmaking technique called the "white line." This concurrence of energy ignited Provincetown's continuous growth as an art colony. By 1934, German-born Abstract Expressionist Hans Hofmann (1880–1966) had opened his school of painting, teaching innovative thinking and liberal concepts.

The town also attracted radical thinkers—political activists and social advocates who birthed American theater with the Provincetown Playhouse. In 1915, a group of talented writers and artists, dissatisfied with the commercialism and stage conventions of the time, came to Provincetown to produce their own plays. A short time later they became known as the Provincetown Players, and Eugene O'Neill, one of its members, changed the course of American theater. Tennessee Williams spent four summers in Provincetown's West End in the 1940s, writing some of his best-known plays. These activities attracted new actors such as Paul Robeson and Olivia de Havilland. Bette Davis was rumored to have moonlighted as an usherette.

The Provincetown Playhouse moved several times, and its final Gosnold Street location, owned by Adele Heller, was burned down by two arsonists in 1977.

In 1924, Frank Shay, one of the original Provincetown Players, started the Barnstormers Theatre at 27 Bradford Street after the Provincetown Players moved to New York. That building still stands.

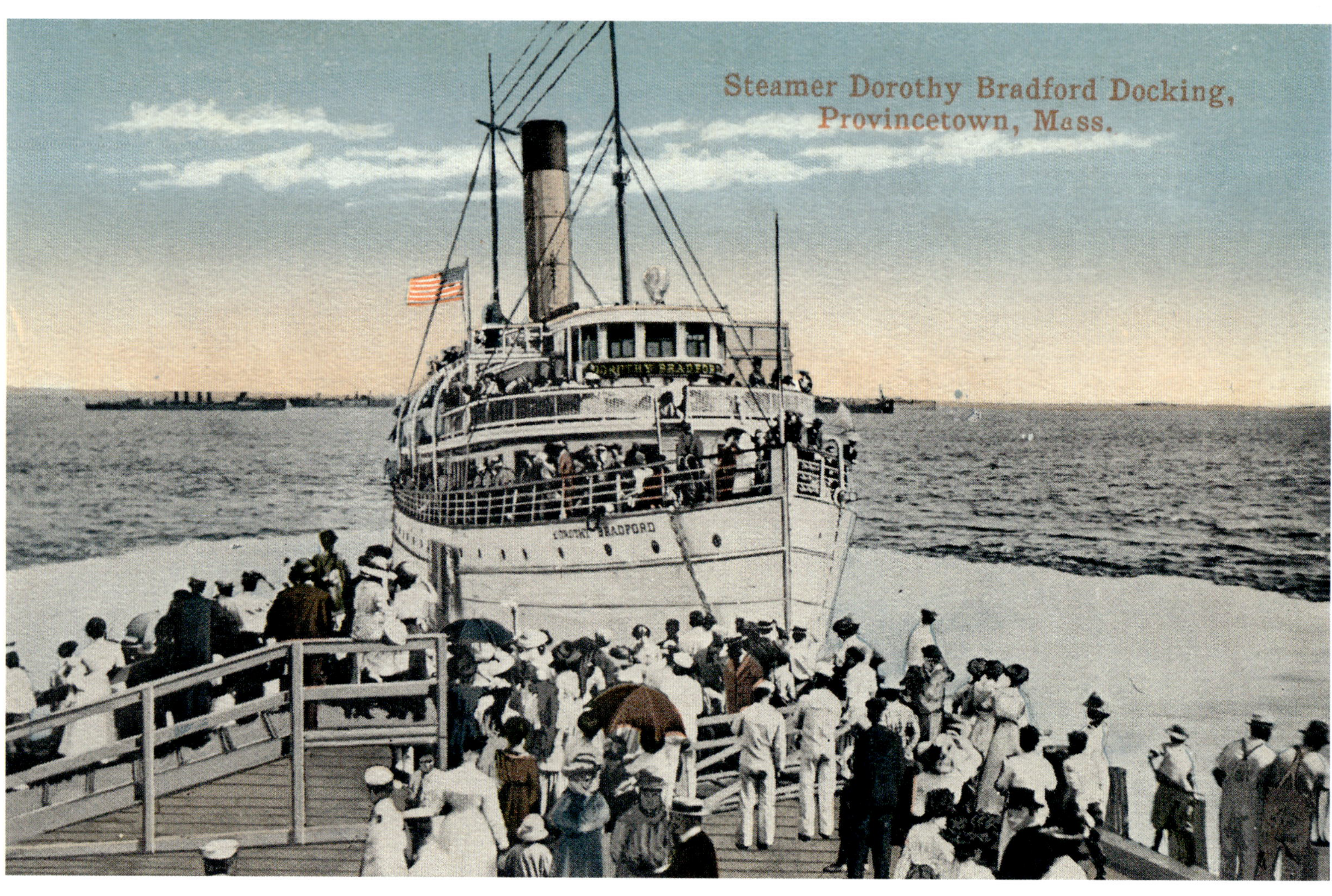
Steamer Dorothy Bradford Docking,
Provincetown, Mass.
DOROTHY BRADFORD
DOROTHY BRADFORD

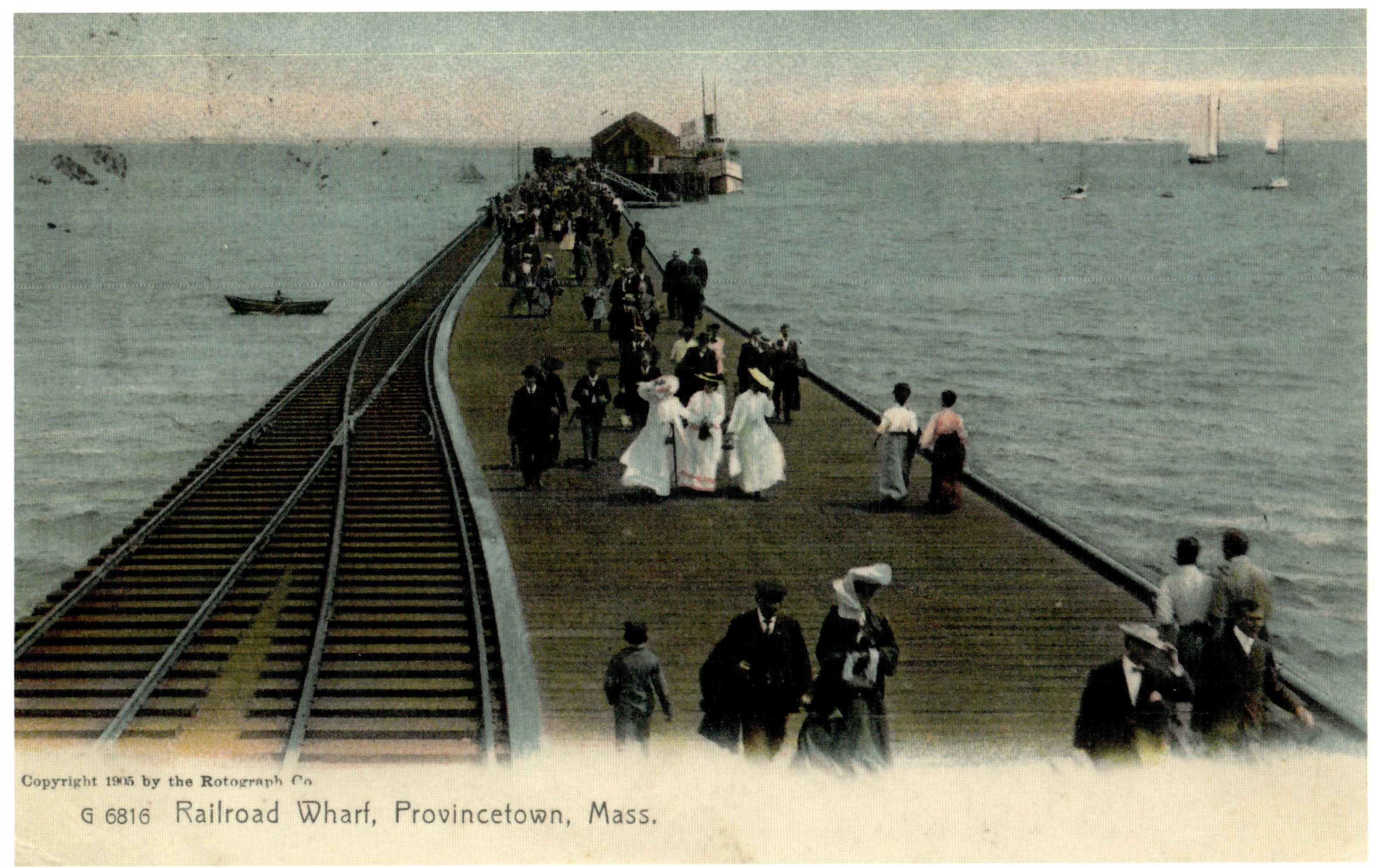
Copyright 1905 by the Rotograph Co.
G 6816 Railroad Wharf, Provincetown, Mass.

American Modern

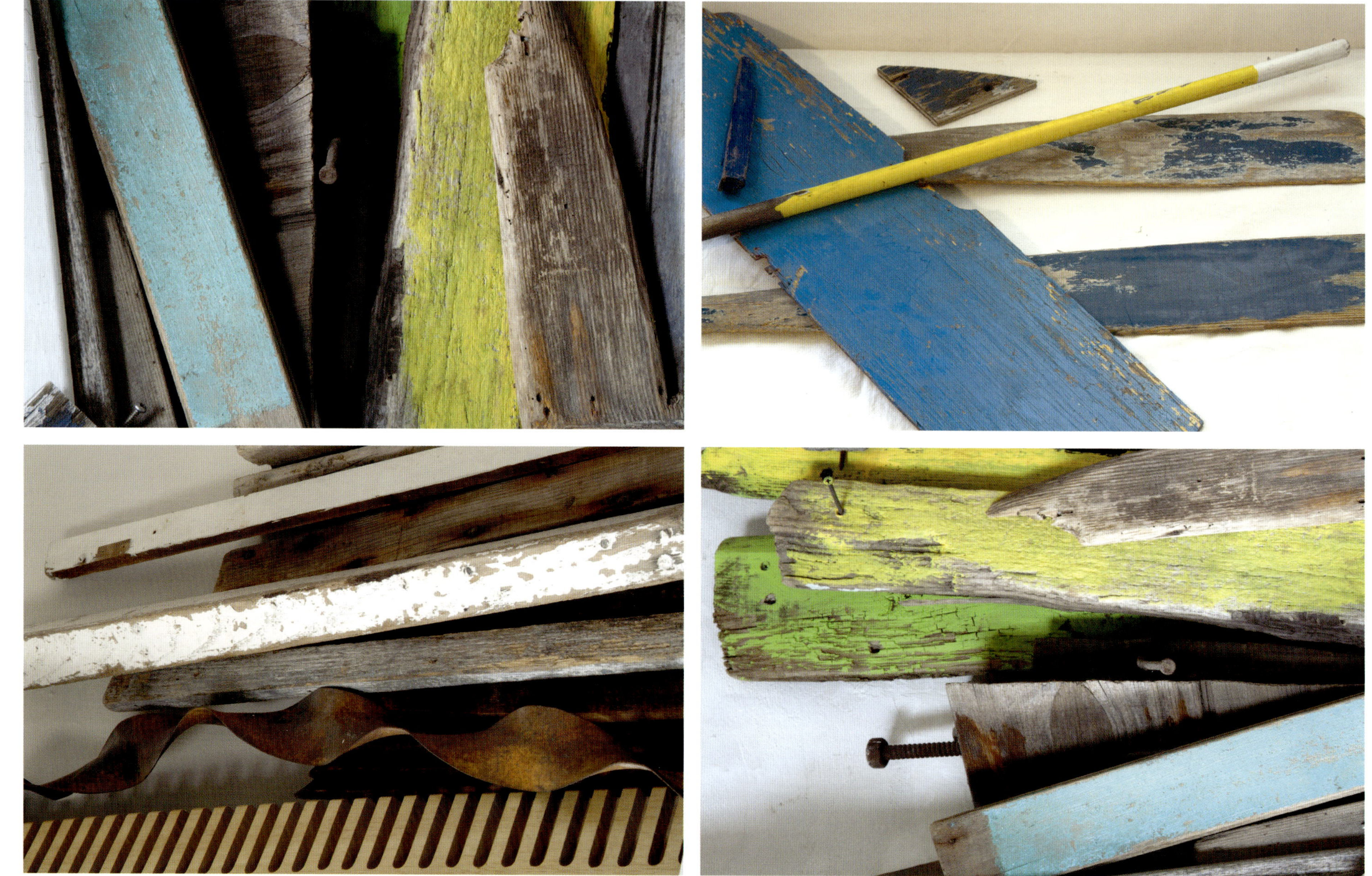

After World War II, the middle-class base expanded with the homecoming soldiers. Funded by the GI bill, many of them went on to further their education, including art school. It was a time of prosperity, expansion, and rapid change, as reflected in the art scene. Provincetown was a focal point for experimentation, and it attracted a contemporary new art movement, the history of which is well documented.

Abstract Expressionist painters Robert Motherwell, Mark Rothko, and Franz Kline galvanized the art world to such an extent that the epicenter relocated from Paris to New York. They were drawn to Provincetown by the cultural atmosphere and natural beauty of the Cape. The excitement drew others too: Willem de Kooning, Milton Avery, Adolph Gottlieb, and many more who spent summers away from New York City, developing their art. It was a heady, infectious, and productive time.

Writers and poets such as Stanley Kunitz, Norman Mailer, and Mary Oliver migrated to Provincetown in the late 1950s and early 1960s. Keeping the beat to this cultural mêlée were the musically gifted, including Billie Holiday, Dizzy Gillespie, Ella Fitzgerald, and Miles Davis, all working the clubs on warm summer nights.

In many Mediterranean cultures, it is a tradition to repaint properties each spring. The Portuguese brought the splattered floor to Provincetown—an economical way to decorate with leftover paint. Given the real-estate boom of the past twenty years, the technique has been virtually renovated into extinction. Only a few examples remain.

There is speculation that the American painter Jackson Pollock (1912–1956) found his oeuvre here, during his brief stay in Provincetown before his stellar ascent as a painter.

The new owner of the Sea Barn, previously the summer home of artist Robert Motherwell (1915–1991), carefully removed and stored the studio floor.

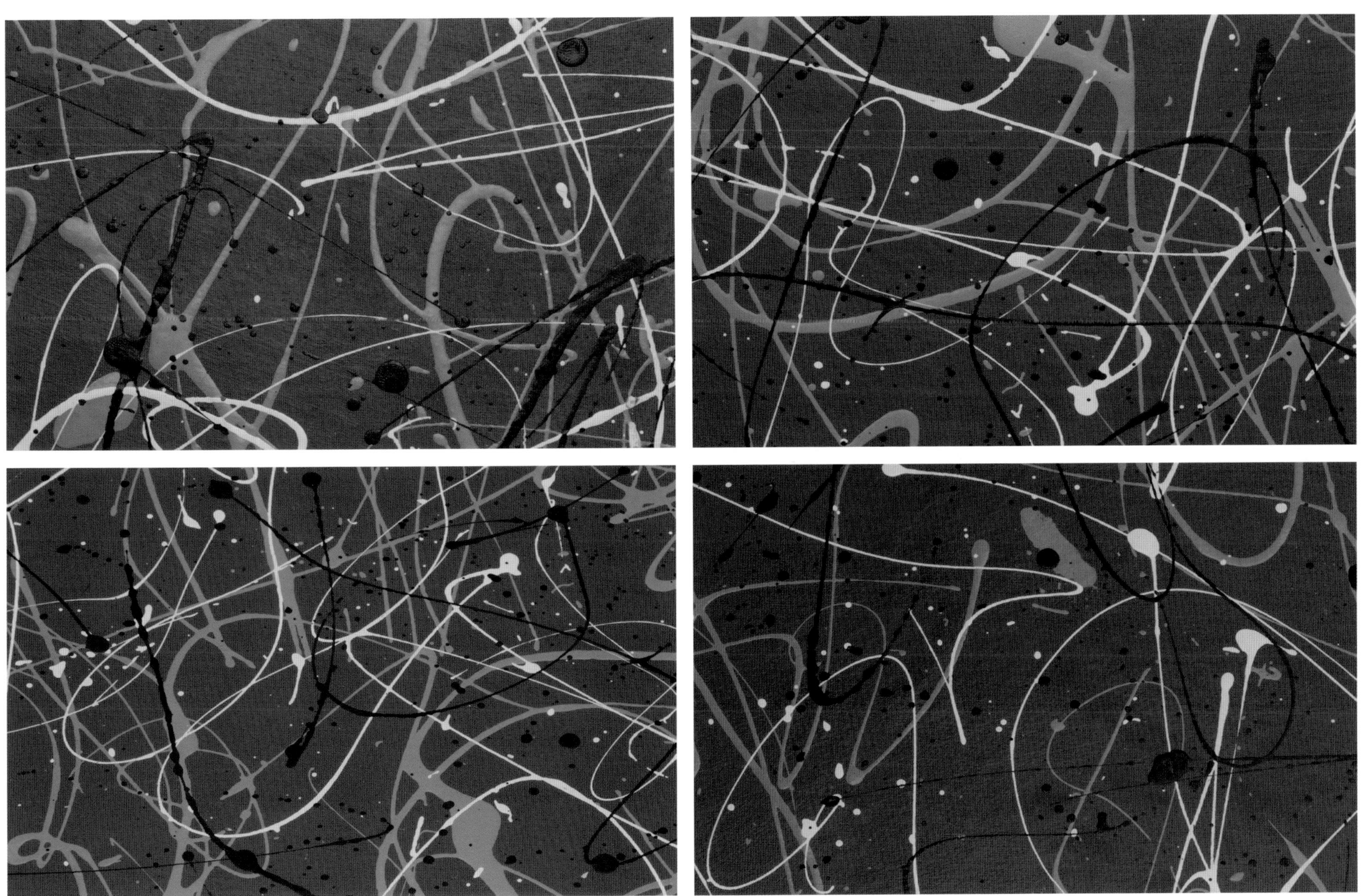

The decade of the 1960s attracted art students, poets, writers, and the like-minded to Provincetown. Referred to as washashores by the locals, they expanded the year-round base and were generously accepted into the community. Within twenty years, property values began to climb and the lifestyle changed again. Today, the Provincetown Art Association and Museum continues to be a rich asset to the community. Other cultural assets are the Fine Arts Work Center, the Provincetown Theater, and the Pilgrim Monument and Provincetown Museum. The town has also evolved into an ecologically aware culture that is committed to preserving its many natural attributes, protected in part by the efforts of the Center for Coastal Studies. Community support for these institutions continues to be the strength of effort to preserve healthy and stable local traditions and infrastructure.

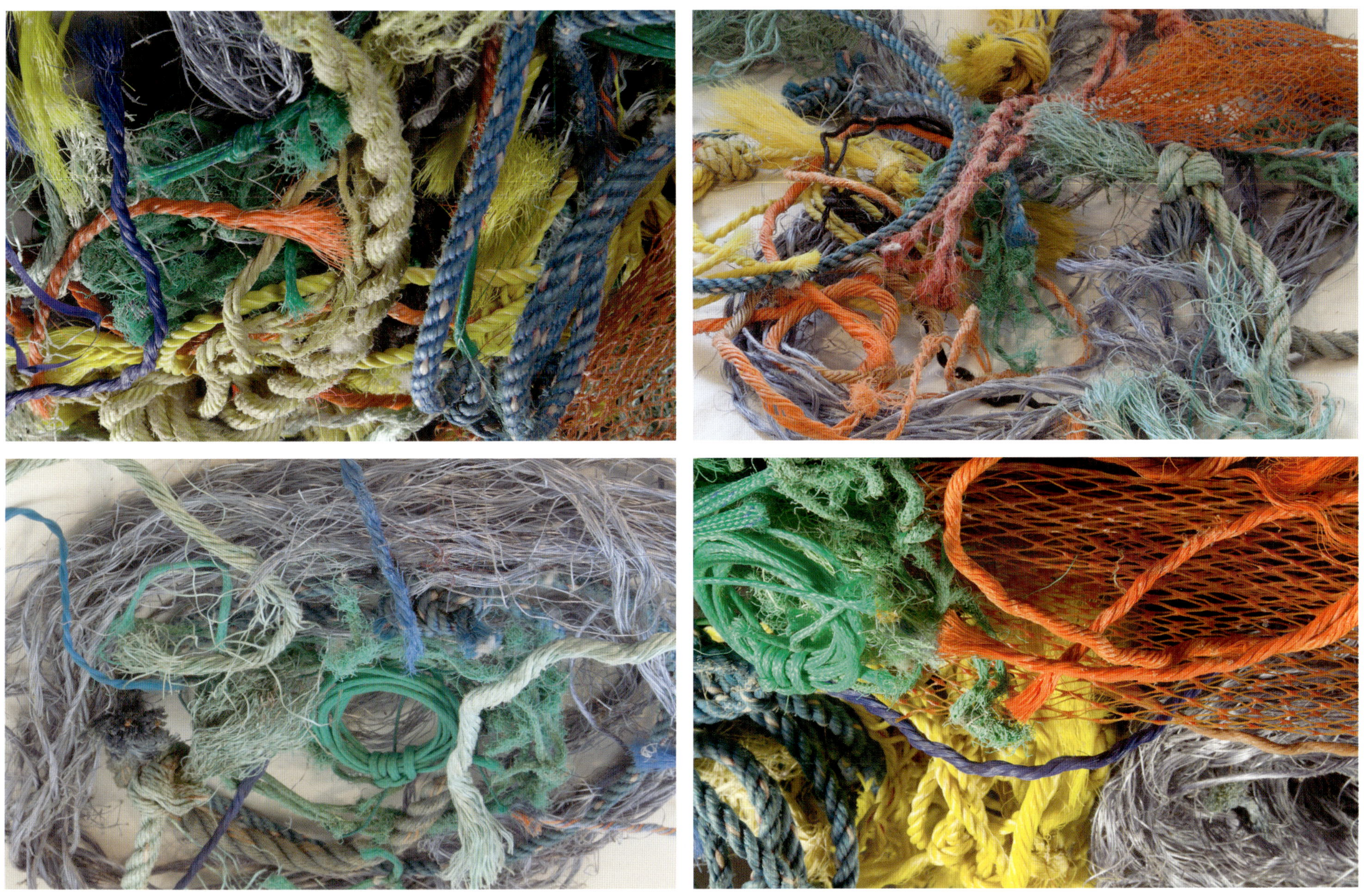

153

"You see color, you see texture, and you see possibility, because whether it's the wood or a nail, sometimes you very simply, beautifully, and elegantly put it together into a construction."

—Judy Berkowitz

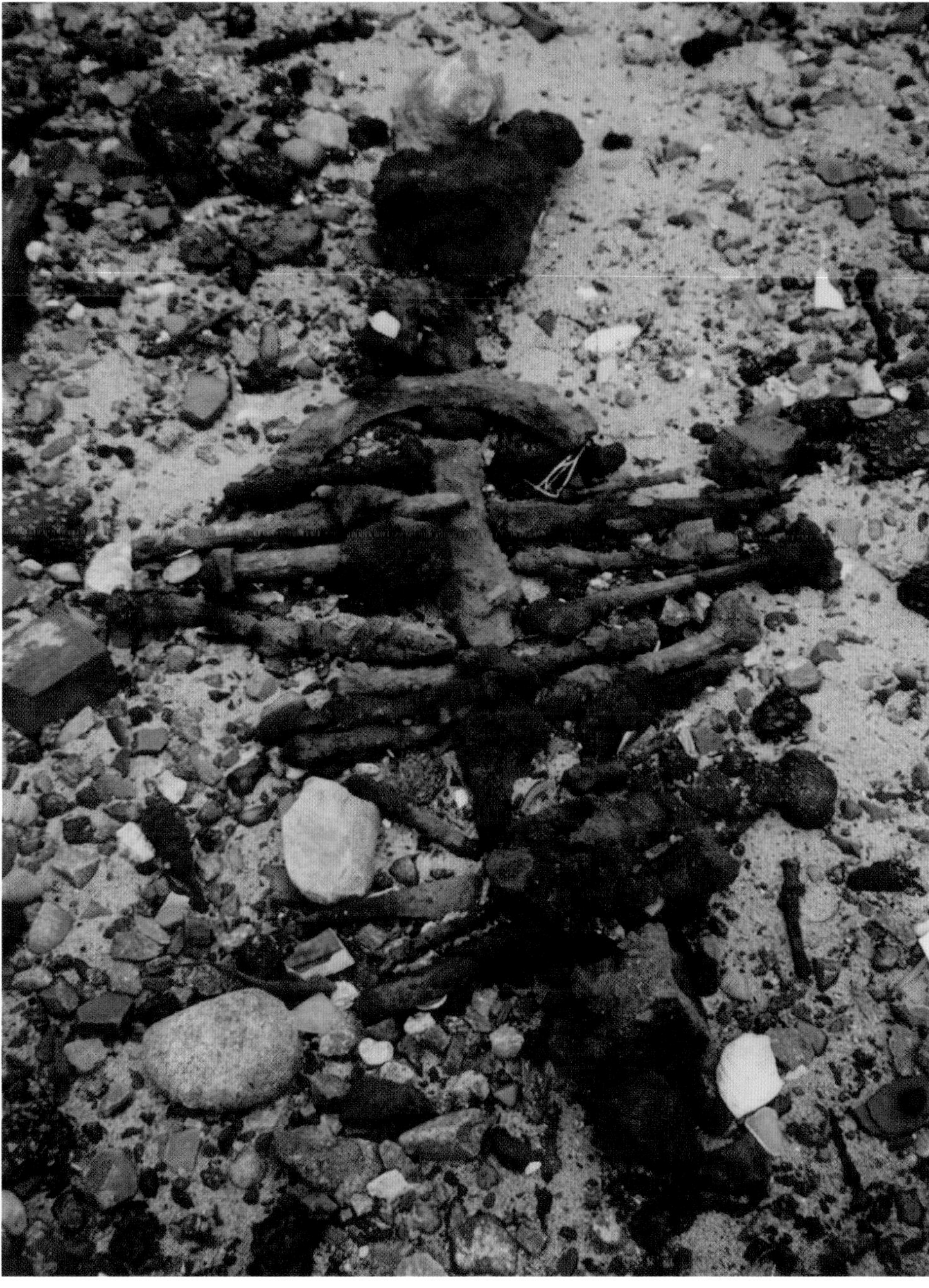

Here lies the remains of the original beachcomber. Exhumed by the scouring tide, the remains appeared at the Old Cold Storage beach for one day in 1995. The shifting winds reburied the remains, and they have not been seen since.

SOURCES

Braginton-Smith, John, and Duncan Oliver. *Cape Cod Shore Whaling: America's First Whalemen*. Yarmouth, MA: Historical Society of Old Yarmouth, 2004.

Heller, Adele. Original playbill of the Provincetown Playhouse on the Wharf, 1976.

Lambert, C. S. *Sea Glass Rare and Wonderful*. Camden, ME: Down East Books, 2017.

LaMotte, Richard. *Pure Sea Glass*. Chestertown, MD: Chesapeake Sea Glass, 2004.

Miller, John, and Tim Smith, eds. *Cape Cod Stories*. San Francisco: Chronicle Books, 1996.

New Bedford Whaling Museum. Whaling Logs. www.whalingmuseum.org.

Shorr, Kathy. *Provincetown: Stories from Land's End*. Beverly, MA: Commonwealth Editions, 2002.

Ward, Katy. "Herring Cove Beach Reveals Its History." *Provincetown Banner*, May 19, 2018.

PHOTO CREDITS

Page 3. Gail Browne beachcombing. *Patricia Burke*

Page 5. Map of Cape Cod. *Municipal Collection / Provincetown History Project Archives*

Page 14. Amy Heller at Cape Cod Museum of Art. *Bart Weisman*

Page 18. Gail Browne in her studio. *Patricia Burke*

Page 18. Gallery window. *Gail Browne*

Page 18. Bookcase with beachcombing treasures. *Gail Browne*

Page 28. Portrait of Paul Bowen. *Pamela Mandell*

Page 31. Ice House Wharf Pilings. *Amy Heller*

Page 64. Ice House. *From the Collection of the Pilgrim Monument and Provincetown Museum, Provincetown, Massachusetts*

Page 65. Advertisement for Consolidated Weir Company. *From the Collection of the Pilgrim Monument and Provincetown Museum, Provincetown, Massachusetts*

Page 65. Black-and-white photograph taken at Old Reliable Wharf, 1960s. *Betty Bodian*

Page 94. Black-and-white photograph of Amy Heller and friend in her homemade boat. *Courtesy of Amy Heller*

Page 155. Beachcomber remains. *Gail Browne*

The Cook Collection photographs: pages 41, 56, 67, 70, 71, 74, 87, 92, 93, 137, 144. *Lisa Tate and Family*

Gail Browne Postcard Collection: pages 13, 45, 50, 61, 68, 91, 146, 147

Art Credits

Page 16
Left to right:
Amy Heller, *Horseshoes*, 2016. Mixed-media LED cyanotype on silk,11 × 8.5 inches

Amy Heller, *Stuck*, 2014. Mixed-media cyanotypes on fabric with rope and acupuncture needles, mounted on mannequin form and turntable, 18 × 6 inches

Amy Heller, *Skates Swimming*, 2006. Cyanotype on fabric, 30 × 26 inches. *Photo by James R. Zimmerman*

Page 17
Top right:
Amy Heller, *Like Mother, Like Daughter*, 2015. Mixed-media LED cyanotype on silk, 8.5 × 11 inches

Bottom:
Amy Heller, *Untitled*, 1989. Time/motion study, black-and-white gelatin silver photograph, 9 × 39.5 inches

Page 19
Left to right:
Gail Browne, *Dunes/Wind*, 2015. Colored shellac inks and walnut ink painting on paper, 38 × 32 inches. *Photo by James R. Zimmerman*

Gail Browne, *Dunes/Moon*, 2015. Colored shellac inks and walnut ink painting on paper, 38 × 32 inches. *Photo by James R. Zimmerman*

Gail Browne, *Dunes, Wind & Rain,* 2015. Colored shellac inks and walnut ink painting on paper, 38 x 32. *Photo by James R. Zimmerman*

Page 20
Left to right:
Gail Browne, *Dusk*, 2018. Linoleum block print on paper, 9 × 9 inches. *Photo by Vincent Guadazno*

Gail Browne, *Harbor*, 2016. Woodblock print on paper collage, 18 × 11 inches. *Photo by Vincent Guadazno*

Gail Browne, *Low Tide*, 2017. Linoleum block print on paper, 9 × 9 inches. *Photo by Vincent Guadazno*

Page 22
Bottom row, left:
Judy Berkowitz, *Untitled*. Hat made with fabric and rope found on the beach

Page 23
Top row, left to right:
Judy Berkowitz, *Untitled*. Wall piece made with wood and washers found on the beach

Judy Berkowitz, *Untitled*. Wall piece made with power saw blades, rusted metal, and rope found on the beach

Bottom row, left to right:
Judy Berkowitz, *Untitled*. Wall piece made with colored wood, metal, and toy marble

Judy Berkowitz, *Untitled*. Wall piece made from wood, rusted metal, and old key found on the beach

Judy Berkowitz, *Untitled*. Wall piece made from wood, rusty metal, chain, and pull chain found on the beach

Page 25
Top row, left to right:
Betty Bodian, *Cult Figure*, 1991. Acrylic on canvas, 36 × 30 inches

Betty Bodian, *Visitation #3*, 1995. Acrylic on canvas, 32 × 30 inches

Bottom row, left to right:
Betty Bodian, *Circus Riders*, 1997. Acrylic on canvas, 32 × 30 inches. Betty Bodian, *Riding the Crest*, 1998. Acrylic on canvas, 20 × 22 inches

Page 27
Top row, left to right, starting second from left:
Varujan Boghosian, *Miss Freedom*, 2003. Mixed-media construction, 20.5 × 13 × 4 inches. *Courtesy of Berta Walker Galleries*

Varujan Boghosian, *From a Chinese Proverb*, 1999. Mixed-media construction, 28.5 × 22 × 4 inches. *Courtesy of Berta Walker Galleries*

Varujan Boghosian, *Self-Portrait as a Lion*, 2009. Paper collage on lithograph, 21 × 16.5 inches

Varujan Boghosian, *Charon Crossing the Styx*, 2007. Mixed media sculpture with clay pipestems, wooden boat, etc.

Bottom row, second from right:
Varujan Boghosian, *Something for Magritte*, 1975. Mixed-media sculpture, 19.5 × 30 × 2.5 inches. *Cape Cod Museum of Art permanent collection, gift of Gilbert and Joyce Franklin, 1991*

Page 28
Top right:
Paul Bowen, *Untitled*, 2000. Two-piece, tandem works, found painted wood, 68 × 30 × 12 inches. *From the Collection of the Provincetown Art Association and Museum, gift of Richard DiFrummolo and Donald Winter, 2010*

Page 29
Top row:
Paul Bowen, wood sculptures at his house in Vermont

Top row, second from right:
Paul Bowen, *Thonet*, 2010. Wood, 23 × 13 × 16 inches. *Courtesy of Albert Merola Gallery, private collection*

Bottom row, left to right:
Paul Bowen, *Brow*, 2014. Rusted wood and ink, 14 × 16 × 4 inches. *Courtesy of Albert Merola Gallery, private collection*

Paul Bowen, *Bridge*, 2014. Walnut ink on paper, 5 × 8 inches. *Courtesy of Albert Merola Gallery, private collection*

Paul Bowen, *Windrush II*, 2002. Redwood, 125 × 193 × 186 inches. *Cape Cod Museum of Art permanent collection with funds from James C. A. and Stephania McClennen, 2002*

Page 30
Paul Bowen, *Good Pickings*, 2005. Walnut ink drawing on paper, 8 × 10 inches. *Courtesy of Gail Browne. Photo by Vincent Guadazno*

Page 151
Floor painting by Gail Browne

Beach Treasures

Judy Berkowitz (JB), Betty Bodian (BB), Varujan Boghosian (VB), Paul Bowen (PB), Gail Browne (GB), and Amy Heller (AH)

Title Page. Ceramic transferware shards, center ceramic shard depicting Provincetown Harbor (GB)

Page 8. Two net weights, inspired by the Chaim Gross sculpture *Tourists* (GB)

Page 10. Pottery shards and other beach treasures (VB)

Page 14. Porcelain doll leg (AH)

Page 17. Jar of sea glass, jar of pebbles, shelf of old bottles (AH)

Page 18. *Bottom, left to right*: pottery shards and other beach treasures on display in window at Gail Browne Gallery; beach treasures displayed in barrister bookcase (GB)

Page 22. *Bottom right:* colored ropes (JB)

Page 23. *Top, left to right:* wood and metal, shelf with pebbles, bench with assorted beach treasures. *Bottom, second from right:* colored ropes (JB)

Page 24. *Left to right*: gold button, type tray with beach treasures, and glass bottles on windowsill in New York City (BB)

Page 26. *Left to right:* metal lion toy with rust concretion, wooden box of pottery shards and other beach treasures (VB)

Page 27. *Bottom, far right:* container of clay pipestems (VB)

Page 28. *Bottom, left to right:* ceramic transferware vase, metal drawer with whale inner ear bones, clay marbles, bones, buttons, and other objects (PB)

Page 29. *Top, far right*: found wood and other objects in studio. *Bottom, second from right*: wood and metal boxes of beach treasures on table (PB)

Page 33. Three views of stone fire starter (GB)

Page 35. Flint (GB)

Page 36. Paint pots and arrowheads (GB)

Page 37. Net weight (GB)

Page 39. Right whale carved from walrus tusk (GB)

Page 42. Inner ear bones of whales (GB)

Page 43. Whale teeth (GB)

Page 46. Carved soapstone head, shallow metal vessel (PB, GB)

Page 47. Three views of ceramic head (GB)

Page 49. Milk bottle buoy (GB)

Page 51. Tool handles, gears, metal odds and ends (JB, GB)

Page 52. Metal gears (GB)

Page 53. Rusted metal nails and assorted pieces of metal, net weights (GB)

Page 54. *Top, left to right*: metal gears, plaques, rusted metal, numbers & letters. *Bottom, left to right*: metal machine parts, metal pieces, keys, screws (GB)

Page 55. Metal badges, medals, locks, and key (GB)

Page 57. Wooden pulleys (GB)

Page 58. *Top*: Wooden oars, metal circular saw blades, brushes. *Center*: rusted metal, oarlocks, assorted tools. *Bottom*: paintbrushes, metal basket, metal tools (JB)

Page 59. Brush handle, wheel hub, pocket knife handles (GB)

Page 60. Pocket knife handles (PB)

Page 62. Wooden pulleys; wooden pulleys and handle (GB)

Page 63. Wooden wheels (GB)

Page 73. Clay pipe bowls (GB)

Page 75. Pyramid of pipestems (PB)

Page 76. Clay pipes and pipe bowls (BB, PB, GB)

Page 77. Glass bottles and beach treasures (BB)

Page 78. Clay pipe bowls (BB, PB, GB)

Page 79. Clay pipe bowls (PB)

Page 80. Clay pipes, bowls, and stems (PB)

Page 81. Clay pipestems, clay pipe and bowl, clay pipestems (PB)

Page 82. Mottled clay pipestems (GB)

Page 85. Clay marbles (GB)

Page 86. Hand-blown glass marble (GB)

Page 88. Glass and clay marbles (GB)

Page 89. Two views of metal toy lion with rust concretions, and miniature ceramic toy lamb, cat, dog, and elephant (VB, GB)

Page 90. Multiple views of French toy metal horse (GB)

Page 95. *Top*: porcelain doll heads. *Bottom*: ceramic hand and ceramic paw, glass doll eye, metal toy soldiers, gun, motorcycle (GB)

Page 96–97. Ceramic and porcelain doll bodies, heads, and fragments (BB, PB, GB)

Pages 98–99. Ceramic and porcelain doll arms and legs (BB, PB, GB)

Page 100. Miniature ceramic toy cups, pitchers, saucers (BB, PB, GB)

Page 101. Ceramic and porcelain doll bodies (GB)

Page 102. Porcelain fragments of doll heads, porcelain fragments of doll legs (PB, GB)

Page 105. Ceramic earthenware shards (GB)

Page 106. Transferware shards (GB)

Page 107. Transferware shards (GB)

Page 108. Ceramic handles, ceramic tops, ceramic handles (GB)

Page 109. Mochaware, Bennington ceramic spouts, salt-glazed stoneware, water drop earthenware, jug spouts (GB)

Page 110. Button and ceramic top, ironstone pitcher, and close-up of pitcher (GB, PB)

Page 111. Close-up of ironstone pitcher, ceramic knobs, ceramic mug covered with limpet shells (PB, BB)

Page 112. Ceramic figurines (PB)

Page 113. Ceramic figurine, ceramic figurine of golfer (PB)

Page 114. Butterfly/dragonfly ceramic transferware shard (VB)

Page 115. Porcelain hand, porcelain leg (PB)

Page 117. Glass cathedral bottle and two other glass bottles; hand-blown bottle on its side is from the seventeenth century (GB)

Page 118. Glass bottle stoppers (GB)

Page 119. Glass bottlenecks (GB)

Page 120. Glass bottle stoppers (GB)

Page 121. Victorian tear-catchers (GB)

Page 122. Glass bottles/inkwells (BB, GB)

Page 123. Glass bottle pontils (GB)

Page 124. Purple glass insulator, green pressed glass (BB, GB)

Page 125. Doctor Hough's Anti-Scrofulous Syrup bottle (BB)

Page 126. Glass bottlenecks, glass handles, hand-blown glass handle (GB)

Page 127. Glass shards (GB)

Page 129. Glass beads (GB)

Page 130–131. Glass beads, charm, Venetian glass, vintage plastic cameo, gold and platinum rings (GB)

Page 132. Three views of pigeon blood ruby stickpin (GB)

Page 134. Ceramic earthenware jugs (GB)

Page 135. Coins (GB)

Page 136. Indian head/Lady Liberty coins (GB)

Page 140–142. Livestock teeth (PB)

Page 148. Painted wood and metal (JB)

Page 153. Colored rope and fishnet (JB)

Page 155. "Skeleton" of machinery parts found on Old Cold Storage Beach (GB)

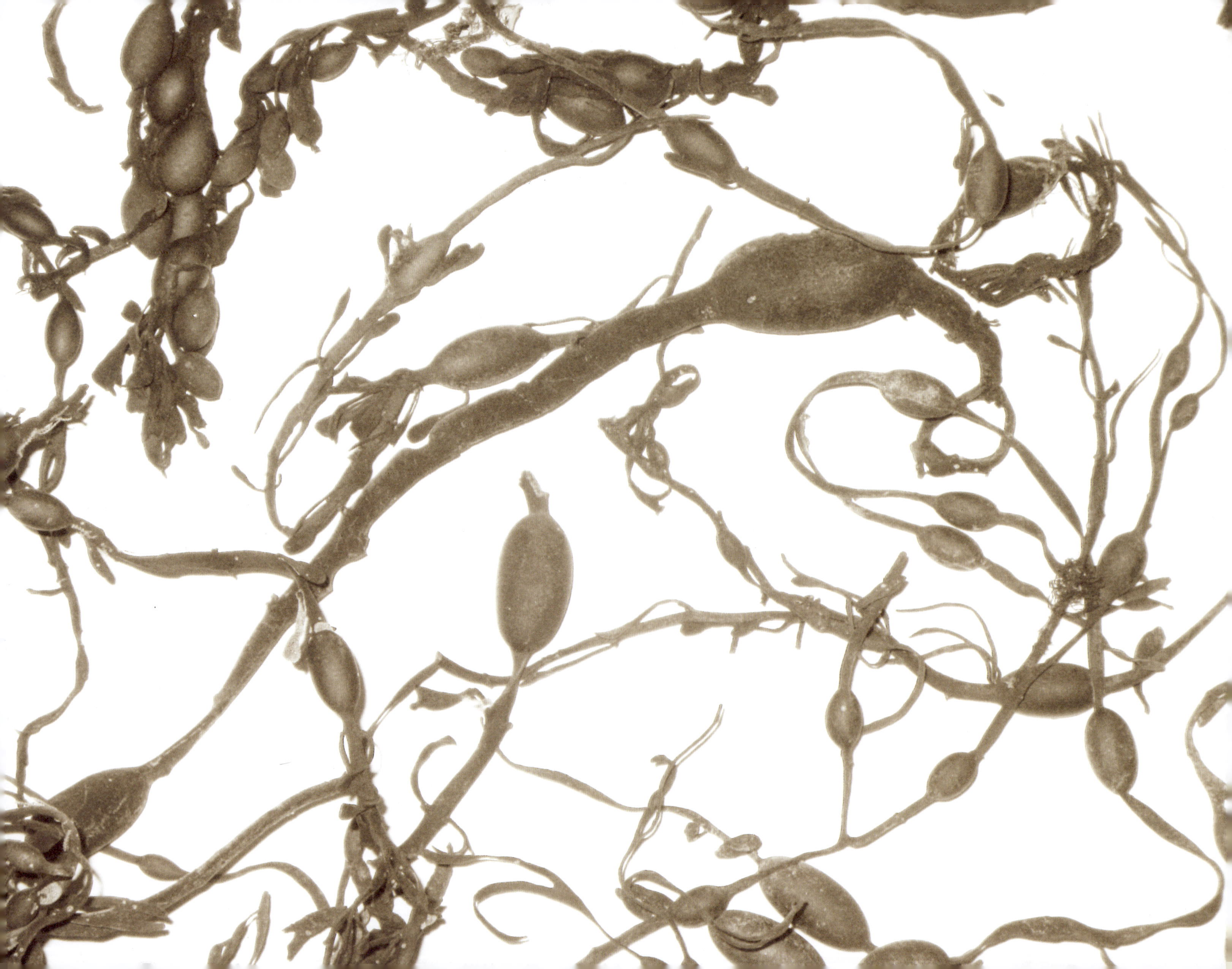